INC 2016

Frankfurt, Germany
19–21 July 2016

Proceedings of the 11th International Network Conference

Editors

Sergej Alekseev
Paul Dowland
Bogdan Ghita
Oliver Schneider

ISBN: 978-1-84102-410-3

© 2016 Plymouth University
All rights reserved
Printed in the United Kingdom

No part of this book may be reproduced, stored in a retrieval system, or transmitted in any form or by any means – electronic, mechanical, photocopy, recording or otherwise, without the prior written permission of the publisher or distributor.

Preface

This book presents the proceedings of the Eleventh International Network Conference (INC 2016), hosted by the Centre of Competence for Computer Networks and Distributed Systems (CCNDS) at Frankfurt University of Applied Sciences and the Centre for Security, Communications and Network Research at Plymouth University, UK, from 19th to 21st July 2016.

A continuing aim of the INC series is to provide an opportunity for those involved in the design, development and use of network systems and applications to meet, share their ideas and exchange opinions. The 2016 event again succeeds in this aim by bringing together leading specialists from academia and industry, and enabling the presentation and discussion of the latest advances in research.

These proceedings contain a total of 30 papers covering many aspects of modern networking, including web technologies, network protocols and performance, security and privacy, mobile and wireless systems, and the applications and impacts of network technology. As such, it is hoped that all readers will find a variety of material of interest. Each paper was subjected to double-blind review by at least two members of the International Programme Committee. We would like to thank all of the reviewers for their efforts, as well as the authors for their willingness to share their ideas and findings.

The conference team is also most grateful to our keynotes speakers for accepting our invitation to share their expertise in the keynote lectures.

We hope that all of our delegates enjoy the conference, and that other readers of these proceedings will be able to join us on a future occasion.

Dr Bogdan Ghita & Prof. Dr Ulrich Trick
Conference Co-Chairs, INC 2016

Frankfurt, July 2016

About the Centre of Competence for Computer Networks and Distributed Systems

The Centre of Competence for Computer Networks and Distributed Systems (CCNDS) is a foundation within the Faculty of Computer Science and Engineering at the Frankfurt University of Applied Sciences. Since 2015 the CCNDS is a newly established partner of the CSCAN network: the Frankfurt Node.

The CCNDS integrates the research and development activities of seven research groups of the Frankfurt University in this field:

- Network Security, Information Security and Privacy
- Operating Systems and Computer Networks
- Mobile Computing
- Telecommunications Networks
- Wireless and Smart Sensor Networks
- Cluster, Grid and Cloud-Computing
- Secure hybrid networks for mobile communication

Our projects revolve around advanced problem solving and the use of new ideas in practice. CCNDS is committed to the training of young scientists and the establishment of an interdisciplinary doctoral partnership.

For further information, please visit the Centre's homepage:
https://www.frankfurt-university.de/fachbereiche/fb2/forschung/kompetenzzentrum-netzwerke-und-verteilte-systeme.html

Address	Centre of Competence for Computer Networks and Distributed Systems, Frankfurt University of Applied Sciences, Nibelungenplatz 1 60318 Frankfurt am Main Germany
Telephone	+49 (0) 69 1533-3673
Fax	+49 (0) 69 1533-2727
Email	alekseev@fb2.fra-uas.de
URL	www.frankfurt-university.de

About the Centre for Security, Communications and Network Research

The INC conference series is organised by the Centre for Security, Communications and Network Research (CSCAN) at Plymouth University, UK.

CSCAN is a specialist technology and networking research facility at Plymouth University. Originally established in 1984 (under the original name of the Network Research Group), the Centre conducts research in the areas of IT Security, Internet & WWW technologies and Mobility, and has a proven pedigree including projects conducted for, and in collaboration with, commercial companies, as well as participation in European research initiatives. Over the years, our research activities have led to numerous successful projects, along with associated publications and patents.

At the time of writing, the Centre has sixteen affiliated full-time academic staff and over seventy research degree projects (at PhD and MPhil levels). The Centre also supports Masters programmes in Electrical and Electronic Engineering; Computer and Computer and Information Security; and, Network Systems Engineering, and hosts a significant number of research-related projects from these programmes.

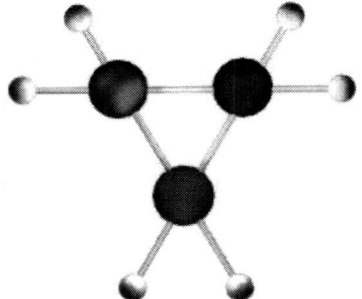

Address	Centre for Security, Communications and Network Research
	Plymouth University
	Drake Circus
	Plymouth
	PL4 8AA
	United Kingdom
Telephone	+44 (0) 1752 586 234
Fax	+44 (0) 1752 586 300
Email	info@cscan.org
URL	www.cscan.org

INC 2016 Committees

International Programme Committee

Nikos Antonopoulos	University of Derby	UK
Dominig ar Foll	Intel Open Source	Brittany-France
Harald Baier	Center for Advanced Security Research, Hochschule Darmstadt	Germany
Frank Ball	Frank Ball Consulting	UK
Udo Bleimann	University of Applied Sciences Darmstadt	Germany
Eugen Borcoci	University POLITEHNICA of Bucharest	Romania
Reinhardt Botha	Nelson Mandela Metropolitan University	South Africa
Aurelian Bria	Ericsson	Sweden
Arslan Brömme	GI BIOSIG	Germany
Phil Brooke	Teesside University	UK
Nathan Clarke	Plymouth University	UK
Jeff Crume	IBM	USA
Mark Culverhouse	Cisco	UK
Mariki Eloff	University of South Africa	South Africa
Christophe Feltus	Luxembourg Institute of Science and Technology	Luxembourg
Klaus-Peter Fischer-Hellmann	Digamma Communications Consulting GmbH	Germany
Ulrich Flegel	HFT Stuttgart, University of Applied Sciences	Germany
Woldemar Fuhrmann	University of Applied Sciences, Darmstadt	Germany
Steven Furnell	Plymouth University	UK
Bogdan Ghita	Plymouth University	UK
Martin Gonzalez Rodriguez	University of Oviedo	Spain
Carsten Griwodz	Simula Research	Norway
Vic Grout	Glyndwr University, Wales	UK
Holger Hofmann	Cooperative State University Baden-Wurttemberg Mannheim	Germany
Martin Kappes	Frankfurt University of Applied Sciences	Germany
Vasilis Katos	Bornemouth University	UK
Sokratis Katsikas	University of Piraeus	Greece
Raj Kettimuthu	Argonne National Laboratory and the University of Chicago	USA
Martin Knahl	Furtwangen University	Germany
Armin Lehmann	Frankfurt University of Applied Sciences	Germany
George Magklaras	University of Oslo	Norway
Dwight Makaroff	University of Saskatchewan	Canada
Jacques Ophoff	University of Cape Town	South Africa
Vassillis Prevelakis	Technische Universität Braunschweig	Germany
Shukor Razak	Universiti Teknologi Malaysia	Malaysia
Andreas Rinkel	University of Applied Sciences Rapperswill	Switzerland
Miguel Rio	University College London	UK
Angelos Rouskas	University of Piraeus	Greece
Oliver Schneider	DIPF – German Institute for International Educational Research	Germany
David Schwartz	Bar-Ilan University	Israel
Ingo Stengel	University of Applied Sciences Karlsruhe	Germany
Kerry-Lynn Thomson	Nelson Mandela Metropolitan University	South Africa
Ulrich Trick	Frankfurt University of Applied Sciences	Germany
Dimitrios D. Vergados	University of Piraeus	Greece
Mathias Wagner	Frankfurt University of Applied Sciences	Germany
Merrill Warkentin	Mississippi State University	USA

Organising Committee

Sergej Alekseev, Hans Ambach, Nathan Clarke, Paul Dowland, Steven Furnell, Bogdan Ghita, Armin Lehmann, Oliver Schneider

Contents

Chapter 1: INC Papers

A Review on Power Consumption Reduction Techniques on OFDM 3
S.Al-Obaidi, M.A.Ambroze, B.Ghita, E.Giakoumidis and A.Tsokanos

Towards an Energy Optimization Framework for Cloud Computing Data Centres 9
S.I.Alshathri

Performance Evaluation of Time-Critcal Smart Grid Applications 13
F.Ball and K.Basu

On the Performance of Anomaly Detection Systems Uncovering Traffic Mimicking Covert Channels 19
J.Bouché, D.Hock and M.Kappes

Using Machine Learning Techniques for User Specific Activity Recognition 25
J.Chawla and M.Wagner

DMC: Distributed Approach in Multi-Domain Controllers 31
S.B.Chundrigar, M-Z.Shieh, L-P.Tung and B-S.P.Lin

Investigating Environmental Causes of TCP Retransmission and Flags in Wireless Networks 37
S.Cunningham, N.Houlden, J.Davies, V.Grout and R.Picking

On Channel Allocation of Directional Wireless Networks Using Multiple Channels 43
H-N.Dai, H.Wang and H.Xiao

What-if Analysis in Wireless Sensor Networks Using Workflow Provenance 49
G.Dogan

Topology Reconstruction for Target Operation Network (TON): A Link Prediction Perspective 55
C.Fan, B.Xiu, Z.Liu, C.Chen and Y.Yang

Mobile Edge Computing: Requirements for Powerful Mobile Near Real-Time Applications 63
H.Frank, W.Fuhrmann and B.Ghita

Acceptance Factors of Wearable Computing: An Empirical Investigation 67
L.Gribel, S.Regier and I.Stengel

VirtualStack: Adaptive Multipath Support through Protocol Stack Virtualization 73
J.Heuschkel, A.Frömmgen, J.Crowcroft and M.Mühlhäuser

A Field Study on Linked and Open Data at Datahub.io 79
T.Heuss, J.Fengel, B.Humm, B. Harriehausen-Mühlbauer and S.Atkinson

QoE Enhancements in IEEE 802.11e EDCA for Video Transmission through Selective Queueing N.Khambari, B.Ghita, D.Lancaster and L.Sun	85
Low Complexity Channel Estimation Method for IEEE 802.11p Vehicle Communications C-M.Li and F-M.Wu	91
A Framework for OpenFlow-like Policy-based Routing in Hybrid Software Defined Networks A.Mishra, D.Bansod and K.Haribabu	97
A View of WSN-Facilitating Application's Design and a Cloud Infrastructure in Academic Environment and Research A.Novinskiy	103
Bitcoin Network Measurements for Simulation Validation and Parameterisation M.Fadhil, G.Owen and M.Adda	109
P2P-based M2M Community Applications M.Steinheimer, U.Trick, W.Fuhrmann and B.Ghita	115
Identity-as-a-Service (IDaaS): A Missing Gap for Moving Enterprise Applications in Inter-Cloud T.H.Vo, W.Fuhrmann and K.P.Fischer-Hellmann	121
Efficient Test Case Derivation from Statecharts-based Models P.Wacht, U.Trick, W.Fuhrmann and B.Ghita	127

Chapter 2: Posters

Deploying Contextual Computing in a Campus Setting F.Aversente, D.Klein, S.Sultani, D.Vronski and J.Schäfer	135
Assay of Multipath TCP for Session Continuity in Distributed Mobility Management M.Dawood, W.Fuhrmann and B.Ghita	141
Algorithm for Generating Peer-to-Peer Overlay Graphs based on WebRTC Events C.von Harscher, M.Schindler, J.Kinzig and S.Alekseev	147
SIP Automated Test Platform Y.Kirkagac, S.Simsek and D.Yavas	153
The Usage of Body Area Networks for Fall-Detection L.La Blunda and M.Wagner	159
Optimization of Wireless Disaster Network through Network Virtualization A.Lehmann, A.P.Tchinda and U.Trick	165

Evaluating Framework for Monitoring and Analyzing WebRTC Peer-to-Peer Applications   171
M.Schindler, C.von Harscher, J.Kinzig and S.Alekseev

A Mobile Solution for Language Communication with Deaf-Blind People Using Arduino and   177
Android
A.L.N. Vieira, F.F.Novaes, D.M.Silva, L.Santos, S.Belozi and T.Castro

Author Index   181

Chapter 1

INC Papers

A Review on Power Consumption Reduction Techniques on OFDM

S. Al-Obaidi[1], M. Ambroze[2], B. Ghita[3]
Centre for Security, Communications
and Network Research (CSCAN)
Plymouth University, UK
{sameer.al-obaidi[1], M. Ambroze[2],
bogdan.ghita[3]}@plymouth.ac.uk

Elias Giakoumidis
Centre for Ultra-high bandwidth
Devices for Optical Systems (CUDOS)
and Institute of Photonics Systems
Optical Science[2] (IPOS)
University of Sydney, Australia
e.giacoumidis@physics.usyd.edu.au

Athanasios Tsokanos
School of Computer Science,
University of Hertfordshire, UK
a.tsokanos@herts.ac.uk

Abstract— Orthogonal Frequency Division Multiplexing (OFDM) modulation format is an excellent candidate for next generation networks due to its properties of high transmission speed, high spectral efficiency, and versatility. However, this technique does suffer from high power consumption caused by extensive signal processing and computational complexity. In order to solve this problem, many methods have been used such us Fast-OFDM, Dynamic Signal-to-Noise ratio (DSNR), Adaptive Cyclic Prefix (ACP), Adaptive Loading Algorithms (ALA), Asymmetrically Clipping Optical-OFDM (ACO-OFDM) and Asymmetrically Companded OFDM. In this paper, we review the aforementioned methods along with their advantages and drawbacks.

Keywords— OFDM; Power consumption; Optical OFDM.

I. INTRODUCTION

Our modern way of living has created an incredible demand for resources that is damaging the eco-balance of our planet. In particular, due to the explosive growth of the Internet and the number of bandwidth-hungry services such as mobile networks, cloud computing, and high-resolution video, it is envisaged that the energy consumption of future networks will dramatically increase in the next few decades [1]. A simple solution towards a 'Greener' world is the reduction of the power consumption of electronic communication devices. In the next generation of networks, two of the most important factors will be energy efficiency and capacity management [2]

One of the most promising modulation techniques for next generation networks is Orthogonal Frequency Division Multiplexing (OFDM), due to its high capacity and flexibility, but it suffers from high consumption power due to complex Digital Signal Processing (DSP) operations [3]. FFT/IFFT (Fast Fourier Transform/ Inverse FFT) is one of the key operations in OFDM. Most power consumption in an OFDM transceiver is derived by IFFT/FFT operation. Various methods of reducing power consumption in OFDM have been develop addressing this problem have been developed in [4, 5, 6, 7, 8, and 9]. In Fast-OFDM, the IFFT/FFT blocks are replaced by the FCT/IFCT (fast cosine transform / inverse FCT) to enable not only twice the bandwidth efficiency compared to conventional OFDM but also to reduce the processing power by employing real arithmetic operations only, and single-quadrature modulation formats (such as Amplitude Shift-Keying). The Dynamic Signal-to- Noise Ratio (SNR) method uses variable length FFT/IFFT, which controls the precision of the processing calculation. The Adaptive Cyclic Prefix (ACP) method focuses on controlling the length of the Cyclic Prefix to eliminate fibre-link distortions in long-haul networks. Adaptive Loading Algorithms (ALA) methods focus on individual OFDM subcarriers by selecting the best modulation format (from Binary Phase Shift-Keying up to 256-Quadrature Amplitude Modulation, QAM) and by adjusting the optimum power per subcarrier. Asymmetrically Clipping Optical-OFDM (ACO-OFDM) and Asymmetrically Companded OFDM are two techniques that used to control the amplitude of the signal transmitted over a communication channel.

This paper presents a review of most important methods for reducing the DSP power consumption in OFDM. Most of them focus on processing operations described in section A and B such as Fast-OFDM and DSNR. In section C focuses on ACP by adding (Cyclic Prefix) CP, and section D focus on the ALA method for OFDM. Finally, section E and F is focuses on the ACO-OFDM and Asymmetrically Companded -OFDM techniques.

II. POWER CONSUMPTION METHODS

A. Fast OFDM

The main goals of next generation networks research are to reduce power consumption and increased network capacity. One of the most widely employed modulation schemes for this purpose is OFDM by means of IFFT/FFT as a basic operation. This part consumes a lot of DSP power when compared with other operations due to a large number of mathematical operations [5].

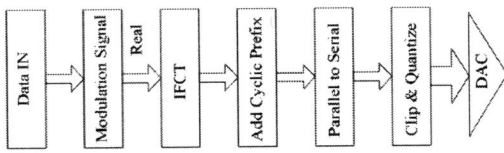

Fig. 1. Transmitter components of F-OFDM

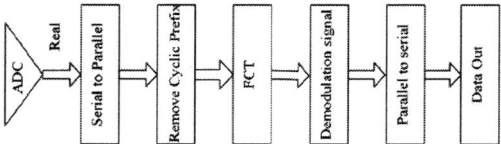

Fig. 2. Receiver components of F-OFDM

Related modulation techniques will be explained in the next section based on the IFFT/FFT but Fast-OFDM is based on IFCT/FCT (which replace the IFFT/FFT blocks) and has improved the bandwidth efficiency (twice the bandwidth efficiency) in comparison to conventional OFDM [10]. Consequently, Fast-OFDM can transmit more bits per channel compared to conventional OFDM because it reduces the frequency space between subcarriers. Other benefits include a reduction in DSP complexity, hardware components and operation time [11]. The most important feature in Fast OFDM is that its power consumption is reduced compared to conventional OFDM [12]. In figure (1-2) a typical block diagram of a Fast-OFDM (denoted as F-OFDM) transceiver is presented.

B. Dynamic Signal to Noise Ratio (DSNR)

There are many important factors in next generation network transponders. These include energy efficiency, network capacity, and flexibility. OFDM is one of the preferable modulation techniques for the next generation networks. However, it suffers from high energy consumptions due to complex Digital Signal Processing (DSP) operation in IFFT/FFT [13]. The number of inputs to IFFT/FFT depends on the number of sub-carriers used. A large number of sub-carriers increase the number of inputs to FFT/IFFT resulting in greater power consumption and the occupation of a large chip area [14]. The method which reduces power consumption by controlling the number of bits entering IFFT/FFT operations is named DSNR. The DSNR techniques control the calculation precision of the (FFT /IFFT) function of the DSP operation dynamically satisfying a Bit Error Rate (BER) requirement [15]. More specifically, this technique reduces the number of bits used in FFT/IFFT calculations resulting in a reduction in power consumption. The quantization and rounding error is used to control the calculation precision in the IFFT/FFT and manages the number of bits used in the OFDM frame generation [12]. Therefore, power consumption is improved by using the minimum number of bits while satisfying the optimum BER. In 2012, a research group from Japan worked on controlling the precision calculation of IFFT/FFT using DSNR to reduce the calculation in IFFT/FFT [5]. The block diagrams of the transmitter and receiver as shown in figure (3). This model includes Bit Length converter (BLC) to convert the symbol to a number of bits. The precision control uses to control the number of bits input to IFFT/FFT and select the minimum number of bits required for calculation result in a reduction in power consumption.

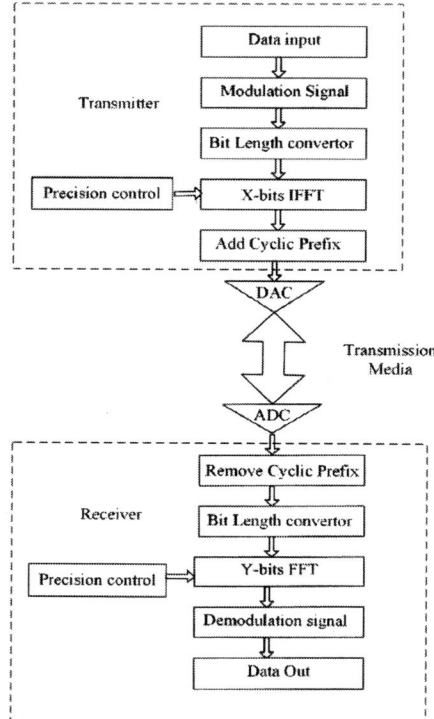

Fig. 3. OFDM Transceiver using Dynamic Signal to Noise Ratio.

C. Adaptive Cyclic Prefix

High-speed transmission can use a multicarrier modulation technique based on orthogonal carriers such as OFDM. If the distance between subsequent symbols is reduced, it can result in interference or overlapping of the OFDM symbols. However, inter-symbol interference (ISI) can be viewed also as a result of multipath propagation added after being transformed from a frequency to time domain by using IFFT [16]. However, the signal distortion and noise are increased due to overlapping. This effect is diminished by adding a cyclic prefix (CP) and fixing the distance between symbols. Adding a CP is performed by taking a copy of the last fraction of each symbol in the time domain and adding it to the front of the corresponding symbol to reduce the effect of the symbol overlapping or ISI, as in Figure (4). A cyclic prefix mechanism can be implemented by putting a gap between adjacent symbols and filling the gap using CP. The mechanism structure of CP is shown in Figure (5). There are two types of CP: fixed length type CP can be added between the symbols in the transmitter side after processing
IFFT to extend the time domain period and it is equal size length between all the symbols. The other type is variable length CP [3].

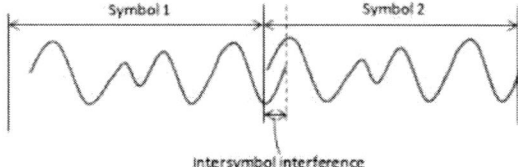

Fig. 4. Inter Symbol Interference (ISI) Structure [6]

A fixed type CP on OFDM increase the number of bits used in transmission and the variable length CP reduced the number of bits and consume less power when compared to fixed size CP [17]. In 2008, a group from Bangor University experimented on Adaptive Cyclic Prefix (ACP) [18]. They work on a variable length CP which depends on the receiver side BER, selected a length of CP that best satisfied the BER of the transmitted signal as shown in Figure (6).

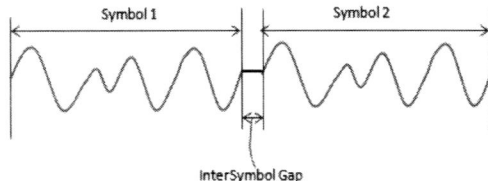

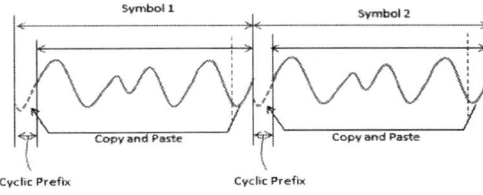

Fig. 5. Mechanism of Cyclic Prefix [6]

This method controlled the length of the CP by selecting the optimum BER on the receiver side and sending a feedback signal to the transmitter this controlling the CP length. In addition, ACP provides a reduction in the unused space of a CP and increases the bandwidth, resulting in an improvement of the transmission performance. A group in Italy also worked on ACP along with a bit loading (BL) algorithm, using a different modulation technique achieving a further reduction in terms of power consumption while improving SNR [19].

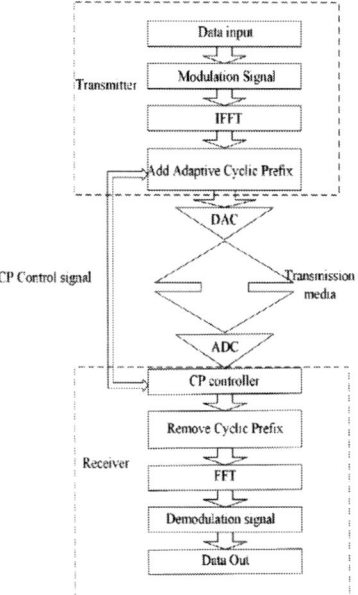

Fig. 6. OFDM Transceiver using Adaptive Cyclic Prefix

D. Adaptive Loading Algorithm

Improvements in the system flexibility and transmission performance along with in power consumption in OFDM can be achieved by increasing the utilization of each individual sub-carrier by applying various adaptive loading algorithms. The three types of algorithms are the following: BL (Bit Loading), PL (Power Loading), and BPL (Bit and Power Loading). Firstly, the Bit Loading algorithm means that the signal has identical signal power with a different signal modulation. This algorithm can control the number of bits per subcarrier depends on BER by optimizing the modulation format level. The BL algorithm occurs in frequency domain before modulation in the transmitter side, and then after demodulation in the receiver the Optical OFDM system enables the variation of the signal modulation format level for each individual subcarrier having identical power for all subcarriers [20]. This technique reduces the total energy consumption when compared without using BPL [21]. Secondly, a PL algorithm manipulates the electrical subcarrier power with the same modulation format for all sub-carriers [22]. Finally, a BPL algorithm adjusts both modulation and power for each subcarrier individually [23]. Although a large transmission bit rate can be achieved with the BPL algorithm, this algorithm suffers from high computational complexity in a transceiver due to complex FFT/IFFT mathematical operations. Transmission performance is usually best for BPL and worse for PL [7]. A diagram showing the interaction of the three ALA methods equipped with an OFDM transceiver is shown in Figure (7).

In 2010, the photonics group Bangor university conducted a Field-Programmable Gate Arrays (FPGA) experiment on a Multi-Mode Fibre (MMF) system channel using OFDM for short distances <800m [24]. They found that:
• BPL had the best transmission performance and PL has the worst.
• The transmission capacity difference between the BPL and PL algorithms that increases with both transmission distance and DAC/ADC sampling rate and is independent of the signal bit rate.
In 2011, a joint group from Photonics UK and AIT Greece investigated the optimization of an adaptive loading algorithm using Single Mode Fibers SMF system undertaken for distance <100km [25]. They have found that
• The transmission performance is best for BPL and worst for PL.
• Transmission capacity differs between algorithms which is independent from the transmission distance and launched optical power. However, when employing large numbers of subcarriers with higher DAC/ADC sampling rate BPL should be adopted.

The most significant technique used to reduce power in IMDD is DC-bias Optical OFDM (DCO-OFDM). A DC current is added to the OFDM signal to make it positive in all the subcarriers carrying data [8]. The configuration of the DCO-OFDM transceiver is shown in Figure (8) using both real and imaginary parts of the signal. Another method is Asymmetrically Clipped (ACO-OFDM), which sets the negative parts of the signal to zero and a positive part carrying data. The imaginary part of the OFDM signal is set to zero using Hermitian symmetry shown in Figure (9). Dividing the signal into two parts (real and imaginary), while the odd subcarriers carry data [26].
The ACO-OFDM method is more efficient in small constellations such as QAM (16, 32) than DCO-OFDM. However, DCO-OFDM is more efficient in large constellations using more power when compared to ACO-OFDM but it is efficient because of the two-part signal used instead of one [27]. These two methods above have been also implemented in real time FPGA [28].
Asymmetrically clipping DC Bias Optical OFDM (ADO-OFDM) combines aspects of both AC-OOFDM and DC-OOFDM [29] and uses even and odd subcarriers to carry data. The odd subcarriers are modulated by ACO-OFDM and the even subcarriers are modulated by DCO-OFDM [30] as it is shown in Figure (10). This technology improves the spectral efficiency of ACO-OFDM and power efficiency of DCO-OFDM improving BER and SNR of the transmitted signal [9].

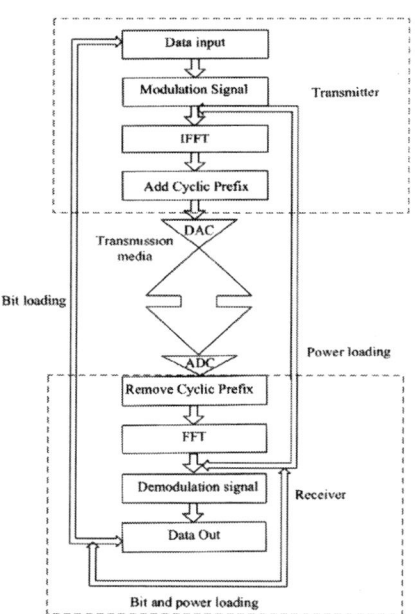

Fig. 7. Interaction of the three adaptive algorithm methods with an

E. Asymmetrically Clipping DC Bias Optical OFDM (ADO-OFDM)

To convert a signal from electrical to optical in OFDM data transmission over an optical channel, Intensity Modulation Direct Detection (IMDD) can be used. This technique uses only the positive real part of the signal because the intensity of light cannot be negative.

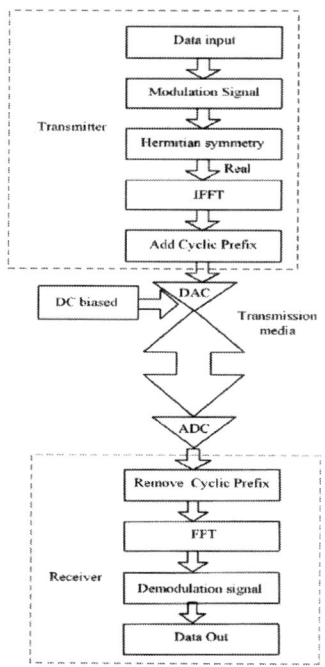

Fig. 8. DC-OOFDM Transceiver

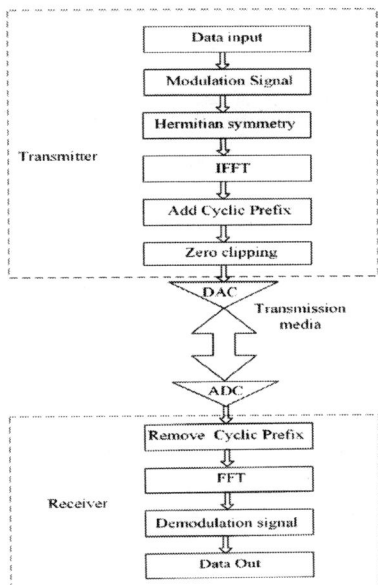

Fig. 9. ACO-OFDM transceiver

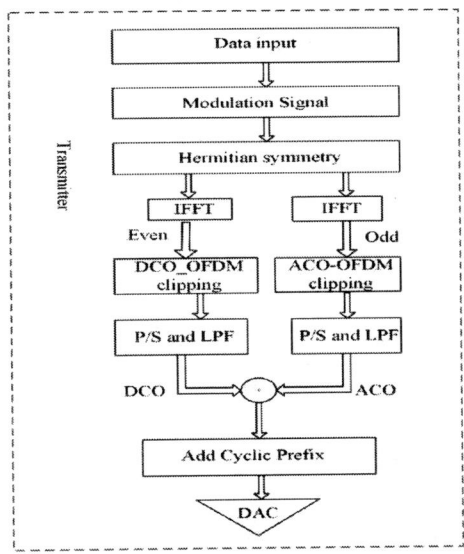

Fig. 10. ADO-OFDM transmitter

F. Asymmetrically Companded DCO-OFDM

IMDD uses only the real positive part of a signal. A theoretical technique proposed by a French group has the potential to reduce the power consumption in DCO-OFDM. The procedure of this method focuses on compressing the negative part of the bipolar real OFDM signal, which means reducing the negative peaks of the signal and then adding DC-Bias to the signal [31]. The amount of remaining negative peak is reduced so less amplitude affected by clipping. In the receiver side DC-bias and CP is remove then inverse companding transform (expander) applied to expand a compressed transmitted signal. The configuration system companded DCO-OFDM is described in figure (11). This technology can reduce the Peak Average Power Ratio (PAPR) in a transmitted optical OFDM signal, increases the bit rate and significantly reduces the complexity of the system [32].

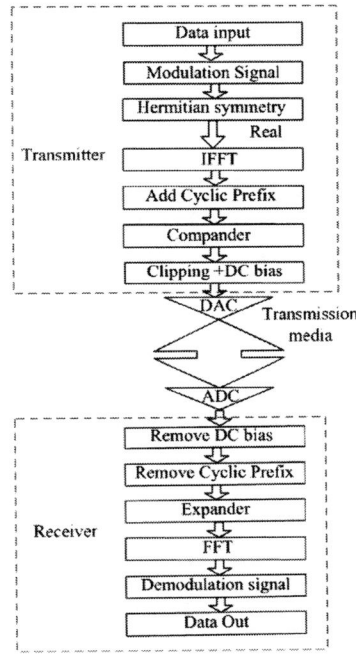

Fig. 11. Configuration system of Compand DC-OFDM

CONCLUSION

One of the main goals for next generation networks is reducing the power consumption, and various power-efficient multi-carrier modulation schemes have been described in this paper. In Fast-OFDM a FCT/IFCT is used instead of FFT/IFFT, while other methods exist such as DSNR to control the length of IFFT/FFT or by clipping/compressing a part of the signal such as in ACO-OFDM, DCO-OFDM, ADO-OFDM and Companded DCO-OFDM. Other methods control the length of the spectrum such as the Adaptive CP, which controls the length of the CP added between adjacent symbols Finally, ALAs can control the power and modulation for each subcarrier individually such as the BPL with high complexity but high performance or the PL algorithm with low complexity but low performance.

ACKNOWLEDGMENT

This project is part of a PhD research currently being carried out at Centre for Security, Communications and Network Research (CSCAN), Plymouth University, U.K. The deepest gratitude and thanks to Baghdad University and The Higher Committee for Education Development in Iraq(HCED) for funding this PhD research.

REFERENCES

[1] A. Scarfo, "All Silicon Data Center, the Energy Perspectives," in 2013 27th International Conference on Advanced Information Networking and Applications Workshops, 2013, pp. 1617–1622.

[2] T. E. H. El-Gorashi, X. Dong, and J. M. H. Elmirghani, "Green optical orthogonal frequency-division multiplexing networks," IET Optoelectron., vol. 8, no. 3, pp. 137–148, Jun. 2014.

[3] Chiwoo Lim, Youngbin Chang, Jaeweon Cho, Panyuh Joo, and Hyeonwoo Lee, "Novel OFDM Transmission Scheme to Overcome ISI Caused by Multipath Delay Longer than Cyclic Prefix," in 2005 IEEE 61st Vehicular Technology Conference, 2005, vol. 3, pp. 1763–1767.

[4] H. Nakamura, H. Kimura, S. Kimura, K. Asaka, and N. Yoshimoto, "First Demonstration of Energy Efficient IM-DD OFDM-PON using Dynamic SNR Management and Adaptive Modulation," 39th Eur. Conf. Exhib. Opt. Commun. (ECOC 2013), no. 1, pp. 669–671, 2013.

[5] H. Kimura, T. Shimada, H. Nakamura, S. Kimura, and N. Yoshimoto, "Dynamic SNR management using variable precision DSP for energy efficient OFDM-PON," in 2012 17th Opto-Electronics and Communications Conference, 2012, pp. 138–139.

[6] A. A. Al-jzari and I. Kostanic, "Effect of Variable Cyclic Prefix Length on OFDM System Performance over Different Wireless Channel Models," Univers. J. Commun. Networ, vol. 3, no. 1, pp. 7–14, 2015.

[7] X. Jin, R. Giddings, and J. Tang, "Experimental Demonstration of Adaptive Bit and/or Power Loading for Maximising Real-Time End-to-End Optical OFDM Transmission Performance," Opt. Fiber Commun. Conf. Fiber Opt. Eng. Conf. 2011, vol. 1, p. JWA029, 2011.

[8] M. F. Sanya, L. Djogbe, and A. Vianou, "DC-Biased Optical OFDM for IM / DD Passive Optical Network Systems," vol. 7, no. 4, pp. 205–214, 2015.

[9] W. N. Wan Ngah, S. J. Hashim, A. F. Abas, P. Varahram, and S. B. Ahmad Anas, "Reduction of Peak to Average Power Ratio in Coherent Optical Orthogonal Frequency division multiplexing using companding transform," 2014 Ieee Reg. 10 Symp., pp. 177–180, Apr. 2014.

[10] E. Giacoumidis, A. Tsokanos, C. Mouchos, G. Zardas, C. Alves, J. L. Wei, J. M. Tang, C. Gosset, Y. Jaouën, and I. Tomkos, "Extensive Comparisons of Optical Fast-OFDM and Conventional Optical OFDM for Local and Access Networks," J. Opt. Commun. Netw., vol. 4, no. 10, p. 724, Sep. 2012.

[11] E. Giacoumidis, I. Tomkos, and J. M. Tang, "Performance of Optical Fast-OFDM in MMF-Based Links," Optical Fiber Communication Conference and Exposition (OFC/NFOEC), 2011 and the National Fiber Optic Engineers Conference. pp. 1–3, 2011.

[12] H. Kimura, H. Nakamura, S. Kimura, and N. Yoshimoto, "Numerical Analysis of Dynamic SNR Management by Controlling DSP Calculation Precision for," vol. 24, no. 23, pp. 2132–2135, 2012.

[13] H. Kimura, K. Asaka, H. Nakamura, S. Kimura, and N. Yoshimoto, "Energy efficient IM-DD OFDM-PON using dynamic SNR management and adaptive modulation.," Opt. Express, vol. 22, no. 2, pp. 1789–95, Jan. 2014.

[14] R. Bouziane, P. a Milder, R. J. Koutsoyannis, Y. Benlachtar, J. C. Hoe, M. Glick, and R. I. Killey, "Dependence of Optical OFDM Transceiver ASIC Complexity on FFT Size," Digit. Signal Process., vol. 1, pp. 45–47, 2012.

[15] H. Kimura, H. Nakamura, K. Asaka, S. Kimura, and N. Yoshimoto, "16QAM signal transmission experiment for dynamic SNR management on IM-DD OFDM-PON," 2013 18th OptoElectronics and Communications Conference held jointly with 2013 International Conference on Photonics in Switching (OECC/PS). pp. 1–2, 2013.

[16] Y. S. Cho, J. Kim, W. Y. Yang, and C. G. Kang, MIMO-OFDM Wireless Communications with MATLAB 2010.

[17] J. N. Bae, Y. H. Kim, and J. Y. Kim, "MIMO OFDM system with AMC and variable CP length for wireless communications," 2009 9th Int. Symp. Commun. Inf. Technol. Isc. 2009, pp. 16–20, 2009.

[18] E. Giacoumidis, J. L. Wei, X. Q. Jin, and J. M. Tang, "Improved transmission performance of adaptively modulated optical OFDM signals over directly modulated DFB laser-based IMDD links using adaptive cyclic prefix," Opt. Express, vol. 16, no. 13, p. 9480, Jun. 2008.

[19] S. D'Alessandro, A. M. Tonello, and L. Lampe, "Bit-loading algorithms for OFDM with adaptive cyclic prefix length in PLC channels," 2009 IEEE Int. Symp. Power Line Commun. its Appl. ISPLC 2009, no. 1, pp. 177–181, 2009.

[20] P. Rana and R. Saini, "Performance of Different Bit Loading Algorithms for OFDM at PLC Channel," in 2012 Second International Conference on Advanced Computing & Communication Technologies, 2012, pp. 486–489.

[21] T. N. Vo, K. Amis, T. Chonavel, and P. Siohan, "A Computationally Efficient Discrete Bit-Loading Algorithm for OFDM Systems Subject to Spectral-Compatibility Limits," IEEE Trans. Commun., vol. 63, no. 6, pp. 2261–2272, Jun. 2015.

[22] R. P. Giddings, X. Q. Jin, and J. M. Tang, "First experimental demonstration of 6Gb/s real-time optical OFDM transceivers incorporating channel estimation and variable power loading.," Opt. Express, vol. 17, no. 22, pp. 19727–38, Oct. 2009.

[23] E. Bedeer, O. a. Dobre, M. H. Ahmed, and K. E. Baddour, "Optimal bit and power loading for OFDM systems with average BER and total power constraints," GLOBECOM - IEEE Glob. Telecommun. Conf., pp. 3685–3689, 2012.

[24] E. Giacoumidis, X. Q. Jin, a Tsokanos, and J. M. Tang, "Statistical Performance Comparisons of Optical OFDM Adaptive Loading Algorithms in Multimode Fiber-Based Transmission Systems," IEEE Photonics J., vol. 2, no. 6, pp. 1051–1059, Dec. 2010.

[25] E. Giacoumidis, J. L. Wei, A. Tsokanos, A. Kavatzikidis, E. Hugues-Salas, J. M. Tang, and I. Tomkos, "Performance optimization of adaptive loading algorithms for SMF-based optical OFDM transceivers," 2011 16th Eur. Conf. Networks Opt. Commun., pp. 56–59, 2011.

[26] J. Armstrong, B. J. C. Schmidt, D. Kalra, H. a. Suraweera, and A. J. Lowery, "Performance of asymmetrically clipped optical OFDM in AWGN for an intensity modulated direct detection system," GLOBECOM - IEEE Glob. Telecommun. Conf., pp. 6–10, 2006.

[27] R. Islam, P. Choudhury, and M. A. Islam, "Analysis of DCO-OFDM and Flip-OFDM for IM / DD Optical-Wireless System," pp. 32–35, 2014.

[28] P. Saengudomlert, E. Sauvage, and K. Sterckx, "Optimised field programmable gate array implementation of a dual-mode orthogonal frequency division multiplexing optical wireless communication transmitter," IET Optoelectron., vol. 8, no. 6, pp. 232–238, Dec. 2014

[29] S. D. Dissanayake and J. Armstrong, "Comparison of ACO-OFDM, DCO-OFDM and ADO-OFDM in IM/DD Systems," J. Light. Technol., vol. 31, no. 7, pp. 1063–1072, Apr. 2013.

[30] N. Wu and Y. Bar-Ness, "l ower bounds on the channel capacity of ASCO-OFDM and ADO-OFDM," in 2015 49th Annual Conference on Information Sciences and Systems (CISS), 2015, pp. 1–5.

[31] Barrami, Y. Le Guennec, E. Novakov, and P. Busson, "An optical power efficient asymmetrically companded DCO-OFDM for IM/DD systems," in 2014 23rd Wireless and Optical Communication Conference (WOCC), 2014, pp.1–6.

[32] Y. Rahmatallah, N. Bouaynaya, and S. Mohan, "Bit Error Rate Performance of Linear Companding Transforms for PAPR Reduction in OFDM Systems," 2011 IEEE Glob. Telecommun. Conf. - GLOBECOM 2011, pp. 1–5, 2011.

Towards an Energy Optimization Framework for Cloud Computing Data Centers

Samah Ibrahim Alshathri
Department of Information Technology, College of Computer and Information Sciences
Princess Nourah Bint Abdulrahman University
Riyadh, Kingdom of Saudi Arabia
Samah_sh3@hotmail.com

Abstract— The cloud computing concept has emerged as a powerful mechanism for data storage by providing a suitable platform of data centers. Recent studies show that energy consumption of cloud computing systems is a key issue. Therefore, the energy consumption should be reduced to minimize performance losses, achieve the target battery lifetime, satisfy performance requirements, minimize power consumption, minimize the CO_2 emissions, maximize the profit, and maximize resource utilization.
In this paper, we present a taxonomy of cloud computing systems and we will discuss many energy optimization considerations. Further, our paper focuses on virtualization, migration and task scheduling algorithms to minimize energy consumption in the cloud data centers. Applying a new idea of scheduling algorithms will help to control and optimize the mapping process time between the data center servers and the incoming tasks. This will perform an optimal deployment of the data center resources to achieve good computing efficiency, network load minimization and reducing the energy consumption in the data center. To evaluate the scheduler's efficiency we use one of the different kinds of simulators that were developed specifically for cloud computing environment.

Keywords—component; cloud computing; scheduling algorithm; green computing; energy optimization, virtualization, simulation.

I. INTRODUCTION

Typically, the constant changes in computers and communications technology led to the need of on-demand network access to shared computing resources to reduce cost and time and this is known as Cloud computing, which delivers computing services to users as a pay-as-you-go manner by emerging several distributed and high-performance computing concepts. The cloud makes reaching any information or source possible from anywhere eliminating the setup and installation step, such that the user and the hardware may co-exist in different places. This comes beneficial for the users or the small companies that cannot pay for the hardware, storage or resources as the big companies. The cloud users do not need anything but the Internet connection to reach their cloud providers without the need of paying for licenses or worry about the installation and updating any resources.

II. THE CLOUD COMPUTING CONCEPT

The cloud consists of either one or multiple data centers where each data center is built using a large number of storage units, servers and communication infrastructure and these resources are provided by cloud vendors using the pay-as-use scheme [1]. Cloud computing defined as follows:

- Reference [2] defines the Cloud computing in terms of its utility to the end user: "A Cloud is a market-oriented distributed computing system consisting of a collection of interconnected and virtualized computers that are dynamically provisioned and presented as one or more unified computing resource(s) based on service-level agreements established through negotiation between the service provider and consumers."

- National Institute of Standards and Technology (NIST) [3] defines cloud computing as follows: "Cloud computing is a model for enabling convenient, on-demand network access to a shared pool of configurable computing resources (e.g., networks, servers, storage, applications, and services) that can be rapidly provisioned and released with minimal management effort or service provider interaction. This Cloud model promotes availability and is composed of five essential characteristics, three service models, and four deployment models."

A. Benefits of Cloud Computing

The following main benefits are the reasons behind the growing demand of cloud computing industry [4]:
- No software is needed for the users.
- Rapid implementation.
- Ease of maintenance.
- Reliability.
- Automatic updating.
- Flexibility of picking several service providers.
- Elastic and on demand basis existence of infrastructure.

- Reduced costs of deployment of services

III. ARCHITECTURAL CONSIDERATIONS

Cloud computing designers are able to explain the main cloud practices and benefits to the end users. Therefore, moving to cloud computing infrastructure requires the following hardware and software components:

A. Cloud Elements

The cloud architecture is based on the incoming tasks, data center broker and the main data center that have all the hosts, Virtual Machines (VMs), network connection and many other components. The key cloud elements are [5]:
- Data Center:

It encapsulates the hosts (memory, cores, capacity, and storage) and the existing connection between them. Every data center has a set of policies to control its components.
- Consumers/Brokers:

The broker acts as an intermediary between the customer and the cloud where it submits service requests from anywhere in the world to the cloud.
- Service Allocator:

It is the interface between the Cloud infrastructure and user.
- VMs:

Multiple virtual machines created on one physical machine to meet the need of processing multiple tasks on a single device.
- Physical Machines:

Physical machines are the main servers used in the data center which they can be virtualized later to meet the processing demands.
- Cloudlet:

The cloudlets are the number of tasks plus the amount of storage needed to process these tasks.
- Memory Provisioner:

It has the physical memory allocation policies for the VMs.
- Cloud Coordinator:

Responsible for the communication between multiple data centers and their brokers and supervise the internal state of the data center itself for load balancing decisions.
- Cloudlet scheduler:

The scheduler defines the police of execution of the incoming tasks.

B. The service Level Agreement (SLA)

It is defined as "a contract document or a formal negotiated agreement based upon the purpose and objectives that exists between the Cloud Service Providers and the cloud users."[6]. SLAs provide the user first with a clear view to the cloud environment, security, management policies and service monitoring as shown in *Fig. 1*.

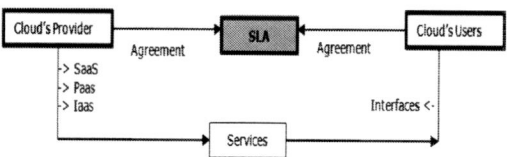

Figure 1. Service Level Agreement

C. Existing models

There are four main types of clouds. The user or company needs usually to define the cloud type that belongs to one of the following categories [3]:
- Public Cloud

The public cloud is about offering the cloud infrastructure to all the users and enabling the consumer to get the services with very little financial cost. This type cloud provides services to multiple customers.
- Private Cloud

It is a cloud created to be used by a specific organization or a precise user to have the ultimate control, security, and quality of service of the data.
- Community Cloud

It is a shared cloud infrastructure between two or more organizations to serve a common function or purpose.
- Hybrid Cloud

The hybrid cloud is simply a combination of two or more of the previously defined clouds type and bound them together as a unit.

D. Types of cloud Services

The cloud providers offer many types of services to their users [7]:

- Infrastructure-as-a-Service (IaaS)

It is the first layer of cloud computing. The provider here offers the hardware and the minimum limit of software for users to develop their work on the cloud infrastructure, and the user in this type gets the service and the ability to configure the settings and implementation of the software and programming environment (e.g., Rackspace).

- Platform-as-a-Service (PaaS)

PaaS is the second layer of cloud computing. It is the type of service where the user can build the service, and the application needed from the sources supplied from the Internet. The user who gets the PaaS service cannot have a complete control over the service. The existence of a software layer between the user and the hardware prevents him from getting a full control. This service eliminates the rule that says that the user has to be an expert to deal with such a service (e.g. Google App Engine).

- Software-as-a-Service (SaaS)

SaaS is considered as the final layer of the cloud services. It is the model in which the user can access an application that is hosted by the provider from a variety of devices through the Internet without the need of any installation, data loss or storage space (e.g. Google Docs) [8].

IV. ENERGY OPTIMAZATION EVOLUTION

Cloud computing researchers are seeking to optimize the energy and they are facing many challenges including virtualization, migration and scheduling.

A. Virtualization

The Virtualization has been around now for more than a decade. It is the creation of a logical number of VMs on the same physical machine. It plays a decisive role in the cloud environment, and it is the heart of the cloud computing industry. Virtualization is a way to reach the ultimate and efficient use of resource's storage, and it provides data center deployment of new methods with reliable management for data to achieve green computing through the best utilization of data center resources. The motivation behind the establishment of virtual machine is to process different tasks on a single host. Each VM acts as a one physical server with its own RAM, CPU, NIC and hardware disk. The benefits of creating virtual machines in the data centers are [9]:

- Reduce infrastructure costs.
- Save energy.
- Faster server provisioning.
- Improve recovery.
- Isolate applications.
- Flexibility.
- Reliability.
- Ease of testing and developing phase.

B. VM Migration

It is an essential to manage cloud computing resources dynamically that's why the VM migration is becoming increasingly used in cloud computing. VM migration is transferring VM from a physical server to another, which grants workload balancing, hardware maintenance, high availability services and consolidated management [9].

The biggest advantages of using the live VM migration are:

1- To have a server consolidation which allows the maintenance of the virtual machine offline whenever needed or for upgrading without shutting down the whole system.

2- Maintain the load balancing in the data center.

We can turn off hosts when using VM Migration in the data center to have a better energy efficiency using server consolidation.

In any VM Migration process, two key questions will rise:

Q1. Which VM to migrate from an overloaded server?

Q2. Which server to pick as destination?

Answering these questions usually depends on the data center processing policy and the user demands.

C. Scheduling Techniques

The research community continually investigated the energy usage since the number cloud users is increasing [10]. One of the best ways to control the energy consumption within the data center is the use of a good scheduling technique. Scheduling algorithm is a way of managing and controlling the process of assigning incoming tasks to servers regarding the cloud user demands.

V. CLOUD ENVIRONMENT SIMULATION

The fast growth of cloud research area implied the necessity of implementing tools to design an efficient data center infrastructure. A number of simulators have been precisely developed for cloud computing environments such as GreenCloud, CloudAnalyst, Cloudsim, Networkcloudsim, EMUSIM and MDCSim but only a few of them are available as an open source platform. Cloudsim simulator is the most sophisticated one among them all [11].

A. Cloudsim Simulator

Cloudsim is a novel Simulation-based approach for modeling and simulation the data center environments. It is the most popular cloud simulation tool that offers major benefits to cloud customers such as testing their services without any cost and the capability of making the needed adjustments to their data center structure before the real deploying it in the real-world [1]. The development of cloudsim simulator was in the CLOUDS laboratory at the computer since and software engineering department of the University of Melbourne.

B. Features Of Cloudsim Simulation

Cloudsim simulator is a free simulator and widely used by research scholars and practitioners. It offers many features to the users such as cloudlets creation and execution, load balancing, energy optimization, task scheduling and resource provisioning.

VI. CONCLUSION

Recent researches are struggling with the energy consumption rates in the cloud computing environment due to the escalating energy-hunger and CO2 emissions in the loud computing data centers.

This paper presented a survey on cloud computing and discussed the importance of minimizing the energy consumption of data centers. We introduced the main cloud architectural elements, models and services for a better understanding to reach the ultimate power optimization. Our idea is jointly based on virtualization, VM migration and scheduling under the regulations of the service level agreement. We introduced also a set of cloud computing simulators focusing on cloudsim as one of the most-used tools. Our future work consists to develop a novel framework to minimize the power consumption in cloud computing data center using cloudsim simulator.

REFERENCES

[1] Buyya, R., Ranjan, R. & Calheiros, R.N., 2009. Modeling and simulation of scalable cloud computing environments and the Cloudsim toolkit: Challenges and opportunities. Proceedings of the 2009

International Conference on High Performance Computing and Simulation, HPCS 2009, pp.1–11.

[2] Buyya, R., Yeo, C.S. & Venugopal, S., 2008. Market-Oriented Cloud Computing: Vision, Hype, and Reality for Delivering IT Services as Computing Utilities. 2008 10th IEEE International Conference on High Performance Computing and Communications, pp.5–13. Available at: http://ieeexplore.ieee.org/lpdocs/epic03/wrapper.htm?arnumber=4637675.

[3] NIST, 2011. The NIST Definition of Cloud Computing Recommendations of the National Institute of Standards and Technology. Nist Special Publication, 145, p.7. Available at: http://www.mendeley.com/research/the-nist-definition-about-cloud-computing/.K. Elissa, "Title of paper if known," unpublished.

[4] Apostu, A. et al., 2013. Study on Advantages and Disadvantages of Cloud Computing - the Advantages of Telemetry Applications in the Cloud. Recent Advances in Applied Computer Science and Digital Services, pp.118–123.

[5] Manasa, H.B. & Basu, A., 2013. Energy Aware Resource Allocation in Cloud Data center. , International Journal of Engineering and Advanced Technology (IJEAT), 2(5), pp.277–281.

[6] Dash, S.B. et al., 2014. Service Level Agreement Assurance in Cloud Computing : A Trust Issue. International Journal of Computer Science and Information Technologies, 5(3), pp.2899–2906

[7] Arabi, E. et al., 2013. Intelligent Strategy of Task Scheduling in Cloud Computing for Load Balancing. International Journal of Emerging Trends & Technology in Computer Science , 2(6), pp.12–22.

[8] Hussin, M., Lee, Y.C. & Zomaya, A.Y., 2011. Priority-based scheduling for large-scale distribute systems with energy awareness. Proceedings - IEEE 9th International Conference on Dependable, Autonomic and Secure Computing, DASC 2011, pp.503–509.

[9] Ahmad, N., Kanwal, A. & Shibli, M.A., 2013. Survey on secure live virtual machine (VM) migration in cloud. Conference Proceedings - 2013 2nd National Conference on Information Assurance, NCIA 2013, (November 2015), pp.101–106

[10] Baliga, B.J. et al., 2011. Green Cloud Computing : Balancing Energy in Processing , Storage , and Transport. , 99(1), p.149.

[11] Malhotra, R. & Jain, P., 2013. Study and Comparison of CloudSim Simulators in the Cloud Computing. The SIJ Transactions on Computer Science Engineering and its Applications (CSEA), 1(4), pp.111–115.

Performance Evaluation of Time-Critical Smart Grid Applications

Frank Ball
Frank Ball Consulting
Oxford UK
frank_ball@ntlworld.com

Kashinath Basu
School of Computing
Oxford Brookes University
Oxford UK
kbasu@brookes.ac.uk

Abstract— This paper focuses on the Firm Real-Time requirements of Time-Critical Wide Area Measurement and Control systems, that are expected to play a major role in future Smart Grids. It analyses the operation of these systems and identifies their communication traffic characteristics. It shows that these characteristics are significantly different to those of the current Near Real-Time Wide Area Measurement applications that provide visualization to support manual grid control. It then discusses the performance evaluation of these time critical systems and presents the first stage in a body of work aimed at developing models and techniques to carry out the performance evaluation process. It presents some preliminary results and outlines the direction for future work.

Keywords—Smart grid, time-crical applications, performance evaluation

I. Introduction

A communication network is an essential component of a smart grid system. Its role is to support a wide range of applications, many of which have very similar requirements to those of current Internet applications. In particular, they have the general requirements for security, resilience, reliability and wide area interconnectivity. However, a number of classes of smart grid applications, particularly those intended for controlling smart grids in the near future, have requirements that are significantly different from those of any existing Internet application. This is due to their Firm-real-time end-to-end delay bound requirements. Furthermore the delay bound specified for each individual type of time-critical application refers to the combined delay resulting from both application level processing time and communication latency. For the most time-critical of these applications, delay targets in the orders of 3ms, 10ms and 16ms have been stipulated. Although no separate targets has been set for communication delay, it has been suggested by some that 1ms to 2ms would be an appropriate goal for the delay component of the communication network [1] [2].

Time-critical smart grid applications are responsible for state estimation, control, protection, and ensuring the stability of power generation and distribution. Their domains of operation include both the local area for internal sub-station control, and the wide area for protection, control, and maintaining wide area awareness. Currently, when operating in the wide area, the role of these applications is generally limited to providing visualization for wide area awareness. Applications that provide visualization have near-real-time requirement and can tolerate latencies in the order of 100ms. Currently, automatic control, for which the more stringent delay requirements apply, is mainly limited to the local area. However, the goal for the future is to extend automatic control into the wide area. This goal is motivated by the fundamental objectives of the Smart Grid. That are: firstly, to provide greater efficiency in the use of current energy generation; and secondly, enable the inclusion of a wide range of renewable, but more variable, energy sources. Extending automatic control into wide area presents the additional challenge of providing low latency in a larger scale network and over greater distances. Distances in the orders of 100km, 160km, 200kms, or even greater, are not unusual, and therefore, the effects of propagation delay will be significant. Furthermore, failures in the smart grid control system can lead to serious consequences, making it essential that delay targets for the system can be guaranteed prior to the system becoming operational.

Due to the stringent nature of the latency requirements, it has suggested that point to point fibers between each device and the controller may be needed to minimize delay. However, this would result fiber capacity being significantly underutilized. Furthermore, the data generated by these application is also used for historic purposes, such as post event analysis. Therefore, using an integrated multiservice networking approach would be desirable, provided that latency requirements can be guaranteed.

The aims of our investigation are: firstly, to derive generic and parameterized models to support the performance evaluation of Time-Critical Synchrophasor Measurement and Control Systems; and secondly, to develop techniques and methods to evaluate the temporal performance of models based on specific systems. These models will be based on the generic concept of packet switching, so as to be applicable both level 2 and level 3 switching. Therefore, throughout the discussion we will use the term forwarding device rather than router or switch. This paper present the first stage of this investigation in which we analyze the data flow patterns of Synchrophasor Measurements Systems and identify the characteristics of the network traffic they will produce. We show these characteristics to be significantly different to those of the Near-Real-Time control applications in current use, and that a different interpretation of the QoS parameters to that generally applied to streaming applications, will be needed. The remainder of the paper is structured as follows: section 2 provides a brief overview of requirements of Wide Area Measurement System and highlights the points that relate to time-critical applications; Section 3 describes the operation of a Synchrophasor Measurement System, introduces their constituent devices, and outlines the current operation of this type of system. It then discusses how the more stringent delay requirements of proposed future systems present a significant challenge to the performance of the system; section 4 presents an analysis of the traffic characteristics and performance parameters that relate to these systems and briefly presents some results from a preliminary performance evaluation. Finally; section 5 concludes and outlines future work.

II. WIDE AREA MEASUREMENT SYSTEMS

A Wide Area Measurement System (WAMS) [3] is an advanced sensing and measurement system used to continuously monitor the power grid. System state and power quality are monitored using information obtained from Phasor Measurement Units (PMUs), which are devices deployed throughout the grid. To support robustness and reliability, it is current practice to deploy PMUs as redundant pairs. PMUs provide accurate system state measurements in real-time. The information generated within a WAMS is used not only by time-critical applications, but may also be required as historical information to be used, for example, in post event analysis.

To support the range of communication needed by a WAMS, Wide Area Measurement Systems for Data Delivery (WAMS-DD) have been proposed. Bakken et al [1] present a thorough and extensive survey of wide area control in a smart grid and a detailed analysis of the overall requirements of a WAMS-DD. From this analysis they produce a comprehensive set of both requirements and guidelines for the implementation of a WAMS-DD. The requirements that are particularly relevant to the time-critical applications can be summarized as follows: the smart grid communication system must provide a wide range of QoS and a "one sizes fits all" approach is not possible; the time-critical control applications require firm end-to-end deterministic guarantees that must be provided over the entire grid; and these guarantees must be given to each individual message and not based on a weaker aggregation over long periods of time.

The guidelines that follow on from these requirements are as follow: don't depend on priority guarantees that are based on preferential treatment in times of heavy traffic, as they cannot provide firm end-to-end delay bounds, i.e. use mechanisms that provide strong class isolation; avoid post-error recovery mechanisms since these can add considerable latency in the case of dropped packets, this guideline proposes that a better alternative would be to send each message over multiple disjoint paths; use static routing not dynamic, much stronger latency guarantees can be given using complete knowledge of the network topology; forwarding decisions should be based on packet header only; exploit a priori knowledge of predicable traffic; exploit the much smaller scale of a WAMS-DD system in comparison to the Internet. It should be noted that these particular guidelines are intended mainly for supporting the time-critical traffic classes. In particular the constraint of static routing need not apply to other classes of traffic, provided that the forwarding devices can support a combination of both static and dynamic routing.

III. SYNCHROPHASOR MEASUREMENT SYSTEMS

A Synchrophasor is a measurement of the amplitude and angle of a sinusoidal waveform (in this case the waveform of power cycle) that is timestamped using a UCT (Universally Coordinated Time) mechanism facilitated by GPS [4]. These synchronized measurements provide a comprehensive picture of state of the power system. These measurements are taken by a PMU which is a specialized device that periodically samples the power cycle and calculates the synchrophasor measurement. Generally, six measurements are taken from the current and voltage for each of the three phases. These measurements are then encapsulated into a single fixed length message for transmission. Although that length may differ between different configurations of the device, generally, PMU devices are configured at the initialization stage of the system and remain unchanged once the system is operational. A message length (including protocol overheads) in the order of 1000bits is typical of many examples quoted in the literature. The frequency at which measurements are taken can vary depending on the requirements of the control application and the frequency of the power cycle, currently values of 10hz, 30hz, 50hz, and 60hz are employed with 120hz being considered as a target for the future. In this paper, discussion will be based on the case of a 60hz power cycle and a 60hz phasor sampling period.

PMUs are deployed throughout the grid, generally within substations, and are connected by direct communication links, or a substation LAN, to a local Phasor Data Concentrator (PDC). This device checks the validity of the messages before forwarding them as a batch, via a WAN, to a Super Phasor Data Concentrator (SPDC), which in turn has a direct connection to the Controller, as shown in figure 1. The end-to-end latency of the system is defined as the time between the timestamp value of the message and completion of the control decision process.

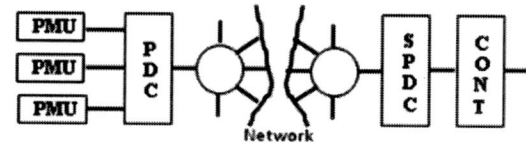

Fig. 1. Synchrophasor Date Flow Architecture

PMU processing involves taking a number of evenly spaced samples over the duration of one power cycle with half the samples being taken before the UTC time stamp and the remainder taken after it. This means that there is delay of 8.35ms after the timestamp before further processing can take place. Following the sample phase a signal processing algorithm is used to calculate amplitude and angle of the synchrophasor. This information is then encapsulated into a message before being transmitted. In the case of less time-critical synchrophasor based applications, e.g. visualization, that is a Near Real-Time process, the latency requirements are in the order of 100ms. For this types of application the main constraint on the performance of the PMU is that processing of the samples must be complete before the end of the next sampling period. See below in Figure 2.

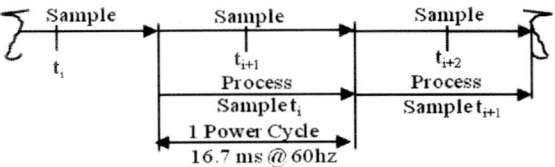

Fig. 2. PMU Processing Cycle

Also in these less time-critical cases the PCD device can apply traffic shaping to its output. For example, for a local PDC serving 20 PMU devices that each produce one message of 1000bits, the PDC can smooth out the packet stream over the 6.7ms period resulting in a sustained rate of 1.2 Mb/s which is in the same order as figures widely reported in the literature [4]. In this case the traffic characteristics are very similar to that of other streaming applications. However, for more the time-critical synchrophasor based application, e.g. Wide Area Automatic Control, processing times will be subject to more stringent constraints and traffic smoothing will not generally, be possible. This will result in a traffic profile that is significantly different from that of the Near Real-Time case.

The ultimate requirement for synchrophasor based wide area control applications is to carry out the measurement-to-decision process within one power cycle [1] [2]. Figure 3 shows how meeting this requirement significantly changes the processing cycle from that shown in figure 2.

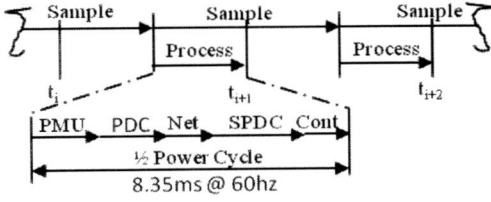

Fig. 3. PMU to Control Processing Cycle

The latency targets become an order on magnitude lower and therefore performance evaluation will need to be carried out at the micro second level. The evaluation process will need to consider the synchrophasor measurement and control system as a whole, although a degree of decomposition is possible as will be shown in section 4. There is a consensus that this class of application requires a Firm Real-Time guarantee that has a hard deadline but for which some missed deadlines and losses may acceptable [1][2][3]. However, the term "some" is a rather vague parameter and as an alternative we propose the use of Probabilistic Hard Real-Time, that offers a more precise definition, i.e. for a latency bound T, the following condition must hold,

$$P(t > T) \leq 10^{-x} \qquad (1)$$

This allows the application to choose a desired value for x, and during evaluation the requirement can be related directly to high percentiles of a delay distribution. However, in order to provide this guarantee to each individual message, as advised in the guidelines presented in section 2, this condition must be applied to each source individually, and not to the aggregation of the batch in each cycle.

Currently, there is a wide range in the performance capabilities of PMU and PDC devices. [5]. Although PMUs are subject to compliance testing for correctness of measurement and quality of data, as yet there are no compliance requirements for their temporal performance. PDCs are not subject to compliance testing, and in some cases they have be implemented on general purposes computational engine including windows PCs. Clearly, if these more stringent requirements are to be met PMUs, PDCs, the SPDC and the controller will need to become, not only faster, but true Real-Time devices with performance requirements being built into their design. Any auxiliary function that they provide, including reconfiguration and device updating should not be allowed to interfere with the time critical functions. Similar requirements will apply to networking equipment. In particular forwarding devices will need to be provide to provide strict priority queuing to time-critical class of traffic. Ideally, forwarding should operate at line rate, with queuing only taking place at the output links. If this is not the case, full details of internal operation and performance at the microsecond level may be required for accurate evaluation. Also, in all cases it will be essential that packet classification operates line rate for strict priority queueing to be maintained.

Due to the nature of PMU and PDC operations there is some interdependency between latency in the network and the latency of the devices. In particular, PDCs wait until all the messages they expect to receive in a given cycle have arrived before starting to process them. To allow for message losses the PDC sets a waiting time. Once this time has expired, it starts to process the messages that have arrived in time. Messages from that cycle that arrive later are discarded, and therefore, missing the deadline set by the waiting time, is equivalent to loss. The same process is employed by the SPDC. Clearly, setting an appropriate value for the waiting time will require information relating to network latency, and in turn the waiting time settings will affect the overall latency of the system. Although attempting to meet these stringent requirements may appear to be a difficult task, there are a few points that help to mitigate the problem. Also, most of these points aid the application of the guidelines outlined is section 2.

Firstly, the system will be based on static infrastructure, and mobility will not be an issue; secondly, device configuration can occur prior to the system becoming operational; Thirdly, full information regarding the number of PMUs, PDCs, forwarding devices and their interconnections, together with link distances, can be made available prior to evaluation; finally, apart from distance, these networks will be of relatively small scale. One further point is that the cost of using more expensive high performance equipment throughout, and redundant equipment for robustness and reliability, may not be a major issue. It has been reported that equipment costs only account for about 5% of the total cost of installing a synchrophasor measurement system [6]. Therefore, if the findings of this report represent a general case, then as an example, trebling the current cost of equipment should only add about 10% to the total bill.

IV. TRAFFIC CHARACTERISTICS AND EVALUATION OF FIRM REAL-TIME SYNCHROPHASOR SYSTEMS

The primary traffic sources are the PMUs that produce a single message for each cycle, in synchrony with each other. However, unless the PMUs are connected to the local PDC by a LAN, the PDC will be the first point of contact with the communication infrastructure. To simplify discussion we will focus on the case of PMUs being directly connected to the PDC, as shown in figure 1.

Once the PDC has finished performing its internal functions it will start to transmit the messages over the network. The output from the PDC will be in form of a short burst of packets, the duration of which will depend on the number of messages and the rate at which the PDC can operate. Ideally the PDC should be designed to operate and the line rate of the communication link. Once the burst has been sent, there will be no further transmissions until the next cycle. In the case of a local PDC serving 20 PMU devices that each produce one message of 1000bits, and a link rate of 500Mb/s the burst duration would be 40µs. alternatively, for a link rate of 100Mb/s (or in the case of a PDC that can only operate at that speed) the burst duration would be 200µs. In both cases the burst duration is very short in comparison to the cycle time of 16.7ms. In cases such as this, the concept of a stream with an average, or sustained, rate is not relevant. However, as all the messages are created at the same time, and are all bound for the same destination, bursts originating from different PCDs could interact with each other as they pass though the forwarding devices along paths that fan-in to the SPDC, as shown below in figure 4.

For economy of space, and to simplify discussion, the system shown in figure 4 is of a very small scale grid, although the overall link distances considered (71km, 111km and 121km) are not untypical for grids discussed in the literature. A more realistic scale would be in the order of 15 to 25 forwarding devices with paths involving between 3 to 20 hops and a median of between 7 and 10 hops [7]. The propagation delays shown on the links are based on the widely quoted figure for optical fiber transmission of 5µs/km.

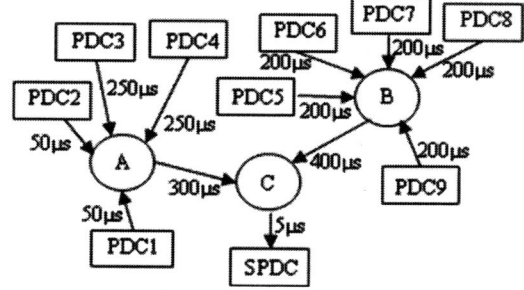

Fig. 4. PMU Message Fan-In to SPDC

Due to the variation in distance and the number of PDCs feeding in to each forwarding node and other factors, there may be a significant difference in the latency between different PDCs and the SPDC. However, since the SPDC has to wait for the whole batch of message to arrive before beginning to process them the maximum delay from the entire set is the important one. Although the main objective is to evaluate the end-to-end latency of the entire system, because the PDC process the messages as a batch before beginning to transmit them, it is possible to evaluate the communication latency in isolation. In turn this evaluation will advise the setting of the SPDCs waiting time. From the perspective of the network the PDC is just a source that periodically creates short burst of packets. Evaluating network latency involves working down through the levels of the fan-in, starting at the PDC level and evaluating the effects that each set of PDCs has on the forwarding node to which it is connected. Using propagation delay and burst lengths as parameters, the convergence and overlapping of bursts arriving at the queue need to be calculated and the effects on the queue, i.e. maximum queue length and busy periods, evaluated. Following this, the output process from the queue, which is related to the queue's busy periods, needs to be derived for use in the next stage down. Once the processing has been completed for all forwarding nodes at that level, the set of derived output process can then be used to continue the process at the next level down, and so on until the SPDC is reached. In the case of deterministic output from the PDCs evaluation can be readily achieved using a combination of arithmetic and basic network calculus [8].

Using the deterministic assumption, we carried out this process to evaluate the model shown in figure 4. The settings were as follows: propagation delays are as shown on the links in figure 4; Each PDC serving 20 PMUs each of which produces 1 message; message length 1000bits; link rates 500Mb/s, for all links; line rate switching devices with queuing at the output link only, and a fixed forwarding latency of 10µs per device; and line rate transmission from the PDCs. A link rate of 500Mb/s is relevant, as this is the data rate supported by the fiber optic carriers contained within an OPGW (Optical Ground Wire Systems) cable [9]. These cables provide both protection and communications and can be installed on high voltage pylons. Therefore, it is most likely that they will be used for communication at this level in the grid. The results of this evaluation are shown below in table 1.

TABLE I.   LATENCY VALUES IN MICRO SECONDS

PDC No.	1,2	3,4	5,6,7,8,9
Latency[max]	455	685	855
Queue[max]	40	40	160
Queue[total]	40	70	190
Latency[prop]	355	555	605
Latency[fwd]	20	20	20
PMU tx. time	40	40	40

These values are relevant only to this one particular simple example and do not represent a typical case. However, they do serve as a scaled down example that shows the range of difference between the latency of individual paths. Even in this simple example we can see that the difference between the maximum and minimum latencies is quite significant. Also, as we would expect, Propagation delay is by far the dominant factor. However, whilst in the worst case queuing latency accounts for only about 21% of the total delay, it is not insignificant.

The highest overall total latency in this example relates to the set of PMUs 5-7, and this value would be the one used to determine the setting for the SPDC's Waiting-Time parameter. The total latencies for the other two sets of PMUs (1-2 and 3-4) are both significantly less than this value, i.e. 400µs and 170µs respectively. Given that the QoS target is based on the delay value of the path with the overall maximum latency, then, in this particular case, it is implicit that both of these latency values could be increased to some degree without this QoS parameter being affected. Provided, however, that any such increase does not result in an adverse effect on the existing maximum delay path

We believe that such significant differences between the individual delay paths could be exploited during the evaluation and design stages. For example, the evaluation presented above is based on a Preemptive Strict-Priority Queuing discipline being applied in all forwarding devices. Whist this particular queuing discipline provides the highest degree of class isolation to real-time class of traffic, it can have an adverse effect on lower priority classes by interrupting the transmission of their packets. Non-Preemptive Strict-Priority Queuing does not allow the transmission of packets to be interrupted and therefore is less harsh on lower priority traffic, although in certain circumstances it can lead to additional delays for real-time messages due to the residual service time of a lower class packet that may already in transmission. However, these additional delays would most likely to be acceptable in the cases presented above. Finally, Rate Based-Priority Queuing offers even better relative-fairness to the lower priority classes but results in a lower forwarding rate for the real-time class. However, this forwarding rate can be set to achieve a particular delay constraint using an appropriate evaluation technique. These possibilities suggest that a three stage evaluation approach could be beneficial. The first stage could be based on further developments of the process we have used to evaluate the example given above, and would provides results in a similar form to those presented in table 1. The second stage would involve identifying those paths that could tolerate a significant increase in latency, then evaluating the effects of substituting Non-Preemptive Strict-Priority Queuing with either Preemptive Strict-Priority Queuing or Rate Based-Priority Queuing on particular individual forwarding devices. Finally, the third stage would carry out a re-evaluation of the complete system as modified according to the finding of stage 2. The points raised in this paragraph will be taken into consideration during our future work.

In general, we expect that the significance of queueing delay and difference between maximum and minimum path latency may both increase in line with the scale of the system. However, as yet we have not had the opportunity to test the effects of scale. Although the evaluation process for the deterministic case is relatively straight forward, it is somewhat laborious, and time consuming. To overcome this problem we have been developing a utility that provides a degree of automation. A prototype of this utility has very recently been completed and is currently being tested. Furthermore, at this stage our models can only identify the set of PDCs to which the worst case latency applies. Extension of the model into the application level devices will be required to identify the individual PMU source involved. This will be more important in future work in which a probabilistic interpretation of the delay bound, as defined by equation in section 3, will be applied.

We do not consider the process that we have used in this preliminary evaluation to be a general solution to the problem of evaluating the performance of Synchrophasor Measurement and Control Systems. However, we do see it as a useful part of its analysis, that can also serve as a starting point toward the development of a more comprehensive solutions. Currently, the evaluation process is based on a single layer Message Flow/Queuing Network Model (QNM) abstraction, with the delay effects of communication layering being subsumed into the elements of this single layer abstraction. In the next stage of our work we will develop the flow model further so that it can fully capture the delay path as it passes up, down and across the communication layers. For accurate evaluation all potential sources of delay that are above a certain level of significance will need to be investigated and generally every process along the delay path may need to be considered in greater detail.

Although there is no principled reason why PMUs and PDCs could not be designed in such a way as to produce deterministic output, implementation convenience and other pragmatic factors will inevitably result in some degree of variability. Therefore the next stage of our investigation will be to modify and extend the evaluation process to accommodate variation. However, for accuracy, this will require that values for the parameters of variability are made available. Ideally, any such information should include probability distributions. Furthermore, variability within the devices will need to be stable. Clearly the property of stability is something that should be expected from Real-Time devices, i.e. it should not be possible for any auxiliary operations to interfere with real-time processing. In the case of PMUs, PDCs and forwarding devices, the required information could be obtained as part of compliance testing, and the viability of extending compliance tests to include these requirements will be part of our ongoing investigation.

Currently, we are developing performance models for PDCs with the aim of capturing a number of possible alternative processing structures. In conjunction with this we are investigating the application of a convolutional approach for deriving the distribution of burst duration from the distribution of inter-packet transmission intervals produced by the PDC. Although the convolution process requires the assumption of mutual independence, which may not always be valid in all cases, biased convolution approaches have been developed and used for evaluating Probabilistic Hard Real-Time System [10]. This part of the investigation is in very early stages and development of the PDC model is still ongoing.

V. CONCLUSION AND FUTURE WORK

This paper has addressed the requirements of Time-Critical Wide Area Measurement and Control systems. Systems that are intended to facilitate automatic control in future Smart Grids. It has examined their operation and analyzed their communication traffic characteristics. It has shown that these characteristics are significantly different to those of the current near real-time wide area measurement applications that provide visualization to aid manual grid control. Therefore, it recognizes that they will also have significantly different QoS requirements. In particular the delay targets are an order of magnitude less, and therefore, evaluation will need to be carried out at the micro second level. Furthermore, the communication delay bound ultimately applies to the maximum delay for a set of messages that are created simultaneously at the beginning of a periodic cycle. If the maximum delay can vary between batches, then the delay bound refers to the maximum possible delay for all batches, over the operational period of the system. However, this requirement can be based on a probabilistic interpretation. Also, due to the wide range of difference in latency that can be expected between different paths through the fan-in to the SPDC, it may be possible to concentrate effort on those paths that are nearest to the limit in terms of latency.

The paper has also discussed the problem of evaluating the performance of these time critical system in advance of their deployment, and has presents the first stage in a body of work aimed at developing models and techniques to facilitate the performance evaluation process. It has presented some preliminary results and outlined the direction for the next stage of the investigation.

We have outlined the direction of our investigation for the immediate future and once the PDC models have been developed we will use them to investigate the effects of variable bust duration. These models will also be used to support the development of a theoretical basis for PDC performance compliance testing. Our future work will also need to addresses the problems of non-line-rate forwarding devices. This will require a similar approach to that we using to evaluate PDCs except the internal queueing model will, most likely, be more complex. To develop the internal queuing model will require detailed analysis of multiple delay paths and the numerous sources of delay contained within the device. However, such information may not be readily available, particularly in the case of propriety equipment and therefore alternative options may need to be considered. Given that one of our main aims is to develop generic and parameterized models for performance evaluation, part of our future work will be to consider the viability of using such models as an alternative to enable the manufacturer to supply the information required for performance evaluation, without having to provide details of the actual implementation. Also, as a another alternative, we will address the viability of obtaining the required information through measurement, that could possibly be carried out during compliance testing.

Finally, as the investigation progresses we will need to consider the results of our work within a wider contextual framework. We believe that the paradigms of Software Defined Networking (SDN) and Software Defined Infrastructure (SDI) are appropriate areas to consider for this purpose. Mainly due to their ability to provide isolation between the function of flow and control. Also, the systems that our models are intended to support are closed loop control system that operate over a communications network. Therefore, we will also need to consider the implications of our work within the context of Networked Control Systems (NCS) research.

REFERENCES

[1] Bakken, D.E.,Bose, A., Hauser, C.H.,Whitehead, D.E., Zweigle, G.C.,"Smart Generation and Transmission With Coherent, Real-Time Data", Proceedings of the IEEE, Vol 99, No 6, June, 2011.

[2] K. C. Budka,. J. G. Deshpande, T. L. Doumi,. M. Maddan and T. Mew, "Communication Network Architecture and Design Principles for Smart Grids", Bell Labs Technical Journal, vol. 15 No. 2, pp 205-228, 2010.

[3] R. B. Bobba, J. Dagle, E.Heine, H. Khurana, W. H. Sanders, P. Sauer, and T. Yardley, "Enhancing Grid Measurements", IEEE power & energy magazine ",. PP 67-72, January/February 2012.

[4] M. Popovic, P. Gao, D. Tomozei, J. Le Boudec, "On the Necessity of Traffic Shaping for PMU Measurement Data Streams", Power and Energy Automation Conference, Spokane, Washington, USA, March 26-28, 2013. School of Engineering, University of Aberdeen, Aberdeen AB24 3UE, UK

[5] D. M. Laverty, R. J. Best, P. Brogan, I. A. Khatib, L. Vanfretti, and D. J. Morrow," The OpenPMU Platform for Open-Source Phasor Measurements", IEEE Transactions on Instrumentation and Measurement, Vol. 62, No. 4, April 2013.

[6] US Department of Energy "Factors affecting PMU installation Cost", Oct 2014. Smartgrid.Gov

[7] P. Kansal and A. Bose, "Bandwidth and Latency Requirements for Smart Transmission Grid Applications", IEEE Transactions on Smart Grid, Vol. 3, No. 3, pp 1344-1352, September, 2012.

[8] W.M. Sofack, M. Boyer, "Non Preemptive Static Priority with Network Calculus, " ETFA 2011, pp. 1 9 Sept. 2011

[9] M. H. Yaghmaee, Z. Yousefi, M. Zabihi and S. Alishahi,"Quality of Service Guarantee in Smart Grid Infrastructure Communication using Traffic Classification", C I R E D 22nd International Conference on Electricity Distribution. Stockholm, 10-13 June, 2013.

[10] G. Bernat A. Colin S. M. Petters,"WCET Analysis of Probabilistic Hard Real-Time Systems", 23rd IEEE Real-Time Systems Symposium, RTSS 2002., 279 - 288

On the Performance of Anomaly Detection Systems Uncovering Traffic Mimicking Covert Channels

Johannes Bouché, Denis Hock, Martin Kappes
University of Applied Sciences Frankfurt am Main
Frankfurt am Main, Germany
e-mail: {johannes.bouche|dehock|kappes}@fb2.fra-uas.de

Abstract—Anomaly Detection Systems aim to construct accurate network traffic models with the objective to discover yet unknown malicious network traffic patterns. In this paper, we study the use of the same methods in order to create a covert channel which is not discovered by Anomaly Detection Systems and can be used to exfiltrate (malicious) traffic from a network. The channel is created by imitating current network traffic behaviour as detected by passive network analysis. Moreover, we present methods for calculating thresholds for the bandwidth of the channel such that, with high probability, the resulting traffic falls within the margins of the Anomaly Detection System under consideration. We also present results of practical experiments with commonly used Anomaly Detection Systems showing the practical applicability of our approach.

Keywords—Anomaly Detection; Mimicry; Covert Channel;

I. Introduction

Since the initial scientific publication of Dorothy Denning [1], the popularity of Aonmaly Detection is constantly increasing. Also, methods to subvert such systems have been proposed. Today, attackers utilize sophisticated heuristic algorithms and statistical methods in order to prevent the detection of their activities by 'Intrusion Detection Systems (IDS)' and network-based Anomaly Detection. One possibility to prevent detection is a so called 'Mimicry attack' which aims at mimicking legitimate user behaviour in order to bypass intrusion detection systems and to evade discovery. The objective of these technqiues is the unrecognized infiltration (e.g. malicious code) and exfiltration (e.g. sensitive information) of data using 'Covert Channels (CC)'. Jaskolka [2] defined them as: "(...) any communication channel that can be exploited to transfer information in a manner that violates the system's security policy". Thus, 'Mimicry-Attacks' are a special case of a 'Covert Channel'. In this paper, we assume that an attacker (or malicious insider) has already gained access to a victim's device including unrestricted access to network traffic and study the possibilities of hiding the attacker's traffic from detection by an Anomaly Detection System through mimicking legitimate traffic. As we will show, covert channels which perform even well enough to hide Botnet Command & Control traffic can be created, particularly if the methods used by the Anomaly Detection System are known.

The remainder of the paper is organized as follows. First, we present an overview of SnortAD and its prediction models for detecting anomalies. Then, we analyze the performance of covert channels in the presence of such Anomaly Detection Systems and highlight their limitations to detect covert channels with artificially generated data. In Section 2, we describe a practical experiment we conducted. By using the same prediction models as the target system, only acquired by passive traffic capturing, we calculate a traffic profile below the thresholds of the Anomaly Detection System and demonstrate that, indeed, the Anomaly Detection System does not report any anomalies.

II. Related Work

Anomaly Detection [1], has been been continuously expanded and improved. Two productivly used systems are SnortAD [3] and PHAD [4]. To the best of our knowledge, a performance evaluation of covert channels mimicking normal traffic based on packet rates and the introduction of a method to ensure that covert channel traffic does not exeed the threshold of an Anomaly Detection System has not been under investigation before.

Wendzel et al. [5] presents a recent overview of covert channels. There are also several detection methods, such as Reyes et al. [12] or Cabuk et al. [13] methods based on packet timings. Mimicry Attacks were first investigated in Wagners [6] work, who introduced 'Anagram'. The IDS 'Siren' [7] analyses how to find mimicry attacks by injecting human input into traffic, Pukkawanna et al. [8] uses a Kullback-Leibler (KL) divergence-based method on the port/pair distribution to detect Denial of Service attacks mimicking normal traffic. Wang et al. [9] detects suspicious payloads which mimic normal packet content with high-order n-grams. Casenove et al. [10] conducted a mimicry attack with covert channels by a so-called Polymorphic Blending Technique in order to exfiltrate data from a network. Wright et al. [11] is using a technique similar to the mimicry attack to prevent statistical analysis and extend the users privacy.

III. Method

To perform realtime Anomaly Detection in productive environments, Snort utilizes the preprocessor module SnortAD. In absence of other reliable solutions, we decided to use this well-known combination as a base for our experiments.

In the following, we address the mechanics of Snort and SnortAD with focus on the used AD models and most notable facts. We propose a theoretical background to infer the performance of payload injection in a covert channels and uncover weaknesses and limitations of Anomaly Detection affording to unveil those. We close this section unfolding to what degree we can utilize these findings improving the mimicry attack.

A. Snort and SnortAD

The rationale behind Snort is simple: A dedicated Snort host running in 'Single Sensor Mode' receives copies of all transported packets within the observed target network. At runtime these packets are passed through the preprocessing engine, enabling SnortAD to perform mandatory actions and raise alarms on occurrence of potentially anomalous network behavior. SnortAD can log packet volumes of several well-known protocols such as ARP, TCP, or DNS by fixed time intervals into a logfile. For each protocol, the total number of packets, bandwidth, amount of transferred bytes as well as the flow direction is collected and stored as a vector. The logfile is essentially a continuous set of vectors, representing a time series over several intervals. With a sufficient amount of data, the logfile can be used to predict future traffic with one of four different prediction models, described in the next subsection. These prediction models calculate and store a so called 'Confidence Band' - a minimum and maximum value representing the expectation for future traffic - for each protocol in an so called 'Profile'. After the generation of such the profile, SnortAD can be utilized to recognize anomalies outside the predicted Confidence Band.

B. SnortAD Prediction Models

Here, we briefly detail the working principles of the prediction models. SnortAD Profiles contain a list of predicted min/max packet volumes for each observed protocol, which is a effective and lightweight manner of storing and examining results. However, the aggregation also leads to various negative consequences as demonstrated in our practical evaluation. Depending on the underlying algorithm, a hostile machine could misuse this behavior to conduct a covert channel for data exfiltration.

Since SnortAD is a volume based Anomaly Detection System, meaning that any anomaly is based on extra ordinary packet volumes, we can define that an covert channel is successful when we can hide a Message M in an N-length packet communication without exceeding SnortAD's Confidence Band. SnortAD uses historical data to calculate a time series prediction of the next incoming packet frequencies. Which means, it measures at regular and discrete time intervals Δ_t the number of packets $p_1, p_2, ..., p_n \in \mathbb{N}$ where p_i is the measurement taken at $t_i = t_{i-1} + \Delta_t$. The chosen prediction model possesses major importance for the resulting detection accuracy. In the following subsection we briefly describe the used prediction models of SnortAD.

TABLE I
NOTATION IN THIS PAPER

Symbol	Description
p_i	Number of Packets on measurement i
t_i	Starttime of window i
α	smoothing factor for level
β	smoothing factor for trend
γ	smoothing factor for season
δ_i	parameter for autoregression

1) 'Moving Average' model (AVG): The 'Average' prediction model transforms the data represented in the logfile into a prediction model defined by arithmetic mean packet counts $\bar{p}$ for a moving window of size k within the logdata.

$$AVG_i = \frac{\sum_{j=i-k}^{i-1} p_j}{k} \quad (1)$$

Depending on the chosen size for the window, the weight of an individual outlier shrinks or grows. In that sense the model has no effective method to eliminate artifacts, negatively influencing the prediction result.

2) 'Holt-Winters' Prediction (HW): The 'Holt-Winters' model applies exponential smoothing to the supplied data and can be seen as an addition to the 'Moving Average' technique. It is used to smoothen the predicted values in a way, that the effect of collected outliers are lowered. To do that, the algorithm needs an scaling factor greater or equal to 1. A scaling factor of 1, produces just the given input as result and higher values will emphasize the distance between the resulting minimal and maximal values, effectively enlarging the region of accepted or normal network traffic. The major benefit of using this method is, that it does not need a minimum amount of input values and already works as expected with at least two observation points. The additive Holt-Winters model breaks the time series into level L_i (an approach to remove noise by subtracting the season), trend P_i (a forecast of changes in the level) and season S_i (an index for the expected level at t_i), and smooths each of the components with its own constant α, β and γ in range [0,1].

$$HW_i = P_i + L_i + S_i \quad (2)$$
$$P_i = \beta(L_i - L_i - 1) + (1 - \beta)P_{i-1} \quad (3)$$
$$L_i = \alpha(p_i - S(i - k)) + (1 - \alpha)(L_{i-1} + P_{i-1}) \quad (4)$$
$$S_i = \gamma(p_i - L_i) + (1 - \gamma)S_{i-k} \quad (5)$$

3) 'Brutlag' Prediction (BL): The 'Brutlag' method utilizes the 'Holt-Winters' model to provide predictions. This method compares actual data of the last period with fitted 'Holt-Winters' values for the same point of time [3]. This technique tries to equalize the impact of seasonality, by utilizing the trend of past periods:

$$BL_i = HW_i + m \cdot d_{i-k} \quad (6)$$

, where d is a predicted deviation and m a scaling factor. This type of prediction is also able to distinguish between different kinds of periodicity, e.g. daily or weekly and introduces therefore a more general prediction, less prone to outliers and singular events. The result is then again scaled with an scaling factor suggested to be chosen between 2 and 3.

4) *'Autoregression' Prediction (AR)*: The 'Autoregression' prediction method utilizes linear regression for variables and their past values and predicts an error value, which is used to define the upper and lower border of a future Confidence Band. Therefore the method compares actual data of one observation point, compared to all past observations of the same period and category. In the context of SnortAD this model tries to emulate the past behavior and occurred patterns. The model accepts a scale factor passed as input variable which will not affect these patterns but will change the scale of the series itself. This approach is therefore also not aware of outliers and seasonal effects. We forecast each point using a linear combination of past values, where δ denotes a parameter to affect the output.

$$AR_i = \delta_0 + \sum_{j=1}^{k} \delta_j p_{t-j} \quad (7)$$

All models above conduct a time-series analysis and operate on a given set of input data and at least a scale factor as parameter. They are in general agnostic to any semantics of the analyzed data and they are all prone to singular events, such as outliers.

C. Limits for Payload Injection in a Covert Channel

In the last section we described the general working principles of all models used by SnortAD. Despite the fact, that every algorithm has it's own purpose and objective, they still have a common vulnerability to covert channels. This limitation is exemplary described on the 'Holt-Winters (HW)' algorithm, but the given assumptions hold for the other prediction algorithms as well. Hereinafter, we provide the theoretical background of traffic mimicking attacks against SnortAD and describe in which way methods for data exfiltration could be determined.

Based on the output curve of a HW model, SnortAD calculates two thresholds for each category of network traffic – a minimum and a maximum – simply be subtracting and adding the standard deviation multiplied with a scale factor from the training data d. We reconstruct this Anomaly Detection method to check the theoretical performances. Based on these experiments we can estimate the maximum rate of hidden transmission for M.

For an initial experiment we can generate a random set of normal distributed data and use the Holt Winters Algorithm to reproduce a smoothed curve as a prediction of the future 50 values. Figure 1 shows a data set with $N = 10000$, $\mu = 100$ and $\sigma = 0.1$. The learned data is black, while the output of the Hold Winters prediction grey dotted. Figure 2 shows a detailed view of the Holt Winters prediction, including the minimum and maximum range, calculated with a scale factor of 1 and the standard deviation of the original data. Note, that the minimum and maximum range would also appear in all other SnortAD models, the used model only affects the trends based on the previous input.

The advantage of a time series prediction in contrast to threshold values based on average frequencies is the adaption to daily and weekly traffic trends. The netflow traces in

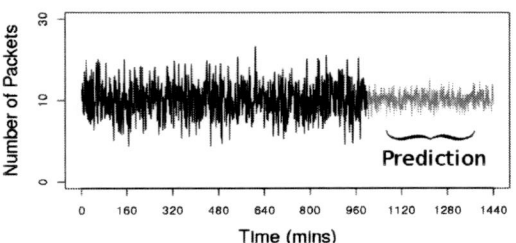

Fig. 1. Normal distributed test data and Holt Winters prediction

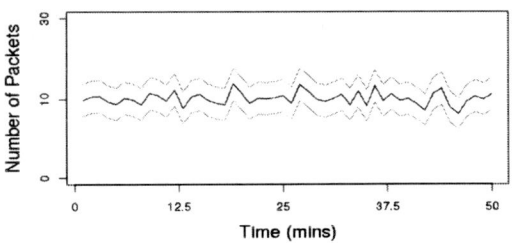

Fig. 2. Holt Winters prediction and min/max range

Figure 3 have been captured on a German medium sized ISP and show the typical traffic trends for one week. The y-axis shows the amount of flows, the x-axis is the time (24 hours). Each circle shows the amount of netflows for one minute, while the dotted line shows the mean amount of flows. Another typical behavior is the change of variance in the amount of traffic.

This fact is interesting, because SnortAD relies on the standard deviation to calculate the thresholds. However, the min/max ranges are consistent throughout the complete predicted interval. Hence, the high variance areas also increase the ranges for low variance intervals. Figure 4 shows two generated time series, where the black curve represents 10.000 points of learned data and the bright curve represents the predicted min and max areas for the next 5000 values calculated with the Holt Winters model. The area of high variance only affects the global min/max range of the output. As the authors of SnortAD did, we define the region between all minimum and all depending maximum values for a given set intervals as 'Confidence band (CB)' [3].

We can conclude, that these drifts from low to high variance either produce false positives or bloat the min/max range unnecessary which provides target for malicious traffic. In that sense, we define values, exceeding thresholds and generating false positives, as outlier. Based on the mean-value μ and standard deviation σ of the training data d, an outlier

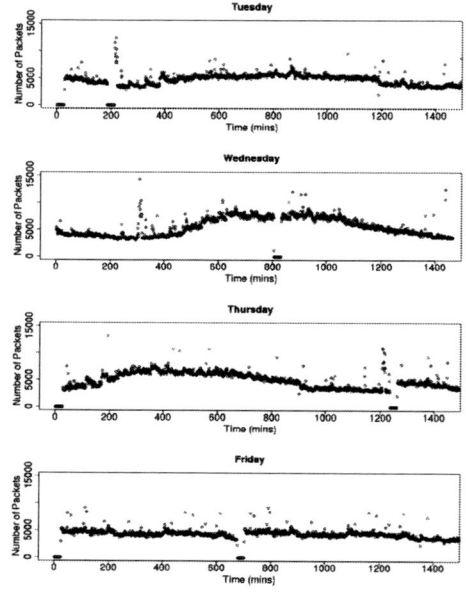

Fig. 3. Daily traffic trends (Tue-Fri)

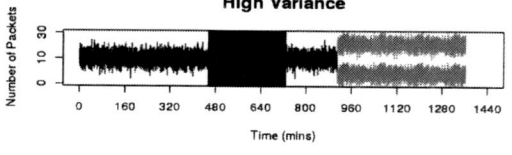

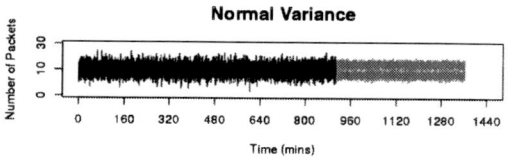

Fig. 4. Holt Winters prediction with and without a high variance area

o is any value included in the following set (8):

$$o = \{p|p > \mu + \sigma\} \wedge \{p|p < \mu - \sigma\} \quad (8)$$

Based on this conclusion, we calculate the minimal scale factor to ensure that SnortAD does not produce false positives. A naive approach to calculate the scale factor would be to use the distance to mean from our global extrema. Using the highest absolute value (11) calculated from the maximal positive (9) and negative (10) distance to the arithmetic mean $\bar{x}$ of the training data d, we can use the standard deviation s (12) to receive the scale factor.

$$maxDist_{pos} = max(d) - \bar{x} \quad (9)$$
$$maxDist_{neg} = min(d) - \bar{x} \quad (10)$$
$$maxDist = max(|maxDist_{pos}|, |maxDist_{neg}|) \quad (11)$$
$$sf = \frac{maxDist}{s} \quad (12)$$

The scale factor sf depends upon outliers, or more precisely the distribution of values. The effect of skewed distributions on standard deviation and arithmetic mean is well known.

Figure 5 shows how many values are within the allowed area (mean +- standard deviation). If the distribution is more skewed we observe less outlier, which are the further away from our allowed area.

To conclude this section, we summarize that the examined algorithm (HW) provides in general an upper and lower border (min/max ranges) for future values, received from a scale factor and an input set of intervals, containing observed packet amounts. These future min/max ranges are used by SnortAD to distinct between an legitimate or anomalous traffic amount and the distance between a min and max value is negatively influenced by singular events in the input data. To compensate that, the underlying scale factor has to be adjusted accordingly, in order to ensure that all legitimate values remain inside of the predicted min/max range for a given interval. Therefore a naive approach to determine an appropriate scale factor was given, including a description of the implications for inappropriately chosen scale factors.

D. Exploiting limitations of prediction models

The last part of this section, we focus on the implementation and practical evaluation of our observations. We present a method to calculate a packet volume threshold for a hidden message to in order to be unnoticeable. To do that, we detail considerations of network administrators and show how to calculate the estimated duration and bandwidth for a covert channel with fixed message length.

Since an attacker trying to evade detection by an IDS, can use our described drawbacks to his advantage, we assume a scenario where an malicious insider wants to exfiltrate sensitive data from the victim network to the outside without being noticed by SnortAD. We also assume that an already infected host can collect the same network traffic as the Snort sensor does. In contrast to the administrators of the victim network, which have to consider their specific demands when they choose prediction model and parameter, an attacker could, instead of guessing the correct algorithm and scale factor, easily create profiles for all available models and choose very restrictive or conservative parameter. Since the predictions are essentially min/max ranges for future time series, the administrators have to provide scale factors resulting in confidence bands, which are large enough to accept all legitimate traffic (including legitimate outliers) without triggering false-positive alarms. Furthermore, they need scale factors to be small enough to only accept the legitimate traffic. In our initial experiments we have chosen

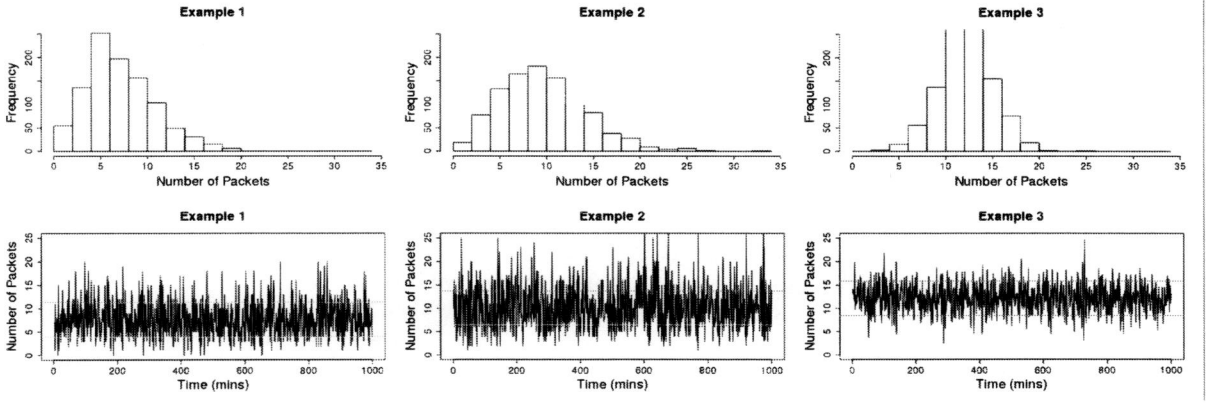

Fig. 5. Outliers in contrast to distribution

rather restrictive scale factors of 1.3 (AVG, HW, AR) or 2 (BL). In the previous section we also explained, how a reasonable scale factor could be predicted more realistically. Since we can guess the necessary scale factor conservatively, we are in the situation to generate profiles for all used algorithms and combine them to a fifth 'Covert Channel profile (CCP)', containing the minima of all MAX-values as well as the maxima of all min-values. Through this combination we obtain a confidence band in which we most likely can send data without conflicting the rules of the observing IDS. This is the case, since the administrators definitely have chosen one of the four provided algorithms and most likely have chosen a scale factor larger than ours, in order to avoid false positive alerts. If that is the case, and the attacker is still able to monitor the current network traffic, he can choose the desired protocol as well as a given message for exfiltration and utilizing the created CCP to exactly determine when he can send unnoticed packets to our destination and how. The amount of packets which can be send, is obtained by subtracting the packet counters of the involved protocol categories from protocol categories in the CCP. For a message of fixed size, the attacker can then calculate the estimated duration and necessary packet counts for a undetected data exfiltration.

IV. RESULTS

For the following evaluation, we created a virtual target network - including an malicious host, a snort sensor and a gateway connected to the Internet - to prove and verify our assumptions. We generated a symbolized normal communication of our virtual environment, in the further section referred to as background traffic, by on-the-fly re-injecting prerecorded traffic samples. This artificial background traffic has been used during the conducted learning phase of SnortAD. The resulting profiles for all available algorithms (see Section 2) were obtained with a scale factor of 2 and a daily periodicity over a total period of four weeks. Altogether, we conducted three tests containing low ('Set 1'), medium ('Set 2') and high ('Set 3') variance background traffic, which was created by re-injecting the prerecorded traffic samples with differing sending rates. According to our defined scenario, the malicious host captures the same traffic as the snort sensor to process an equivalent model of network traffic in order to secretly exfiltrate sensitive data to an controlled host on the Internet. We proceeded to this scenario by creating a combined profile of all implemented algorithms. Using the method described in the previous chapter, we obtained a conservative scale factor of 1.3 on the malicious host, which was used to predict future send rates over a length of 60 seconds. In consonance with the captured background traffic, our protocol of choice to establish the covert channel was HTTP, which was abundant and showed a reasonably high variance in terms of sending rate and total amount of send packets.

Table II provides the obtained average min/max packet counts over a period of 28 days for each test set, as well as the utilized network bandwidth. As can be seen, the total amount of packets, as well as the utilized bandwidth roughly doubles with each set. Table III shows an excerpt of the SnortAD

TABLE II
CAPTURED PACKETS COUNTS AND TRAFFIC UTILIZATION

	Total #Pkt	HTTP #Pkts	HTTP Up	HTTP Down
Set1	9079-9277	8768-8921	12.4-12.6 KB/s	46.6-47.9 KB/s
Set2	9250-18078	8913-17432	12.6-24.6 KB/s	47.5-93.3 KB/s
Set3	9242-736039	8984-34674	12.6 48.9 KB/s	47.5-186.5 KB/s

profiles, the average minimum and maximum packet counts for the category 'HTTP' defining the confidence band for each algorithm (Section 2) are used by the snort sensor to determine anomalous behavior. In that sense packet amounts lower than the min-value or higher than the max-value, will be considered as anomaly and lead to a preprocessor alert inside snort. Table IV shows the combined profile as created by the malicious host. To obtain the minimal Covert Channel

TABLE III
SNORT SENSOR ALGORITHM PREDICTIONS (HTTP)

	AVG	HW	BL	AR
Set1	8605-9074	8605-9072	8601-9074	8606-9073
Set2	3851-17120	2909-19248	4634-17559	9528-17722
Set3	0-56153	0-56201	0-17823	0-56099

Profile (CCP), we simply choose the highest minimum value and smallest maximum of each interval and all of the above algorithms. The amount of packets per interval predicted for the CCP, represent the upper and lower border of a corridor in which an attacker can most likely send undetected traffic. These borders were obtained by scaling the CCP down to 10 percent. The 'Center' of the Covert Channel Profile, which is the maximum amount of packets the malicious host sends, is defined by subtracting the min-value from the max-value and through the division of the result by two. Defining a fixed message size of 1MB as exfiltration data and by assuming a payload of 1000 bytes per send packet, we can calculate the time needed to transfer a Message M via our covert channel. Recapitulatory, our results show that an malicious insider is

TABLE IV
COMBINED PROFILE AND COVERT CHANNEL PREDICTION FOR 1MB MESSAGE (HTTP)

	Combined	Covert Channel	Center	Duration
Set1	8726 - 8954	872 - 895	3	9.38h
Set2	6931 - 14355	693 - 1435	248	0.13h
Set3	34700 - 40051	347 - 4005	524	0.03h

able to find a sufficient confidence band (CB) to extract traffic unseen. The maximum performance of the covert channel is predfined by the variance in the underlying traffic and influences the required time to send all data. Since we can assume at least a decent variance in most protocols, we assume that an attacker is always able to find such a channel, given that the time is not a critical factor for the exfiltration. The proper knowledge of actual payload data is not essential to perform this operation, since SnortAD is merely a paket counter, solely relying on statistical data obtained from the network, not taking into account the semantics or payloads of transported data. Therefore an attacker has to mimick only the bandwidth of the monitored network and does not have to care about actual contents of single packets. In that sense, the creation of such an covert channel is also possible on any other network protocol (e. g. HTTPS, SMTP, FTP), providing enough variance at a given time window.

V. CONCLUSION AND FUTURE WORK

Many Anomaly Detection Systems rely on the assumption that malicious traffic is different from the norm. A sophisticated stealthy attack, such as our proposed mimicry attack can be very challenging to detect. Our aim was to study how efficiently mimicking traffic can hide covert channels from Anomaly Detection Systems. We showed that we can indeed easily hide traffic. We outlined the mechanics of the Anomaly Detection Plug-in SnortAD and concluded how the variance of legitimate network traffic can negatively affect the confidence band. We detailed how to exploit this weakness by calculating how much additional volume of network traffic can be send unseen and were able to estimated duration and bandwidth for a covert channel with fixed message length. Our results showed that even small networks offer enough variance to easily hide data equivalent to several HTTP pages, which is sufficient to hide botnet command and control traffic, within a small amount of time. Since SnortAD is based purely on packetcounts, we did not focus much on our method to inject specific payloads. However, we assume that the mentioned techniques are not only possible within the HTTP protocol, but also within encrypted protocols such as HTTPS. Therefore we state, that the time to transport hidden messages is in fact the only constraint to conduct such an attack successfully. We are well aware that our exemplarily used Anomaly Detection System SnortAD represents only one of many possible systems but we are confident that other systems can be circumvented in a similar way whenever someone with malicious intend has the same network insights as the Anomaly Detection System and other mitigation methods are not implemented. While we deliberately wanted to keep the initial experiment simple and representative for a wide range of network traffic, a future prospect is to evaluate this approach in industrial environments and the associated protocols which are lately threatened by 'Advanced Persistent Threats (APT)' such as stealthy botnets and other malware.

VI. REFERENCES

[1] Dorothy E Denning. An intrusion-detection model. *Software Engineering, IEEE Transactions on*, (2):222–232, 1987.

[2] Jason Jaskolka and Ridha Khedri. Exploring covert channels. In *System Sciences (HICSS), 2011 44th Hawaii International Conference on*, pages 1–10. IEEE, 2011.

[3] Maciej Szmit, Slawomir Adamus, Sebastian Bugala, and Anna Szmit. Implementation of brutlag's algorithm in anomaly detection 3.0. In *FedCSIS*, pages 685–691, 2012.

[4] Matthew V Mahoney and Philip K Chan. Phad: Packet header anomaly detection for identifying hostile network traffic. 2001.

[5] Steffen Wendzel and Jörg Keller. Hidden and under control. *annals of telecommunications-annales des télécommunications*, 69(7-8):417–430, 2014.

[6] David Wagner and Drew Dean. Intrusion detection via static analysis. In *Security and Privacy, 2001. S&P 2001. Proceedings. 2001 IEEE Symposium on*, pages 156–168. IEEE, 2001.

[7] Kevin Borders, Xin Zhao, and Atul Prakash. Siren: Catching evasive malware. In *Security and Privacy, 2006 IEEE Symposium on*, pages 6–pp. IEEE, 2006.

[8] Sirikarn Pukkawanna, Youki Kadobayashi, and Suguru Yamaguchi. Network-based mimicry anomaly detection using divergence measures. 2015.

[9] Ke Wang, Janak J Parekh, and Salvatore J Stolfo. Anagram: A content anomaly detector resistant to mimicry attack. In *Recent Advances in Intrusion Detection*, pages 226–248. Springer, 2006.

[10] Matteo Casenove. Exfiltrations using polymorphic blending techniques: Analysis and countermeasures. In *Cyber Conflict: Architectures in Cyberspace (CyCon), 2015 7th International Conference on*, pages 217–230. IEEE, 2015.

[11] Charles V Wright, Scott E Coull, and Fabian Monrose. Traffic morphing: An efficient defense against statistical traffic analysis. In *NDSS*, 2009.

[12] Guido Pineda Reyes and Pepijn Jansen. Covert channel detection using flow-data. 2014.

[13] Serdar Cabuk, Carla E Brodley, and Clay Shields. Ip covert channel detection. *ACM Transactions on Information and System Security (TISSEC)*, 12(4):22, 2009.

Using Machine Learning Techniques for User Specific Activity Recognition

Jaideep Chawla, Matthias Wagner
Research Group WSN & IOT
Frankfurt University of Applied Sciences
Frankfurt Am Main, Germany
Email: j.chawla|mfwagner@fb2.fra-uas.de

Abstract—This paper explores the possibility of using wireless sensor networks and a machine learning based approach to classify activities performed by the wearer. The network consists of inertial sensors mounted on the non-dominant wrist of a user. This wrist mounted module sends data to a smartphone present in the user's pocket via Bluetooth Low Energy (LE). The sensors present in the smartphone themselves are used to collect movement data of the user. In addition to this network structure no particular care is given to the orientation of the wrist based device and smartphone. The motivation behind this network structure is to develop a Human Activity Recognition (H.A.R.) system which causes minimal to no inconvenience to the user. Movement data (acceleration and orientation) was collected from 8 subjects for movement based activities like walking, jogging, running, cycling and some basic weight training based exercises and features were extracted from the raw data. The extensive list of features was reduced using a correlation based subset evaluation method. The performances of four different classification algorithms namely the K Nearest Neighbor, Support Vector Machine, Artificial Neural Network and Classification and Regression Tree (CART) was evaluated for classification accuracy. Classification accuracy in excess of 90 percent was obtained which points to the possibility using such a system for Real Time Human Activity Recognition while causing minimal inconvenience to the user.

Keywords: human activity recognition, body area networks, inertial sensors, wearables, machine learning, classification

I. Introduction

Human activity recognition (H.A.R.) is the capture and analysis of various types of movement that a human can exhibit. It includes but is not limited to locomotion(translation), gestures, change of orientation of the body or a limb (via movement of joints). Capturing different types of human movement has its uses in fields like medicine, sports, surveillance and gesture recognition. We focus on macro level movements of the body such as locomotion, change of orientation and movement of the joints. Traditionally such forms of motion capture and analysis was done using video motion capture but with advancements in sensor and the ubiquitous nature of inertial sensors which are now available in almost all the smart devices (phones and digital watches) it is equally feasible to use a wireless sensor network on the human body for the purpose of H.A.R.

If done in a reliable manner, implementation of human activity recognition can be used for medical purposes. A good example is tracking of patient activity while performing a 24 hour ambulatory blood pressure monitoring. Patients are required to maintain a diary and note all the activities performed by them over a 24 hour period. This process could be automated with better accuracy if combined with an activity recognition system. Another possible application area is the monitoring of generalized tonic-clonic seizures(GTCS). This type of seizure manifests itself as rapid jerking movements in the limbs of the patient. Biniczky et al [1] assessed the reliability of a wrist worn wireless accelerometer for detecting generalized tonic clonic seizures and were able to achieve an accuracy of 89.7% in detecting GTCS with a false alarm rate of 0.2 false alarms per day. Automatic tracking of daily activity levels can also help in managing caloric expenditure especially if combined with a daily reporting and notification system.

We considered various locations sensors could be placed on the body and the subjects involved in the data collection phase of the experiment were also questioned as to where they would prefer (if at all) to have sensors on the body and amongst the 8 users all of them unanimously agreed to having a sensor placed on the non dominant wrist. It is also important to note that smart watches and fitness bands which are mounted on the non dominant wrist of the user themselves contain accelerometers and have been widely accepted by the demographic of consumers who use smart devices.

The prime motivation behind this paper is to evaluate the accuracy of a two node sensor network for H.A.R. for various fitness based activities (not limited to running,walking or bicycling as is the case with current fitness tracking systems). H.A.R. has been of interest to researchers since the 1980's and the field has seen two distinct approaches for implementation:

- Sensor based
- Vision based

Vision based activity recognition involves the use of some form of video as an input in order to detect the activity being performed. Inspite of its merits a video based approach cannot be implemented in a pervasive manner i.e. it cannot be used to track daily activity of a person because a person cannot be recorded everywhere she/he is present. This paper focuses on a sensor based single user activity recognition. This approach is based very strongly on statistically modeling the data being recorded by the sensors and using it as an input for a machine learning based algorithm. The second motivational factor behind the research is do develop a system which is able to learn various types of activities, hence the term "user specific has been used to highlight the fact that the research is not limited to analyzing if the approach can classify a fixed set of activities but rather a wide variety of activities so that the system is as versatile as possible while still not hindering any day to day activity of the user.

The research was conducted in a four step process

1) **Set up a wireless sensor network and collect data from 8 different users for 6 activities**: A wireless sensor network was built with a focus on ease of use and comfort therefore only a single wrist mounted module was built as a prototype which communicates with a smartphone present in the user's pocket.
2) **Extract features from the raw data collected**: The data itself generated by the sensors and collected by the smartphone cannot directly be used for the purpose of training a data mining model for activity recognition. The data needs to be converted into features.
3) **Select features using a correlation based subset filter**: An initial set of 75 features was reduced to 13 features using this approach.
4) **Evaluate 4 data mining models for accuracy**: The data mining algorithms were evaluated using a split of 66% towards the training data set and 34% towards the validation data set.

II. RELATED WORK

The devices currently present in the market are dependent on human input of the data required to track the activity performed by a user. A fair amount of research on H.A.R. has been performed using various types of devices containing a different mix of sensors. Accelerometers are utilized by many researchers as they can provide information that is significantly distinct for different types of activity[3]. With the proliferation of accelerometers in devices like smartphones and smart watches it is theoretically possible to implement activity recognition in a way that can be made available out of the box. Such implementations also make it easy to provide solutions geared towards a specific use case for example assistance of an elderly population. Chernbumroong et al.[8] conducted a survey on 18 participants regarding the usefulness,effectiveness, adoption willingness and the concerns of using smart home technologies for assisting elderly people. Their study was inconclusive towards the willingness of adoption of such technology but it does raise the question of the user friendliness of such devices. It is also important to consider that a for the purpose or a survey a count of 18 participants is a very small sample space to derive any conclusions. If H.A.R. is to be used to assist daily living of any population demographic it becomes important to keep psychological factors also into consideration along with the technology used in such a system. Although Gao et al.[2] evaluated the difference in accuracy of a single versus multi sensor approach and came to the conclusion that a multi sensor approach is able to achieve higher accuracies using limited features(using only mean and standard deviation) the feasibility of using multiple sensors on a human body without hindering day to day activities needs to be evaluated before such a system is to be made commercially available. Chernbumroong et al.[4] used a single wrist mounted accelerometer present in a sports watch to identify activities of daily living (ADL) like lying, walking, sitting, standing and running. Data was transmitted to a laptop and features were extracted from the data. The list of features consisted of 13 features. Two data mining models (Decision tree and artificial neural networks) were evaluated for classification accuracy. The researchers were able to achieve an accuracy of maximum 94.13%. There are multitudes of options available when it comes to data mining model all with their own merits and demerits. Kao et al.[5] used a similar setup of a wireless node on a user's wrist and collected data for ADL. In their case activity classification was performed using fuzzy basis function based classifiers. System performance was also evaluated by them in order to calculate the amount of time required by an embedded system to perform various calculations. The system in question was an Intel®Xscale PXA270 which was running at 520 MHz. A common criticism to both these approaches is that none of these venture to analyze the feasibility of their system when it comes to activities beyond those performed in daily living. If a user is performing activities other than walking or running then the systems proposed by these authors holds no merit to these types of users.

In order to use a data mining model it is essential to extract features from the data. Accelerometers provide a continuous stream of data therefore it is required transform the stream into a discrete form. The most popular way of doing so is to "window" the data and calculate features from the data. Windowing is the most popular technique for feature extraction.[3],[5],[6],[7],[4] and [9] use an overlapping window method to segregate the data and extract features from it. The windows are then labeled according to the activity that was performed. We chose a window size of 2 seconds as per Nyan et al[10] and Wang et al[11]. It also makes computational sense to use as small a window of data without it being too small leading to loss of information of the movement in the selected window size. Real time implementation of H.A.R. will be less computationally expensive on a smaller window size since the algorithm that calculates features works over a smaller sample size hence using less time and computing power.

III. DATA COLLECTION AND PREPROCESSING

A. System description

The prototype consisted of a board (Adafruit ™ Flora), a 3 axis sensor (consisting of an accelerometer, gyroscope and magnetometer) and a Bluetooth module working on the Bluetooth 4.0 low energy protocol as shown in Figure 1.

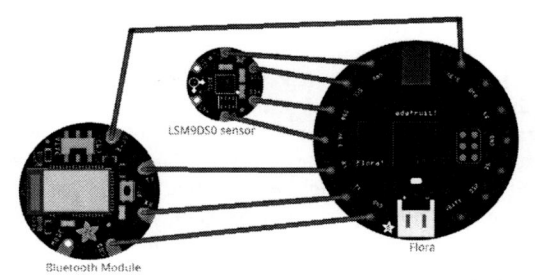

Fig. 1: Schematic of the wrist mounted prototype.

The phone used for data collection was a One Plus One™ which has a battery capacity of 3100 mAh. Battery consumption was calculated by running the application along with the prototype connected to the phone via Bluetooth LE. This resulted in a battery consumption of about 2 -4 % per hour. On a 100% charge that results theoretically in a battery life of **25 hours** for the smartphone. In actual day to day usage it can be much less depending upon multiple factors that can affect the battery life of a smartphone. These include (but are not limited to):

- Signal quality of cellular network : lower signal strengths results in higher battery consumption as the phone tries to lock on to the strongest possible signal.
- Use of mobile internet instead of Wi-Fi can possibly lead to increased battery consumed
- Use of Sensors : More the sensors being used by the smartphone more the battery consumption will be
- Power consumption by applications running in the background

All of these factors combined could possibly reduce the battery life of the smartphone being used in such an application. More research is required to have an accurate estimate of power consumption of a smartphone being used.

B. Data Collection

Implementation of Human Activity Recognition requires a trained classification algorithm. In order to train a data mining algorithm it was necessary to first collect data which is as close as possible to data which will be generated in real life usage of our application. To make sure the data was as close as possible to real life we took the following measures :

- No cables were used. The prototype and the smartphone communicate in a wireless manner using bluetooth even during the data collection phase.
- When it comes to the orientation of the devices set up on the body no particular care was taken regarding the orientation of the devices in order to make sure the data generated is as close as possible to how it will be generated in real life.

Data for the following movement was collected in an environment as close to real life as possible with the prototype mounted on the left wrist and the data collection device kept in the right pocket. Movement was initiated after clicking the data collection button on the smartphone. No pre processing of the data occured at this stage. The data was stored in a CSV file. The following data was gathered by application present on the smartphone

- Timestamp when the reading was taken
- Orientation values : roll, pitch and heading(yaw)
- Acceleration experienced by the sensor over the three axes (x,y,z). Please note that these are the axes of the sensor present on the device
- end of line character

TABLE I: Data format

timestamp	pitch	roll	heading	acc_x	acc_y	acc_z
1446921069	-81.12	-38.21	-8.39	0.14	-0.59	0.75

The phone based sensors were programmed to collect data at the rate of 25 Hz and the wrist mounted prototype collected data at a rate of 5 Hz. On trying a faster refresh rate for the prototype the bluetooth connection between the phone and the prototype used to terminate. A possible explanation could be because the communication happens via Universal Asynchronous Receive and Transmit (UART). Such communication requires a UART buffer which is of a limited size. Higher refresh rates possibly lead to an overflow in the UART buffer which then results in the communication being terminated.

The accelerometer on the wrist based prototype was set to a range of +-6G. As per Chen et al[12] the peak G's measured while collecting data while measuring falls were 6.9 G's for falling backwards and 12.7 G's for falling sideways. Should we choose to extend our system to be able to detect falls the LSM9DS0 sensors allows a range of measurement of 16 g's.

C. Feature Extraction

To calculate features a complete signal of duration 12 seconds for a particular activity was taken and was divided into windows of 2 seconds each using a sliding window method. These two second windows were then used to calculate features. The initial list consisted of 75 features which involved performing the following operations on the data for acceleration and orientation collected for the different axes of movement:

- mean
- standard deviation
- maximum and minimum amplitude
- root mean square
- inter-quartile range

From a list of 75 features a final set of 17 features was chosen using a correlation based filter method. Correlation based feature selection is dependent upon the concept of 'merit' of a feature. Good feature subsets contain features highly correlated with the classification, yet uncorrelated to each other [14]. Correlation here refers to the Pearson's correlation coefficient. Pearson's correlation coefficient is defined via

$$R(i) = \frac{Cov(X_i, y)}{\sqrt{var(X_i)var(y)}}$$

where cov refers to the covariance and var reference to the variance The acceptance of a feature calculated via "Merit"

$$M_S = \frac{k\overline{r_{cf}}}{\sqrt{k+(k-1)\overline{r_{ff}}}}$$

where $\overline{r_{cf}}$ is the correlation of the feature to the classifier, $\overline{r_{ff}}$ is the correlation of the feature to other features and k is the number of features

There is no 'one size fits all' approach to feature selection. It depends a lot on the type of features we are working with. Wherever possible it is a good practice to involve the use of a subject matter expert to get a better insight into the set of features to make sure the feature selection techniques are not skipping features which could be important.

IV. Evaluation

In order to select the best possible algorithm for H.A.R. the algorithms chosen were evaluated for classification accuracy and the time required to train the algorithms.

A. Algorithms considered for evaluation

We evaluated the following models :
- kNN: K nearest neighbor classification
- ANN:Artificial Neural Network(Single layer perceptron)
- SVM:Support vector machines
- CART:Classification and Regression Tree

B. Protocol for evaluation of algorithms

In order to evaluate the algorithms for their accuracy of classification data was collected from 8 different subjects each performing the following activities:

1) walking
2) jogging
3) running
4) push-ups
5) squats
6) bench press
7) deadlifts
8) cycling

The activities performed by the subjects were dependent on their discretion and no care was taken to by the subjects to perform the activities in a certain standard manner since our focus is to provide a user specific solution to cater to the activities performed by an individual. The data of all the users was then collected and aggregated into a single file and features were extracted for the various activities. A total of 522 instances of data were generated after extracting features from the raw data streams of various users. These were split into 66 % towards training the data mining algorithm and 34 % towards validation of the model. The results of the evaluation have been provided in table 2.

NA refers to the fact that the time required to build the model was less than a second. Further evaluation was done to assess the classification accuracy corresponding to different activity types performed. The first column consists of percentage of correctly classified instances with all the features and the second column consists of classification accuracy of the algorithm after correlation based feature selection was performed. In three cases using a smaller set of features extracted using correlation based subset selection led to a minor decrease in accuracy of classification but led to a significant decrease in the time required to build the model. These metrics however are preliminary and more testing needs to be done with a wider population to be able to properly analyze the accuracy this approach can realize.

V. Conclusion

Looking at the algorithm evaluation table it can be observed that when all the features were used for the purpose of model evaluation the artificial neural network provided the highest accuracy(96.77%) but also took the longest time to train. The training dataset itself consists of 522 instances of data of which 66% were used to train the model. Even though the machine on which the models were trained is not as powerful as the servers which are used today it nevertheless can be inferred that using the ANN classifier with all the features is not feasible to use for an activity recognition system which needs to learn new types of movements continuously during it's operating lifetime. Using the reduced set of features decreased the training time to 1.42 seconds which is a significant amount but still does not compare to the K nearest neighbor algorithm which took very little time to train yet providing an accuracy of 96.16% when all features were used and 95.31% on the reduced set of features.

For a limited dataset the results point to the feasibility of KNN as a classifier of choice for the problem of classifying human activity but given the small size of the study certain points/limitations need to be taken into consideration:

- The data was collected mostly in a fitness studio with subjects who are well trained and perform the movements with the correct form. This can lead to similarities in the data collected from different users. It is imperative to collect data from a general population to properly determine the accuracy of the algorithm.
- The quantity of data collected needs to be more in order to accurately analyze the time taken to train the models.
- The reliability of data transmission for Bluetooth low energy needs to be analyzed to see if is feasible to use when deploying the system to run on a real time basis.

Deploying such a system on a real time basis presents the challenge of having not only a reliable classification but the right hardware also needs to be used.The hardware tasked with measuring data for H.A.R. can be preferred to have the following characteristics

- Non pervasive: should not hamper with day to day activities of the wearer
- Long battery life: should not consume a lot of power or need frequent charge cycles
- Reliable connectivity:connection with a smartphone or ay other data collection device should be reliable

TABLE II: Algorithm Evaluation

Activity—Algorithm	KNN		CART		ANN		SVM	
	All	CFSS	All	CFSS	All	CFSS	All	CFSS
Time to train	NA	NA	0.25 seconds	0.06 seconds	13.64 seconds	1.42 seconds	0.21 seconds	NA
Jogging	89.6%	87.2%	93.2%	88.9%	91.3%	92.7%	86%	82.6%
Running	100%	100%	92.1%	94.4%	100%	97%	100%	89.2%
Walking	94.6%	95.9%	94.6%	90.9%	95.9%	86.4%	95.9%	95.8%
Pushups	100%	100%	92.3%	100%	100%	100%	93.3%	100%
Squats	100%	100%	100%	77.8%	100%	100%	100%	88.9%
Bench Press	91.6%	89.3%	100%	95.3%	91.6%	90.1%	89.3%	86.4%
Deadlifts	100%	100%	98.7%	97%	100%	96.9%	98.7%	96.3%
Cycling	93.5%	90.1%	91.6%	90.1%	95.4%	93.5%	92%	94.3%
Average accuracy	**96.16%**	**95.31%**	**95.31%**	**91.8%**	**96.77%**	**94.57%**	**94.4%**	**91.68%**

- Storage: some form of storage on the device(for example flash memory) could be useful to store data in the event that no connectivity options are available.

An all round device which exhibits all the features mentioned above is significantly difficult to come by in the market. Wrist devices which use the Android wear™ operating system are possible options as they provide a sensor API that allows us access to raw data stream of sensors and include accelerometers, gyroscopes and magnetometers. Another option is to develop a custom board with all the requisite sensors and communication modules. The advantage of developing a custom board is the flexibility in developing your own firmware. The obvious disadvantage is that the equipment required to fabricate such boards is not cost friendly and will not be feasible for a home user looking to implement H.A.R. As future work we are looking to analyze the power consumption of our approach while using three distinct devices:

- A smart watch.
- A fitness band.
- a microcontroller mounted with sensors on a small printed circuit board

We believe that given the right hardware it is possible to implement a reliable and accurate human activity recognition system in the near future to assist users for a myriad of purposes and with the collection of more data and advancements in smart devices it is looking increasingly feasible.

REFERENCES

[1] Beniczky, S., Polster, T., Kjaer, T. W. and Hjalgrim, H. (2013), Detection of generalized tonicclonic seizures by a wireless wrist accelerometer: A prospective, multicenter study. Epilepsia, 54: e58e61. doi: 10.1111/epi.12120

[2] Lei Gao, A.K. Bourke, John Nelson, "Evaluation of accelerometer based multi-sensor versus single-sensor activity recognition systems", Journal of medical Engineering and Physics 36 2014, 779 - 785.

[3] Prkk, J., Ermes, M., Korpip, P., Mntyjrvi, J., Peltola, J. and Korhonen, I. Activity Classification Using Realistic Data From Wearable Sensors, IEEE Transactions on Information Technology in Biomedicine, vol. 10, no. 1, pp- 119-128, Jan 2006.

[4] Chernbumroong, S.; Atkins, A.S.; Hongnian Yu, "Activity classification using a single wrist-worn accelerometer," in Software, Knowledge Information, Industrial Management and Applications (SKIMA), 2011 5th International Conference on , vol., no., pp.1-6, 8-11 Sept. 2011

[5] Tzu-Ping Kao; Che-Wei Lin; Wang, Jeen-Shing, "Development of a portable activity detector for daily activity recognition," in Industrial Electronics, 2009. ISIE 2009. IEEE International Symposium on , vol., no., pp.115-120, 5-8 July 2009

[6] Siirtola, P.; Laurinen, P.; Haapalainen, Eija; Roning, J.; Kinnunen, H., "Clustering-based activity classification with a wrist-worn accelerometer using basic features," in Computational Intelligence and Data Mining, 2009. CIDM '09. IEEE Symposium on , vol., no., pp.95-100, March 30 2009-April 2 2009

[7] Yang J-Y, Chen Y-P, Lee G-Y, Liou S-N, Wang J-S. Activity recognition using one triaxial accelerometer: a neuro-fuzzy classifier with feature reduction. Lect Notes Comput Sci. 2007;4740:395400.

[8] Chernbumroong, Saisakul; Cang, Shuang; Atkins, Anthony; Yu, Hongnian; ,Elderly activities recognition and classification for applications in assisted living,Expert Systems with Applications,40,5,1662-1674,2013,Elsevier

[9] MANNINI, A., S. S. INTILLE, M. ROSENBERGER, A. M. SABATINI, and W. HASKELL. Activity Recognition Using a Single Accelerometer Placed at the Wrist or Ankle. Med. Sci. Sports Exerc., Vol. 45, No. 11, pp. 21932203, 2013.

[10] M. N. Nyan, F. E. Tay, K. H. Seah, and Y. Y. Sitoh, Classification of gait patterns in the time-frequency domain, J.Biomech., vol. 39, pp. 26472656, 2006.

[11] N. Wang, E. Ambikairajah, N. H. Lovell, and B. G. Celler, Accelerometry based classification of walking patterns using time-frequency analysis,in Proc. 29th Annu. Conf. IEEE Eng. Med. Biol. Soc., Lyon, France, 2007,pp. 48994902.

[12] J. Chen, K. Kwong, D. Chang, J. Luk, and R. Bajcsy. "Wearable sensors for reliable fall detection". In Proceedings of the 27th Annual International Conference of the IEEE EMBS,pages 35513554, Shanghai,China, Sept 2005. IEEE.

[13] Stephen J. Preece, John Yannis Goulermas, Laurence P. J. Kenney, and David Howard, "A Comparison of Feature Extraction Methods for the Classification of Dynamic Activities From Accelerometer Data".IEEE TRANSACTIONS ON BIOMEDICAL ENGINEERING, VOL. 56, NO. 3, MARCH 2009

[14] Senliol, Baris, et al. "Fast Correlation Based Filter (FCBF) with a different search strategy." Computer and Information Sciences, 2008. ISCIS'08. 23rd International Symposium on. IEEE, 2008.

DMC: Distributed Approach in Multi-Domain Controllers

Shahzoob Bilal Chundrigar[1], Min-Zheng Shieh[1], Li-Ping Tung[2], and Bao-Shuh Paul Lin[1,2]
[1]Department of Computer Science, National Chiao Tung University, Hsinchu, Taiwan
[2]Microelectronics and Information Research Center, National Chiao Tung University, Hsinchu, Taiwan
Shahzoob.bilal@yahoo.com, mzshieh@nctu.edu.tw, lptung@nctu.edu.tw, bplin@mail.nctu.edu.tw

Abstract— **Multi-domain networks are vital to datacenters, home and enterprise networks. The networks require an independent and private control plane. Thus, the networks must be resilient and easily scalable. The emergence of Software Defined Networking (SDN) protocols simplifies the evolution of networks by decoupling the control plane from the data plane. In this paper, a Distributed approach in the Multi-domain Controllers architecture (DMC) is introduced. It interconnects heterogeneous networks to form a wide area network (WAN) while preserving the privacy of their domains. It also deals with the link failure across the domains, making it resilient. The controller manages its own network domain and exchanges minimal information among neighbor controllers. It applies a light weight control carrier (i.e., RabbitMQ) that reduces overheads. The application has been implemented on top of the RYU control platform.**

Keywords—Multi-domain; Distributed SDN; Multi Controllers;

I. INTRODUCTION

Within the past few years, Software Defined Networking (SDN) [1] has gained immense interest from the industry and academia [2]. It solves many challenging concerns of legacy networks by transferring the intelligence from traditional network devices to a centralized control plane. It has been declared as the future paradigm of networking; aimed at decoupling the control plane from the data plane and network programming. The centralized control plane, often known as the controller, manages the universal view of the network via a southbound interface. OpenFlow [3], specified by the Open Networking Foundation (ONF), is currently the leading protocol specifying the southbound interface.

SDN centralizes the network control plane that provides abilities to program, monitor, and manage networks efficiently. However, a dramatic increase of the network scale may force a single controller to drop an increasing number of incoming packets; it could become the bottleneck of the entire network. This unified approach may not be suitable for interconnecting multi-domain networks while dealing with potential scalability concerns [4].

Recent proposals have been offered to physically distribute the SDN control plane. A distributed control plane is divided into two categories: (1) distributed but logically centralized, and (2) hierarchically distributed.

Hyperflow [5], Onix [6] and Devolved Controllers [7] maintain a network-wide centralized view while distributing the network control plane. In the hierarchical distribution, Kandoo [8] reduces the load of the control plane by processing frequent events in the local controllers and rare events in a global controller. These approaches manage the scalability of the control plane within a single domain. Multi-domain networks are the core of datacenters, home, and enterprise networks. Therefore, a SDN-driven solution is required, where a domain can scale and interconnect amongst other domains resiliently and preserve their privacy.

This paper proposes a novel Distributed approach in Multi-domain Controllers (DMC). It is not only able to handle the scalability of a single domain but can also interconnect multiple domains regardless of the geographical locations of the datacenters, telecommunication, home, and enterprise networks. This paper emphasizes on interconnecting multiple domains but it can be applied to a single domain, intuitively.

In DMC, a centralized controller is in charge of its own domain, and fulfills the necessities of itself and sharing minimal information (i.e., host addresses) in order to entertain end-to-end services among neighbor domains to ensure privacy. Controller to controller communication is made possible by a light-weight control channel that utilizes the messaging mechanism, RabbitMQ [9], which is one of the implementations of AMQP [10]. Additional overheads are reduced because only minimal required information is passed through the light-weight control channel in order to compute routes across domains, as well as to ensure user-to-user connectivity. It manages link failure across the domains and maintains communications smoothly with minimum link recovery time. The DMC is implemented on top of the RYU [11] control platform. The control plane has been declared as the best controller in a recent survey [12]. To the best of our knowledge, this is the first distributed application implemented on the RYU [11] control platform.

The remainder of the paper is organized as follows. In Section II, related work is discussed. Section III introduces the DMC architecture and implementations. Results are presented in Section IV, and Section V concludes the paper.

II. RELATED WORK

The concept of introducing Multi-controllers in the control plane to solve scalability issues is well known, with many solutions proposed in this area. Hyperflow [5] introduces a cloud of controllers sharing the same consistent network-wide view by synchronization using a distributed file system. Onix [6] takes it one step further and introduces the platform on which a distributed control plane could be implemented. It also uses a distributed file system. ElastiCon [13] and Devolved controllers [7] address the control plane scalability issue in datacenters by dynamically configuring switches to controllers. ASIC [14] introduced the traditional load balancer in their architecture, which balances the load by diverting incoming packets to different controllers.

Kandoo [8] takes the scalability concern to another level by introducing a hierarchical architecture. It proposes two layers of controllers: (1) the root controller maintains network-wide view and processes rare events, whereas (2) the local controllers do not have any knowledge of the network-wide state and are subjected to frequent events. However, all the above mentioned approaches only deal with the scalability concerns in a single domain.

Zerrik et. al. [15] introduced a decentralized hierarchical architecture comprising of direct and parent controllers. The direct controllers serve local requests, and the parent controllers are responsible for inter-domain requests. This approach interconnects the multi-domain. It neither preserves privacy across multi-domain due to parent controllers having network-wide view, nor deals with link failure at the switch granularity level.

DISCO [16] introduced a semi-distributed architecture, where controllers are in charge of their domains and pass the information to other domains via a logical channel. Controllers utilize this information to gain a network-wide view. It uses mainly agents to share the network wide information across the domains. However, it does not preserve privacy as a controller can take over another domain's controller in the case of controller failure.

TABLE I. COMPARISONS OF RELATED WORK

Approach	Architecture	Area	Privacy	LF	CF
Hyperflow [5]	Logically Centralized	Single Domain	No	No	Yes
Onix [6]	Logically Centralized	Single Domain	No	Yes	Yes
Kandoo [8]	Hierarchical	Single Domain	No	No	No
Zerrik et al. [15]	Hierarchical	(Single, Multi) Domain	No	No	Yes
DISCO [16]	Semi-Distributed	(Single, Multi) Domain	No	Yes	Yes
DMC	Distributed	(Single, Multi) Domain	Yes	Yes	Yes

The related work in terms of issues is summarized in Table I. Five criteria are defined: Architecture, Area (single domain (sd), multi-domain (md)), Privacy (isolation between multiple controllers), Link failure at switch level (LF), and Controller failure (CF). The DMC provides a distributed control plane in the multi-domain networks based upon a messaging mechanism. The DMC scales the control plane that resiliently interconnects multiple domains while preserving privacy by sharing minimal information.

III. ARCHITECTURE AND IMPLEMENTATION

The overall architecture and implementation of the DMC is presented and illustrated in three phases. First, the controller design is mainly based on events and connected via the REST (representational state transfer) interface. Second, routing module, being responsible for computing intra- and inter-domain routes, is described. Finally, the monitoring channel that is subject to any link failure is elaborated.

A. Controller Design

Each domain is supervised by its own independent controller that enables end-to-end services. It establishes a control channel with its neighboring domains to exchange minimal information. This enables end-to-end services without the intervention of a controller in the neighbor's network, resulting in a private domain.

The controller is purely event driven. The overall architecture is depicted in Fig. 1. It provides networking services to its own domain and also communicates with the neighboring domains via the control channel. The channel provides a communication bus in the east/west directions with neighboring domains. It is integrated with the REST interface that allows the user to configure IP addresses on switch interfaces. When data is posted or deleted via the REST

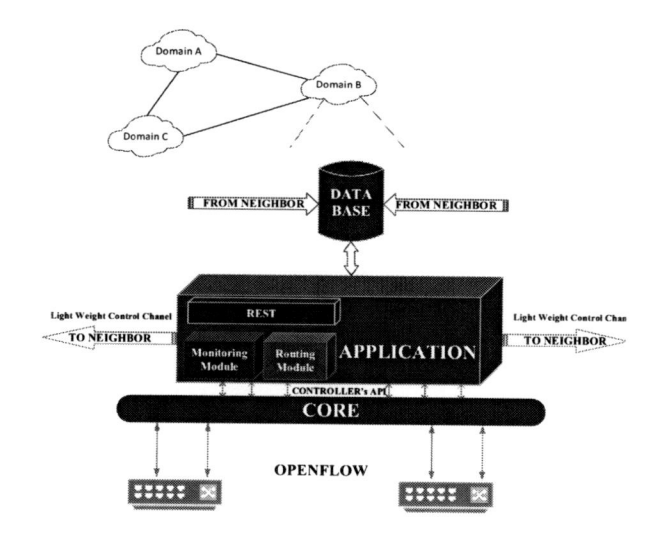

Fig. 1. DMC overall architecture

interface, the controller generates an event that performs three tasks: (1) updates information in the database, (2) updates neighbor domains via the control channel, and (3) requests the controller to perform actions such as setting up the interfaces of a switch.

A centralized database is utilized in each domain to store the information from the neighboring controllers and from its own domain. It stores information such as the categorization of switches (edge and middle) and the network addresses of switch interfaces. The information may be enhanced or used by different modules. The core component provides all the events/API's of OpenFlow [3], enclosed in RYU [11], such as `packet_in`, `packet_out`, etc.

RabbitMQ [9] is utilized to create a light-weight messaging channel. The control channel exchanges minimal information between controllers to carry out end-to-end services. Information that is shared and stored in the database includes the network addresses of switch interfaces in the domain. The Routing Module enriches the information and utilizes it to generate dynamic routes across the domain. The control channel offers a publish/subscribe model among controllers, where each controller is a publisher and a subscriber at the same time.

Both reactive and proactive approaches are used in the architecture in order to keep minimizing the load on controller. All the routes installed by the controller in a switch are prioritized. Proactive flows at the network level are enforced on a switch by applying the REST interface, whereas Reactive flows are calculated dynamically by the controller through the inspection of the first packet. As the first packet is received by the switch, it checks whether the destination network exists in its flow table or not. If it exists, the packet is sent to the controller that floods an ARP (Address Resolution Protocol) request to all the nodes. The destination node responds to the ARP request and hence, the controller knows the MAC address and port connected to that host. Based on that information, the controller installs the high priority flow to the switch.

B. Routing Module

The Routing Module is responsible for the calculation of intra-domain and inter-domain routes. Once this module is triggered, it pushes network level routes proactively using the REST interface to the switch, whereas end-to-end routes are calculated actively by the controller. Fig. 2 illustrates a typical implementation of the DMC.

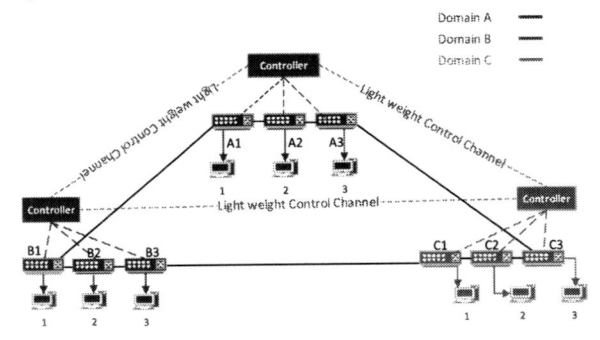

Fig. 2. A typical implementation of DMC

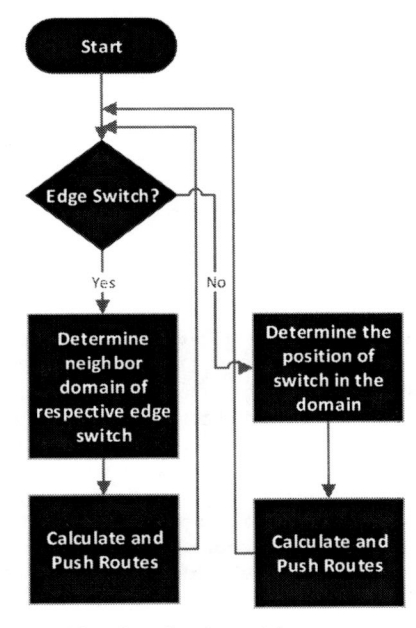

Fig. 3. High level flow chart of routing module

The controller computes the intra-domain routes and sets up gateways for the inter-domain communication. It identifies whether if a switch is an edge or a middle switch. In the case of an edge switch, it locates the connecting domain and sets up the respective edge switch as the gateway. For the middle switch, it finds the position in its domain and sets up its respective gateways.

The high-level flowchart is illustrated in Fig. 3. For better understanding, let's consider the following two scenarios as shown in Fig. 2:

a) Intra-Domain : To develop a route from Switch A1 to A3, since the controller has a global view of its own domain, it recognizes a middle switch between the targets. It identifies the path from A1 to A3 via A2 and vice versa. Thus, the routes are pushed to the respective switches by the controller.

b) Inter-Domain : The objective is to develop a route between Switch A2 and B2 in Fig. 3. Switch A2 is in domain A, and switch B2 is in domain B. In this case, the destination network address is not registered in the controller's domain, and it does not have any view of other domains. It refers to the database and determines which neighbor is registered with the destination network address. After recognizing the domain, it identifies the edge switch connected to that neighbor in Fig. 2. Switch A1 is directly connected to the Domain B, whereas Switch A3 is also connected but it needs to pass Domain C in order to reach its target. The controller picks the best edge connecting switch on the basis of number of hops and identifies the route via Switch A1 to that domain. Consequently, the controller pushes these infomation to the corresponding switch and vice versa.

C. Monitoring Module

It ensures end-to-end connectivity between nodes in the case of a link failure across domains. The goals of a monitoring module are to: (1) trigger an event when a link is compromised, (2) identify an alternative route, (3) delete previous routes, and (4) push new routes via the controller. An OpenFlow event `EventOFPPortsStatus` is used to find the status of the link. The Module is triggered when a link failure occurs, resulting in retrieving the information of the previous route from the database. It deletes the previous route, computes an alternate route, and pushes the route to the switch for further communication.

Consider a scenario in Fig. 2 where Host 2 of Domain A is communicating with Host 1 of Domain B. Here, the routing module has calculated a route where switch A1 and switch B1 are gateways of domain A and domain B, respectively. Once a link failure occurs which results in an triggered event, the monitoring module will be activated and will read the central database and retrieves the previous route. It calculates the second best route on basis of hop counts. The new path is now where switch A3 and switch B3 will serve as the gateways of domain A and B, respectively. Once the routes are calculated, it deletes the previous routes and pushes the new ones via the controller to the switches. It makes the inter-domain connectivity more resilient, resulting in an efficient and reliable network. In the meantime, it guarantees traffic reachability with a fast convergence time.

IV. EVALUATION

In order to provide illustrations for how the DMC operates, an emulation experiment was carried out. This is described below.

A. Experiment Setup

In the experiment, three domains enclosed in a private cloud having three hosts each are used. The topology depicted in Fig. 2, represents a WAN covering the three domains. A domain can be any network, ranging from enterprise to home. The DMC is mounted on the RYU [11] control platform. Each centralized controller is in charge of its own network domain and exchanges minimal information with the neighboring domains. The network is emulated by applying Mininet [17]. The Mininet [17] is hosted on a dedicated Virtual Machine (VM), and controllers are hosted on separate VMs. A Single machine is used to host all VMs, mininet and controllers VM uses the LAN segmentation which gives the feel of a WAN. The hosts, connected to the network domains, are user terminals and provided with 100 Mbps links.

1) Flow Setup Time:

The flow setup time is one of the outstanding issues highlighted in [20]. The reactive approach makes an SDN architecture more dynamic and robust but also induces flow setup delays. In the reactive approach, the first packet of the flow is sent to the controller for the route calculation. The DMC offers both approaches to minimize the load on the controller. It also allows the controller to respond to the flows more quickly, making it robust and dynamic.

Considering the example in Fig. 2, proactive flows are installed when the user configures the defined interfaces and the routing module is triggered. These flows are only installed on the network level, concluding that the flows still do not have any node level knowledge. When a host makes a communication path with another host in the same domain or in another domain, the controller pushes the intelligence to the switch at the node level and this makes the communication possible.

The flow setup delay results obtained are presented in Fig. 4, indicating ten different inter-domain flow requests were sent to the controller by different switches. Average response time noticed from the controller is 5.2 milliseconds.

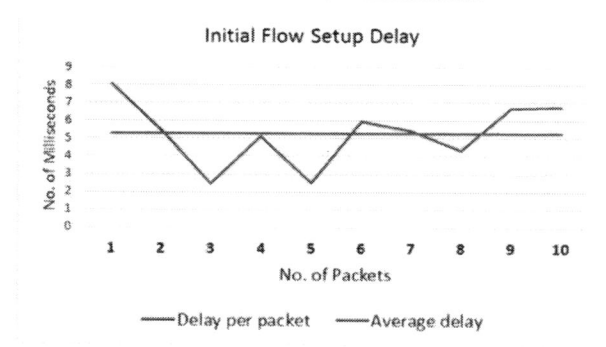

Fig. 4. Flow-setup delay

2) Packet Exchange:

This experiment was conducted to examine the effect of the size of packets exchanged between the domains to make the DMC functional. The DMC utilizes AMQP [10] packets to exchange the minimal information that uses a mere few bytes. The DMC efficiently reduces the additional overheads and results in a very smooth communication. To determine the size of the packets, Wireshark [19] is used. In the topology depicted in Fig. 2, a controller shares less than 1 KB data with other controllers, decreasing the overheads to a great extent and helping the topology to scale and evolve without worrying about the footprint of control information.

Considering the example in Fig. 2, every domain utilizes 3 switches and each switch represents a network. As the user configures the DMC domain, the Control Channel passes the network address information (i.e., internal address) and also shares the edge address connecting to the neighbor of the respective neighboring domains. In the topology depicted in Fig. 2, three network addresses (there are 3 networks in a domain) and one edge address is passed to every connected domain.

Fig. 5 represents the results of the Packet Exchange from one domain to another. Also, it displays the amount of information in bytes to another domain. DMC reduces the overhead to a great extent and doesn't cause flow overhead in the controller to controller communication. DMC promises to dedicate controller for its domain while offering multi-controller communication. Each controller in a domain shares their network addresses and connecting edge address to the neighboring domain, and this information regarding message size is depicted in Fig. 5. For further explanation, since each domain has three different networks in the scenario presented in Fig. 2, the first three bars in Fig. 5 denotes the network addresses of each network listed under the domain, and final bar represents the edge network address connected to the adjacent domain. Total overhead of each message is 220 bytes, consisting 88 bytes of header and 122 bytes of the content body.

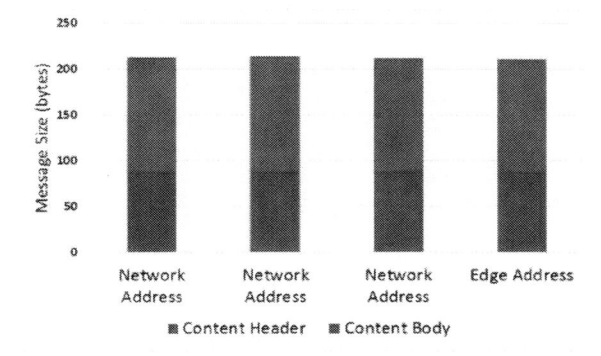

Fig. 5. Message size of control packets from one domain to another

3) Link Recovery:

This experiment test how the monitoring module reacts to the link failure and computes an alternative route in minimal time. The TCP traffic is generated using iPerf [18] between host A of Domain A and Host B of Domain B, as shown in Fig. 2. The link was disconnected at time t = 2.2 s by the using "link down" command. To determine the link recovery time, packets are inspected using Wireshark [19] on both hosts. As the link goes down, the monitoring module senses that, immediately computes an alternative route and pushes it to the switch. As shown in Fig. 6, the link was up again by t = 3.7 s, hence the link recovery time was 1.5 s.

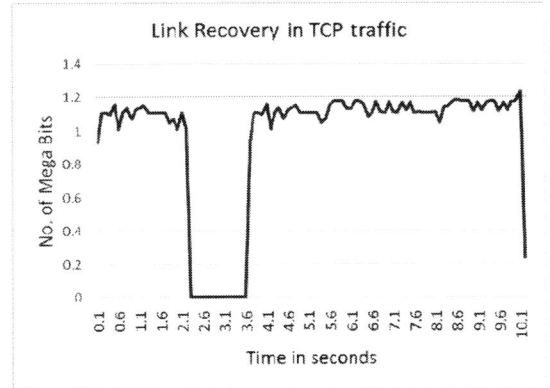

Fig. 6. Time taken for link recovery

V. CONCLUSION

This paper proposes a Distributed approach in Multi-domain Controllers. The proposed model interconnects multiple domains in a resilient, scalable and secure manner. The DMC relies on the centralized controller in each domain that exchanges minimal information across other controllers to provide end-to-end network services. It implements a light-weight control channel that reduces the additional overheads by sharing only the host information to other domains. Unlike other approaches, it secures privacy as the controller is solely confined to the view of its own domain. The approach is implemented on top of the RYU control platform [11] and has been evaluated for inter-domain link failure.

Future work would include the addition of a master/slave architecture within a domain, as that would be beneficial in the case of a controller failure. If a controller fails within a domain, the slave controller takes over and continues exchanging information with neighboring controllers, and this would result in a smooth communication throughout the entire network.

ACKNOWLEDGEMENT

This research was supported in part by the Ministry of Science and Technology of Taiwan and National Chiao Tung University under Grants: MOST 104-3115-E-009-007, MOST 104-2221-E-009-023, MOST 104-2622-8-009-001, and ICTL-105-Q707.

REFERENCES

[1] M.-K. Shin, K.-H. Nam and H.-J. Kim "Software-defined networking (SDN): A reference architecture and open apis," in *Proc. International Conference on ICT Convergence* (ICTC), 2012, Korea, pp. 360-361.

[2] "Software-Defined Networking: The New Norm for Networks." [Online]. Available: http://www.opennetworking.org/

[3] "Open Networking Foundation (ONF)." [Online]. Available: http://www.opennetworking.org/

[4] S. Yeganeh, A. Tootoonchian, and Y. Ganjali, "On scalability of software-defined networking," *IEEE Communications Magazine*, vol. 51, no. 2, pp. 136–141, February 2013

[5] A. Tootoonchian and Y. Ganjali, "Hyperflow: a distributed control plane for openflow," in *Proc. INM/WREN*, pp. 3-3,2010.

[6] T. Koponen, M. Casado, N. Gude, J. Stribling, L. Poutievski, M. Zhu, R. Ramanathan, Y. Iwata, H. Inoue, T. Hama, S. Shankar "Onix: a distributed control platform for large-scaleproduction networks," in *Proc. OSDI*, pp. 351-361, 2010.

[7] A.-W. Tam, K. Xi, and H. Chao, "Use of devolved controllers in datacenter networks," in *Proc. IEEE INFOCOM workshops* pp. 596-601, 2011.

[8] S. H. Yeganeh and Y. Ganjali, "Kandoo: a framework for efficient and scalable offloading of control applications," in *Proc. HotSDN*, pp. 19-24, 2012.

[9] "RabbitMQ." [Online]. Available: http://www.rabbitmq.com

[10] "AMQP." [Online]. Available: http://www.amqp.org

[11] "Ryu OpenFlow Controller." [Online]. Available: http://osrg.github.io/ryu/

[12] R. Khondoker, A. Zaalouk, R. Marx, and K. Bayarou, "Feature-based comparison and selection of Software Defined Networking (SDN) controllers," in *Proc. 2014 IEEE World Congress on Computer Applications and Information Systems* (WCCAIS), pp. 1-7, 2014.

[13] A. Dixit, F. Hao, S. Mukherjee, T.V. Lakshman and R. Kompella "Towards an elastic distributed sdn controller" in *Proc. 2nd ACM SIGCOMM workshop on Hot topics in software defined networking*, pp. 7-12, 2013.

[14] P. Lin, J. Bi, H. Hu "ASIC: An Architecture for Scalable Intra-domain Control in OpenFlow" in *Proc. 7th international conference on Future Internet Technologies*, pp. 21-26, 2012.

[15] S. Zerrik, M. Bakhouya, J. Gaber "Towards a Decentralized and Adaptive Software Defined Networking Architecture," in *Proc. Fifth International Conference of Next Generation Networks and Services (NGNS)*, pp. 326-329, 2014.

[16] K. Phemius, M. Bouet and J. Leguay, "Disco: Distributed multi-domain SDN controllers" in *Proc. 20th IEEE netw. Oper. Manag. Symp.*, pp. 1-4, 2014

[17] "Mininet." [Online]. Available: http://mininet.org

[18] "IPerf." [Online]. Available: https://iperf.fr/

[19] "Wireshark." [Online]. Available: https://www.wireshark.org/

[20] B.Astuto, M.Mendonca, X.Nguyen, K.Obraczka and T.Turletti, "A Survey of Software-Defined Networking:Past, Present and Future of Programmable Networks," *IEEE Communication Survey and Tutorials*, vol. 16, no. 3, pp. 1617-2014, 2014.

Investigating Environmental Causes of TCP Retransmission and Flags in Wireless Networks

Stuart Cunningham, Nigel Houlden, John Davies, Vic Grout, and Richard Picking
Creative and Applied Research for the Digital Society (CARDS)
Glyndŵr University
Wrexham, Wales, UK
{s.cunningham | n.houlden | j.n.davies | v.grout | r.picking}@glyndwr.ac.uk

Abstract—**Wireless computer networks are pervasive, but recent work has identified that there remain performance issues that prevent users from utilizing the full capacity of wireless equipment. Much research has taken place to compare the performance of different configurations of wireless networks to one another, but there has been little done recently to determine the effect that the physical environment has upon wireless performance. In this study, we compare TCP retransmission and flag proportions of captured network traffic over a wired and two wireless connection conditions, to determine what extent the physical environment is impacting upon performance in contemporary, real-world networks. Though limited by the practicalities of conducting our experimental work, our analysis indicates that physical environment is not playing a substantial role in the underutilization of conventional wireless networking capacity.**

Keywords—reliability; retransmission, wi-fi; wireless; 802.11.

I. INTRODUCTION

This paper attempts to determine the extent to which the physical environment around a real world wireless network affects its performance. We propose that an effective strategy to determine the influence of these factors is to perform a series of experiments that compare undertaking a large data transfer between a wired and wireless network configuration. In fact, we consider the comparison of the wired network performance to two wireless situations, neither of which permits line of sight between the receiving computer and access point. The aim of this work then is to compare results for these three conditions by considering packet retransmission and flagged packet ratios.

The remainder of this paper is organized as follows: in section 2 we provide background and our motivation on the subject. In section 3 environmental causes of wireless networking errors are outlined. Section 4 discusses the experimental setup that we employed and the results obtained. Finally, in section 5 we provide discussion on the outcomes of the research, limitations therein, and directions of future work.

II. BACKGROUND

Recently published work sought to investigate the phenomenon of impeded throughput in 802.11 networks, with a particular focus upon determining causal factors or conditions. A particular strength in this recent article is that experimental data is captured in real-world networks, thereby acknowledging and incorporating the range of environmental and usage situations that are likely to inhibit throughput in the day-to-day user experience of 802.11 networks [1].

As such, the research detailed in [1] shares aspects of rationale and intention with the work that is presented here. These are twofold: First, the desire to conduct research into real-world wireless networks as opposed to those in a controlled, laboratory setting. Second, to determine, since a period of over 10 years has passed since initial work into throughput in wireless networks was conducted, showing throughput of 41% and 55% [2]; 28% of data transmissions being retransmitted data [3]; and that link reliability can be indicated by measuring packet retransmission [4], if the performance of contemporary 802.11 networking equipment still suffers with the same degree of problems caused by the physical environment and conditions. As such, the work presented here builds, and seeks to expand upon, aspects highlighted in the work of Murray *et al.*, specifically by attempting to determine if physical and environmental factors where the network is deployed are contributory to the level of retransmission encountered in 802.11 networks.

Ensuring optimum performance of wireless networks is more and more important given their pervasive nature and the increasing number of devices to be connected, due to the growth in mobile devices, sensor devices, and the broader Internet of Things (IoT). As such, performance and fairness of access are paramount [5].

One limitation in the current literature is that evaluation of wireless network performance predominantly is concerned with comparing variations in wireless configuration and standards, rather than evaluating performance due to physical factors by benchmarking results against a wired network. However, one notable work that does employ wired and wireless comparison, of peer-to-peer software performance, is that of Quan, Lee and Pinkston [6].

Another example, work by Sallabi Abu Odeh, and Shuaib is commendable for experimental work in a real world environment, although their analysis is oriented around the use of overlapping and non-overlapping channels [7]. An earlier work by Doefexi, Armour, Lee, Nix, and Bull also examined wireless network performance in an office scenario, but only considered a comparison between 802.11a and 802.11g [8].

III. INVESTIGATING CAUSES OF WIRELESS PACKET RETRANSMISSION

A. Scope for Investigation

Based on the literature discussed in the previous section, it seems that retransmission rates for packets in wireless networks is a topic that has not received significant attention, especially in determining the cause of this phenomenon with respect to the physical environment where the network is installed. The work that has been done on the topic is largely descriptive and explorative. To this extent, there is scope for future research in two main categories: first, to gather larger volumes of data on networks of varying scale and size in order to *validate* that these retransmission rates are representative of the wider phenomenon and, second, to take a more controlled and deductive approach in determining the *causes* of the observed retransmission rates.

The theme of validation has been discussed, so far as is possible, in the previous literature review. It is not the main intention of this study to attempt to recreate or extend any of these previous studies to determine the reliability and transferability of these figures. This is not to dismiss such an activity as being without value, but it is of size and scope that is presently impractical. For researchers interested in this avenue, we suggest several replications will be of use as well as extending the work to undertake similar studies in wireless networks of variable size, hardware configuration, and traffic loading.

The focus of this paper, therefore, is in undertaking an initial probe as to the cause of the reportedly high retransmission rates of previous studies. We begin this task by considering the technological and physical properties of wireless transmission and its environment, which separates it from its wired counterpart. Following this, we undertake an initial pilot study to illustrate how the problem might be approached on a larger scale in future.

B. Environmental Causes of Packet Retransmission

All computer networks are prone to errors in transmission and this is an acknowledged impediment in data transfer, regardless of whether the network is wired or wireless. In the focus of this research, we are primarily interested in determining the characteristics of wireless networks that introduce scope for errors, and hence retransmission, over and above those encountered in wired equivalents.

Given that errors in data networks are generally caused by attenuation and noise [9] it is upon these lines that we outline possible causes of error in wireless scenarios.

In terms of attenuation, wireless networks are particularly prone. Data exchanges are affected by natural attenuation of the signal as a function of distance between a node and access point. In practical situations attenuation is also impacted by the fact that there is rarely line of sight between node and access point. This is especially the case since wireless networks are designed to allow users to be mobile and therefore the intermittent, possibly persistent, obstruction or occlusion of the wireless signal will occur. As such, attenuation beyond distance will be hard to guarantee or predict, since various obstructions will be made from different density materials, and therefore absorption coefficients, reflective characteristics, and absorptive surface areas will vary [10].

In terms of noise in wireless networks, contemporary standards are generally robust, although naturally still impaired by electromagnetic interference and impulse noise cause by other microwave frequency devices in the vicinity.

In this work, issues of noise from causes such as electromagnetic interference are considered beyond the scope and control of the experimental work conducted here. It is intended that these factors will appear only as background noise given the scale of the intended study.

IV. EXPERIMENTAL STUDY

A. Aims

The main intention of the experimental work documented here is to identify the extent to which physical conditions, such as reflection and absorption of the wireless signal, significantly contribute to performance differences when compared to wired networks. The null hypothesis of the work is that differences experienced in performance between wired and wireless networks are down to other factors, whilst the alternate hypothesis is that physical conditions around the network access point and receiving node are likely to cause performance differences between wireless and wireless conditions.

Ideally, conducting several repetitions of a pairwise experiment in a highly controlled environment would be used to investigate these hypotheses. For example, the ideal research design would be within a microwave anechoic chamber, which would allow for one experimental configuration with 100% absorption in the room and a clear line of sight connection between an access point (AP) and computer as the control condition. The test configuration would then take place by installing a highly reflective box within the anechoic chamber whilst still maintaining line of sight between the AP and the computer. Under both conditions, a series of data transfers would then be initiated, over a fixed period of time, and the number of packet errors logged. Analysis of this data would therefore indicate if any significant difference in the number of packet errors were attributable to the reflections caused inside the test condition.

However, this ideal situation is, at the present time, not practicable. Furthermore, it does not represent the experience of wireless network users in real world scenarios. To this extent, we conduct experimental work under conditions of convenience in a real world setting to evaluate any differences between a wired connection; a wireless connection without line of sight; and a wireless connection without line of sight and with no unobstructed signal path.

B. Methodology

Data was captured on five days, selected by the researchers at convenience, over a two-week period. Samples were captured during working days and hours of the University, again at the convenience of the researchers. A MacBook Pro laptop computer was located on a desk, at a height of 73 cm above the floor, in an office at the University and the Wireshark 1.12.7 software was used to capture network packets. The built-in Ethernet and wireless adapters of the computer were used.

There was a wireless AP located in the corridor outside the office, the model of which was a Cisco Aironet. The AP was located on a wall at a height of 250 cm above the floor. The wall dividing the office from the main corridor is made of plastered brick and has a thickness of approximately 45 cm. The office door is 4 cm thick, wood with a large glass panel occupying around 60% of the door area. In the corridor outside there is a double fire door of 4.3 cm thickness with a small glass panel in each door. The physical environment around the office, computer, and AP are illustrated in **Fig. 1**. From this information, the straight-line distance between the AP and computer is calculated as being approximately 906 cm.

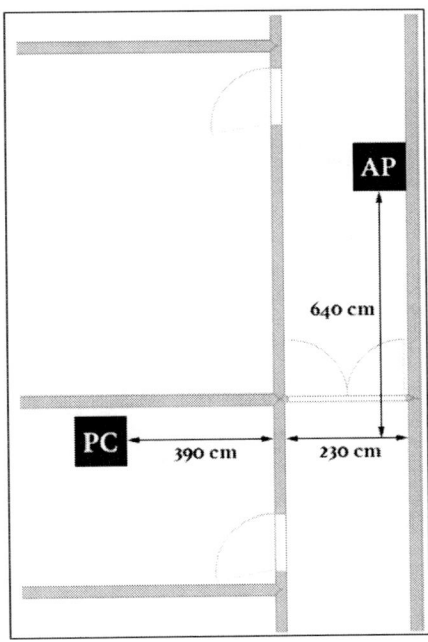

Fig. 1: Experiment Physical Setup

The overarching aim of the experiment was to capture substantial amounts of network traffic over three connection conditions: wired Ethernet; wireless with the office door open; and wireless with the office door closed. To generate a predictable amount of traffic during the captures and to keep the majority of the data under experimental control, a large video was loaded into the Firefox web browser that had duration of 61 minutes and 18 seconds (the video used is at https://www.youtube.com/watch?v=dVfmS-dG38U) and was viewed at Full HD (1080p) resolution. Wireshark was set to capture for a fixed time period of 65 minutes on each occasion. This allowed the researchers to begin the capture, load Firefox and the YouTube video, skip any pre-viewing adverts, and set the video resolution to Full HD. The YouTube video was chosen since it is a non real-time source and hence uses the TCP protocol to deliver the video data. These parameters aside, no other controls were exerted over the experiment, such as the state of the fire door in the corridor, people in the office or corridor outside, or the overall usage of the wired and wireless networks of the University when captures were made. It is intended that these extraneous factors will be normalized out of the data by the size of the packet captures.

It is important to stress that each triplet of connection condition captures were not recorded simultaneously. Instead, they were recorded in a linear sequence, chosen at random.

C. Results

The five capture sessions resulted in a total of 16798416 packets. These are broken down into the separate five capture sessions represented, in chronological order, in the results and analysis as labels S1 through S5. Although time was fixed at 65 minutes for each capture, the number of packets varied due to network conditions. The mean number of packets per capture condition is 1119894. **TABLE I** provides an overview of the data captured.

TABLE I. SUMMARY OF PACKETS CAPTURED BY CONNECTION CONDITION

Sess.	Experiment Condition	Total	TCP	TCP Retransmission	Bad TCP
1	Wired	1216691	1203401	773	26720
	Wireless DoorOpen	1090689	1090208	758	29837
	Wireless DoorClosed	1156434	1155994	3659	57015
2	Wired	1144501	1131097	1426	39970
	Wireless DoorOpen	1247702	1247071	4940	83872
	Wireless DoorClosed	1064452	1063877	331	22033
3	Wired	1174117	1154817	15544	111902
	Wireless DoorOpen	1081932	1081462	623	28180
	Wireless DoorClosed	1100937	1100574	10882	95085
4	Wired	1123591	1106750	565	23218
	Wireless DoorOpen	1202512	1201998	5061	106416
	Wireless DoorClosed	1066336	1065822	7023	76111
5	Wired	937030	914674	7432	91214
	Wireless DoorOpen	1273043	1272461	5061	95189
	Wireless DoorClosed	918449	917897	19290	121338

The work of this paper is primarily concerned with TCP packets and the number of these that have reported issues. Hence, the analysis focuses on the presence of 'Bad TCP' packets, as defined by Wireshark as being all TCP packets that have been flagged, with the exception of updates to the sender's TCP buffer. As another explicit measure in this experiment the number of TCP packets that have been retransmitted are also shown, which is a subset of the Bad TCP packets.

D. Analysis

1) TCP Retransmission

The initial analysis of the data captured is concerned with the proportions of TCP packet retransmission rates (percentage of all TCP packets), over the five sessions and this is illustrated in Fig. 2. In terms of TCP retransmission rates over all five of the sessions, the wired condition experienced 0.467%; the wireless with the door closed 0.776%; and wireless with the door open 0.279%.

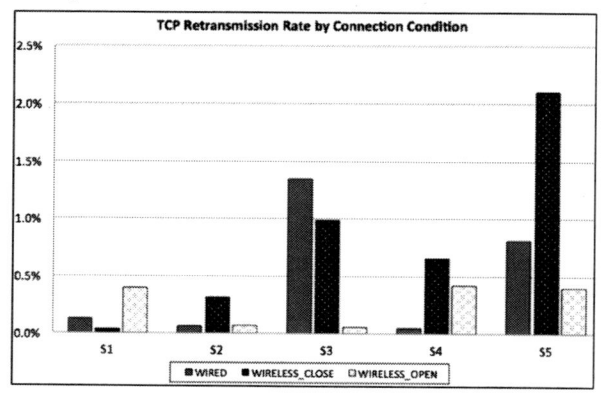

Fig. 2: Proportion of TCP Packets Retransmitted by Connection Condition

From inspection it is seen that there is a degree of fluctuation and variation within the results and across the five sessions. Generally, both wireless connections have higher rates of retransmission, although it is noteworthy that in S3 and S5 the retransmission rates in the wired connections have increased. Indeed, in condition S3 it is unusual that the wired connection condition has a higher retransmission rate than both wireless conditions. Aside from that anomaly, the results broadly fit what would be expected: that the wireless connection with the office door closed, results in a larger number of retransmissions than those where the door is open, suggesting that the presence of the door means the signal is suffering from more attenuation and negative reflection.

A repeated-measures Analysis Of Variance (ANOVA) with a Greenhouse-Geisser correction was employed to objectively analyze the TCP retransmissions rates. Prior to this analysis, the percentage values were transformed using the arcsin function, which changes the binomially distributed percentage scale to one that is normally distributed so as to allow for the ANOVA test to be conducted. The arcsin transformation function in degrees of a percentage value x represented as a proportion (i.e. 25% is recorded as 0.25) is, as follows

$$\arcsin(x) = \left(\sin^{-1}(\sqrt{x})\right)\frac{180}{\pi} \quad (1)$$

The test concluded that there was not a statistically significant difference between the connection conditions ($F(1.734, 6.937) = 1.153, p > 0.05$).

2) Bad TCP Packets

Similar analysis is then conducted regarding the Bad TCP proportions that have been recorded during the data capture experiment, to determine if this broader set of information can also indicate if reduction in performance is related to the connection condition. An illustration of Bad TCP (as percentage of all TCP packets) is shown in Fig. 3. In terms of Bad TCP packet rates over all five of the sessions, the wired condition experienced 5.317%; the wireless with the door closed 7.005%; and wireless with the door open 5.829%.

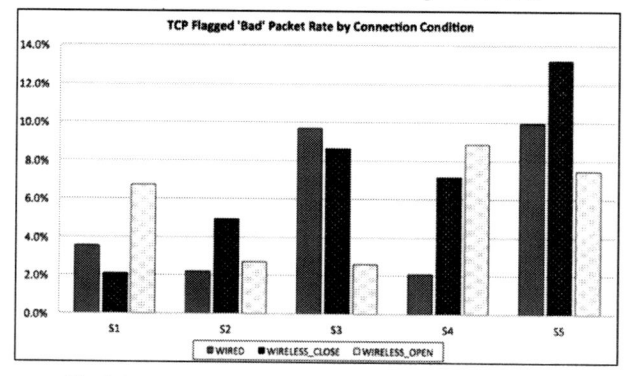

Fig. 3: Proportion of Bad TCP Packets by Connection Condition

This analysis shows an unexpected degree of variation in the results. There are no easily identifiable trends, when looking across all of the capture sessions, especially once the TCP retransmissions, as accounted for in the previous subsection, are factored out of the analysis. Whilst the total figures are broadly inline with what would be expected, on a session-by-session basis it is hard to identify any particular outcome.

A repeated-measures ANOVA with a Greenhouse-Geisser correction was again employed to objectively analyze the Bad TCP rates upon the percentage values transformed using the arcsin function. The test concluded that there was not a statistically significant difference between the connection conditions ($F(1.539, 6.158) = 0.389, p > 0.05$).

3) TCP Packet Lengths

As a final piece of analysis, the packet lengths used across each of the three connection conditions was investigated, since the presence of any major problems on the wireless network conditions would show as a reduction in packet lengths. This is illustrated in Fig. 4.

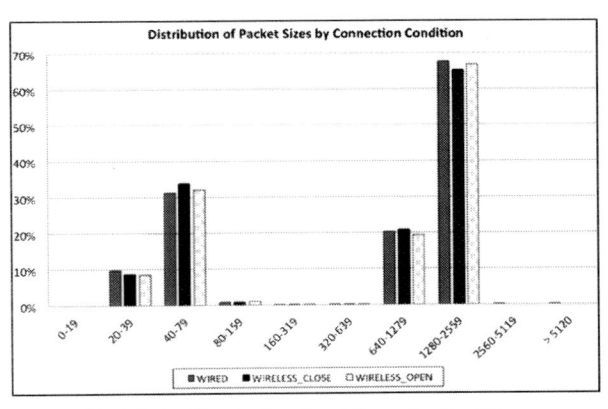

Fig. 4: Packet Sizes by Experiment Connection Condition

Distribution of packet lengths does not appear to have been impacted by the connection conditions evaluated in the study, indicating that there have not ben any exceptional problems in the delivery of the video data in the experiment.

V. DISCUSSION AND FUTURE WORK

The work presented here shows lower than anticipated presence of issues with the two wireless connection conditions being evaluated. Further, the analysis of experimental results concludes that there are no significant differences between the two wireless conditions and the wired counterpart. As such, this evidence would suggest that issues relating to and overall link quality and TCP issues are not related to the physical environment. These results, as measured in this paper, seem to be out of step with the general experience of others in the literature. However, there are a number of methodological limitations that may be contributing to these results and that warrant future investigation.

One issue stems from the non-concurrent capture of the data that has been analyzed. Whilst each session was undertaken on the same day these captures were, by design, taken at different times of day, albeit randomized over all conditions. To an extent, this partly negates the use of repeated measures ANOVA, although it was the closest to the ideal condition as could be practically obtained at this time.

Another factor to be considered is the distance between the AP and computer used in the experiments. Placed at a straight-line distance of 906 cm, the receiving computer, it is suggested, was working with a good level of signal strength and quality, albeit attenuated by the thick walls. A more effective analysis might have implemented the experimental conditions at greater distances and by measuring Signal-to-Noise Ratio (SNR) at each point.

Thus, future work proposed should attempt to take multiple measures of performance, in parallel data capture situations, so as to allow for an unquestionable triplet-wise comparison of the results. Other modifications, such as: altering distances, presence of obstructions and occlusion between the AP and computer, and measuring SNR to determine if this correlates with packet loss and/or retransmission proportions, should also be pursued. Ultimately, it is hoped that work can be undertaken in a microwave anechoic chamber, as indicated in section 4, which will serve to provide a more conclusive, though not real world, test bed for future work to use as a reliable benchmark.

REFERENCES

[1] D. Murray, T. Koziniec, M. Dixon, K. Lee, "Measuring the reliability of 802.11 WiFi networks," in *Internet Technologies and Applications (ITA), 2015*, pp.233-238, 8-11 Sept. 2015

[2] J. Jun; P. Peddabachagari, M. Sichitiu, "Theoretical maximum throughput of IEEE 802.11 and its applications," in *Network Computing and Applications, 2003. NCA 2003. Second IEEE International Symposium on*, vol., no., pp.249-256, 18-18 April 2003.

[3] M. Rodrig, C. Reis, R. Mahajan, D. Wetherall, J. Zahorjan, "Measurement-based characterization of 802.11 in a hotspot setting," in *Proceedings of the 2005 ACM SIGCOMM workshop on Experimental approaches to wireless network design and analysis 2005* Aug 22 (pp. 5-10). ACM.

[4] A.P. Jardosh, K.N. Ramachandran, K.C. Almeroth, E.M. Belding-Royer, "Understanding link-layer behavior in highly congested IEEE 802.11 b wireless networks," in *Proceedings of the 2005 ACM SIGCOMM workshop on Experimental approaches to wireless network design and analysis 2005* Aug 22 (pp. 11-16). ACM.

[5] H. Shi, R.V. Prasad, E. Onur, I.G., Niemegeers, "Fairness in wireless networks: Issues, measures and challenges," *Communications Surveys & Tutorials*, IEEE. 2014 May;16(1):5-24.

[6] L. Quan, K.G. Lee, T.M. Pinkston, "Performance analysis of unstructured peer-to-peer schemes in integrated wired and wireless network environments," In Parallel and Distributed Systems, 2005. Proceedings. 11th International Conference on 2005 Jul 20 (Vol. 1, pp. 419-425). IEEE.

[7] F.M. Sallabi A.O. Abu Odeh, K. Shuaib, "Performance evaluation of deploying wireless sensor networks in a highly dynamic WLAN and a highly populated indoor environment," In Wireless Communications and Mobile Computing Conference (IWCMC), 2011 7th International 2011 Jul 4 (pp. 1371-1376). IEEE.

[8] A. Doefexi, S. Armour, B.S. Lee, A. Nix, D. Bull, "An evaluation of the performance of IEEE 802.11 a and 802.11 g wireless local area networks in a corporate office environment," In Communications, 2003. ICC'03. IEEE International Conference on 2003 May 11 (Vol. 2, pp. 1196-1200). IEEE.

[9] W. Stallings, Data and computer communications, International ed., Pearson Education, 2014.

[10] J.E. McDonnell, "Characteristics of the indoor wireless propagation environment at microwave and millimetre frequencies," In Radio Communications at Microwave and Millimetre Wave Frequencies (Digest No. 1996/239), IEE Colloquium on 1996 Dec 16 (pp. 13-1). IET.

On Channel Allocation of Directional Wireless Networks Using Multiple Channels

Hong-Ning Dai*, Hao Wang† and Hong Xiao‡
*Macau University of Science and Technology, Macau SAR
hndai@ieee.org
†Norwegian University of Science and Technology, Aalesund, Norway
hawa@hials.no
‡Faculty of Computer, Guangdong University of Technology, Guangzhou, China
wh_red@gdut.edu.cn

Abstract— This paper investigates the channel allocation problem in multi-channel wireless networks with directional antennas. In particular, we propose a general analytical framework on the number of channels, in which we consider a new directional antenna model. This antenna model is more general than existing antenna models since other existing antenna models can be regarded as a special case of our model. Besides, it can accurately depict directional antenna with consideration of side-lobes and back-lobes. Moreover, we derive the upper bounds on the number of channels of such networks to ensure collision-free communications. Our results are also insightful to the network design and network deployment.

Index Terms— Directional Communications; Wireless Networks; Multiple Channels

I. INTRODUCTION

The proliferation of wireless networks as well as various wireless services is driving the new demands on the precious wireless spectrum result. Therefore, how to use wireless spectrum efficiently has received extensive attentions recently. One of current solutions to improve the network performance is to use multiple channels instead of using a single channel in wireless networks. Both the experimental results and the theoretical results [1]–[5] show that using multiple channels can significantly improve the network throughput due to the improved spectrum reuse. However, most of the studies assume that each node is equipped with omni-directional antennas only, which can cause higher interference and result in poor spectrum reuse. We call such multi-channel wireless networks with omni-directional antennas as OMN-Nets.

Recent studies such as [6]–[9] found that using directional antennas instead of omni-directional antennas in wireless networks can greatly improve the network throughput. In contrast to omni-directional antennas, directional antennas can concentrate the radio signal to some directions so that the interference to other undesired directions can be reduced. As a result, the spectrum reuse can be further improved and can consequently enhance the network performance. The integration of directional antennas and multiple channels can potentially improve the network performance further. Some of most recent works such as [10], [11] found that using directional antennas in multi-channel wireless networks can improve the capacity and connectivity. We call such multi-channel wireless networks with directional antennas as DIR-Nets.

However, there are few works on the channel allocation problem with DIR-Nets. Although [12] investigated the channel allocation problem with DIR-Nets, this work only considers an idealistic directional antenna model without consideration of side-lobes and back-lobes of antennas, which can potentially affect the network performance [13]. In this paper, we establish a general analytical framework on the channel allocation problem with DIR-Nets, in which we consider a new antenna model - Iris. This new antenna model is more general than existing antenna models and can accurately model directional antenna with consideration of side-lobes and back-lobes. We also derive the upper bounds on the number of channels in DIR-Nets.

The rest of this paper is organized as follows. Section II presents the antenna models. We then give the system models in Section III. Section IV next derives the upper bounds on the number of channels to ensure collision-free communications in DIR-Nets. Finally, we conclude the paper in Section V.

II. ANTENNA MODELS

A. Directional Antennas

An antenna is a device that is used for radiating/collecting radio signals into/from space. An omni-directional antenna, which can radiate/collect radio signals uniformly in all directions in space, is typically used in conventional wireless networks. Different from an omni-directional antenna, a directional antenna can concentrate transmitting or receiving capability to some desired directions so that it has better performance than an omni-directional antenna.

To model the transmitting or receiving capability of an antenna, we often use the *antenna gain*, which is the directivity of an antenna in 3-D space. The antenna gain of an antenna can be expressed in *radiation pattern* in 3-D space as the following equation [13],

$$G(\vec{d}) = \eta \frac{U(\vec{d})}{U_{ave}} \quad (1)$$

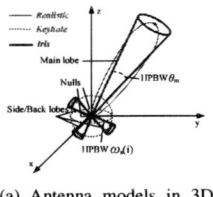

(a) Antenna models in 3D space

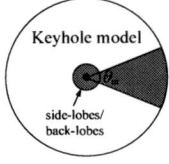

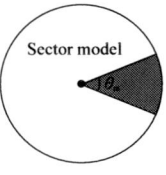

(b) Keyhole model

(c) Sector model

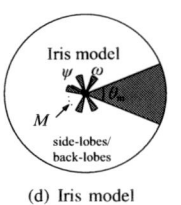

(d) Iris model

Fig. 1. Directional Antenna Models

where $U(\vec{d})$ is the power density in the direction $\vec{d}$, which is denoted by a vector, U_{ave} is the average power density over all directions and η is the efficiency factor, which is set to be 1 since an antenna is often assumed to be lossless.

It is obvious that an omni-directional antenna has the gain $G_o = 1$ (or 0 dBi) since it radiates the radio signal uniformly in all directions. Different from an omni-directional antenna, a directional antenna can radiate or receive radio signals more effectively in some directions than in others. A directional antenna consists of the *main-lobe* (or *main-beam*) with the largest *radiation intensity* and the *side-lobes* and *back-lobes* with the smaller radiation intensity. A typical antenna radiation pattern of a Uniform Circle Array (UCA) in 3-D space is shown in Fig. 1(a).

To accurately depict a directional antenna, we introduce the following properties:

- *Main beam* (main lobe) is the radiation *lobe* with the *maximum* antenna gain.
- *Half Power Beam Width* (*HPBW*) is the angular width between the half-power (-3 dB) points of the main lobe.
- *Side/Back lobes* are the radiation lobes with *maximal* antenna gain (i.e., the local maximal values).
- *Nulling capability* is the capability of a directional antenna employing *nulls* to counteract unwanted interference in some undesired directions.

B. Simplified Directional Antenna Models

It is complicated to compute the antenna gain of a realistic antenna in each direction. Besides, realistic antenna model can not be used to solve the problem of deriving the optimal bounds on the network connectivity [14]. Thus, several simplified directional antenna models have been proposed. In particular, an approximated antenna model has been proposed in [15] and been widely used in [6], [14]. This model is named as *Keyhole* antenna model due to the geometrical analogy to the archaic keyhole in 2-D plane. As shown in Fig. 1(a), Keyhole model consists of one main beam with *beamwidth* θ_m (equal to the HPBW θ_m of a realistic antenna) and side/back lobes approximated by a sphere (the dash line). We next derive the antenna gain of Keyhole model in 2-D plane.

As shown in Fig. 1(b), Keyhole model consists one main-lobe (a sector) with beamwidth θ_m and side-lobes back-lobes denoted by a circle. Since the sum of the radiated power in each direction of an antenna is equal to the radiation power P [13], we have

$$G_m(\vec{d}) \cdot U_{ave} \cdot \theta_m + G_s(\vec{d}) \cdot U_{ave} \cdot (2\pi - \theta_m) = P \quad (2)$$

where $G_s(\vec{d})$ denotes the gain of the back-lobes and the side-lobes and $P = 2\pi \cdot U_{ave}$.

Then, we have

$$G_m = \frac{2\pi - G_s \cdot (2\pi - \theta_m)}{\theta_m} \quad (3)$$

$$G_s = \frac{2\pi - G_m \cdot \theta_m}{2\pi - \theta_m}, \quad (4)$$

where we ignore the vector notation $\vec{d}$ in G_m and G_s for simplicity since they are uniform within θ_m and $2\pi - \theta_m$, respectively.

Sector model [10], [16] is another simplified directional antenna model, which can be regarded as a special case of Keyhole model. As shown in Fig. 1(c), Sector model consists only one main lobe and all the side/back lobes are ignored, i.e., $G_s = 0$. Therefore, we have

$$G_m = \frac{2\pi}{\theta_m}. \quad (5)$$

C. Iris Antenna Model

Either Sector antenna model or Keyhole antenna model somehow over-simplify the radiation pattern of a realistic directional antenna. For example, the sector model may "over-estimate" the performance since it ignores the side-lobes and the back-lobes, which however significantly affect the network performance [17]. The keyhole model may "under-estimate" the performance since it regards all the side-lobes and back-lobes as a circle and ignores the nulling capability of an antenna [7], which somehow can cancel the interference to other nodes.

To overcome the limitations of existing antenna models such as Keyhole and Sector models, we propose a new directional antenna model to approximate the radiation pattern of realistic antennas. Our model consists of one sectoral main beam and several sectoral side/back lobes. We name this model as *Iris model* since it is geometrically analogous to an Iris flower. Fig. 1(a) shows our Iris model, in which the sectoral main beam is analogous to the petal of Iris flower and the sectoral side/back lobes are analogous to the sepals of the flower. We then derive the antenna gain of Iris model in 2-D plane as follows.

For simplicity, each side-lobe is regarded to be identical and is uniformly distributed in $2\pi - \theta_m$ (the separation angle between any two adjacent lobes are ψ) as shown in Fig. 1(d).

We denote the number of side-lobes by M, which depends on the number of side/back-lobes in realistic antennas. There is a constraint on the number of side-lobes M, the angle of each lobe ω and the separation angle ψ, which are denoted as the following equation

$$\theta_m + M \cdot \omega + (M+1) \cdot \psi = 2\pi \tag{6}$$

Similarly, we can calculate the gain of the main-lobe and the gain of each side/back-lobes. First, we have

$$G_m \cdot U_{ave} \cdot \theta_m + M \cdot G_s(\vec{d}) \cdot U_{ave} \cdot (2\pi - \theta_m) = P \tag{7}$$

where $P = 2\pi \cdot U_{ave}$.

We then have

$$G_m = \frac{2\pi - M \cdot G_s \cdot (2\pi - \theta_m)}{\theta_m} \tag{8}$$

$$G_s = \frac{1}{M} \cdot \frac{2\pi - G_m \cdot \theta_m}{2\pi - \theta_m} \tag{9}$$

Generality of Iris model: Our proposed Iris model is more general than existing antenna models. In particular, other antenna models such as Sector model, Keyhole model and omni-directional model can be regarded as special cases of our Iris model under the following scenarios.

(1) Keyhole model is a special case of our Iris model: When $M = 1$ and $\theta_m = 0$, there is only one side-lobe, which is a circle with angle $2\pi - \omega$. In this configuration, our model becomes Keyhole model and G_m and G_s in Eq. (8) and Eq. (9) are consistent with those in Eq. (3) and Eq. (4), respectively.

(2) Sector model is a special case of our Iris model: When $M = 0$, there is no side/back-lobes and our model becomes the sector model. The main antenna gain $G_m = \frac{2\pi}{\theta_m}$, which is consisted with Eq. (5) in the sector model.

(3) Omni-directional model is a special case of our Iris model: When $M = 0$ and $\psi = 0$, $\theta_m = 2\pi$, our model becomes the omni-directional model and $G_m = G_o = 1$.

III. SYSTEM MODELS

A. Interference Model

We propose an interference model to analyze DIR-Nets. Our model only considers directional transmission and directional reception, which can maximize the benefits of directional antennas.

Two nodes X_i and X_j can establish a bi-directional *link* denoted by l_{ij} if and only if the following conditions are satisfied.

(1) X_j is within the *transmission range* of X_i and X_i is within the *transmission range* of X_j.

(2) X_j is covered by the antenna beam of X_i. Similarly, X_i is also covered by the antenna beam of X_j.

(3) No other node within the *interference range*(the interference range is used to denote the maximum distance within which a node can be interfered by an interfering signal) is simultaneously transmitting over the same channel and in the same direction toward X_j.

We call two nodes in *conflict* with each other if they are located within the interference range of each other and their

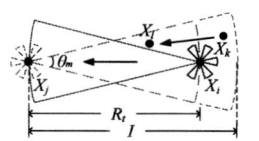

Fig. 2. The Interference Model.

antenna beams are pointed toward each other. For example, in Figure 2, node X_k within the interference range of node X_j may conflict with X_j. Link l_{ij} *conflicts* with link l_{kl} if either node of one link conflicts with either node of the other link.

We next analyze the interference range.

B. Interference Range

We denote the node whose transmission causes the interference to other nodes as the *interfering* node. The node whose reception is interfered by other *interfering* nodes is denoted as *interfered* node.

We assume that the interfering node transmits with power P. The received power at the interfered node at a distance d from the interfering node is denoted by P_r, which can be calculated by

$$P_r = C_1 G_t G_r P \frac{1}{d^\alpha}, \tag{10}$$

where C_1 is a constant, G_t and G_r denote the antenna gain of the interfering node and the antenna gain of the interfered node, respectively, and α is the path loss factor usually ranging from 3 to 5 [18].

When an interfering node interferes with an interfered node, the received power at the interfered node P_r is required to be no less than a threshold P_0, *i.e.*, $P_r \geq P_0$. We then have

$$P_0 = C_1 G_t G_r P_t \frac{1}{I^\alpha}, \tag{11}$$

where I is defined as the *interfering range*.

Solving this equation, we have

$$I = \left(\frac{C_1 G_t G_r P_t}{P_0}\right)^{\frac{1}{\alpha}}. \tag{12}$$

Eq. (13) is a general expression of the interference range for both OMN-Nets and DIR-Nets. With regard to an OMN-Net, the interference range denoted by I_o can be trivially calculated as follows,

$$I_o = \left(\frac{C_1 P_t}{P_0}\right)^{\frac{1}{\alpha}}, \tag{13}$$

where $G_t = G_r = G_o = 1$ as shown in Section II.

TABLE I
FOUR SCENARIOS.

Scenarios	Interfering node	Interfered node	Interference Range
I	Main beam	Main beam	I_{mm}
II	Main beam	Side-lobes	I_{ms}
III	Side-lobes	Main beam	I_{sm}
IV	Side-lobes	Side-lobes	I_{ss}

It is more complicated to derive the interference range I for DIR-Nets due to the directivity of antennas. In particular, we

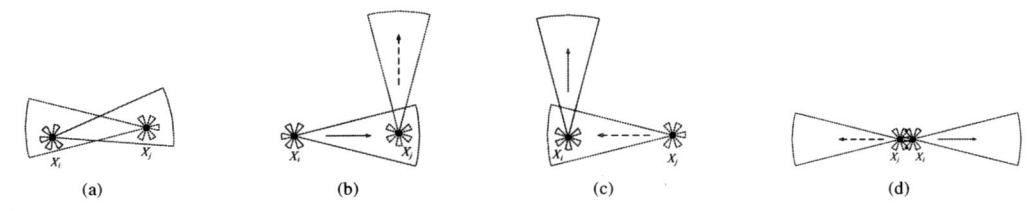

Fig. 3. Four scenarios: (a) Scenario (I), (b) Scenario (II), (c) Scenario (III), (d) Scenario (IV).

categorize our analysis into four different scenarios as shown in Table I.

In Scenario I, two nodes X_i and X_j interfere with each other if and only if they fall into the interference range of each other and their main antenna beams are pointed toward each other, as shown in Figure 3(a). In this case, the interference range denoted by I_{mm} can be calculated by

$$I_{mm} = \left(\frac{C_1 G_m G_m P}{P_0}\right)^{\frac{1}{\alpha}}, \quad (14)$$

where we replace both G_t and G_r in Equation (13) by G_m.

In Scenario II, the main antenna beam of the interfering node X_i is pointed to the interfered node X_j, which also falls into the interference range of X_i. However, the main beam of the interfered node X_j is not necessarily pointed to the interfering node X_i. Due to the existence of the side-lobes and the back-lobes, the reception of node X_j is interfered by node X_i, as shown Figure 3(b). Thus, the interference range denoted by I_{ms} can be calculated by

$$I_{ms} = \left(\frac{C_1 G_m G_s P}{P_0}\right)^{\frac{1}{\alpha}}, \quad (15)$$

where we replace G_t and G_r in Equation (13) by G_m and G_s, respectively.

Similar to Scenario II, the interference range in Scenario III, which is denoted by I_{sm}, can be calculated by

$$I_{sm} = \left(\frac{C_1 G_s G_m P}{P_0}\right)^{\frac{1}{\alpha}}, \quad (16)$$

where we replace G_t and G_r in Equation (13) by G_s and G_m, respectively.

It is obvious that $I_{ms} = I_{sm}$. Thus, we regard I_{ms} as I_{sm} interchangeably throughout the remaining paper.

In Scenario IV, the side-/back-lobes of the interfering node X_i and the interfered node X_j cover each other. Thus, we can calculate the interference range denoted by I_{ss}

$$I_{ss} = \left(\frac{C_1 G_s G_s P}{P_0}\right)^{\frac{1}{\alpha}}, \quad (17)$$

where we replace both G_t and G_r in Equation (13) by G_s.

C. Definitions

In this paper, we assume that there are n nodes in a plane and each node has only one antenna, which allows only one transmission or reception at a time. We also assume that each node is equipped with an identical antenna with the same beamwidth θ_m. Each node also has the same *transmission range* R_t and the same *interference range* I. Typically, I is no less than R_t, i.e. $I \geq R_t$.

We then have the following definitions.

Definition 1: Link Set. A link set is defined as a set of links among which no two links in this set share common nodes. Such a link set is denoted as LS. A link set is used to describe a set of links that need to act simultaneously.

Definition 2: Valid Assignment. A valid assignment to a link set is an assignment of channels such that no two conflicting links are assigned an identical channel. A link set is called a *Schedulable Link Set* if and only if there exists a valid assignment for the link set.

Definition 3: Node Density. There are n nodes randomly located in the plane. Let S denote the (infinite) set of sectors on the plane with interference range I and angle θ_m. The number of nodes within sector s is denoted as $N(s)$. The density of nodes is defined as $D = \max_{s \in S} N(s)$.

Note that we define

Then we give the definition of the upper bound on the number of channels to ensure collision-free communications in DIR-Nets.

Definition 4: Upper Bound on the number of channels. There exist possibly many valid link sets, which represent different combination of communication pairs among the nodes. The problem is to find a number, denoted as U, such that any link set LS derived from n nodes is schedulable using U channels. In other word, U is the upper bound of channels needed to ensure a collision-free link assignment.

The link assignment problem can be converted to a *conflict graph* problem, which is first addressed in [19]. A conflict graph is used to model the effects of interference.

Definition 5: Conflict Graph. We define a graph in which every link from a link set LS can be represented by a vertex. Two vertices in the graph are connected by an edge if and only if the two links conflict. Such a graph is called a conflict graph. The conflict graph G constructed from link set LS is denoted as $G(LS)$.

IV. UPPER BOUNDS ON THE NUMBER OF CHANNELS

A. Background Results

By constructing the conflict graph for a link set, and representing each channel by a different color, we found that the requirement that no two conflicting links share the same channel is equivalent to the constraint that no two adjacent vertices share the same color in graph coloring. Therefore, the problem of channel assignment on a link set can be converted to the classical vertex coloring problem (in graph theory, the vertex coloring problem is a way of assigning "colors" to vertices of a graph such that no two adjacent vertices share the same color) on the conflict graph. The vertex coloring problem, as one of the most fundamental problems in graph theory, is known to be NP-hard even in the very restricted classes of planar graphs [20]. A coloring is regarded as valid if no two adjacent vertices use the same color.

The minimum number for a valid coloring of vertices in a graph G is denoted by a *chromatic* number, $\chi(G)$. There are two well-known results on the upper bound of $\chi(G)$, which will be used to derive our results.

Lemma 1: [21] If $\Delta(G)$ denotes the largest degree among G's vertices, i.e., $\Delta(G) = \max_{v \in G} Degree(v)$, then we have

$$\chi(G) \leq \Delta(G) + 1$$

∎

B. Upper Bounds on the Number of Channels

Before the derivation of upper bounds on the number of channels in DIR-Nets, we have the follow lemma to analyze the interference range I according to the aforementioned scenarios in Section III-A.

Lemma 2: When the main beamwidth θ_m is narrow, we have $I_{ss} \ll I_{ms} \ll I_{mm}$.

Proof. First, we have

$$\frac{I_{ss}}{I_{ms}} = \frac{(\frac{C_1 G_s G_s P}{P_0})^{\frac{1}{\alpha}}}{(\frac{C_1 G_m G_s P}{P_0})^{\frac{1}{\alpha}}} = (\frac{G_s}{G_m})^{\frac{1}{\alpha}}. \quad (18)$$

Similarly, we have

$$\frac{I_{ms}}{I_{mm}} = (\frac{G_s}{G_m})^{\frac{1}{\alpha}} \quad (19)$$

As shown in Eq. (8) and Eq. (9), when the beamwidth θ_m is narrow (e.g., $\theta_m \leq 10°$), $G_s \ll G_m$. Since the path loss factor α usually ranges from 2 to 5, it is obvious that $I_{ss} \ll I_{ms} \ll I_{mm}$. ∎

We then derive the upper bounds on the number of channels to ensure collision-free communications in DIR-Nets with Sector antenna model.

Theorem 1: If there are n nodes in a planar area with the density D and each node is equipped with a directional antenna, for any valid link set LS derived from the n nodes, the corresponding conflict graph $G(LS)$ can be colored by using $2D + \frac{2DM\omega}{\theta_m} \cdot \left(\frac{G_s}{G_m}\right)^{\frac{2}{\alpha}} - 1$ colors.

Proof. We first derive the results based on *Sector* model (as shown in Fig. 4).

Consider link l_{ij} that consists of nodes X_i and X_j, as shown in Fig. 4. The interference region is denoted as two sectors with radius I and angle θ_m (the gray area in Fig. 4). From the definition of node density, each sector has at most D nodes. Other than nodes X_i and X_j, there are at most $D-1$ nodes in either sector. After we combine the nodes in the two sectors, the gray area contains no more than $2D - 2$ nodes excluding nodes X_i and X_j.

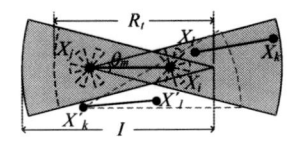

Fig. 4. Side/back-lobes included in interference region

Suppose link l_{kl} is one of the links that conflicts with l_{ij}. It is obvious that at least one node of that link, e.g., X_k, should be in X_j's interference region, the gray sector centered at X_j in Fig. 4. At the same time, the antenna of X_k should be pointed to X_j if it can interfere with X_j. Thus, X_k's interference region must also cover X_j. So, $|X_k - X_j| \leq I$. Since the antenna beam of the other node X_l should be turned toward X_k, it must also fall in the interference region of X_j, as shown in Fig. 4. Hence, $|X_l - X_j| \leq I$.

It seems that any link that conflicts with link l_{ij} must fall in the gray area representing the interference regions of nodes X_i and X_j. However, consider the case that X'_k and X'_l form a link l'_{kl} in Fig. 4. X'_l is outside the gray region of l_{ij}, but X'_k can interfere with X_i since its beam covers X_i. So, a link conflicting with link l_{ij} must contain at least one node falling in the gray area. Therefore, there are at most $2D - 2$ links that conflict with l_{ij}.

We then extend the proof with consideration of side/back-lobes that are not completely covered by interference region as shown in Fig. 5. We denote the distance between X_i and X_j by d. To ensure that X_i can communicate with X_j, we require $d \leq R_t$, where R_t is the transmission range of X_i. The area of the interference region (including the interference region of the main beam as well as the interference region of the side-/back-lobes) varies with the different distance d. However, d cannot be too large, otherwise X_i and X_j cannot communicate with each other. It holds that $d \leq R_t$. When $d = R_t$, the analysis is the same as the above sector case. So, we omit the detailed analysis here.

When the distance d is decreased, the interference region caused by the side-/back-lobes may not be totally covered by the interference region of the main beam. For example, when d becomes much more smaller than R_t, as shown in Fig. 5, where the side-lobes and back-lobes, which cannot be totally covered by the interference region of the main lobes. In this case, the interference region has the maximum coverage area.

We then calculate the number of nodes in this interference region. The number of nodes falling into the side-lobe area is bounded $2 \cdot \frac{D}{\frac{\theta_m}{2} \cdot I_{mm}^2} \cdot M \cdot \omega \cdot I_{ss}^2 = \frac{2DM\omega}{\theta_m} \cdot \left(\frac{G_s}{G_m}\right)^{\frac{2}{\alpha}}$. Hence, the maximum degree of the vertices of G is $\Delta(G) \leq 2D + \frac{2DM\omega}{\theta_m} \cdot \left(\frac{G_s}{G_m}\right)^{\frac{2}{\alpha}} - 2$. From Lemma 1, the conflict graph can be colored by using $2D + \frac{2DM\omega}{\theta_m} \cdot \left(\frac{G_s}{G_m}\right)^{\frac{2}{\alpha}} - 1$ colors. ∎

C. Discussions and implications

From the results, we found that the number of channels to ensure collision-free communications in DIR-Nets heavily depends on (i) the node density D and (ii) the antenna model (i.e., θ_m, ω and M). In particular, our results indicate that the

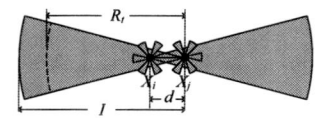

Fig. 5. Side/back-lobes not completely included in interference region.

higher node density results the more number of channels to ensure collision-free communications. Our findings imply that in the next generation wireless communication systems (e.g., 5G cellular networks), the fined-grained channel allocation mechanisms shall be designed, which however causes the new research challenges [22].

Besides, directional antennas have higher spectrum reuse than omni-directional antennas. One evidence is that the node density of OMN-Nets is larger than that of DIR-Nets as indicated in [5], [12]. Thus, if there are only limited channels available in a network, we can use directional antennas to cater for the collision-free transmission. In millimeter wave (mmWave) communication networks (i.e., potential solutions to 5G communication systems) [23], in order to overcome the high attenuation of mmWave radio signal (the radio frequency is above 30GHz), directional antennas are compulsorily equipped with wireless devices. One of research issues in such mmWave networks is how to assign channels to improve the spectrum reuse. Our study in this paper offers a solution to such new challenge.

V. CONCLUSIONS

How to efficiently use the radio spectrum has received extensive attentions recently. Some of previous works concerned with using multiple channels in wireless network with omni-directional antennas. The performance improvement is limited due to the broadcasting features of omni-directional antennas, which have high interference. There are other works considering wireless networks with directional antennas, which concentrate the transmission to some desired directions and consequently improve the network performance. But, there are few studies on integrating directional antennas with multiple channels together. This paper is one of pioneer works in the new area. In particular, we establish an analytical model to analyze the maximum number of channels to ensure the collision-free communications in DIR-Nets. More specifically, we propose a novel antenna model - Iris to completely depict the features of realistic antennas. On one hand, this model depicts directional antennas more accurately than other existing simple antenna models. On the other hand, this model is more general since other existing models can be regarded as special cases of our Iris model. Besides, our theoretical results also offer many useful insights to design wireless networks.

ACKNOWLEDGEMENT

The work described in this paper was partially supported by Macao Science and Technology Development Fund under Grant No. 096/2013/A3 and the NSFC-Guangdong Joint Fund under Grant No. U1401251. The authors would like to thank Gordon K.-T. Hon for his constructive comments.

REFERENCES

[1] P. Bahl, R. Chandra, and J. Dunagan, "SSCH: Slotted seeded channel hopping for capacity improvement in ieee 802.11 ad-hoc wireless networks," in *Proceedings of Mobicom*, 2004.
[2] R. Draves, J. Padhye, and B. Zill, "Routing in multi-radio, multi-hop wireless mesh networks," in *Proceedings of Mobicom*, 2004.
[3] M. Kodialam and T. Nandagopal, "Characterizing the capacity region in multi-radio multi-channel wireless mesh networks," in *Proceedings of MobiCom*, 2005.
[4] P. Kyasanur and N. H. Vaidya, "Capacity of multichannel wireless networks: Impact of number of channels and interfaces," in *Proceedings of MobiCom*, 2005.
[5] L. Cao and M.-Y. Wu, "Upper bound of the number of channels for conflict-free communication in multi-channel wireless networks," in *Proceedings of IEEE WCNC*, 2007.
[6] P. Li, C. Zhang, and Y. Fang, "The Capacity of Wireless Ad Hoc Networks Using Directional Antennas," *IEEE Transactions on Mobile Computing*, vol. 10, no. 10, pp. 1374–1387, 2011.
[7] J. Zhang and S. C. Liew, "Capacity improvement of wireless ad hoc networks with directional antennae," *Mobile Computing and Communications Review*, vol. 10, no. 4, pp. 17–19, 2006.
[8] H.-N. Dai, K.-W. Ng, and M.-Y. Wu, "On collision-tolerant transmission with directional antennas," in *Proceedings of IEEE WCNC*, 2008.
[9] ——, "On busy-tone based MAC protocol for wireless networks with directional antennas," *Wireless Personal Communications*, vol. 73, no. 3, pp. 611 – 636, 2013.
[10] H.-N. Dai, K.-W. Ng, R. C.-W. Wong, and M.-Y. Wu, "On the Capacity of Multi-Channel Wireless Networks Using Directional Antennas," in *Proceedings of IEEE INFOCOM*, 2008.
[11] H. Xu, H.-N. Dai, and Q. Zhao, "On the connectivity of wireless networks with multiple directional antennas," in *the 18th IEEE International Conference on Networks (ICON)*, 2012.
[12] H.-N. Dai, K.-W. Ng, and M.-Y. Wu, "Upper bounds on the number of channels to ensure collision-free communications in multi-channel wireless networks using directional antennas," in *Proceedings of IEEE WCNC*, 2010.
[13] C. A. Balanis, *Antenna Theory : Analysis and Design*, 3rd ed. New York: John Wiley & Sons, 2005.
[14] M. Kiese, C. Hartmann, and R. Vilzmann, "Optimality bounds of the connectivity of adhoc networks with beamforming antennas," in *IEEE GLOBECOM*, 2009.
[15] R. Ramanathan, "On the performance of ad hoc networks with beamforming antennas," in *Proceedings of MobiHoc*, 2001.
[16] S. Yi, Y. Pei, and S. Kalyanaraman, "On the capacity improvement of ad hoc wireless networks using directional antennas," in *Proceedings of ACM MobiHoc*, 2003.
[17] R. Ramanathan, J. Redi, C. Santivanez, D. Wiggins, and S. Polit, "Ad hoc networking with directional antennas: A complete system solution," *IEEE JSAC*, vol. 23, no. 3, pp. 496–506, 2005.
[18] T. S. Rappaport, *Wireless communications : principles and practice*, 2nd ed. Upper Saddle River, N.J.: Prentice Hall PTR, 2002.
[19] K. Jain, J. Padhye, V. N. Padmanabhan, and L. Qiu, "Impact of interference on multi-hop wireless network performance," in *Proceedings of ACM MobiCom*, 2003.
[20] D. B. West, *Introduction to graph theory*, 2nd ed. Upper Saddle River, N.J.: Prentice Hall PTR, 2001.
[21] A. Panconesi and R. Rizzi, "Some simple distributed algorithms for sparse networks," *Distributed Computing*, vol. 14, no. 2, pp. 97–100, 2001.
[22] T. Wang, Y. Sun, L. Song, and Z. Han, "Social data offloading in d2d-enhanced cellular networks by network formation games," *IEEE Transactions on Wireless Communications*, vol. 14, no. 12, pp. 7004–7015, 2015.
[23] J. Qiao, X. Shen, J. W. Mark, Q. Shen, Y. He, and L. Lei, "Enabling device-to-device communications in millimeter-wave 5g cellular networks," *IEEE Communications Magazine*, vol. 53, no. 1, pp. 209–215, January 2015.

What-if Analysis in Wireless Sensor Networks Using Workflow Provenance (Position Paper)

Gulustan Dogan
Yildiz Technical University
Istanbul, Turkey
gulustan@yildiz.edu.tr

Abstract—Over the time sensor network readings become large datasets. A user reading the sensed data will not totally comprehend the readings without learning the path taken and understanding the dataset. As this is an accepted fact, the idea of including the provenance data while publishing sensor readings has been around for many years. First, the readings were annotated with data provenance such as reading time, node id. Since only keeping data provenance was not sufficient, the idea of storing workflow provenance arose. Workflow provenance illustrate the path taken to produce the readings and provenance models capture a complete description of evaluation of a workflow. As provenance is crucial for wireless sensor networks to support reproducibility, debugging and result comprehension, they have been an increasingly important part of wireless sensor networks. In our paper, we argue that sensor network provenance systems should support what-if analysis and debugging in order to allow users do modifications, see the results visually without actually running the workflow steps and be able to debug the workflows to figure out the anomalies in a wireless sensor network.

Keywords—Workflow Provenance, Trust, Wireless Sensor Networks, Fault Tolerance, Distributed Intelligence, Self Organization.

I. INTRODUCTION

Wireless sensor networks (WSN) are used in many applications such as battlefield surveillance, air pollution monitoring, forest fires detection, biological, chemical attack detection. Due to their nature, wireless sensor networks are more error-prone than traditional networks. However in some critical sensor networks there is no central authority monitoring to find faults. Fault management and trust assessment are very crucial in order to sustain these real-time and mission critical networks. Information trust in a WSN depends on several factors such as its path, the trust of the source (sensor), time elapsed after the transmission, past behaviors, trust history of the nodes. Doing what-if analysis involves understanding the causal chains of past events which is provided by provenance. With provenance there are solid references of the phases data goes through and the event chains [2].

In our model provenance is kept for trust history and other information such as node location, node type, data type. Moreover provenance is used in order to find out causes of faulty behavior, to figure out the circumstances that will determine the connectivity of the network, to produce trusted data after elimination of the causes.

Previously we have done several work on provenance and sensor networks [3, 4, 5, 6, 8, 11]. In one of our work [3] we have built an architecture called ProTru for trust assessment using provenance. Our architecture is a generic architecture for all network types. Trust assessment of the nodes are done locally and network restructuring is done based on the trust calculations such as deleting untrusted nodes. Our trust metrics are data accuracy and data freshness. We decide about accuracy based on data similarity. In this paper, we modify this model for improved self organization and cognitive capabilities in wireless sensor networks. We extend our previous model so that it can remember the past network snapshots by storing dataflow provenance graphs. For wireless sensor networks remembering the past dataflows is very helpful for self organizing of the data. We came up with this idea by looking into nature. There are many examples of path recordings in the nature. One example is foraging behavior in ant colonies. Ants leave pheromones on the paths they follow so that they can later remember the paths they took when carrying food to their nests. The central dataflow provenance repository gives the wireless sensort network the ability to remember the paths data followed as pheromones in ant colonies.

This paper is organized as follows. Related work is presented in Section 2. In Section 3 and Section 4 we describe our architecture briefly and explain the central dataflow provenance model. Section 5 concludes the paper.

II. RELATED WORK

There has been some work on fault tolerance in sensor networks. Paradis and Han survey fault-tolerance techniques for sensor network applications such as ESRT, PSFQ [1, 14, 17]. To our knowledge, there is not any work on using provenance specifically for fault tolerance in sensor networks. The interest of our paper differs from all of the above as we are using provenance locally to do what-if analysis and to capture network snapshots for self organization.

There is some work on cognitive networks. Traditional networks only deal with amount of data transmitted however cognitive networks also deal with content of the information delivered. It is closely related to provenance in the sense that provenance can keep information about the content [13]. In cognitive networks, elements in networks have states that are changing based on the content of the information received. This idea is close to our idea of nodes in a network that are in specific states at a given time and are behaving according to a Finite State Machine [13]. A cognitive model takes the data and converts it into intelligent information. Apart from the provenance research, there have been many ideas of increasing the intelligence within a multihop network. Intelligence can mean a range of behaviors from a sensor that turns on a light to much more complicated computing and

49

actions. We cannot relate all possible uses of the term here, we use it in a broader sense meaning the capability of the network to provide an immediate and detailed data trust.

There are several research threads that can be differentiated from the use in our architecture. One important common theme in making intelligent decisions within a network has been to better balance the traffic. Kelly provided a technique that makes use of local knowledge at a node to improve the traffic flow versus link capacity within the network [10]. Heo and Varshney made use of mobility to better position sensors in an area to improve coverage and energy efficiency [9]. Close to the ideas presented in our paper, Zahedi et al. have considered a two-tiered fault detection system for a sensor field that is collecting information [20]. Fusion node for a group of sensors weighs the usefulness of the inputs based on how accurate the result is compared to its likeliness for a misbehaved value. Our model is broader than the approaches listed as it is a general architecture applicable to different wireless network types. It is also more powerful as it is making use of provenance to create a distributed intelligence. Our approach is also novel in the sense that while storing rich trust and provenance information in vectors, we transmit one trust value over the network conserving network bandwidth utilization and reducing energy consumption. In addition, the two way communication (push and pull) between intermediate node and its children makes it possible to have an up-to-date trust picture of the network. Moreover by centrally storing the network pictures, our network gains a very valuable capability of remembering past flows.

Provenance has been studied in Sensor Network community. Provenance aware sensor data storage systems are proposed. In these systems, sensors collect provenance information of the data they are sensing or the processes they are running [12]. Furthermore, provenance information associated with sensor data has been used in answering domain specific complex queries [15]. Park and Heidemann explore the need for data provenance in a information network to understand how processed results are derived and to correct anomalies [16]. In addition, provenance-aware Open Provenance Model based sensor systems have been implemented in different domains [7, 18]. There has been work presenting frameworks for provenance-aware information networks where data fusion methods are implemented [19]. However, to our knowledge this is the first work where what-if analysis using provenance in wireless sensor networks is discussed.

III. Network Model and Architecture

In this section, we briefly summarize our architecture ProTru [3]. More detailed theoretical explanation of the framework is presented in our paper.

A. Leaf Nodes

They are the source nodes (identified by a unique id). Leaf nodes collect and then disseminate information but do not receive information from other nodes. All nodes in our network as well as leaf nodes have vectors of reputation and provenance. $trust_{accuracy}$ and $trust_{freshness}$ values computed using the values in the vectors are forwarded along with the data while provenance and reputation vectors are kept at the nodes. In this system, nodeid is concatenated to the (data, $trust_{accuracy}$, $trust_{freshness}$) tuple forwarded along in order to have the dataflow information which is required for creating the graphs at the central provenance graph repository.

B. Intermediate Nodes

They are computationally more powerful nodes receiving information from a group of nodes, doing calculations on the received information such as fusing, and transmitting the information for the group forward. Intermediate nodes are identified by a unique id and they are the leaders of a group of leaves. Intermediate nodes receive two trust values along with the data; $trust_{accuracy}$ and $trust_{freshness}$. As the information is computed and fused, outlier nodes are found out by the intermediate node as the result of comparisons of several (data, $t_{accuracy}$, $t_{freshness}$) tuples received. For instance an intermediate node can fuse temperature data coming from two nodes, let's say $node_1$ sends the tuple (d_1, $t_{accuracy1}$, $t_{freshness1}$) and $node_2$ sends the tuple (d_2, $t_{accuracy2}$, $t_{freshness2}$) with trust values very close to each other. However the fusion node might realize that quality of d_2 is much better than d_1 and it can send a *decrease your trust value* message to the $node_1$. The algorithms used for data value comparisons and fusion are described in more detail in our paper [3]. Differently than ProTru, nodeid numbers of the sensor nodes which trasnmitted the data used in the fusion are concatenated to the (data, $trust_{accuracy}$, $trust_{freshness}$) tuple forwarded along in order to have the dataflow information which is required for creating the graphs at the central provenance graph repository.

C. Central Node

It is the top level of hierarchy which is a central station receiving values from intermediate nodes and calculating the final value. Intermediate nodes will send computed fused data, corresponding trust value and nodeid numbers of the tranmsitting nodes to central node. Due to distributed nature of our architecture, central node does not make decisions, it calculates the final result by taking the weighted average of incoming (data,trust) tuples. It also stores the coming result and dataflow graph at the central provenance storage after labeling it either bad or good based on a trust threshold.

ProTru architecture is extended by adding a central provenance repository of dataflow graphs. In our previous work, we designed a system called DustDoctor which troubleshoots a sensor network by doing mining on provenance graphs [11]. In this work we will use the same approach in DustDoctor to troubleshoot the wireless sensor network and find out the untrusted nodes. In DustDoctor we reported the faulty node by a GUI however the system we are proposing in this paper is much more powerful in the sense that based on the outcome the network will re-organize and heal itself.

IV. Provenance

In wireless sensor networks, time of creation of the leaf node data, the id of the Leaf Node creating the data, how much energy is left on the Leaf Node, how many times Leaf Node was turned of, the id of the central node leaf node is reporting to (dataflow) are part of the provenance data.

In most network systems, there is a central or distributed provenance storage system [12]. Provenance is stored for later reuse and reference. We will transmit the workflow provenance to a central storage. We will keep the amount of provenance data at the required minimum level not to consume much energy for transmission.

All the workflow provenance data flowing over the network will be kept in the Central Storage. Workflow provenance records will be stored in the Central Storage. The historical data will also be available in the Cental Storage for network maintenance such as figuring out the leaf nodes that are silent for very long time, determining the group of leaf nodes that are misreporting. Final decision regarding the location estimation will be done at the Headquarter.

Provenance collecting and processing is very costly. However richer provenance is better for more efficient network restructuring. Therefore how much provenance to collect is an important choice.

A. What-if Analysis

Workflow provenance will help wireless sensor network in making cognitive decisions in case of a failure. An example scenario where workflow provenance will be useful is as follows. When a computation node is not receiving correct and sufficient input from the nodes it is data dependent, it should take an action to find a correct result. One possible action can be asking to another Intermediate node. This behavior can be implemented by a control flow statement such as "If the incoming edges do not send reliable data then ask to Intermediate node X".

There is also what-if analysis available in our system using the historical data stored in the Central Node. Mining the data, it can be found out how the network will respond if the target moves along a specific path.

- By what-if analysis, administrators can understand the impact of their decisions before they are actually made.
- Using historical provenance data stored in the system, what-if analysis can be done.
- By inspecting provenance graphs, network behavior under certain circumstances can be modeled.
- Solutions will be modeled and verified before deployment.

We make the workflow provenance store-able so "what-if" scenarios can be tested to further improve the debugging capabilities. One feature which will greatly improve the capability of having workflow provenance (graphs) will be to be able to mine the workflow provenance. That is, in effect, the current idea of workflow provenance as a graph is similar to a flow chart or an xlm diagram. Suppose instead of the nodes being labeled with the provenance, the system also stores the path followed to generate the data. The idea is that given the set of input values, and the sequence of the execution of the historical workflow provenance would give same outputs.

Below we will list some of the benefits of storing the workflow provenance. If for some reason the system (including the person reading the output) feels there are unusual results, one could manually request the workflow to be analyzed by graph mining algorithms. Or more powerfully one could add or subtract nodes (or branches from the provenance graph to

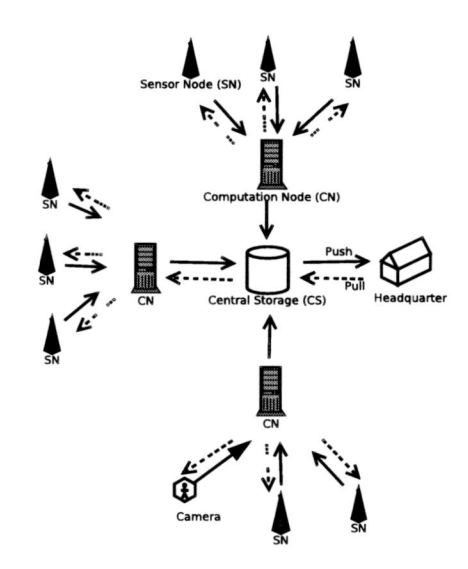

Figure 1: Network Architecture

provenancegraph	timestamp	trustvalue
	2011-01-19 03:14:07	λ
....	....	....

Figure 2: Central Workflow Provenance Storage Scheme

examine the changes. An example is if one suspects a sensor that is collecting data that is being fed into the system to be deviating from accurate results, one could remove it from the workflow and re-analyze.

Examples of Provenance Queries that can be run on workflow provenance:

- Find the groups that have been sleeping in the last six time intervals
- Find the intermediate nodes with an averaged trust value of less than ξ in the last time period
- Find the closest and most-trusted nodes to add to the group with decreasing trust value
- Find the intermediate nodes sending conflicting computation results with the rest of the network
- Find the intermediate node (closest one) to take control of the untrusted intermediate node group

Workflow provenance will be used in analyzing dataflow graphs of the wireless sensor network. For example in a case that an intermediate node is waiting for information coming from a leaf node but that node fails to send the information, the intermediate node will have the information of other possible leaf nodes that might have the same kind of information it is waiting for. With this model we have a snapshot of the network at specific time intervals which we can refer to do some conclusions such as regrouping the fused leaf nodes, omitting a leaf node, changing the dataflow scenario.

In addition to support for alterations of processes and data provenance graphs should also support meta analysis such as concatenating provenance graphs which can be useful for researchers in combining the results of different experiments. In addition to this, for efficiently doing the what-if analysis, sub-graphs should support independent modifications to illustrate conditions and changed subgraphs should be recomposed. These features will give researchers the opportunity of discovering creative experiments.

V. CONCLUSION

Dealing with provenance in systems where data moves along such as wireless sensor networks is an open research area because it is hard to manage provenance when objects are mobile or distributed. Various solutions have been proposed to this problem but solutions are often domain-specific. A true solution will require architectural changes to the applications at the main levels such as hardware, network, operating system. Using provenance for what-if analysis is novel method with a low communication overhead compared to other approaches. Moreover transmitted data for what-if analysis is kept small making the model lightweight making our model efficient for wireless sensor networks. In addition support for multiple metrics makes the architecture flexible for different wireless sensor network domains such as industry, military, healthcare. Dataflow graphs become a reference and serve as a memory for self-organization of the network. Besides the use we have illustrated in this paper, the central provenance graph repository can be used for many purposes as various intelligence can be deduced from the recorded provenance graphs which is an area that we will explore as the continuation of this work.

ACKNOWLEDGEMENT

This research was sponsored by the Technological Research Council of Turkey and was accomplished under Project Number TUBITAK 2232 114C143. The views and conclusions contained in this document are those of the authors and should not be interpreted as representing the official polices, either expressed or implied, of the Technological Research Council of Turkey or the Turkish Government.

REFERENCES

[1] Ö. Akan and I. Akyildiz. Event-to-sink reliable transport in wireless sensor networks. *IEEE/ACM Transactions on Networking (TON)*, 13(5):1003–1016, 2005.

[2] J. Cheney, S. Chong, N. Foster, M. Seltzer, and S. Vansummeren. Provenance: a future history. In *Proceeding of the 24th ACM SIGPLAN conference companion on Object oriented programming systems languages and applications*, pages 957–964. ACM, 2009.

[3] G. Dogan and T. Brown. Protru: Leveraging provenance to enhance network trust based on distributed local intelligence. Technical Report TR2011427, City University of New York, http://tr.cs.gc.cuny.edu/tr/, December 2011.

[4] G. Dogan and T. Brown. Using provenance in sensor network applications for fault-tolerance and troubleshooting. In *International Conference on Sensor Networks*. SENSORNETS, 2012.

[5] G. Dogan, T. Brown, K. Govindan, M. Khan, T. Abdelzaher, P. Mohapatra, and J. Cho. Evaluation of network trust using provenance based on distributed local intelligence. In *Military Communications Conference*. IEEE, 2011.

[6] G. Dogan, E. Seo, T. Brown, and T. Abdelzaher. Leveraging provenance to improve data fusion in sensor networks. In *SPIE Defense, Security, and Sensing*. SPIE, 2012.

[7] T. D. H. Eric G. Stephan and B. D. Ermold. Leveraging the open provenance model as a multi-tier model for global climate research. 2010.

[8] K. Govindan, W. X., M. Khan, G. Dogan, G. Zeng, K. Powell, T. Brown, T. Abdelzaher, and P. Mohapatra. Pronet: Network trust assessment based on incomplete provenance. In *Military Communications Conference*. IEEE, 2011.

[9] N. Heo and P. Varshney. An intelligent deployment and clustering algorithm for a distributed mobile sensor network. In *Systems, Man and Cybernetics, 2003. IEEE International Conference on*, volume 5, pages 4576–4581. IEEE, 2003.

[10] F. Kelly and R. Williams. Dynamic routing in stochastic networks. *IMA Volumes in Mathematics and its Applications*, 71:169–169, 1995.

[11] M. Khan, H. Ahmadi, G. Dogan, K. Govindan, R. Ganti, T. Brown, J. Han, P. Mohapatra, and T. Abdelzaher. Dustdoctor: A self-healing sensor data collection system. In *Information Processing in Sensor Networks (IPSN), 2011 10th International Conference on*, pages 127–128. IEEE, 2011.

[12] J. Ledlie, C. Ng, and D. A. Holland. Provenance-aware sensor data storage. *Data Engineering Workshops, 22nd International Conference on*, 0:1189, 2005.

[13] S. Misra, S. Misra, and I. Woungang. *Selected Topics in Communication Networks and Distributed Systems*. World Scientific Pub Co Inc, 2009.

[14] L. Paradis and Q. Han. A survey of fault management in wireless sensor networks. *Journal of Network and Systems Management*, 15(2):171–190, 2007.

[15] H. Patni, S. Sahoo, C. Henson, and A. Sheth. Provenance aware linked sensor data. In *Proceedings of the Second Workshop on Trust and Privacy on the Social and Semantic Web*, 2010.

[16] J. H. Unkyu Park. Provenance in sensornet republishing. In J. Freire, D. Koop, and L. Moreau, editors, *Provenance and Annotation of Data and Processes*, volume 5272 of *Lecture Notes in Computer Science*, pages 280–292. Springer Berlin / Heidelberg, 2008.

[17] C. Wan, A. Campbell, and L. Krishnamurthy. Pumpslowly, fetch-quickly (psfq): a reliable transport protocol for sensor networks. *Selected Areas in Communications, IEEE Journal on*, 23(4):862–872, 2005.

[18] J. M. A. R. R. K. Yong Liu, Joe Futrelle. A provenance-aware virtual sensor system using the open provenance model. 2010.

[19] X. W. L. M. D. H. J. M. A. R. R. K. Yong Liu, Barbara Minsker. A new framework for on-demand virtualization, repurposing and fusion of heterogeneous

sensors. 2009.

[20] S. Zahedi, M. Szczodrak, P. Ji, D. Mylaraswamy, M. Srivastava, and R. Young. Tiered architecture for on-line detection, isolation and repair of faults in wireless sensor networks. In *Military Communications Conference, 2008. MILCOM 2008. IEEE*, pages 1–7. IEEE, 2008.

Topology Reconstruction for Target Operation Network (TON): A Link Prediction Perspective

Changjun Fan, Baoxin Xiu *, Zhong Liu, Chao Chen, Yao Yang
Science and Technology on Information Systems Engineering Laboratory
National University of Defense Technology
Changsha, Hunan, P. R. China, 410073

Abstract—Information is crucial in the military area, how to purify the obtained information and improve its quality is of great significance. This paper aims to shed some lights from the perspective of target operation network topology reconstruction. First, formalized it as a TON structure reconstruction problem; then proposed a link reliability index, named LR, based on which to identify the spurious edges and predict the missing edges; a greedy algorithm based on LR was designed to reconstruct the observed network; finally, experiments on the public data validated the effectiveness of the reconstruction algorithm, the reconstructed network is closer to the true network in nine topological indexes, including clustering coefficient, assortativity, congestion, synchronization, propagation threshold, network efficiency, betweenness mean standard deviation and natural connectivity, compared to the observed network, which means our reconstruction algorithm could narrow the structural gap between the observed network and the true one.

I. Introduction

In real battle field, however advanced and excellent the reconnaissance means and information collecting works are, it's still rather difficult to guarantee the information to be 100% accurate due to some objective or subjective reasons. In sensitive area, like military battlefield, a small error might cause a huge catastrophe to the outcome of a battle, therefore, a scientific method to refine the information from the battle and to make it a further step closer to the truth before putting them into real uses will be of significant importance for commanders to hold the battle situation, make operational plans, and make decisions. Analysis of the battle field information processing from the perspective of target operation network could be described as the problem of TON structure reconstruction, more specifically, abstract a observed target operation network from the information collected, refine the network by identifying the false information and predicting the missing information and thus obtain reconstructed network closer to the truth than the observed one, so as to lay the foundation for the following central analysis based on network topology. This paper proposed a link prediction based reconstruction model for target operation network based on FINC operation network model, to meet the practical demand of real situations.

FINC is the abbreviation of Force, Intelligence, Networking, C2(command and control)[1][2][3][4][5]. In the process of modeling, triangular nodes represent intelligence units, such as radar, and rectangular nodes stand for operational units, such as missile positions, and the circular nodes indicate command and control units, such as command post. Meanwhile, the edge of the network is used to represent information transmission links, which can be both direct and indirect, edge weight represents the information transmission time delay. Thus we may agree that military system or military network model based on FINC model is able to analyze indexes such as system information delay, reconnaissance performance and synergy ability. The existing FINC model is a military network model based on social network theory, nodes in which could have different properties and structures, meanwhile it's also a well-behaved method to analyze military network's command and communication capability.

Link prediction refers to a prediction of existing probability of nonexist edges in the network[6][7][8]. In the area of computer science, many studies have been conducted on link prediction[9][10]. Exterior information, logically speaking, may obtain higher accuracies, yet the access to those information is difficult to get. Recently link prediction based on network structure has been a heated topic[6][7][8]. It's easier and more reliable to obtain the network structure information than the exterior information, meanwhile network structure based methods are more generative. Current methods can be divided into two main parts according to the prediction theory: similarity based methods and likelihood based methods. Similarity based methods also divide into local information based methods, path based methods and random walk based methods, likelihood based methods divide into hierarchical structure models and stochastic block models. All in all, the effect of link prediction based reconstruction methods is mainly determined by link prediction index chosen. Current link prediction indexes are mainly based on the network topology, for two main reasons, one is the easy access to the network topology information, the other is the satisfactory prediction accuracies of them. Of course there is little evidence shows the combination of exterior information could lead to worse prediction. Provided that the obtained information is correct enough, it's true that the more the available information is, the closer it will get to the truth.

The remaining parts of this paper is arranged as follows: Section 2 formalize the problem this paper aims to address; Section 3 model the link reliability, and proposed the LR index; Section 4 put forward a local greedy search algorithm for TON structure reconstruction; Section 5 conducts experiment

*Correspondence to: baoxinxiu@163.com

on the public dataset, and validates the algorithm proposed before. The last section conclude the paper.

II. PROBLEM FORMULATION

A target operation network $G(V, E, A, L)$, where V stands for a set of nodes, E indicates edges, A is a set of node types, including C2 nodes, fire nodes and information nodes; L stands edge types, including reporting relationship, command relationship, and communication relationship; The problem of TON reconstruction task is to find out a strategy $\{E_{mising}, E_{spurious}\}$, and obtain $maxR(G + \{E_{mising}\} - \{E_{spurious}\})$, here $\{E_{mising}\}, \{E_{spurious}\}$ represent missing edges and spurious edges respectively, $R()$ is the calculation of TON reliability.

How to identify the spurious edges and predict the missing edges, and how to determine each number to obtain the optimal TON reliability, is the core problems we are to address in this paper. Inspired by link prediction research, this paper proposed link prediction based method for TON structure reconstruction. Three definitions are given first:

Definition 1. *(Link Prediction):* *Given network $G(V, E)$, based on the obtained network structure, to predict the occurrence possibility $f(v_i, v_j)$ for those nonexist edges.*

Definition 2. *(Link Reliability):* *It refers to the possibility of whether the link really exists. The higher the reliability, the more possible that there exists certain kind of links between two operation units.*

Definition 3. *(TON Reliability):* *It refers to the degree of structure similarity between the observed TON and the real one.*

III. LINK RELIABILITY MODEL FOR TON

As mentioned before, the observed network is a noisy incomplete network, not all the reliability of the observed edges are 1, nor the reliability of non-observed edges equal to 0. In fact, a credibility evaluation for all the edges of the observed network is needed, so as to provide basis for the subsequent spurious edges recognition and missing edges prediction.

While under the circumstance of unknown real network and other information, it remains a great challenge to calculate each edge's link reliability based on the observed network only. However, for target operation network, the analysis of its reconstruction should be well combined with the specific features.

Three hypothesis are put forward before modeling the link reliability of target operation network:

Hypothesis I: The link connection probability between between nodes is correlated with nodes type.

There are three types of nodes in TON: fire nodes, command and control nodes and information nodes. The nodes type do generate impacts on linking behaviors, for instance, there are no possible links between fire nodes, which is a reason for choosing the stochastic block model, for its basic hypothesis is whether nodes are connected in a network is determined by the cluster they belong to.

Hypothesis II: The link reliability of the exist edges may not be 1.

For the observed network contains some noise, i.e., spurious edges, link reliability of these edges are not 1.

Hypothesis III: The link connection probability between nodes is correlated with their indirect connection stregth.

Generally speaking, if there are more reachable paths between two nodes, which means their indirect connection strength is strong, it is more likely to generate direct connections between these two nodes.

As a resul, this paper takes two factors into modeling, which are nodes types, represented as T, and nodes indirect connection strength, represented as S; let R stands for the link reliability, then

$$R = f(T, S) \quad (1)$$

Now the quantitative effects of these two factors on link reliability evaluation are analyzed as follows:

A. Influence of the node type

This section quantify the nodes types' influence on link reliability based on stochastic block model.

Theorem 1: For an target operation network $G(V, E, A, L)$, let σ_x denotes the type number of node v_x, and r_{σ_x, σ_y} stands for all of the possible connections between these two types of nodes. $l^o_{\sigma_x, \sigma_y}$ represents the observed edge numbers between σ_x type nodes and σ_y type nodes. Then link reliability for $\{v_x, v_y\}$ is:

$$p(A_{xy} = 1 | A^o) = \frac{l^o_{\sigma_x, \sigma_y} + 1}{r_{\sigma_x, \sigma_y} + 2} \quad (2)$$

Proof of Theorem 1 sees in Appendix.

B. Influence of the network topology

The definition of indirect connection strength between two nodes is defined as the number of reachable paths between them. Weight of the path is determined by its length, the shorter the path is, the bigger the weight is.

Definition 4. *(Indirect Connection Strength):Indirect Connection Strength S_{xy} between node v_x and node v_y refers to the weighted sums of the reachable paths with different lengths between these two nodes.*

According to Definition 4, the mathematical expression of S_{xy} is given as follows:

$$s_{xy} = \sum_{l=1}^{\infty} \alpha^l |paths^{<l>}_{x,y}| = \alpha A_{xy} + \alpha^2 (A^2)_{xy} + \alpha^3 (A^3)_{xy} + \cdots \quad (3)$$

where $\alpha > 0$ is an adjustable parameter controlling the path weight, and $|paths^{<l>}_{x,y}|$ is the l-length path numbers. When

α is less than the reciprocal of the maximum eigenvalue of adjacency matrix A, S_{xy} can also be expressed as:

$$S = (I - \alpha A)^{-1} - I \qquad (4)$$

C. Link Reliability Index

Based on the following three points, we get the following conclusions by using the simplest form of product:

$$R = T * S \qquad (5)$$

Firstly, the influences of two factors are all positive, which means, the higher value T or S is, the higher link reliability value is;

Secondly, if any value of these two factors is 0, the link reliability value is 0.

Thirdly, the value of link reliability could be adjusted through normalization.

Therefore, with formula (2) and (4), the value of link reliability for v_x, v_y could be calculated as:

$$r_{xy} = g_{xy} \times s_{xy} = \frac{l^o_{\sigma_x \sigma_y} + 1}{r_{\sigma_x \sigma_y} + 2} \times [(I - \alpha A)^{-1} - I]_{xy} \qquad (6)$$

And we call the link reliability index LR.

IV. TON RECONSTRUCTION ALGORITHM BASED ON LINK RELIABILITY INDEX

Section 3 put forward the Link Reliability index for TON, the following definitions of the missing edge and the spurious edge are given based on this index:

Definition 5. *(Missing Edge):The missing edges are those nonexist edges with higher LR values, referring to the actual missing edges due to incomplete information.*

Definition 6. *(Spurious Edge):The spurious edges are those exist edges with lower LR values, referring to the actual nonexist edges due to noisy information.*

Rank all the edges in TON (including exist edges and nonexist edges) in the descending order, and identify missing edges and spurious edges according to Definition IV and IV, the biggest problem here is to determine the number: the missing edge number and the spurious edge number. This section aims to address the problem.

Definition II explains the physical meaning of TON Reliability, here give its calculation:

$$Reliability_{A^o} = \prod_{A^o_{ij}=1, i \leq j} r_{ij} \qquad (7)$$

Formula (7) is the product of reliability of all the observable links, i.e., the similarity degree of the topology of an observed target operation network to the topology of a real network is determined by the reliability of all the observable links; if all the observable links are more credible, the topology of the observed network is closer to the real one.

This is a typical combinational optimization problem: solution space is all possible combinations of missing edges number and spurious edges number, objective function is TON reliability. Traditional enumeration algorithm is of $O(|E|^2)$ time complexity, which is computational prohibitive for networks with large amount of edges. This section put forward a local greedy search algorithm (1),which is based on the hypothesis that the number of missing edges equal to the spurious one.

Algorithm 1 TON Reconstruction Algorithm Based on Equal Numbers of Missing Edges and Spurious Edges

---

1: **Step 1:** Divide the edges in the observed network A^o into two categaries, exist edges E_{exist} and non-exist edges $E_{nonexist}$, calculate each LR values for all edges,and rank the edges of E_{exist} in an ascending order(thus edges ranked higher indicate higher probability of the spurious edge),rank the edges of $E_{nonexist}$ in a descending order(thus the edges ranked higher indicate higher probability of the missing edge);
2: **step 2:** Get each edge from E_{exist} and $E_{nonexist}$ one by one, e^{exist}_i and $e^{nonexist}_j$, reliability values are r^{exist}_i and $r^{nonexist}_j$ respectively, calculate $\delta = r^{nonexist}_j / r^{exist}_i$;
3: **step 3:** If $\delta > 1$, means the reconstruction strategy (remove the spurious edges e^{exist}_i and add the missing edges $e^{nonexist}_j$) increases the reliability of TON, thus accept it; drop it if not, and repeat Step 2;
4: **step 4:** Repeat the previous three steps until the continuous drop number reaches 5, stop the algorithm.

As a local greedy search algorithm, Algorithm 1 just output a near-optimal solution, and it is based on the assumption that the number of missing edges equals to the spurious one, which is always not accurate in reality. As a result, a more reliable reconstruction algorithm deserves a further research.

An incomplete target operation network with noise can be refined after Algorithm 1, its topological structure is reconstructed to be closer to the real one, which is beneficial to the subsequent analysis based on TON topology.

V. EXPERIMENTS

This section validates the effectiveness of algorithm 1.

A. Data Description

A public reported data is chosen as the experimental data. It contains 89 entities, including 12 C2 units, 26 fire units and 51 information units, and 150 observable links,including 16 F-I(Fire-Information) links, 26 F-C(Fire-C2) links, 51 I-I(Information-Information) links, 30 I-C(Information-C2) links and 17 C-C(C2-C2) links, the relationship of these entities are shown as Figure 1.

Among them, blue nodes represent C2 units, such as control center and command post; red nodes stands for fire units, such as various missile positions; green nodes represents information units, such as various optical fiber stations and radar stations. Edges with different colors stand for different types of links, purple edges stand for optical fiber communication links, red edges represent command and control links and blue edges stand for reporting links.

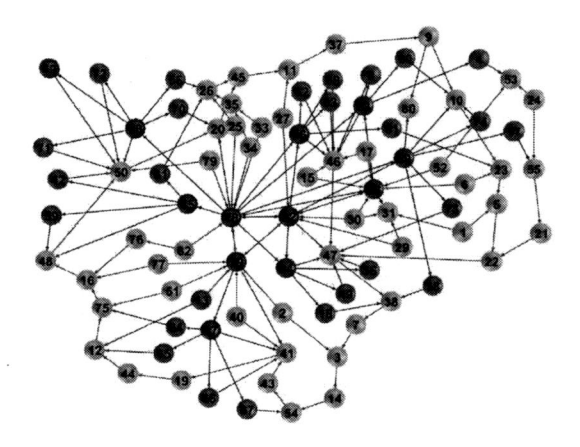

Fig. 1. TON Topology of the Experimental Data

B. Evaluation Indexes

Before evaluating our method's ability in reconstructing TON structure, there is a basic hypothesis here that the experimental data is the real battle field situation, this paper made it as the true network, and assumed the observed network by randomly adding or removing some edges. Evaluation indexes are put forward to quantify the algorithm's ability in narrowing the structure gap between the reconstructed network (from observed network) an the true one.

1) Evaluation Index for Link Reliability: For an observed network A^O, calculate each edge's LR value (including both exist edges and nonexist edges). When evaluating algorithm's ability in predicting missing edges, divide all the nonexist edges ($A^O_{ij} = 0$) into two types, one is the missing edge N_{01} ($A^O_{ij} = 0, A^T_{ij} = 1$); the other is the true nonexist edge $N^0 0$ ($A^O_{ij} = 0, A^T_{ij} = 0$). Now randomly select one edge in N_{01} and in N_{00}, if the edge from N_{01} has a higher LR value than the one from N_{00}, add one score; if two values are equal, add 0.5 score. After comparing $||N^{01}|| \times ||N^{00}||$ times, if one score exists n' times, and 0.5 score exists n'' times, we got $n' + 0.5n''$ scores, the algorithm's ability in predicting missing edges is calculated as:

$$AUC\_Missing = \frac{n' + 0.5n''}{||N^{01}|| \times ||N^{00}||} \quad (8)$$

Similarly, the algorithm's ability in identifying spurious edges could be calculated as:

$$AUC\_Spurious = \frac{n' + 0.5n''}{||N^{11}|| \times ||N^{10}||} \quad (9)$$

where N^{11} ($A^O_{ij} = 1, A^T_{ij} = 1$) represent true exist edges; N^{10} ($A^O_{ij} = 1, A^T_{ij} = 0$) represent spurious edges.

Obviously, if all scores are generated randomly, $AUC \approx 0.5$. Therefore, AUC value measures the extent our LR index is superior to other link prediction index.As a matter of fact, AUC is equivalent to Mann-Whitney U statistical test and Wilcoxon rank-sum statistical test[11] in its form.

2) Evaluation Index for TON Reconstruction: How to measure the structural gap between the reconstructed network A^R and the true network A_T, reference [12] utilized five network structural indexes, clustering coefficient, assortativity, cogestion, synchronization and propagation threshold respectively. Here we adopted four more topological indexes: network efficiency, average betweenness, betweenness mean square deviation and natural connectivity. Following are the further explanations of them:

Network efficiency[13]: $L = \frac{1}{N(N-1)\sum_{i \geq j} \frac{1}{d_{ij}}}$, defined as average reciprocal of the distance between any two nodes, reflecting the network connectivity;

Mean betweeness[14]: $\overline{B} = \frac{1}{N}\sum_{i=1}^{N} b_i$, defined as the average betweenness for all nodes, reflecting the network congestion;

Betweenness mean square deviation[15]: $\sigma = \sqrt{\frac{1}{N}\sum_i (b_i - \overline{B})^2}$, defined as the mean square deviation of the betweeness for all nodes;

Clustering coefficient[14]: $C = \frac{1}{N}\sum_{i=1}^{N} \frac{E_i}{1/2k_i(k_i-1)}$, defined as the average connecting ratio of neighboring nodes in the network, reflecting the clustering degree of nodes in the network;

Assortativity[16][17]:
$r = \frac{W^{-1}\sum_k u_k v_k - [W^{-1}\sum_k a/2(u_k v_k)]^2}{W^{-1}\sum_k \frac{1}{2}(u_k^2+v_k^2) - [W^{-1}\sum_k 1/2(u_k+v_k)]^2}$, where u_k, v_k are the two nodes' degrees of the edges k, W the total edge number. Value of r ranges between [-1,1], when $r > 0$, the network is assortative; when $r < 0$, the network is disassortative; and when $r = 0$, the network is not related. $|r|$ reflects the assortativity degree of networks.

Natural Connectivity[18]: $\overline{\lambda} = ln(\frac{1}{N}\sum_{i=1}^{N} e^{\lambda_i})$, and λ_i is the eigenvalue of adjacent matrix $A(G)$ in G, reflecting the network vulnerability.

Congestion[19][20]: $Congestion = max(b_i)$, defined as the biggest betweenness of of nodes in the network, reflecting the biggest congestion in the network;

Synchronization[21][22]: $Synchro = max(\lambda_i)/min(\lambda_i)$, defined as the ratio of the biggest eigenvalue and the smallest negative eigenvalue of the network Laplacian matrix, reflecting the network's synchronization ability.

Propagation threshold[23]: $Spreading = <k>/<k^2>$, k is the network degree distribution defined as the ratio of first-order moment and the second-order moment, reflecting the propagation threshold of the network.

After calculating the above indexes value for the real network, the observed network and the reconstructed network, the following formulas are used to measure these networks' structural gaps:

Relative error of the observed network and the real network is defined as:

$$RE^O = (X(A^O) - X(A^T))/X(A^T) \quad (10)$$

Relative error of the reconstructed network and teh real network is defined as:

$$RE^R = (X(A^R) - X(A^T))/X(A^T) \qquad (11)$$

$X(A)$ stands for one index value from the above nine indexes.

As a result, comparison of two values RE^O and RE^R could be used to see whether the reconstructed network is closer to the true network than the observed network.

C. Results Analysis

1) Evaluation Results for LR: We choose Katz, the index performing best among structural similarity based link prediction indexes, and SBM, the index performing best among likelihood based link prediction indexes, as comparisons with the index LR, calculate the values of $AUC\_Missing$ and $AUC\_Spurious$ for each index, to measure their ability in predicting missing edges and identifying spurious edges.

First we evaluate their ability in predicting network's missing links, adjust the ratio of edges randomly removed (missing edges), and calculate $AUC\_Missing$ value each time, results shown as Figure 2 (each point in the figure is the average value for 100 times computation).

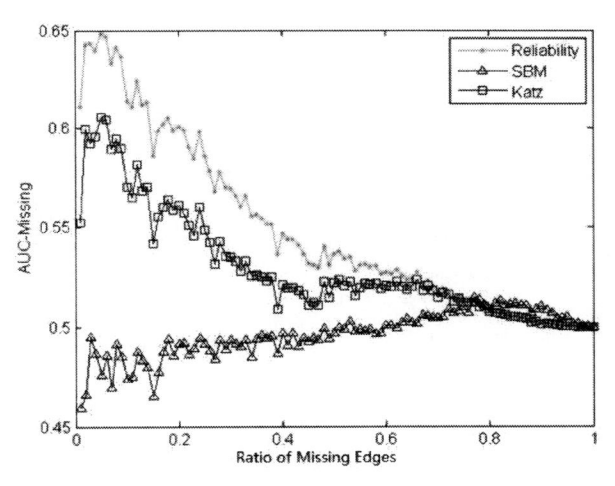

Fig. 2. Comparisons between Reliability and other indexes in predicting missing edges.

It can be seen from Figure 2 that LR index performs better than other two indexes as the ratio of missing edges is less than 0.77; as the ratio is over 0.77, LR performs a little worse than SBM, and the same as Katz. Overall, LR performs no worse than other two indexes for 97.03% times.

Similarly, when comparing ability in identifying spurious edges, adjust the ratio of edges randomly added (spurious edges), and calculate $AUC\_Spurious$ value each time, results shown as Figure 3 (each point in the figure is the average value for 100 times computation).

It can be seen from Figure 3 that LR index always performs better than other two indexes,

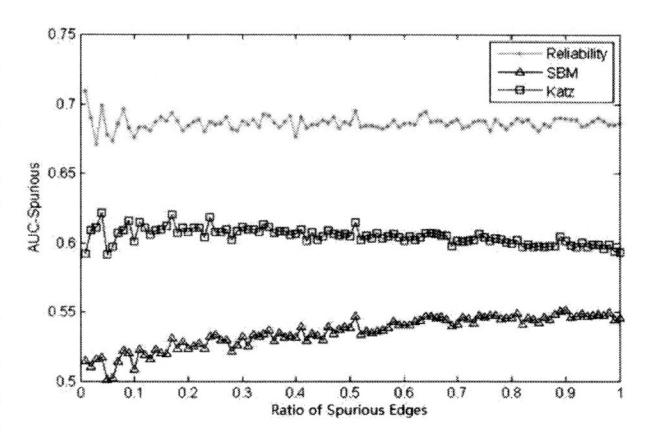

Fig. 3. Comparisons between Reliability and other indexes in detecting false edges.

Combined with Figure 2 and Figure 3, LR index is a better link prediction index in purifying the network noise, i.e., identify spurious edges and predict missing edges.

2) Evaluation Results for TON Reconstruction: Here we validate the effectiveness of the reconstruction algorithm. First, adding some noise on the true network, and obtain the observed network A^O, assume the ratio of missing edges is α, the ratio of spurious edges is β, let $\alpha = \beta = p$, and call p as the observed error. After the reconstruction algorithm, the reconstructed network A^R is got, measure the closeness of A^O, A^R and A^T by calculating RE^O and RE^R. If $RE^R < RE^O$, means the A^R is closer than A^O to A^T, the reconstruction algorithm is validated then.

Make p changes from 0 to 1, and the step is set 0.05, calculate the nine topological indexes above, results are shown as Figure 4(each point in the figure is the average value for 100 times computation).

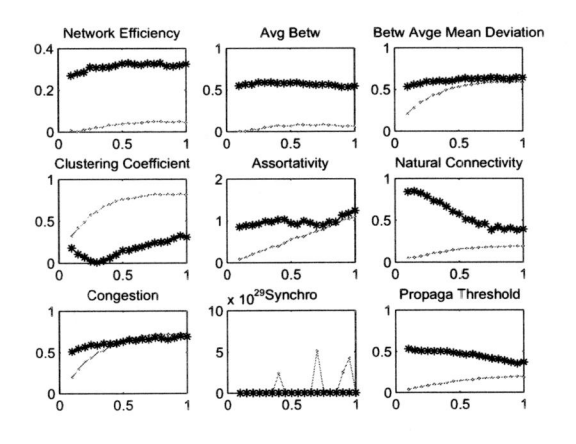

Fig. 4. Comparisons of RE^O and RE^R in nine topological indexes

In Figure 4, black '.' stands for RE^O value, and green '*' stands for RE^R value, it can be seen that except the congestion index and Clustering Coefficient index, RE^R is less than RE^O all the time. For congestion index, as p less than 0.5, RE^R is less than RE^O; for clustering coefficient index, A^R seems farther to A^T than A^O; for synchronization index, since there existing some abnormal points, which stretches the vertical coordinate axis in a large scale, and make it difficult to judge. All in all, comparisons on nine topological indexes show the reconstructed network is closer to the true one than the observed network.

VI. Conclusion

In this paper, we put forward a target operation network structure reconstruction algorithm and validate it in the public data, experimental results indicate the algorithm is able to effectively narrow the structure gap between the observed network and the real one to some certain extent. Firstly, a link reliability index, called LR, was proposed based on the hypothesis that the existing possibility between two nodes is mainly determined by their types and topological locations, and verified that LR could better identify spurious edges and predict missing edges, compared with SBM and Katz index; then network reliability index, based on LR, was put forward, we designed a locally greedy search algorithm based on the assumption that the spurious edge number equals to the missing edge number to reconstruct the TON structure. The experimental data consists 89 units and 155 links, let it be the true network, and assumed an observed network through adding some noise (randomly remove some missing edges and add some spurious edges). Nine indexes were utilized to measure the algorithm performance, experiments on the observed network showed that the reconstruction algorithm could effectively narrow its gap with the true one for each index, since there are both static structural index and dynamic structural index in these nine indexes, they comprehensively represent all the structural characteristics for a network, as a result, the reconstructed network is closer to the real one in topology.

Acknowledgment

This work is partially supported by National Natural Science Foundation of China (No.71471176, No.61303266) . All authors acknowledge the National University of Defense Technology.

References

[1] H. C. White, S. A. Boorman, and R. L. Breiger, "Social structure from multiple networks. i. blockmodels of roles and positions," *American journal of sociology*, pp. 730–780, 1976.
[2] C. J. Anderson, S. Wasserman, and K. Faust, "Building stochastic blockmodels," *Social networks*, vol. 14, no. 1, pp. 137–161, 1992.
[3] P. Doreian, V. Batagelj, and A. Ferligoj, *Generalized blockmodeling*, vol. 25. Cambridge university press, 2005.
[4] Y. Guo-li, H. Jin-cai, and Z. Wei-ming, "Combat system quantitative assessment method based on finc model," *Computer Engineering*, vol. 37, no. 10, 2011.
[5] E. M. Airoldi, D. M. Blei, S. E. Fienberg, and E. P. Xing, "Mixed membership stochastic blockmodels," in *Advances in Neural Information Processing Systems*, pp. 33–40, 2009.
[6] L. Lin-yuan, "Link prediction on complex networks," *Journal of University of Electronic Science and Technology of China*, vol. 39, no. 5, pp. 651–661, 2010.
[7] L. Lü and T. Zhou, "Link prediction in complex networks: A survey," *Physica A: Statistical Mechanics and its Applications*, vol. 390, no. 6, pp. 1150–1170, 2011.
[8] L. Lin-yuan and Z. Tao, *Link Prediction*. Higher Education Press, 2013.
[9] R. R. Sarukkai, "Link prediction and path analysis using markov chains," *Computer Networks*, vol. 33, no. 1, pp. 377–386, 2000.
[10] A. Popescul and L. H. Ungar, "Statistical relational learning for link prediction," in *IJCAI workshop on learning statistical models from relational data*, vol. 2003, Citeseer, 2003.
[11] F. Wilcoxon, "Individual comparisons by ranking methods," *Biometrics bulletin*, vol. 1, no. 6, pp. 80–83, 1945.
[12] R. Guimerà and M. Sales-Pardo, "Missing and spurious interactions and the reconstruction of complex networks," *Proceedings of the National Academy of Sciences*, vol. 106, no. 52, pp. 22073–22078, 2009.
[13] D. J. Watts and S. H. Strogatz, "Collective dynamics of small-worldnetworks," *nature*, vol. 393, no. 6684, pp. 440–442, 1998.
[14] X. WANG, X. LI, and C. Guanrong, "Network science: An introduction," 2012.
[15] T. Nishikawa, A. E. Motter, Y.-C. Lai, and F. C. Hoppensteadt, "Heterogeneity in oscillator networks: Are smaller worlds easier to synchronize?," *Physical review letters*, vol. 91, no. 1, p. 014101, 2003.
[16] M. E. Newman, "Assortative mixing in networks," *Physical review letters*, vol. 89, no. 20, p. 208701, 2002.
[17] M. E. Newman, "Mixing patterns in networks," *Physical Review E*, vol. 67, no. 2, p. 026126, 2003.
[18] J. Wu, M. Barahona, Y.-J. Tan, and H.-Z. Deng, "Robustness of regular ring lattices based on natural connectivity," *International Journal of Systems Science*, vol. 42, no. 7, pp. 1085–1092, 2011.
[19] G. Yan, T. Zhou, B. Hu, Z.-Q. Fu, and B.-H. Wang, "Efficient routing on complex networks," *Physical Review E*, vol. 73, no. 4, p. 046108, 2006.
[20] R. Guimerà, A. Díaz-Guilera, F. Vega-Redondo, A. Cabrales, and A. Arenas, "Optimal network topologies for local search with congestion," *Physical Review Letters*, vol. 89, no. 24, p. 248701, 2002.
[21] A. Arenas, A. Díaz-Guilera, J. Kurths, Y. Moreno, and C. Zhou, "Synchronization in complex networks," *Physics Reports*, vol. 469, no. 3, pp. 93–153, 2008.
[22] M. Barahona and L. M. Pecora, "Synchronization in small-world systems," *Physical review letters*, vol. 89, no. 5, p. 054101, 2002.
[23] R. Pastor-Satorras and A. Vespignani, "Epidemics and immunization in scale-free networks," *Handbook of graphs and networks: from the genome to the internet*, pp. 111–130, 2005.

APPENDIX
PROOF OF THEOREM 1

The stochastic model is introduced first before the proof.

Stochastic block is one of the most pervasive networks [1][2][3][5]. This model divides the nodes in the network into several groups, and whether the two nodes are linked is determined by the group they belong to. In other words, the roles of all nodes in the same group are identical. The stochastic block model is particularly suitable for situations when nodes' roles exert significant influences on their linking behaviors. A stochastic block model is composed by two parts: one is the plans that the network is divided into a number of groups; the other is the linking probability matrix between two nodes that come from two different groups. Let Ω represents all the grouping plans, given a specific plan $P \in \Omega$ and a specific linking probability matrix Q, a stochastic block model $M = (P, Q)$ is then determined. The current structure from an observable network can be regarded as from an unknown stochastic block model. Suppose the current network structure is A^o, psi represents a specific property, then the probability that this network with the property is:

$$p(\psi|A^o) = \int_\Theta p(\psi|M)p(M|A^o)dM \quad (12)$$

where Θ stands for the set of total stochastic block models, $M \in \Theta$ refers to a specific stochastic block model, and $p(\psi|M)$ represents the probability that the observed network generated by model M has property psi, and $p(M|A^o)dM$ stands for the probability that the observed network is actually generated by model M. According to Bayes Theory, we have:

$$P(M|A^o)p(A^o) = p(A^o|M)p(M)$$

since:

$$p(\psi|A^o) = \frac{\int_\Theta p(\psi|M)p(A^o|M)p(M)dM}{\int_\Theta p(A^o|M')p(M')dM'} \quad (13)$$

Next, formula(13) is utilized to prove the theorem.

Proof. Let the property ψ be $A_{xy} = 1$, probability $p(A_{xy} = 1|A^o)$ represents the link reliability of $\{v_x, v_y\}$, according to formula(13):

$p(A_{xy} = 1|A^o)$
$= \frac{1}{Z}\sum_{P\in\Omega}\int_0^1 |Q|p(A_{xy} = 1|P,Q)p(A^o|A,Q)p(P,Q)dQ$

where $|Q|$ stands for the numbers of matrix elements, which are equal to the square of the number of groups in the network, and

$$Z = \sum_{P\in\Omega} |Q|p(A^o|P,Q)p(P,Q)dQ \quad (14)$$

since $p(A_{xy} = 1|P,Q) = Q_{\sigma_x,\sigma_y}$, then

$$p(A^o|P,Q) = \prod_{\alpha\leq\beta} Q_{\alpha\beta}^{l^o_{\alpha\beta}}(1-Q_{\alpha\beta})^{r_{\alpha\beta}-l^o_{\alpha\beta}} \quad (15)$$

Take formula (15) into formula (14), and get

$$Z = \sum_{P\in\Omega}\prod_{\alpha\leq\beta}\int_0^1 Q_{\alpha\beta}^{l^o_{\alpha\beta}}(1-Q_{\alpha\beta})^{r_{\alpha\beta}-l^o_{\alpha\beta}}dQ_{\alpha\beta} \quad (16)$$

Let

$$H = \prod_{\alpha\leq\beta}\int_0^1 Q_{\alpha\beta}^{l^o_{\alpha\beta}}(1-Q_{\alpha\beta})^{r_{\alpha\beta}-l^o_{\alpha\beta}}dQ_{\alpha\beta} \quad (17)$$

Next we prove:

$$H = exp\{-\sum_{\alpha\leq\beta}[ln(r_{\alpha\beta}+1) + ln\binom{r_{\alpha\beta}}{l^o_{\alpha\beta}}]\} \quad (18)$$

Proof. With Beta integral formula:
$\int_0^1 t^{a-1}(1-t)^{b-1}dt = \frac{(a-1)!(b-1)!}{(a+b-1)!}$

we have:

$\int_0^1 Q_{\alpha\beta}^{l^o_{\alpha\beta}}(1-Q_{\alpha\beta})^{r_{\alpha\beta}-l^o_{\alpha\beta}}dQ_{\alpha\beta} = \frac{l^o_{\alpha\beta}!(r_{\alpha\beta}-l^o_{\alpha\beta})!}{(r_{\alpha\beta}+1)!}$
$= \frac{1}{r_{\alpha\beta}+1}\frac{l^o_{\alpha\beta}!(r_{\alpha\beta}-l^o_{\alpha\beta})!}{r_{\alpha\beta}!}$

and

$lnH = \sum_{\alpha\leq\beta} ln(\frac{1}{r_{\alpha\beta}+1}\frac{l^o_{\alpha\beta}!(r_{\alpha\beta}-l^o_{\alpha\beta})!}{r_{\alpha\beta}!})$
$= -\sum_{\alpha\leq\beta}[ln(r_{\alpha\beta}+1) + ln\binom{r_{\alpha\beta}}{l^o_{\alpha\beta}}]$

Thus

$H = exp\{-\sum_{\alpha\leq\beta}[ln(r_{\alpha\beta}+1) + ln\binom{r_{\alpha\beta}}{l^o_{\alpha\beta}})]\}$ □

According to formula (18),

$$Z = \sum_{P\in\Omega} H = \sum_{P\in\Omega} exp\{-\sum_{\alpha\leq\beta}[ln(r_{\alpha\beta}+1) + ln\binom{r_{\alpha\beta}}{l^o_{\alpha\beta}})]\} \quad (19)$$

and

$p(A_{xy} = 1|A^o)$
$= \frac{1}{Z}\sum_{P\in\Omega}\prod_{\alpha\leq\beta}\int_0^1 p(A_{xy} = 1|P,Q)Q_{\alpha\beta}^{l^o_{\alpha\beta}}(1-Q_{\alpha\beta})^{r_{\alpha\beta}-l^o_{\alpha\beta}}dQ_{\alpha\beta}$
$= \frac{1}{Z}\sum_{P\in\Omega}\prod_{\alpha\leq\beta}\int_0^1 Q_{\sigma_x,\sigma_y}Q_{\alpha\beta}^{l^o_{\alpha\beta}}(1-Q_{\alpha\beta})^{r_{\alpha\beta}-l^o_{\alpha\beta}}dQ_{\alpha\beta}$

1°. when $(\sigma_x, \sigma_y) \neq (\alpha, \beta)$,

$\prod_{\alpha\leq\beta}\int_0^1 Q_{\alpha\beta}^{l^o_{\alpha\beta}}(1-Q_{\alpha\beta})^{r_{\alpha\beta}-l^o_{\alpha\beta}}dQ_{\alpha\beta}$

$$= exp\{-\sum_{\alpha \leq \beta, (\sigma_x,\sigma_y) \neq (\alpha,\beta)} ln(r_{\alpha\beta}+1) + ln\binom{r_{\alpha\beta}}{l^o_{\alpha\beta}})\}$$

2°. when $(\sigma_x, \sigma_y) = (\alpha, \beta)$,

$$\int_0^1 Q_{\sigma_x,\sigma_y} Q_{\alpha\beta}^{l^o_{\alpha\beta}} (1-Q_{\alpha\beta})^{r_{\alpha\beta}-l^o_{\alpha\beta}} dQ_{\alpha\beta} = \int_0^1 Q_{\sigma_x\sigma_y}^{l^o_{\sigma_x\sigma_y}+1}(1-Q_{\sigma_x\sigma_y})^{r_{\sigma_x\sigma_y}-l^o_{\sigma_x\sigma_y}} dQ_{\sigma_x\sigma_y} = \frac{(l^o_{\sigma_x\sigma_y}+1)!(r_{\sigma_x\sigma_y}-l)!}{(r_{\sigma_x\sigma_y}+2)!}$$

$$= \frac{l^o_{\sigma_x\sigma_y}+1}{r_{\sigma_x\sigma_y}+2} exp\{[ln(r_{\alpha\beta}+1) + ln\binom{r_{\alpha\beta}}{l^o_{\alpha\beta}})]\}$$

Combine the above two situations, and reliability for link $\{v_x, v_y\}$ could be calculated as formula(20):

$$p(A_{xy}=1|A^o) = G_{xy} = \frac{1}{Z} \sum_{P \in \Omega} \frac{l^o_{\sigma_x\sigma_y}+1}{r_{\sigma_x\sigma_y}+2} H \qquad (20)$$

And the expression of Z, H see as formula (19) and formula (??).

For a specific TON, node type have been fixed, which means the division plans P are also fixed, then :

$$p(A_{xy}=1|A^o) = g_{xy} = \frac{l^o_{\sigma_x\sigma_y}+1}{r_{\sigma_x\sigma_y}+2} \qquad (21)$$

Theorem 1 has been proved. □

Mobile Edge Computing: Requirements for Powerful Mobile Near Real-Time Applications

Harald Frank
IQDoQ
Document Management Company of MATERNA
Bad Vilbel, Germany
harald.frank@iqdoq.de

Woldemar Fuhrmann
Department of Computer Science
University of Applied Sciences Darmstadt
Darmstadt, Germany
woldemar.fuhrmann@h-da.de

Bogdan Ghita
Centre for Security, Communications and Network Research
University of Plymouth
Plymouth, United Kingdom
bogdan.ghita@plymouth.ac.uk

Abstract— The progressive distribution of the components in Mobile Edge Computing at different locations, need to be controlled from a centralized logical unit. This paper proposes a new controlling unit between the mobile transport network and the cloud infrastructure, called Mobile Edge Computing Manager, which reuse the concept of the Black Rider, which is context- and policy-based itself. This centralized processing unit bundled informations from the mobile transport network as well as from the cloud-infrastructure. The paper provides a first architectural overview.

Keywords—component; Mobile Edge Computing, Mobile Cloud Computing, Black Rider, policy

I. Introduction

The Vision of Mark Weiser in 1991 [1] become slowly reality. Ubiquitous and pervasive computing is ready to be the basis of the internet of things in the near future.

Mobile Edge Computing (MEC) enables powerful application on mobile devices in near real-time quality. This was reached by the extension of the original Mobile Cloud Computing (MCC) concept via the introduction of an additional infrastructure component, the so called "Cloudlet". The cloudlet is an additional small data center between the mobile device and the centralized data center. This small data center is usually located in the near of the cell-tower of the radio network. The proposal of the cloudlet is reducing the network latencies between the application on the mobile device and its counterpart in the centralized data center, which is usually far away. The cloudlet consist of an amount of virtual machines, which provide computing resources close to the mobile device.

This is particularly necessary for the envisaged new 5th generation of mobile networks. The planned high data transfer rates, low internal latency and high movement speeds of mobile devices require an appropriate infrastructure on the cloud side, to be able to use it optimally.

MCC and MEC have basically the same objectives, such as the following:

- Extension of the operation time of the mobile terminal with limited battery capacity [2].
- Outsourcing of compute-intensive applications from the mobile device to the cloud, in order to enable applications that are not possible on the mobile device, e.g. real-time applications with high workload.

MEC has the following additional objectives:

- Increase of the quality of experience (QoE) by reducing the response time of the application for the user.
- Reduction of traffic in the packet-core network.

Both MCC and MEC consist of a mobile and a wired infrastructure. The advantages of MEC are only effective, if the application in the cloudlet stays in the close neighborhood of the mobile device over the entire runtime of the applications on the mobile device. Therefore we need to classify the relationship between applications.

On the one hand we have fixed applications, where the server-side application stays at a fixed location in the cloud, and on the other hand we have mobile applications, where the server-side application can follow the mobile device within the cloudlet infrastructure:

- Case 1: Wireless mobile user application – fixed cloud/infrastructure application
- Case 2: Wireless mobile user application - mobile cloud/infrastructure application

There are a variety of proposals and detailed solutions on parts of the issues of MEC. However, an approach is missing that enables the effective control of the combined mobility of applications on the device and on the cloudlet side. In order to minimise the length of the transport path in the fixed network infrastructure the applications have to follow the mobile devices.

Requirements have to be formulated for the control of the mobility of applications taking into account the specific roles of mobile devices, the network providers, the cloudlet providers, and the cloud providers. Furthermore the provision of infrastructure elements from different vendors makes open interfaces necessary. In this context a working group was formed by the ETSI on Mobile Edge Computing [3]. The standardization efforts of ETSI have the goal to avoid proprietary solutions wherever possible.

In [4] the functional entity 'Black Rider' (BR) had been introduced which is able to gather static and dynamic user specific data in a mobile network. These information will be used to improve activities in the mobile network, for example to reduce energy consumption. The BR will be used as an example for the required control unit.

II. RELATED WORK

In earlier days there were mainframes, which were usually placed at a central location. Also virtualization (VSE, VMS, etc.) has already been used, but primarily for separating multiple user environments and executing them in parallel. These mainframe systems had front-end computers, which were partly distributed to connect remote workstations. However, these front-end computers supported only communication functions and did not provide any processing and storage capacity. In these systems the applications on the fixed infrastructure side was static at a fixed location with no need for mobility control.

Nowadays computers are distributed in the cloud and the applications are virtualized. It is not transparent to the user where his applications are stored and processed. With MEC additional mini computing centers (cloudlets) are placed close to the radio interface. This allows the distribution of client- or server-side applications in the immediate vicinity of the mobile user with the objectives to minimize the length of the transmission path and the transmission latencies. Cloudlets support powerful applications with near real-time requirements and help to relieve the battery capacity constraints of the mobile terminals [5]. A typical MEC architecture is shown in fig. 1.

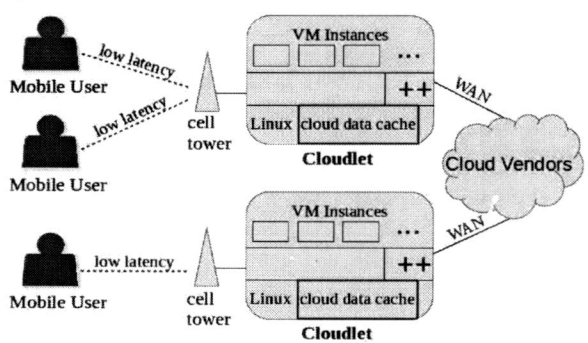

Fig. 1. Typical MEC architecture

Many important building blocks for MEC architectures are already available, for example in the OpenStack extension OpenStack++. Also mechanisms are available for effective moving one VM from one cloudlet to another cloudlet in another location in the network [6].

However, open interfaces between the components of the MEC architecture and the underlying transport networks are not yet defined. Furthermore, the MEC architecture has to support roaming within one provider infrastructure and between different provider infrastructures. Fig. 2 illustrates this situation showing different providers with different cloudlet solutions.

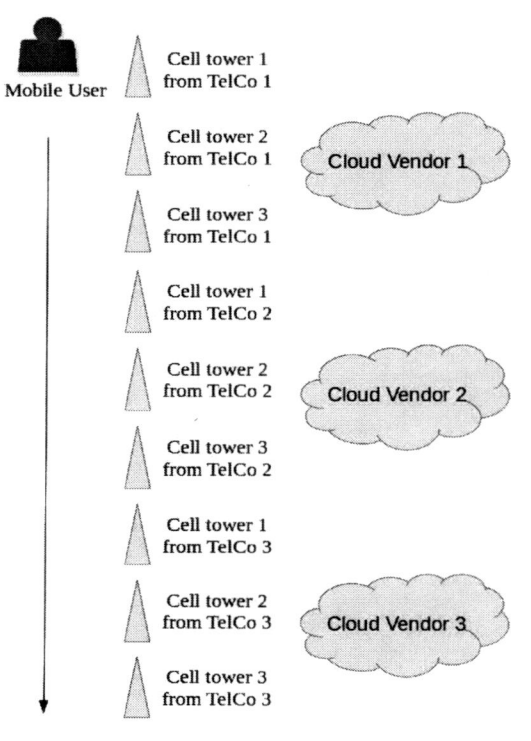

Fig. 2. Different Provider with different Cloudlet Solutions

The BR is a functional entity in a mobile network which is able to gather static and dynamic user specific data, for example related to the mobility management context and bearer management context of the mobile user. These data are stored in a BR Database (BR DB) which complements the centralized database for user data convergence UDR (User Data Repository). The BR is involved in decision making processes of the transport network control, such as handover and traffic offloading, and for that purpose, it can make use of external components, such as mobility analyzers estimating the mobility behavior of a mobile user. Decision made by the BR based on the gathered information and defined policies are propagated by commands to other network elements [7].

III. USE CASE

Critical use cases in MEC are typically scenarios of real-time applications in (fast) moving vehicles, like moving cars, trains or motor cycles. These application run too slow on mobile devices or need too much energy. An example for these is the using of computer graphics or virtual reality applications. In order to display of 3D-pictures of computer tomography a lot of computing power and memory is necessary. Figure 3 show the use case diagram.

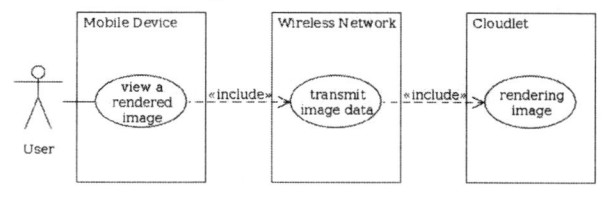

Fig. 3. Display 3D-pictures of computer tomography on a mobile device

In this case a person ride a fast moving train and want to show some 3D-animations of computer tomography data. The person want to zoom in and zoom out because of the limited size of the mobile. In order to render the picture a lot of computing power is necessary. Usually a workstation will be used in a office environment to process the data.

If the render process is located at a central cloud no real-time feeling can be established because of the high latency between the mobile device and the central cloud. To get a near real-time feeling in this scenario, the processing of the data has to be in the near of the mobile device to prevent high latency. This can be reached by the using of cloudlets.

But without the moving of applications between different cloudlets the latency increase by time again. Methods for controlling the positioning of the data and processing-power in order to follow the mobile device is necessary to keep the latency constant on a low level.

IV. REQUIREMENTS

In order to keep the latency constant on a low level with long running applications, the applications on the fixed infrastructure side need to be mobile and have to follow the movement of the mobile user. This require a better control of the serverside applications on the consideration of the mobile device. In order to optimize the control of the mobility of the applications on the fixed infrastructure, a first requirement is to collect necessary informations from different sources. The following informations would be reasonable, because they affects the long term latency of the application:

- Information about the location of the mobile device
- Information about the location of the serverside application (the location of the cloudlet)
- Locations of available cloudlets in the network with their properties.
- Energy consumption of the mobile device
- Capacity status of the battery of the mobile device
- The workload of the cloudlet in the environment of the mobile device
- Radio-Bandwidth of the mobile device
- Latency requirements of the application
- Processing power requirements of the application
- Transmission path length between the mobile device and the processing unit (cloudlet)

The above information can be divided into two groups – static and dynamic information. Static information are typically constant over the runtime of the usage of the application. For example the location of cell towers are mostly fix. Dynamic information changes over the runtime of the application. Examples of this kind of information are the status of the capacity of the battery of the mobile device.

The second requirements for the task is to control the resources reasonable depending of the collected information. Those a unit is necessary. which use this information to optimize the behavior of the applications on the fix infrastructure. Therefore the second requirement for the task to control the mobility of the fixed infrastructure is a centralized component, which collect the information and provide them for optimize the location of the application in the different available cloudlets.

Furthermore, it should be noted that open interfaces are required and roaming within the infrastructure of one provider and between infrastructures of different providers.

V. ARCHITECTURE CONCEPT

Based on the requirements above, an additional central component is necessary, which collect the information and provide the results to other network components. An analog concept exists in the form of the Black Rider, which also collect information and provide these to other network components. However the component Black Rider is justified to collect information about the mobile device, not for the complete infrastructure inclusive cloudlets.

An architecture concept containing the old entity Black Rider an the new entity MEC Manager for the mobility management of the applications in the MEC environment is shown in Fig. 4.

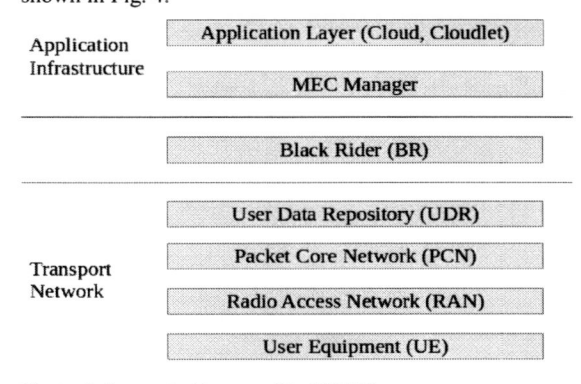

Fig. 4. Reference-Architecture of the MEC Manager

On top there is the application layer including the Cloud and Cloudlets infrastructure. The MEC Manager gets information on the mobility management context and bearer management context of the mobile users from the BR, for example by subscribing appropriate user events, and can make its own decisions on application mobility management within the application infrastructure. The UDR stores all user data, except user content and user context data, which are required for transport network control. The transport network consists of user equipment, radio base stations of the radio access network and the packet core network. Basically, the BR monitors the mobility behavior of the mobile user in the transport network and makes optimized decisions on the traffic distribution in the transport network. Based on these decisions in the transport network, the MEC Manager uses appropriate mobility management and bearer management information from the BR and his own collected information from the cloudlet infrastructure to optimize the behavior of the Application Layer, like movement of VMs between cloudlets in order to improve the QoE for the mobile user.

Thereby the MEC Manager can execute context- and policy-bases decisions to control the components of the cloud infrastructure. By using the MEC Manager important information about the network infrastructure and their conditions are available at a central point in the network. As a result new opportunities for the optimization for other network components are available. In the final architecture parts of the Black Rider architecture can be reused. So a common use of the database of the Black Rider is conceivable.

VI. Conclusion

Starting from simple use-cases, is shown first that an efficient management of application mobility is required. Afterwards requirements for the control of the cloud infrastructure was derived. Next a simple control architecture is developed based on existing blocks as cloudlets and Black Rider. Through the use of the concept "Black Rider" it is possible in principle to establish a central management instance called MEC Manager that enables the distribution and management of mobile applications in the cloud infrastructure.

An evaluation of the new architectural concepts with concrete examples is pending. Likewise, the development of decision strategies for optimization. Furthermore, interfaces between different providers should be defined so that VMs can be transported in cloudlets over provider boundaries.

References

[1] M. Weiser, "The computer for the 21st century," Scientific American, pp. 94-104, September 1991.

[2] R. Want, "The power of smartphones," IEEE Pervasive Computing vol. 13, issue 3, pp. 76-79, 2014.

[3] ETSI Consortium 2016, "Mobile Edge Computing," http://www.etsi.org/technologies-clusters/technologies/mobile-edge-computing.

[4] S. Frei, W. Fuhrmann and B. Ghita, "Generic real-time traffic distribution framework: Black Rider," 22nd International Conference on Computer Communication and Networks (ICCCN 2013), pp. 1-8, 2013.

[5] M. Satyanarayanan, P. Bahl, R. Cáceres and N. Davies, "The case for vm-based cloudlets in Mobile Computing," IEEE Pervasive Computing, 2011.

[6] K. Ha, Y. Abe, Z. Chen, W. Hu, B. Amos, P. Pillai and M. Satyanarayanan, "Adaptive vm handoff across cloudlets," Technical Report CMU-CS-15-113, CMU School of Computer Science, 2015.

[7] S. Frei, W. Fuhrmann and B. Ghita, "Framework for generic context- and policy-based traffic distribution in heterogeneous wireless networks: Black Rider," Workshops of 27th International Conference on Advanced Information Networking and Applications (WAINA), pp. 534-541, 2013.

Acceptance Factors of Wearable Computing: An Empirical Investigation

Lena Gribel[†][††], Stefanie Regier[††], Ingo Stengel[††]

[†] School of Computing, Electronics and Mathematics University of Plymouth, United Kingdom,
[††] Faculty of Computer Science and Business Information Systems
University of Applied Sciences Karlsruhe, Germany,
lena.gribel@plymouth.ac.uk, {stefanie.regier|ingo.stengel}@hs-karlsruhe.de

Abstract—Despite the vast economic potential of wearable technologies, up to now there is only little scientific research on the acceptance determinants of the wearable computing phenomenon. Therefore, the overall aim of this study is to explain psychographic factors that lead to either acceptance or resistance of wearable computing. This paper synthesises a cause and effect model of wearable computing adoption in the European market. The basis of the proposed conceptual framework builds an explorative study consisting of expert interviews and a subsequent qualitative content analysis to identify salient acceptance factors. The results indicate that the strongest factor that supports the acceptance of wearable technologies is perceived usefulness, whilst the main reason for resistance towards these technologies are perceived IT security risks.

Keywords—wearable computing; technology acceptance model; perceived pervasiveness; perceived IT security; Big Five personality traits

I. INTRODUCTION

As a consequence of the proliferation of computer-augmented everyday objects along with the ever-increasing miniaturization of microprocessors, the recent advances in information technologies has considerably changed the manner in which people conceive, experience and employ IT. Regarding this, the convergence of variant Information and Communication Technologies (ICT) entails an evolving paradigm shift in the field of human computer-interaction, promising context-aware and seamlessly integrated on-the-fly computing across heterogeneous circumstances and irrespective of place and time. In this context, the wearable computing paradigm complements the concept of ubiquitous computing, since "wearables" afford a continuous connectivity to the environment by equipping the user with computational capabilities. Not least the forecasted wearable device market value with an amount of 12.6 billion U.S. dollars by 2018 implies the vast economic potential of the respective socio-technological gadgets [1]. Nonetheless, the diffusion of wearable computing highly depends on a variety of factors, which are primarily technological or socio-psychological in nature [2]. In view of the numerous efforts in the area of innovation, which failed due to a lack of consumer acceptance, it becomes clear that facilitation of acceptability is a key issue for entrepreneurship [3].

However, up to now, there is only little scientific research on the acceptance of ubiquitous computing in general and, in particular, on the latent acceptance determinants of the wearable computing phenomenon [4]. Also, it is significant that personality variables in terms of endurable dispositions have seldom been examined within the scope of information systems research [5].

II. CONCEPTUAL BACKGROUND

The convergence of various technological innovations in mobile and ubiquitous computing has fostered a promising new transdisciplinary field referred to as wearable computing with the goal to provide computational services anytime and anywhere in an unobtrusive manner. The universal notion of wearable computing covers a broad spectrum of concepts and implementations: In the broadest sense, the terms "wearable technology" or "wearables" both relate to computer systems or electronic technologies that are body-worn and utilised mostly hands-free [6]. Due to the remaining diversity in possible functional and technical implementations arising from this ambiguous definition, wearable devices are generally particularised and differentiated from other computer types by means of several properties. A first narrower conceptualisation is provided in [7]. Here, wearable computers are attributed by five characteristics:

- Portable while operational
- Enabling hands-free or one-handed utilisation
- Providing sensory features, e.g. Global Positioning System receivers or cameras
- Proactive notifications, attracting the user's attention
- Constantly running and accessible

It has to be stated, that the aspect of portability per se makes up the central differentiator between wearable and ubiquitous computing, since wearable computers are conventionally defined as "fully functional, self-powered, self-contained computers" [8], whereas ubiquitous computing necessitates distributed computing environments, pervading our surrounding world with small-scale, networked ICT components cumulatively.

In contrast to mobile computing, especially the wearable's continuous operating and non-obtrusive character is accentuated in the academic literature. Mann clarifies this by introducing the "personal empowerment" requirement, focusing on a synergetic symbiosis between man and machine [9]. Moreover, given that wearables ought to be non-distracting, easily accessible everyday companions, multimodality has repeatedly been mentioned as another focal capability. In addition to their typically small form factors, intrinsically placing high demands on the design of Input/Output modalities (e.g. gesture-based data entry), the dynamically changing user's environment requires that the interaction modalities ideally should be able to adapt to the given circumstances. Complementarily, Kortuem et al. posit the augmented-reality criterion, that is, wearable computers should be capable of "focusing the user's attention and presenting information in an unobtrusive, context-dependent manner" [10]. Thus, in comparison to the aforementioned taxonomy the attribute "context-awareness" is particularly emphasised. Thereby, context-awareness describes the ability of a system to sense, interpret and respond to certain environmental states.

III. METHODOLOGY

In view of the fact that the attitude formation towards innovative technologies involves multiple interrelated cognitive and affective activities, it is surprising that almost all empirical studies on technology acceptance solely depend on quantitative methodologies [11]. Moreover, up to now academic research in the area of ubiquitous and wearable computing acceptance is still relatively scarce [12]. This makes an initial explorative research study indispensable in order to motivate and legitimise research on intrapersonal factors of wearable technology adoption. In particular, the explorative insights are expected to highlight the need for developing a new multi-factor measurement model of effectuation and causation respectively from a consumer viewpoint. Furthermore, the qualitative study aims to explore subjective beliefs and perceptions adopters have towards wearable computing in order to establish a proper theoretical basis for the development of a coherent system of causal hypothesises.

Thus, seeking for a predictive cause and effect model of wearable technology acceptance, a multi-strategy research will be used, where methodological triangulation will pose a multi-stage research process in which data from a preliminary conceptual study and qualitative research will build the foundation for future quantitative research. The findings from the exploratory approach, yet, will be confronted with relevant theoretical concepts and behavioural models in literature, that relate to the adoption of new information technologies (such as utility and risk perceptions). The resulting categories of beliefs towards wearable computing acceptance will eventually constitute the main content of the Wearable Technology Acceptance Model (Wearable TAM, see Fig.1) that can be further tested quantitatively.

Actually, qualitative research has developed various methodological alternatives to collect verbal data. The different interview methods alternate between the goal of either producing openness or producing structure [13]. Therefore, the choice of a method should be based on the given research objectives as anchor points, which intrinsically pose the need for exploration or rather explanation. Recalling the research goals of the study at hand, the central aim is to develop a comprehensive understanding of which socio-psychological factors influence the decision-making towards the acceptance of wearable computing. Thus, the interviews should be oriented towards a thematic direction. At the same time, this study seeks to reveal *latent* beliefs towards wearable computing adoption in mass markets as a new field. In view of this persistent research gap, the need for a supplementary explorative function to acquire more background knowledge about the study topic becomes acute. Consequently, a semi-structured expert interview appears to be appropriate for the purpose of this study [11].

The target group of expert interviews comprises informants possessing a specific in-practice knowledge within a professional sphere of activity. Considering that qualitative research seeks transferability rather than generalisability of results, an adequate sample size is "one that adequately answers the research question" [14]. Typically, the participants are recruited on the basis of the potential contribution to the body of knowledge its members have in a certain social system. Hence, in qualitative research the sample is usually derived purposefully rather than randomly, focussing primarily on the *information-richness* of each case [15]. Consequently, significant information redundancy marks the point of theoretical saturation, when no further insights or perspectives are forthcoming from ongoing data collection and the conceptual categories or theories of relevance are fully explained.

A. Empirical Setting

The objective of the present sample selection was to attain a sufficient sample heterogeneity in terms of maximal diversity of knowledgeable interview participants. Therefore, sample units from industry and educational sector with different perspectives on wearable computing, with different levels of personal experience and with experiences of different types of wearables - particularly in terms of smart watches and smart glasses - were selected.

Overall, four academics from different research institutions participating in multiple wearable technology projects and three professionals from different companies within the information technology sector were interviewed. All interviewees were particularly involved in diverse wearable computing issues and thus expected to have a higher level of affinity towards wearables and to provide more elaborative beliefs and pre-existing assessments concerning the social and individual-level causal mechanisms and processes involved in the adoption of wearable technologies. Besides the criteria of theoretical purpose and theoretical relevance, the sampling procedure was not controlled by any further selection criteria such as gender, age or social status.

The exploratory study was conducted in fall of 2015. All interviews were performed in German as the native language of the interviewees. The inquiries were carried out as semi-structured, open-ended interviews based on an interview guideline, and took between half an hour and one hour. Three out of the seven interviews were performed face-to-face, whilst the other four were telephone interviews, what allowed for wider geographical access. In terms of the general empirical setting, each interview was conducted at the subject's place of work, resembling "real-world" conditions in favour of ecological validity.

Based on the theoretical findings from literature review, the interview guideline comprised a small set of carefully worded questions, aiming at exploring the general perceptions of wearable technologies as well as the central success factors of their inter-individual acceptance. Subsequent to the introduction phase, the respondents were asked to convey their assessment of the current developments in wearable computing markets. Afterwards, the interviewees discussed the challenges, benefits and barriers to the usage of wearable technologies.

As a theoretical sampling procedure was chosen for this study, data collection was controlled by the emerging codes and categories. Hence, the author simultaneously collected, coded and analysed the material, attempting to "saturate" the relevant concepts and categories. After interviewing the seventh subject, the need for further interviews ceased since no further findings were expected to contribute to the conceptual and theoretical understanding of the subject matter. Consequently, no further interviews were conducted.

B. Qualitative Content Analysis

Following the inductive category development process described by Mayring [16], data analysis started with a material reduction of the transcribed versions of the audiotapes and field notes by discarding those chunks of data that intrinsically do not relate to wearable technology usage. Thereafter, the process of data interpretation commenced by underlining relevant parts of the text with regard to wearable technology acceptance. Subsequently, in-vivo codes were constructed from each marked meaning unit of analysis supported by the text (e.g. via single words, sentences or paragraphs). Afterwards, these codes had been transferred into constructed codes in English, thereby being gradually abstracted into higher order concepts in the course of an iterative process of constant revision. In sum, 67 codes emerged from the analytical process, which constituted the basis for the further content analysis.

To further conceptualise the properties of inter-individual attitude formation in wearable technology markets, similar codes constructed were aggregated into a coherent, overarching concept. For instance, the codes "Status-consciousness" and "Openness to Experience" were clustered into one logical content unit, as all these concepts include personality-related elements relating to behaviourally-relevant traits. Thus, a more abstract, higher-level category was developed, being either one of the codes inferred from the text that readily represents the category in semantic terms or alternatively a newly developed theoretical construct, completely covering the implicit meaning of the code cluster. In the example given above, a new analytical category "Personality" was developed to reflect the common contents of the constructed lower-level codes. Particular emphasis was laid on defining categories that are exhaustive and at the same time mutually exclusive [17]. The code clustering procedure was performed until all constructed codes were assigned to a higher-order category, reflecting a specific theoretical construct. In total, 13 theoretical constructs emerged from the qualitative research phase.

IV. KEY FINDINGS

The results from the qualitative study give manifold insights concerning the inter-individual adoption decision process in wearable technology markets. Table I gives an overview of the main qualitative research findings. As indicated by the frequent referencing to acceptance-related determinants, product growth is actually influenced by various demand factors, such as social acceptability and changes in beliefs. Apart from this, various non-psychographic macro-environmental forces were pointed at, which are, however, outside of the scope of the present study as they cannot be altered by managerial actions. Especially, the points of pricing structures and technical immaturity emerged during the process of coding and analysis. Furthermore, the results show that social influence plays a significant role in wearable computing adoption processes. From a social networks perspective, this suggests that social proof might also have some conative influence on usage decisions in terms of a sociocultural impetus that manifests in a bandwagon-based diffusion.

The strongest intrapersonal factor that is expected to support the acceptance of wearable computing is *Perceived Usefulness*, primarily attributed to work and learning support. Most respondents named hands-free instruction guidelines and real-time notifications as specific product features that they considered beneficial. Furthermore, the wearables' potential provision of assistance in the field of health and fitness - particularly through offering the possibility of continuous self-monitoring - was seen variously as a clear advantage. Based on the interviews, the usefulness of wearables can be mainly ascribed to the unique attributes of the respective, newly emerged computing paradigm. Theses abstract attributes are subsumed under the concept of *Pervasiveness*, meaning that this innovative class of IT systems ought to provide ubiquitous as well as context-aware information services and applications unobtrusively to the greatest possible extent in order to generate substantial benefits. Accounting for the main differences between traditional desktop systems and pervasive or ubiquitous computing models, wearables should be seamlessly integrated into the daily life, proactively enhancing all routine activities [18].

Moreover, from the results of the qualitative study it is apparent that the main reason for wearable computing resistance are IT security concerns. In particular, a majority of respondents reported that they would fear privacy risks in view of the fact that wearables would process highly sensitive personal data at an unprecedented rate. Yet, *perceived risks* outside IT security risks have seldom been mentioned, referring to ambiguous threats and physical risks due to possible distractions.

TABLE I. CODING CATEGORIES OF THE QUALITATIVE STUDY

Category	Code	References	Sources
Acceptance behaviour	Acceptance	9	4
	Socio-psychographic factors of adoption	11	5
Innovativeness	Level of innovativeness	2	1
	Fear of innovations	2	2
	Early Adopter	3	3
IT security aspects	IT security	4	4
	System reliability	1	1
	Third Party Access	2	1
	Sensitive personal data	4	3
	Surveillance	5	3
	Data security threats	11	7
Macro-environment	Technical immaturity	21	7
	Price as an economical factor	10	6
	Competitive factors	3	1
	Political and legal aspects	4	3
Perceived Risk	Physical risks	1	1
	Generally risky	1	1
Perceived Usefulness	Relative Advantage	12	5
	Control of networked devices	2	1
	Work support	24	7
	Health	17	5
	Quantified Self	10	4
	Safety	1	1
	Efficiency enhancement	7	4
	Learning aid	25	5
	Error reduction	3	3
	Entertainment	3	2
	Strengthens social relationships	11	4
	Enhancement of self-confidence	5	3
	Gamification	1	1
	More comfort of life	1	1
	Schedule control	5	3
	Many application scenarios	2	2
	Boosts fitness	7	5
	Continuous and persistent logging	4	3
	More transparency and traceability	1	1
	Ubiquitous connectivity	2	2
Personality	Curiosity	2	2
	Lifestyle	1	1
	Status-Consciousness	4	3
	Open to new ideas and experiences	2	2
	Personal involvement	7	4
Pervasiveness	Sensory features (multimodality)	11	5
	Context-awareness	5	3
	Proactive	7	6
	Convenient	9	4
	Hands-free working	8	3
	Information accessibility	9	6
	Seamless integration into everyday life	5	3
	Real-time operation and output	5	3
	Always on	6	5
	Non-distracting	2	2
	Ubiquitous	1	1
Prior Experience	Prior Experience	3	3
	Familiarisation with wearables	3	3
	No personal experience	1	1
Social Influence	Other-directedness, Imitation	2	2
	Reactions of the social environment	1	1
Trust	Trust in consequences of usage	4	3
	Trust in the system's functionality	2	2
Usability	Fashionability and wearing comfort	6	5
	High demands on effectiveness and efficiency	6	3
	Demands on the range of functions	1	1
	Usability	5	3
Behavioural change Behavioural change	Behaviour modification due to continuous monitoring	2	1
	Mergence of private and business life (BYOD)	3	2
	Lives become more "digitized" as media consumption behaviour changes	2	2

The interview statements show, that trust in the technology itself including its functionality and predictability directly relates to risk perceptions. Besides, based on the interview results prior experience with wearables as well as the degree of personal innovativeness seem to influence how consumers assess the perceived risk and usefulness of such technologies.

Furthermore, the interview analysis revealed that personality-related correlates of behaviour exert actually an important - albeit indirect - influence on wearable computing acceptance. The most common predisposition to behaviour mentioned by the respondents is the personal relevance or involvement with mobile and wearable computing. Since this factor is deemed to directly interact with compound personality traits [19], it may be considered as a more domain-specific trait relevant to consumption behaviour. Additionally, status concerns emerged as another salient socio-psychological variable that affect the decision to adopt wearables.

In order to develop an inter-individual path model of wearable technology acceptance the results from the study were finally confronted with extant theoretical and conceptual models in literature. Overall, the sought Wearable TAM aims at clarifying correlating effects of the identified acceptance factors and to thus holistically explain the consumer's intention to adopt wearable technologies. Due to its efficiency as well as its dominant role within acceptance research, in the context of the present study the Technology Acceptance Model (TAM) by Davis [20] served as a behavioural source model for successively deriving the research hypothesises. This model is specially geared towards understanding acceptance behaviour in technology markets. It conceptualises the behavioural intention to use a new technology as a direct consequence of the *perceived usefulness* and *perceived ease of use* as powerful and simultaneously parsimonious predictor variables.

Since contemporary research gaps as well as the results of the qualitative study prompted this, particular attention was furthermore directed to commensurable theories in the area of IT security and personality psychology for gradually augmenting the TAM with further explanatory variables. More precisely, the well-accepted Five Factor Model (FFM) of personality [21] in conjecture with the so called 3M model by Mowen [22] were employed for the purpose of the present study, resulting in a hierarchically ordered structure of personality-related correlates of behaviour. Besides, the subjectively perceived degree of IT security was modelled in terms of a multidimensional construct by seizing on the classical CIA triad (Confidentiality, Integrity, and Availability) in security literature [23] to be capable of fully evaluating the singular effect of each dimension on consumers' perceptions of security.

As a consequence, drawing on the results of both the qualitative expert interviews and the findings of prior research, the causal Wearable TAM depicted in Fig. 1 could be stepwise deduced in a theory-driven manner. In this acceptance model the behavioural intent to use wearables is defined as a causal effect of cognitive beliefs regarding the degree of both usefulness and pervasiveness of wearable computing. The latent variable of perceived usefulness is conceptualised as a multidimensional construct, reflecting several salient benefits of wearables which primarily relate to efficiency gains. Moreover, the perceived risk of IT security threats as another significant attitudinal component in intention formation is hypothesised to inhibit considerably the willingness to employ smart wearable devices. The effect of trust on consumer's usage intention is in turn supposed to be mediated by security risk perceptions and to thus indirectly influence the criterion variable. Likewise, the pervasiveness construct acts additionally as an upstream model parameter of usefulness perceptions. Furthermore, personal involvement with the product category of interest is also proposed to be positively associated with the adoption decision. Thereby, drawing on the 3M model intrapsychic predispositions are assumed to determine the level of personal involvement with the research subject and to thus find expression in behavioural patterns, as well.

V. CONCLUSIONS AND FUTURE WORK

Overall, the implications from the present exploratory study are substantial from the point of view that they deliver unique insights from a qualitative perspective, since it is the first study focusing on the social and psychological origins and contexts

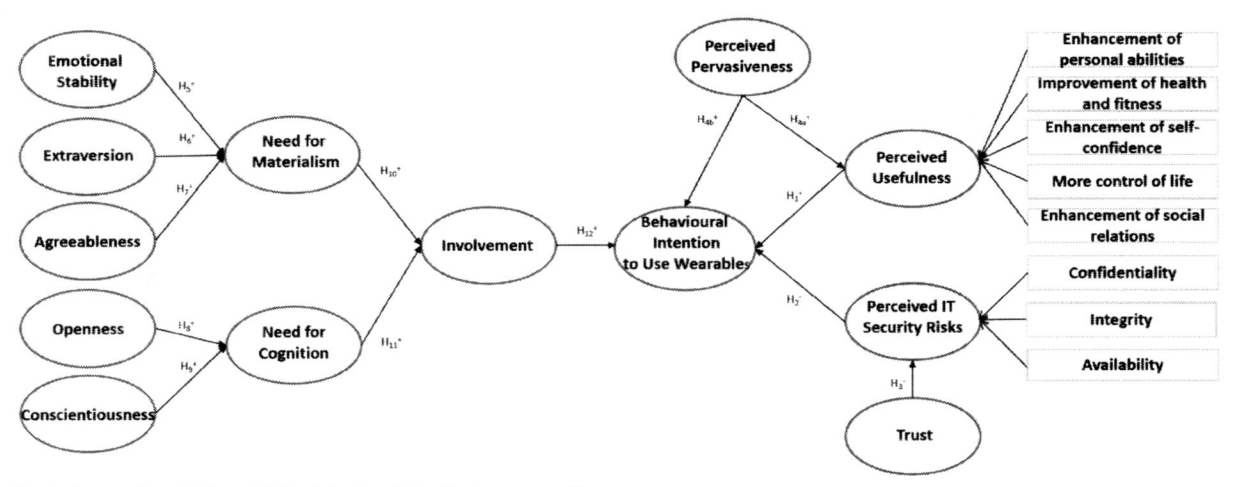

Fig. 1. Structural model for explaining behavioural intention to use wearables

of wearable computing usage intention. These inductive findings provide not only single belief sets, but also a holistic perspective on the acceptance behaviour in innovative IT markets. The empirical results from the expert interviews contribute to information systems research by revealing the substantial role of personality traits on the consumer' willingness to adopt wearable computing. However, it has to be noted that the results are not readily generalizable to the broad consumer market, as they are based on a theoretical sample. Rather, they build the basis for a subsequent development of the future quantitative study to validate the hypothesised Wearable TAM. Therefore, based on the preceding findings a questionnaire survey of consumer attitudes on wearables will be conducted in the next research stage in order to confirm or falsify where appropriate the proposed structure of the measurement model.

References

[1] Statista 2014, „Wearable device market value from 2010 to 2018," Statista Inc., 2012. [Online]. Available: http://www.statista.com/statistics/259372/wearable-device-market-value/.

[2] M. S. Elliott and K. L. Kraemer, Computerization Movements and Technology Diffusion: From Mainframes to Ubiquitous Computing, New Jersey: Information Today, Inc., 2008.

[3] A. Dillon and M. M. Morris, "User acceptance of new information technology: theories and models," *Annual review of information science and technology*, vol. 31, 1996.

[4] C. Buenaflor and H.-C. Kim, "Six Human Factors to Acceptability of Wearable Computers," *International Journal of Multimedia and Ubiquitous Engineering*, vol. 8, 2013.

[5] T. Zhou and Y. Lu, "The Effects of Personality Traits on User Acceptance of Mobile Commerce," *International Journal of Human-Computer Interaction*, vol. 27, 2011.

[6] L. Bass, S. Mann, D. Siewiorek and C. Thompson, "Issues in Wearable Computing: A CHI 97 Workshop," *SIGCHI Bulletin*, vol. No. 4, no. pp. 34-39, 1997.

[7] B. J. Rhodes, "The wearable remembrance agent: a system for augmented memory," *Personal Technologies Journal Special Issue on Wearable Computing*, 1997.

[8] W. Barfield and K. Baird, "Issues in the design and use of wearable computers," *Virtual Reality*, 1998.

[9] S. Mann, "Wearable computing as means for personal empowerment, Keynote Address for The First International Conference on Wearable Computing, ICWC-98," 1998. [Online]. Available: http://wearcomp.org/wearcompdef.html.

[10] G. Kortuem, Z. Segall and M. Bauer, "Context-aware, adaptive wearable computers as remote interfaces to'intelligent'environments," in *16th International Symposium on Wearable Computers*, IEEE Computer Society Press, 1998.

[11] P. Planing, Innovation acceptance: the case of advanced driver-assistance systems, Springer Science & Business Media, 2014.

[12] D. H. Shin, "Ubiquitous computing acceptance model: end user concern about security, privacy and risk," *International Journal of Mobile Communications*, vol. 8, no. 2, 2010.

[13] U. Flick, An introduction to qualitative research, 4 ed., Sage, 2009.

[14] M. N. Marshall, "Sampling for qualitative research," *Family practice*, vol. 13, no. 6, 1996.

[15] M. Q. Patton, Qualitative Evaluation and Research Methods, Newbury Park: Sage, 1990.

[16] P. Mayring, "Qualitative Content Analysis: Theoretical Background and Procedures," in *Approaches to Qualitative Research in Mathematics Education*, Springer, 2015.

[17] K. Krippendorff, "Agreement and information in the reliability of coding," *Communication Methods and Measures*, vol. 5, no. 2, 2011.

[18] D. C. Karaiskos, "A predictive model for the acceptance of pervasive information systems by individuals," PhD Dissertation, Athens University of Economics and Business, 2009.

[19] M. Bosnjak, M. Galesic and T. Tuten, "Personality determinants of online shopping: Explaining online purchase intentions using a hierarchical approach," *Journal of Business Research*, vol. 60, no. 6, 2007.

[20] F. D. Davis, "A Technology Acceptance Model for Empirically Testing New End-user," Wayne State University, Massachusetts, 1985.

[21] R. R. McCrae and P. T. Costa, "Personality trait structure as a human universal," *American psychologist*, vol. 52, no. 5, 1997.

[22] J. C. Mowen, The 3M Model of Motivation and Personality: Theory and Empirical Applications to Consumer Behavior, Springer, 1999.

[23] E. Hartono, C. W. Holsapple, K.-Y. Kim, K.-S. Na and J. T. Simpson, "Measuring perceived security in B2C electronic commerce website usage: A respecification and validation," *Decision Support Systems*, vol. 62, 2014.

VirtualStack: Adaptive Multipath Support through Protocol Stack Virtualization

Jens Heuschkel[1], Alexander Frömmgen[2], Jon Crowcroft[3], Max Mühlhäuser[1]
[1]TK / TU Darmstadt, [2]DVS / TU Darmstadt, [3]SRG / University of Cambridge
{heuschkel, max}@tk.tu-darmstadt.de, froemmge@dvs.tu-darmstadt.de, jon.crowcroft@cl.cam.ac.uk

Abstract—More and more network devices, such as servers or smartphones, have multiple network interfaces. Today's commonly used communication protocols do not leverage these interfaces to increase bandwidth and reliability using multiple network paths. Recent approaches, such as Multipath TCP (MPTCP), clearly show these advantages. However, adaptation of MPTCP is slow as it requires a modified kernel and faces compatibility issues inside the network. MPTCP is also inflexible in the sense that all paths must use TCP. The challenge is to support multipathing on any operating system, with any legacy application using any transport layer protocol.

In this paper, we present *VirtualStack*. VirtualStack manages multiple network stacks per application and decides on the best stack on a per-packet basis. This allows to support multipath using any combination of interfaces and protocols for every application. We evaluate the multipath support by comparing VirtualStack against MPTCP using a combination of TCP and UDP connections. Additionally, we show how rules provide flexible programmings abstractions for VirtualStack.

I. INTRODUCTION

Multihoming is a well known technique to increase reliability and bandwidth, by connecting a device to multiple networks. Most devices today are physically multihomed, i.e., they are equipped with multiple network interfaces. Mobile devices, for example, provide cellular and WiFi interfaces.

Multipath TCP (MPTCP) increases bandwidth and robustness by using these multiple network interfaces and hence multiple paths in parallel [4], [16]. For this purpose, MPTCP uses multiple *TCP subflows* covering different paths. The advantages of MPTCP are obvious and have been shown several times [15], [14]. Apple's natural language user interface *Siri*, for example, is known to use MPTCP.

Unfortunately, outside of data-centers and some lighthouse applications, MPTCP penetration is lagging due to slow adoption by operating system vendors and network operators. As of today, Windows does not support MPTCP, and the MPTCP Linux implementation is neither part of the default Linux kernel nor of the standard Android. Additionally, Internet Service Providers (ISPs) must support the MPTCP header, i.e., must not modify MPTCP headers sent as TCP option [8]. However, many middleboxes in the internet modify or filter options [2], severely limiting the adoption of MPTCP.

MPTCP only supports TCP subflows. We argue that multihoming should be agnostic of the used underlying network protocol. In many situations, a multihoming UDP connection might be more beneficial, or even combinations of protocols on different paths. This increases the flexibility and allows to avoid common pitfalls which impact performance on some link types (e.g., a VPN link[1]). Thus, the challenge is to support multipath on any operating system, with any legacy application using different transport layer protocols.

In this paper, we present how VirtualStack (VS) [7], a framework for protocol stack virtualization, provides flexible multipath connections with multiple different network protocols. VS manages several independent network stacks – from the physical to the transport layer – per application flow. It decides on the best stack on a per-packet basis. This allows to leverage multiple paths, and even to apply different transport protocols per path. Our evaluations show that the increased flexibility of VS does not harm the throughput compared with MPTCP. For scenarios with different transport protocol stacks per sub-flow, VS provides even more performance as it can leverage properties of the underlying network links. We show that this benefit comes with a reasonable low CPU overhead. Furthermore, we show how rules provide a flexible programming abstractions for the VirtualStack.

The contribution of VirtualStack in this paper is twofold:

- VirtualStack enables transparent multipath connections for any application using standard protocols.
- VirtualStack enables flexible multipath connections in the sense that each path can be treated differently.

The remainder of this paper is organized as follows. First, we present the architecture of VS in Section II. Next, Section III presents our performance measurements of the different protocols. Section IV discusses the related work. Finally, Section V concludes the paper and discusses future work.

II. ARCHITECTURE

In this Section, we present the modular architecture of VirtualStack (VS) and discuss the responsibilities and capabilities of its modules.

A. General Considerations

In principle, the desired functionality could be implemented in several ways, e.g., as (a) programming framework, (b) shim layer, (c) or kernel module. In the following, we discuss these approaches and argue for a fourth, superior solution.

(a) A programming framework which provides a modified network socket could easily manage the network connection for the application. This implies, however, that applications

---
[1]http://sites.inka.de/bigred/devel/tcp-tcp.html

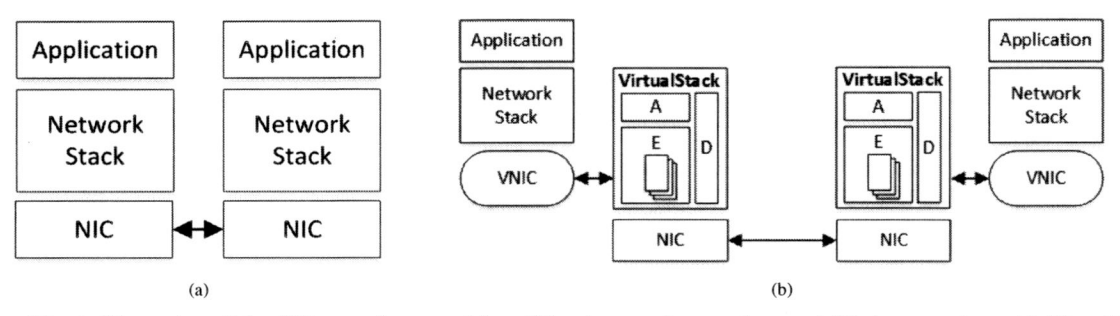

Fig. 1: Illustration of the difference between (a) traditional network operations and (b) the operation with VirtualStack

are prepared to use this framework. Existing legacy applications would not benefit from such a framework. Additionally, developers have to explicitly consider the framework and learn how to use it. Thus, most applications would be written in the same way it is done today without the new functionality.

(b) A shim layer, such as wine [1], is a small library which transparently intercepts API calls. As this implies that the operating systems libraries have to be modified, it is not a optimal solution because operating systems with a closed kernel source wouldn't benefit from the new functionality.

(c) A kernel module suffers from similar problems. Modifying the kernel requires access to the kernel source code. This would work for most Unix/Linux flavors and some BSD systems but not for MAC OSX, iOS or Windows.

In this paper, we tackle these problems and propose a fourth option: Intercepting the network connection with a virtual network interface (VNIC). Using a VNIC – or especially a TUN device – allows us to deploy VS on every operating system that supports VNICs, such as Linux, Windows, Mac OSX, iOS, and Android. Even though we are convinced the proposed VNIC approach is the most suitable, the concepts of VS could inspire the implementation alternatives (a-c).

Figure 1 compares a traditional networking application scenario with VS. Whereas the traditional approach uses a static network stack, VS intercepts the network connection at both hosts. The payload is tunneled through a virtual network interface. VS provides multiple network stacks and adapts the protocol stack for the current network environment. We divide the architecture – illustrated in Figure 2 – in three main modules with different responsibilities: *Analysis* module (Section II-B), *decision* module (Section II-D), and *execution* module (Section II-E). To enable an easy implementation and separate the VS-Core implementation we decide to implement a lightweight interface (Section II-C) to control VS. The decision module is a user-space program which connects to this lightweight interface.

To understand the details of every module, we explain the data-flow – illustrated by the arrows in Figure 2 – inside of VS first. As described above, we use a VNIC (i.e., a TUN device) to get payload (as IP packets) from applications. The received IP packet is processed by the analysis module first. After this step the analysis module passes the packet to the execution module and some meta information to the decision module. The execution module sends the payload over a prepared network connection to its target. Additionally the decision module has the option to send control commands to the execution module.

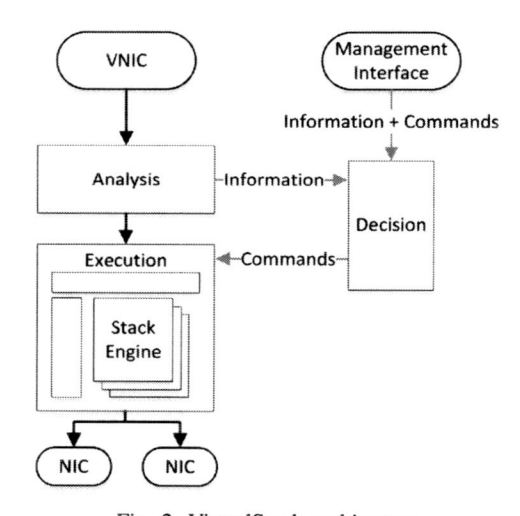

Fig. 2: VirtualStack architecture

B. Analysis Module

The analysis module parses every packet header to identify the corresponding flow. A flow is identified by its *flow id* generated out of three parameters: source port, destination port and destination address. In case the parameters aren't available, the packet is assigned to the flow 0. Every packet from flow 0 is sent over the raw stack (see Section II-E).

Additionally, the analysis module parses the used protocols up to the transport layer (e.g., TCP + IPv4). These meta information are used by the decision module to configure the right endpoint (see Section II-E) and to build an initial stack.

C. Control Protocol

We introduce the control protocol *vs-control* to configure the VS. This protocol decouples the VS from plugable decision modules. The protocol specifies the communication between the decision module and VS in both directions. All registered decision modules are informed about events such as new incoming flows. These events contain additional information, e.g., the *flow id* and the used protocols. The decision module controls VS with the following four basic commands:

- *Build Stack [features] for [FlowId]*: Builds a new network stack with specified features and properties, e.g. a TCP stack with reno congestion control on the LTE link.
- *Set [StackId] for [FlowId] with [quota]*: Sets the specified network stack for the specified flow as active. In case more than one stack is activated, the stacks are used in a weighted round robin manner using the quota.
- *Unset [StackId] for [FlowId]*: Sets the specified network stack for the specified flow as inactive. If every stack is inactive, the default stack – which is the first built stack – is used.
- *Cleanup [FlowId]*: Deletes all stacks to the corresponding flow. After this call, any following packet from this flow is registered as new flow.

These simple but powerful commands allow for plugable decision module which define complex behavior.

D. Decision Module

The decision module is responsible to manage and optimize the flows. Therefore, it requires information about the flows from the analysis module. For every flow it builds a stack engine with an appropriate endpoint and an initial stack. Since the decision module has a management interface, it can communicate with an external optimization instance, e.g., a SDN controller. The optimization instance can send commands or install rules for the best configuration of a connected network path. With these rules the decision engine is capable to build more suitable stacks for a given network environment.

```
agg([flowId].rx.throughput, 5s) < 10Mbps:
  set [TCPoverLTEStack] for [flowId];
```

Listing 1: Example rule which activates an additional LTE flow in case of low WiFi throughput.

We envision decision modules which provide expressive abstractions for complex adaptive behavior. *Event Condition Action* rules for adaptive distributed systems [5], for example, could support the specification of complex adaptation logic. These rules provide concepts to express events and conditions which trigger changes of the protocol stacks. Supposing, for example, an application requires a certain throughput, the rule as shown in Listing 1 turns on LTE in case the WiFi connection is not sufficient. The rules can be evaluation efficiently at the local network device in software and use additional monitoring data and events.

E. Execution Module

The main part of VS is the execution module, illustrated in Figure 3. The module consists of a *flow manager*, multiple *stack engines* and a *raw stack*.

The flow manager assigns every incoming packet to the respective stack engine based on the flow id. If a new flow is registered, the flow manager sets up a new stack engine with the protocols used by the clients. The stack engine is the main component to fulfill the protocol virtualization. It contains the *endpoint* for the application, a *NAT engine*, a *stack manager*, and the corresponding *stacks* of this flow.

After passing the analysis module, every application flow managed by VS is terminated at the associated endpoint. The endpoint acts like a transparent protocol proxy, i.e., it handles the connection to the application and passes the payload to the stack manager. In the case of UDP, for example, the endpoint just sets a pointer to the payload of the packet. TCP is more complex since the endpoint has to handle connection tasks such as handshakes, acknowledgments and retransmissions.

For every new stack, the target server address is given by the *NAT engine*. Typically this is the target address which is parsed by the analysis module. For the transparent redirection of flows, e.g., after a link failure or for load balancing, the target address can be changed.

The *stack manager* is responsible for the actual stacks, that means it builds and uses stacks to send the payload. When a command to build a new stack is received, the stack manager takes the destination address from the NAT engine. The stack manager treats any stack as abstract container, which leads to some degree of freedom. One option is to take a classical protocol combination and utilize the kernel implementations for that. VS provides the additional flexibility to implement new protocols as user-space stack.

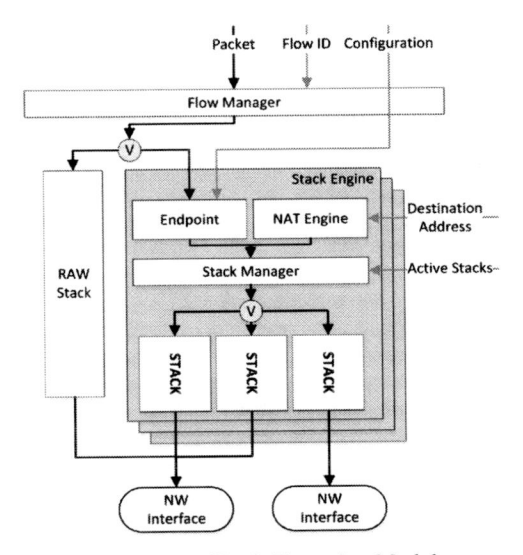

Fig. 3: VirtualStack Execution Module

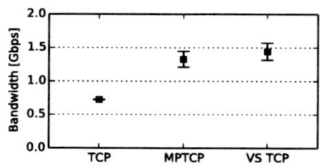

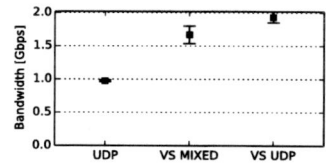

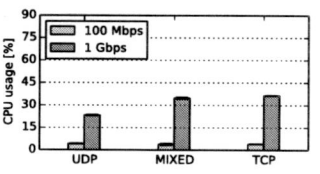

(a) TCP comparison: Throughput for TCP stacks on two 1 Gbps links.

(b) TCP vs UDP: VS throughput in comparison to traditional protocols on two 1 Gbps links.

(c) Overhead: CPU utilization of VS for two parallel links depending on the link speed.

Fig. 4: Performance evaluation results for VS in comparison to different protocols

As described in Section II-D, multiple stacks can be activate within one stack engine. This is useful for multihoming since the decision engine can activate stacks which are bind to different physical interfaces.

The *raw stack* is a special stack engine for unsupported protocols. Incoming packets that cannot be parsed by the analysis module are mapped to *flow 0*, that is assigned to the raw stack. As packets are sent over the raw stack without any changes, VS supports arbitrary applications.

III. EVALUATION

We implemented the VirtualStack (VS) architecture outlined in the previous section and evaluated it with two different setups. First a bare metal setup for performance measurements on physical hardware without any vitualized network parts and second a Mininet [6] setup where we have a controllable environment for demonstrating the operation with ECA rules. Finally, we discuss limitations.

A. General Considerations

VS is implemented as a user-space software in C++. From a performance perspective, it adds another layer of processing to the network interface. Therefore, it is important to mitigate the processing impact as much as possible. VS's implementation is efficiency optimized regarding the CPU, e.g., reduces waiting times for memory operations. Hence, network packets are not copied inside VS. The network packets are read from the TUN device into a kernel buffer. VS then relies on pointers to the respective part of the buffer for any further processing. Therefore, there are only two copy operations of the data in total. First, the copy generated in the kernel-space as the packet is generated. Second, the copy from the kernel-space to the sending buffer of the network device.

For our performance measurement evaluation, we used two machines – a server and a client – each with two 1 Gbps Ethernet network interfaces. They are connected through two physically separated path with CAT6 Ethernet cables. The CPU used for the CPU usage measurements was a mid range commodity CPU (Intel Core i5-4690k) with 3.5 GHz.

For the Mininet evaluation we used one machine with two virtual hosts connected through two separated path, one main channel with 50 Mbit/s (WiFi speed for IEEE 802.11g) and one offloading channel with 20 Mbit/s (typical LTE speed [9]).

The operating system used was Ubuntu 14.04 LTS x64 with a 3.13.0-45-generic kernel for both setups.

To generate the workload, we used a Python-based packet generator and counted the transferred packets. The packet generator creates payloads for packets and sends them through a TCP or a UDP socket. The packet counter counts the number of received packets and calculates the throughput. We verified our results with IPerf [17] measurements for TCP, UDP, and MPTCP. Since the server side implementation of VS – to back-transform the used protocols – is still ongoing we couldn't use IPerf for the measurements with VS.

B. Performance Measurements

We start with building a baseline through measuring the performance of the traditional protocols UDP, TCP, and MPTCP. Since VS is a framework which enables automatic network management and optimization we focus on the standard configurations of the single protocols. This reflects the performance when the application does not tweak the network protocol to optimize the connection (which is in fact the most common situation). The maximum aggregated performance of a multipath connection is limited by the combined performance of the single connections. Our measurements show that VS performance is even closer to this maximum as MPTCP. Further, we show that it is beneficial for performance to use lighter protocols like UDP on reliable links.

To demonstrate its capabilities, we used three different modes: (i) VS TCP, which uses TCP on both channels, (ii) VS UDP, which uses UDP on both channels, and (iii) VS MIXED, which uses an UDP and a TCP channel. We discuss our results in three groups: (a) a TCP comparison, (b) TCP vs UDP and mode comparison, and (c) the induced overhead.

(a) To show that VS is competitive to established methods, we measured TCP and MPTCP as baseline and compared it to VS. Figure 4a illustrates our measurement results regarding the considered TCP flavors. As expected, a single TCP connection has the lowest throughput with 725 Mbps. With a variability ($throughput_{max} - throughput_{min}$) of 1 Mbps, it is the most stable link in our measurements. MPTCP enables an average throughput of 1327 Mbps, which is quite near the assumed optimum of 1450 (two times the TCP connection). The variability over was 119 Mbps. VS in (i) TCP mode creates two traditional TCP connections and distributes the packet load over these two. It enables a throughput of 1433

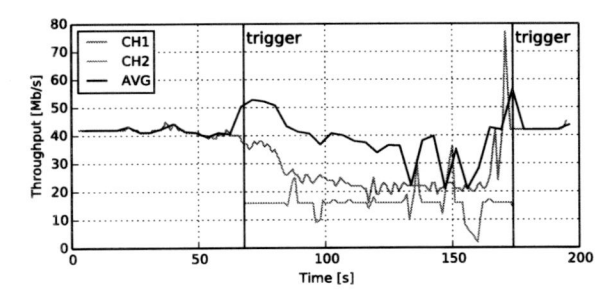

Fig. 5: Throughput for an offloading scenario: main channel (Ch1), offloading channel (CH2), combined (AVG).

Mbps, which is very close to the theoretical optimum and slightly better than MPTCP but has also a slightly higher variability of 127 Mbps. In fact, the measurements show that VS is competitive to MPTCP in terms of throughput, but brings a number of additional features and more flexibility with it. However, VS is able to use MPTCP as transport protocol but opens the possibility to use different protocols on other channels.

(b) As a second common protocol, which is fairly lightweight and therefore promises a higher throughput, we measured UDP (Figure 4b). With regard to theoretical optimum bandwidth, UDP has better performance than TCP since it is a much lighter protocol without the overhead of acknowledgments, retransmissions or congestion control. This restricts the use cases to reliable links or applications which are able to cope with the weaknesses of UDP (e.g., video streaming [13]). Thus, the measured throughput of 973 Mbps is near to the theoretical optimum bandwidth of the link. With VS in (ii) UDP mode, we reach a throughput of 1934 Mbps, which this is nearly the sum of two UDP channels. The variability of 84 Mbps is slightly lower than in TCP mode, which is owed to the missing congestion control.

We further measured this scenario in MIXED mode with different protocols on each of the two channels. This feature is useful, if the connectivity of the device is heterogeneous, e.g., a laptop with an reliable VPN link build on TCP and a unreliable WiFi link. VS in MIXED mode enables a throughput of 1667 Mpbps with a variability of 132 Mbps (Figure 4b). Theoretically, the combination of a TCP and a UDP channel enables 1688 Mbps, which is again just a little more than VS delivers. The shown protocols are the most common protocols on the Internet but it would be possible to use the whole range of available protocols. E.g., in datacenters, where reliable links are available, instead of UDP, DCCP could be used if a congestion control is required.

(c) The higher flexibility comes with a cost. As we described above, we do not copy packets inside VS to reduce any unnecessary waiting time for memory operations and to enable efficient CPU utilization. In Figure 4c, the CPU usage is illustrated. For the used 1 Gbps link, VS needs between 22% and 37% on a single core of our test machine. As we limit the network speed of both interfaces to 100 Mbps, VS uses around 4% of one CPU core. This indicates that VS scales very well, since a 10 times faster link leads just to around 5-9 times higher CPU usage. In fact, this is not much overhead over the TCP encumbered CPU usage. A generally accepted rule of thumb [3] is that 1 Hertz of CPU processing is required to send or receive 1 bit/s of TCP/IP, which would lead to 29% of CPU usage with a 1 Gbpslink. We also observe that the CPU usage does not increase with more flows. That's because the load comes from the number of processed packets, which is limited by the available bandwidth.

We want to create a solution which works, in principle, with every operating system. For this reason, we refrained to use TCP Offload Engine (TOE), which potentially enables significant lower CPU usage [10]. We didn't re-implement all known improvements and techniques from MPTCP. As congestion control we rely on the techniques from TCP on every single path. With UDP we have no congestion control at all. Also the packets need to be reordered on the server side and the round robin scheduling is not convincing on unequal links. In Section V we present some ideas how to solve this.

Our measurements show that multiple paths on devices with multiple network interfaces enable higher throughput. We further demonstrated that the increased flexibility of VS does not harm the performance. VS delivers a wider range of applications since VS is able to freely use available protocols for every network layer up to transport layer.

C. Rule-based Programming

To demonstrate the ease of the rule-based programming abstraction, we executed VS with two simple rules for an offloading scenario (Listing 1). Imagine a live video transfer, which requires at least an average throughput of 30Mbit. With two simple rules, VS can activate a second channel, e.g., a LTE connection, in case the throughput of the primary channel drops suddenly due to congestion. Figure 5 shows an example run in Mininet, where cross traffic leads decreasing throughput on the first channel and therefore triggers the activation of the second channel. A second rule deactivates this channel later, as it detects that the primary channel is sufficient again.

IV. RELATED WORK

In [7], *Heuschkel* et al. presents rough sketch of VirtualStack (VS) and discusses the use-cases (i) protocol transformation, (ii) multipath routing, and (iii) flow migration. The authors evaluated the use-case (i) protocol transformation between UDP and DCCP with a very low switching delay and almost no throughput degradation. The prototype provided a maximal throughput of 4.36 Gbps.

Multipath TCP (MPTCP) is the most related protocol for the discussed features of VS. In [14] and [15], it is shown that MPTCP is capable to improve the performance and robustness of network connections. MPTCP has some limitations as noted previously: the end-to-end path must permit the MPTCP flag, and it is not yet implemented for all operating systems.

Additionally, MPTCP does not provide the flexibility to use different protocols for its subflows.

In [12], *Martins* et al. presents ClickOS, which is a lightweight operating system uses click modular router [11] to enable network flow manipulation. It is also possible to split network flows to multiple path, which could lead to a better performance. It suits perfect the needs for applications regarding network function virtualization. However, it is not intended to run on edge devices, such as mobile devices.

In the IETF Draf [18], *You* presents 3RED TAPS. Like VS it provides a decoupling of applications and the network transport layer. Another common goal is to achieve that decoupling without a customization or reimplementation of the applications. For that, TAPS need a kernel modification to insert their services before the network packets are processed in the kernel. However, VS is intended to decouple the applications from all network matters and not just from the transport layer. Also, VS is build to run on every operating system without modifying the kernel.

In contrast to the related work, this paper presented the first approach to use protocol stack virtualization for combining the benefits of multiple paths and the flexibility of a virtual protocol stack which decouples the application and the network.

V. CONCLUSION AND OUTLOOK

In this paper, we presented VirtualStack (VS), a protocol virtualization framework which decouples the application and the network stack. We discussed how this increases the flexibility, and showed on a concrete example how it enables optimizations. We further showed how protocol virtualization enables multipath communication increasing reliability and throughput. We demonstrated the flexibility of the protocol virtualization concept combine different protocols on different network paths transparently for the application. The decoupled architecture of VS enables existing applications to benefit from multiple paths in the network and the flexibility of different protocols without changes.

We implemented VS as user-space program. Our measurements show that VS delivers at least the same throughput as MPTCP. We further presented measurements to show the performance of a multipath UDP network stack and mixed stack with UDP and TCP on the different paths. Thereby, the overhead of VS in terms of RAM is less than 2 MB in all tested scenarios. The CPU usage depends on the achieved throughput and the underlying links. For a 1 Gbps link VS uses just between 22% and 37% (depending on protocol) of CPU power on a single core. On a 100 Mbps link VS uses just about 4% of CPU power on a single core. Note that it is just the utilization of one core and competes with the common rule of thumb for TCP connections.

In this paper, we discussed how the decision engine can implement adaptive behavior to control the usage of multiple paths in the network. In the future, we will connect existing SDN controllers in the network with the control infrastructure of VS to fully decouple the data plane from the control plane not only *inside* the network, but also on the *end-devices*.

ACKNOWLEDGMENT

This work has been funded by the German Research Foundation (DFG) as part of the projects A02 and B02 within the Collaborative Research Center (CRC) 1053 – MAKI.

REFERENCES

[1] Winehq - run windows applications on linux, bsd, solaris and mac os x. https://www.winehq.org/, 2015.
[2] G. Detal, B. Hesmans, O. Bonaventure, Y. Vanaubel, and B. Donnet. Revealing middlebox interference with tracebox. In *Proceedings of the 2013 conference on Internet measurement conference*, pages 1–8. ACM, 2013.
[3] A. P. Foong, T. R. Huff, H. H. Hum, J. P. Patwardhan, and G. J. Regnier. Tcp performance re-visited. In *Performance Analysis of Systems and Software, 2003. ISPASS. 2003 IEEE International Symposium on*, pages 70–79. IEEE, 2003.
[4] A. Ford, C. Raiciu, M. Handley, and O. Bonaventure. TCP Extensions for Multipath Operation with Multiple Addresses. RFC 6824.
[5] A. Frömmgen, R. Rehner, M. Lehn, and A. Buchmann. Fossa: Learning eca rules for adaptive distributed systems. In *International Conference on Autonomic Computing*, 2015. in press.
[6] N. Handigol, B. Heller, V. Jeyakumar, B. Lantz, and N. McKeown. Reproducible network experiments using container-based emulation. In *Proceedings of the 8th International Conference on Emerging Networking Experiments and Technologies*, CoNEXT '12, pages 253–264, New York, NY, USA, 2012. ACM.
[7] J. Heuschkel, I. Schweizer, and M. Mühlhäuser. Virtualstack: A framework for protocol stack virtualization at the edge. In *Proceedings of IEEE Local Computer Networks Conference*, 2015.
[8] M. Honda, Y. Nishida, C. Raiciu, A. Greenhalgh, M. Handley, and H. Tokuda. Is it still possible to extend tcp? In *Proceedings of the 2011 ACM SIGCOMM Conference on Internet Measurement Conference*, pages 181–194, 2011.
[9] J. Huang, F. Qian, A. Gerber, Z. M. Mao, S. Sen, and O. Spatscheck. A close examination of performance and power characteristics of 4g lte networks. In *Proceedings of the 10th International Conference on Mobile Systems, Applications, and Services*, MobiSys '12, pages 225–238, New York, NY, USA, 2012. ACM.
[10] K. Kant. Tcp offload performance for front-end servers. In *Global Telecommunications Conference, 2003. GLOBECOM '03. IEEE*, volume 6, pages 3242–3247 vol.6, Dec 2003.
[11] E. Kohler, R. Morris, B. Chen, J. Jannotti, and M. F. Kaashoek. The click modular router. *ACM Transactions on Computer Systems (TOCS)*, 18(3):263–297, 2000.
[12] J. Martins, M. Ahmed, C. Raiciu, V. Olteanu, M. Honda, R. Bifulco, and F. Huici. Clickos and the art of network function virtualization. In *11th USENIX Symposium on Networked Systems Design and Implementation (NSDI 14)*, pages 459–473. USENIX Association, 2014.
[13] J. Nightingale, Q. Wang, C. Grecos, and S. Goma. The impact of network impairment on quality of experience (qoe) in h.265/hevc video streaming. *Consumer Electronics, IEEE Transactions on*, 60(2):242–250, May 2014.
[14] C. Paasch, G. Detal, F. Duchene, C. Raiciu, and O. Bonaventure. Exploring mobile/wifi handover with multipath tcp. In *Proceedings of the 2012 ACM SIGCOMM Workshop on Cellular Networks: Operations, Challenges, and Future Design*, CellNet '12, pages 31–36, New York, NY, USA, 2012. ACM.
[15] C. Raiciu, S. Barre, C. Pluntke, A. Greenhalgh, D. Wischik, and M. Handley. Improving Datacenter Performance and Robustness with Multipath TCP. *SIGCOMM Comput. Commun. Rev.*, 41(4):266–277, Aug. 2011.
[16] C. Raiciu, C. Paasch, S. Barre, A. Ford, M. Honda, F. Duchene, O. Bonaventure, M. Handley, et al. How Hard Can It Be? Designing and Implementing a Deployable Multipath TCP. In *NSDI Vol. 12*, pages 29–29, 2012.
[17] A. Tirumala, L. Cottrell, and T. Dunigan. Measuring end-to-end bandwidth with iperf using web100. In *Web100, Proc. of Passive and Active Measurement Workshop*, page 2003, 2003.
[18] J. You. 3red model for taps. Internet-Draft draft-you-taps-3red-model-00, IETF Secretariat, June 2015. http://www.ietf.org/internet-drafts/draft-you-taps-3red-model-00.txt.

A Field Study on Linked and Open Data at Datahub.io

Timm Heuss*[†], Janina Fengel*, Bernhard Humm*, Bettina Harriehausen-Mühlbauer* and Shirley Atkinson[†]
*University of Applied Sciences
Darmstadt, Germany
Email: {Timm.Heuss|Janina.Fengel|Bernhard.Humm|Bettina.Harriehausen}@h-da.de
[†]University of Plymouth,
Plymouth, United Kingdom
Email: {Timm.Heuss|Shirley.Atkinson}@plymouth.ac.uk

Abstract—We describe and conduct a study on datahub.io to explore to what, in practice, Linked and Open Data refers to. We focus on the use of formats, licenses, ages and popularity of the data. An in-depth analysis reveals information about availability, quantity, structure and vocabulary usage of the real-world RDF-based datasets contained. Results show that the most common formats are Microsoft Excel, CSV and RDF. High proportions of structured data is of tabular nature, independent from the format. The heuristics and evaluation methods developed here are released as open source and can be applied to other CKAN-based repositories and RDF-based datasets, too.

I. INTRODUCTION

In 2006, Tim Berners-Lee introduced a 5-star rating or maturity model for data [5]. This model is used to "encourage people [...] along the road to good linked data" [5] and to assess "the openness and linking potential of the data" [9], p. 4. The ranking starts with Open Data, data in any format that is openly licensed (1 star), followed by structured, machine readable formats (2 stars), non-proprietary structured formats (3 stars), RDF (Resource Description Framework) or SPARQL (SPARQL Query Language) endpoints (4 stars) and ends up with the highest maturity class, which is RDF data interlinked with other data [5].

II. MOTIVATION

As there is only a licence-based constraint for the first star, many different file formats might come into question. When building applications based on Linked and Open Data, this question of format becomes important: it requires an entirely different technology stack to integrate, assure quality, and store data from, for example, RDF - compared to the technology needed for data in MS Excel format. And while building apps based on Office formats is straight forward (thank to frameworks like Apache POI [3]), years of experience and complex infrastructure might be required to master the advanced possibilities of RDF, such as OWL (Web Ontology Language) reasoning. Furthermore, integrating different formats is challenging, e.g., if the internal structure of the data differs fundamentally. While data stored in spreadsheets might usually be of tabular nature, RDF-based data, by design, does "not necessarily consist of clearly identifiable 'records'" [17]. RDF knowledge bases are considered to be heterogeneous, non-tabular structures, which do not resemble relational structures [18], p. 455.

Therefore, the question that needs to be answered before putting the data into use is: what are relevant formats when dealing with Linked and Open Data in practice? Under what terms of use may it be reused and processed? If the format is RDF, can it flawlessly loaded and does it require sophisticated tool support (in form of OWL reasoners)? What is the internal structure of the real-world RDF? Does it constitute homogeneous, tabular structures or is it as heterogeneous as often found in large knowledge bases? This field study reported on is conducted using the well-known data portal datahub.io, as it is commonly used as an indicator for the progress of Linked Data, e.g. upon creating the LOD Cloud diagram [22].

III. APPROACH

The field study is designed to consist of three parts. Firstly, the meta information about the data available at datahub.io is extracted and stored in a CSV (Comma Separated Values) file. Secondly, the CSV file is loaded, interpreted and analysed. Based on this meta data, information about formats, popularity, licences, and ages of the datasets can be acquired. Thirdly, based on the meta data, the highest rated RDF-based resources are attempted to be downloaded, imported, and analysed.

The exact analytical process is described in the following. For demonstration purposes, the third part uses excerpts of the New York Times Linked Open Data dataset "People" [7] as an example for the analysis conducted. All scripts, queries, program source code and results are published in the GitHub repositories CKANstats [15] and LODprobe [16].

A. Extraction

Like many other data portals, datahub.io is based on CKAN (Comprehensive Knowledge Archive Network), offering an open, REST-based, JSON-based API [8]. In CKAN-terminology, the actual data is published as a resource, and one or more resources are provided in units named datasets [21]. A Python script named CKANstats.py uses the CKAN-API (Version 3) [19] and extracts the meta information about the datasets registered at datahub.io [20], including: dataset names, licences, a boolean flag if the dataset is openly licensed, the dataset's page views (total + last 14 days), a resource's format statement, download URL and resource's page views (total + last 14 days).

The script stores the retrieved meta information in a CSV file [12].

B. Meta Data Analysis

In order to conduct further analysis with SQL, the first step is to load the CSV file into PostgreSQL (Version 9.4.1) using `COPY datahubio FROM 'datahubio.csv' DELIMITER ',' csv;`. Unfortunately, values found in format column are not unified. For example, there are at least 29 different notations given for specifying a Microsoft Excel resource. Another issue with this column is the fact that in about 20% of the cases, there is no format specification at all.

To address these issues, a generic mapping table has been manually created. It assigns the various source values stated in resource to a unified format definitions. For example, `application/zip+application/vnd.ms-excel` and `microsoft excel` is combined into `Excel`.

Based on the table holding the imported data, a database view is created using this mapping table twice:

- Firstly, the format definition of datahub.io is translated via SQL-like-patterns `left outer join mptbl as a on lower(trim(resource_format)) like lower(a.expr)`.
- Secondly, for every remaining format unknown, it is attempted to join the mapping table an additional time based on the last characters of the resource URL - `left outer join mptbl as b on (a.format = 'n/a' and lower(substring(trim(resource_url) from '...$')) like b.expr)`. So if, for example, a resource has a URL pointing at "example.com/filename.pdf", this is an indication for the file format PDF (Portable Document Format).

Both these joins produce a best-effort corrected view on the meta data extracted. Thus, further analysis is enabled based on this view, and the SQL scripts developed are documented online [15].

C. In-Depth Analysis of RDF-based Resources

The in-depth analysis is conduced for every RDF resource which has ever been visited, ergo having a `resource tracking summary total` larger than 0. At the time of the described metadata extraction this included 606 resources.

In a semi-automated process, each single resource is downloaded using wget (Version 1.15) and loaded into an empty Apache Fuseki (Version 2.0.0 2015-03-08T09:49:20, Xmx set to 14.240M) using s-put and, if that failed, using Fuseki's WWW front end. Errors during this process are logged as follows:

Not Found wget could not download the resource, either because it was no longer available or the connection timed out.

Parse Error Fuseki failed to load the downloaded resource using s-put and Fuseki Web.

TABLE I
EXCERPT OF LODPROBE ANALYSIS RESULT FOR THE NEW YORK TIMES LINKED OPEN DATA DATASET "PEOPLE".

Number of unique subjects: 9958	Count	[0]	[1]	[2]	[3]	[4]	[5]
[0] cc:attribution[...]	4979	-	4979	4979	0	0	0
[1] cc:attributionURL	4979	-	-	4979	0	0	0
[2] cc:license	4979	-	-	-	0	0	0
[3] nyt:associated[...]	4979	-	-	-	-	4281	4281
[4] nyt:first_use	4281	-	-	-	-	-	4281
[5] nyt:latest_use	4281	-	-	-	-	-	-

TABLE II
EXCERPT OF THE PREVIOUS TABLE I, LOADED, MIRRORED, AND CONVERTED AS AN R MATRIX OBJECT.

Number of unique subjects: 9958	[0]	[1]	[2]	[3]	[4]	[5]
[0] cc:attributionName	4979	4979	4979	0	0	0
[1] cc:attributionURL	4979	4979	4979	0	0	0
[2] cc:license	4979	4979	4979	0	0	0
[3] nytdata:associated[...]	0	0	0	4979	4281	4281
[4] nytdata:first_use	0	0	0	4281	4281	4281
[5] nytdata:latest_use	0	0	0	4281	4281	4281

Partly Some files of the resource were loaded, others not. Evaluation is done with the loaded files only.

Out of Memory Fuseki failed to load the resource and reported a out of memory exception or a garbage collection overhead exception.

This process is documented for all 606 resources [13]. Out of these, the resources that could successfully be loaded into Apache Fuseki are the foundation for the subsequent analysis. Thereby, the authors notice that in some cases, RDF dumps could be loaded using s-put, but not via Web front end, and in others vice versa.

The Java tool called LODprobe [16] has been specifically developed for this field study to analyse the inner structure of the RDF-based datasets. Once a dataset is entirely loaded in an empty local Fuseki dataset, LODprobe fires a number of SPARQL queries against the default graph.

As a result, quantities about several basic characteristics of the resources are extracted:

- The number of unique RDF subject identifiers.
- The number of occurrences of each RDF property the default graph contains.
- The number of co-occurrences of two RDF properties, considering every property with each other.

The result is a symmetrical matrix of co-occurrences, accompanied with individual property counts, as excerpted in Table I. For example, the value 4979 in the second row (starting with [1]) and column [2] shows that the RDF property http://creativecommons.org/ns#attributionName ([1]) co-occurs with the RDF property http://creativecommons.org/ns#attribution ([2]) in 4979 subjects.

Considering the co-occurring values of two RDF properties row- or column-wise, further insights into the structure of the resource can be gained. For the example above, the properties [0], [1], and [2] always co-occur. This holds also true for the properties [4] and [5], all co-occur as well. Both property groups seem to be part of distinct entities, as [0], [1], and

TABLE III
METRICS FOR LODPROBE RESULTS, SAMPLE MEASUREMENT RESULTS
FOR THE NEW YORK TIMES LOD "PEOPLE" RESOURCE.

Metric	Sample
LODprobe analysis name	people.csv
Number of unique subjects	9958
Number of properties	20
Minimum height cluster analysis	0
Maximum height cluster analysis	1
Number of cluster groups at h=0.1	3
Number of cluster groups at h=0.2	3
Number of cluster groups at h=0.3	3
Number of cluster groups at h=0.4	3

[2] never co-occur with [4] and [5], as indicated by the zero values in the matrix. This may be concluded that this sample data contains two entities.

In such obvious cases, the result of a LODprobe analysis contains about 20x20 RDF properties with few, clearly identifiable entities. Usually, however, there are more entities, less clear co-occurrences, and / or much more properties.

In a next step, a large-scale analysis of the individual LODprobe outputs is conducted using the scriptable statistics software R. Thereby, a co-occurrence diagonal matrix from the CSV-files is loaded, converted into a numerical matrix and mirrored in a symmetric one. Individual property-counts are moved into the diagonal. Table II shows this for the chosen example. Having the LODprobe results available as R objects allows for further advanced analysis in consecutive order: calculation of the dissimilarity matrix of the LODprobe matrix, followed by a cluster analysis of the dissimilarity matrix. From this cluster analysis, a number of metrics for the structuredness of the individual resources is extracted. This metrics-based analysis is augmented by generating visualisations of the clusters detected. Follow-up analytical steps are:

1) Dissimilarity Calculation: In this step, based on the counted co-occurrences, the dissimilarity of the property-pairs in the matrix is calculated. The work showed that LODprobe results usually contain more zero than non-zero values. Therefore, non-euclidean distance metric has been applied. This field study uses the Gower Distance [10] by utilising the R function `daisy` from the `cluster` package, using `metric = "gower"`.

2) Cluster Analysis: In this step, based on their mutual (dis-)similarity calculated previously, groups or clusters of the properties are searched for. Thereby, the complete linkage method [1] is used (via R's `hclust` using `method ="complete"`), so resulting cluster analyses are usually scaled from a minimum height of 0 to a maximum height of 1.

Table III shows the metrics that are calculated for all LODprobe results for comparison purposes. They characterise a RDF resource: in the case of New York Times LOD "People" dataset, judging by the minimum and maximum height of the analysis, the dissimilarity of groups of properties in the dataset is very high - it is obvious that the RDF resource contains different entities.

Upon considering a number of cluster analyses of different RDF resources, the grouping behaviour of the clusters between the heights 0.1 and 0.4 seems to be most informative. Especially at lower heights of 0.1, 0.2 or sometimes even 0.3, properties usually seem to be clustered based on the logical entities found in the data, just before those clusters are again grouped together with other clusters. In the example above, even at lower heights, the 20 involved RDF properties constitute three groups. This is an indicator that the properties within the groups are very similar, but the groups themselves are very distinctive.

Finally, the collected metrics are compared to metrics computed for synthetically generated resources, simulating the case in which RDF data is truly heterogeneous. Thereby, property occurrence and co-occurrence counts are randomised and then normalised by the amount of actual unique subjects. This is repeated in a Monte-Carlo-like process based on two real examples, a small RDF resource with 9,958 subjects, 20x20 properties, and 1,000,000 simulations and a large one with 694,400 subjects, 222x222 properties, and 15,127 simulations.

In addition to the cluster analysis metrics, dendrograms are generated for each of the 251 LODprobe results to support the interpretation. They are generated using R's 'plot' function with the generated cluster analysis from above, without any further parameters.

IV. RESULTS

With using the described methodology, various insights on real data at datahub.io could be gained.

A. Common Formats

Considering the unified format values, the most frequently used format for data are full-featured spreadsheets such as Microsoft Excel or LibreOffice Calc documents, and CSV, including its variations like TSV [15]. Together, both tabular formats add up to almost one third of all data formats (27%), followed by RDF (11%), PDF (8%), and Images (7%).

With regard of the openness of data, the frequently used data formats are usually not openly licensed: only 21% of the spreadsheets are open, about 59% of the CSV, and roughly 14% of the PDF [15]. RDF, in contrast, is openly licensed in more than three of four cases (76%). The highest openness-percentages can be archived for the formats MARC (Machine-Readable Cataloging) (100%), GTFS (General Transit Feed Specification) (100%), and Beacon (98%).

By using the 5-star rating model [5] to classify the data, over a quarter (25%) of the data is 1-star, 6% 2-stars, 24% 3-stars, and 21% is 4 stars (or more) [15]. Excluded from this is data that is not explicitly openly licensed (about 48%). One fourth of open data formats could not be classified. The low frequencies of 2-star data can be explained by the openness criteria: Most 2 star data is in the Microsoft Excel format and not openly licensed.

B. Popular Formats

Based on existing data, a popularity measure can only be approximated using the tracked visits from the CKAN-API [20]. According to the resource tracking, in the last two weeks before the extraction, 33% of the clicks at datahub.io where on resources with an unknown format, followed by RDF (13%), RDF sample record (10%), CSV (8%), Spreadsheet (7%), SPARQL (6%) [15]. Despite the fact that PDF is quite a quite common format, resources with that format only received 2% of the tracked clicks. The most unpopular types are Links, RSS and Maps with 0,3%, 0,2% and 0,05% of the visits.

C. Licences

A clear license statement of data is important as it defines a terms of use of the referred resource(s). However, similar to the case of the original format information, the licence-field does not contain unified values [15]. Even worse, in more than 40% of the cases, there is no specification of a licence at all. In the remaining cases, properly defined licences (like Creative Commons licences) are mixed with country- or language specific licences, and insufficiently named licences like "None", "Other (Not Open)", or "apache". Moreover, the boolean openness flag is set in 10,612 of the total 20,178 cases, which corresponds to 52.59%.

D. Ages

The extract contains meta information about data up to four years. Judging by the created and revision timestamp, in most cases (80%) this meta information is never updated after the dataset had been put online [15]. Of the remaining cases, more than 10% are updated within less than 50 days.

E. In-Depth RDF Analysis Results

In addition to the previous analyses, based on metadata of all data on datahub.io, the following analyses are limited to specific datasets of the type RDF and that have a popularity ranking larger than zero. At the time of extraction, this included 606 RDF resources.

1) Download and Process Results: In two-thirds of the cases, the download-URL worked and returned a server response (33% of the cases are not found). The downloaded resources, however, could only be flawlessly loaded in about 46,37% of the cases - the rest resulted primarily in parser errors (18,81%). Only a few datasets (0,83%) could not be loaded due to memory deficiencies of the test machine[1] - this includes the knowledge base DBpedia. Additional four resources[2] (0.66%) could only loaded partly, e.g., because they are split-up into several parts.

[1] "dbpedia", "library-of-congress-name-authority-file", "semantic-xbrl", "europeana-lod-v1" and "allie-abbreviation-and-long-form-database-in-life-science"
[2] "jiscopenbib-bl_bnb-1", "geowordnet", "datos-bcn-cl", and "rkb-explorer-citeseer"

TABLE IV
AVERAGE CLUSTER ANALYSIS RESULTS OF OBSERVED DATA AT DATAHUB.IO AND OF ARTIFICIALLY SIMULATED HETEROGENEOUS DATA.

	Average at datahub.io	Simulated Heterogenous (small)	(large)
number of resources	253	1,000,0000	15,127
number of unique subjects	217.659.05 ± 994,267.50	9,958	694,400
min. height	0.00 ± 0.05	0.13 ± 0.03	0.04 ± 0.01
max. height	8.48 ± 79.17	0.58 ± 0.05	0.51 ± 0.02
Total Groups (h=0.0)	28.07 ± 33.03	20	222
Groups at h=0.1	7.66 ± 3.96	20 ± 0.5	210 ± 3.91
Groups at h=0.2	5.05 ± 2.08	16 ± 2	106 ± 13.1
Groups at h=0.3	3.76 ± 1.35	8.6 ± 1.4	20 ± 2.6
Groups at h=0.4	2.96 ± 1.00	4 ± -1	3 ± 1

2) Frequently used Properties: By summing up all individual LODprobe property counts, a big picture of the most frequently used RDF properties and vocabularies can be calculated. In total, over 373 million triples have been analysed, containing nearly 3000 different RDF properties. Unsurprisingly, basic properties are very frequent: every one out of six observed property is a rdf:type assignment, one out of 20 is a rdfs:label.

Regarding OWL, the most frequently used properties with the default namespace http://www.w3.org/2002/07/owl is sameAs - position 19 of the most frequently used properties with more than 4.5 million occurrences, followed by onProperty (Position 948 - 3,213 occurrences) and intersectionOf (position 1,016 - 2,038 occurrences).

3) Homogeneous Structures in RDF: Table IV shows the aggregated results of 253 LODprobe and cluster analyses for distinct resources [11]. On average, a RDF datasets contained 28 (± 33) different RDF properties, which can be grouped in only 7 (± 4) clusters at a height of 0.1 and in only 5 (± 2) clusters at a height of 0.2. Moreover, Table IV compares the measured values with two synthetically generated and simulated heterogeneous RDF datasets of different sizes. In these, there are significantly more cluster groups at lower heights, such as for h=0.1, the number of groups is (almost) identical to the total number of groups.

Accordingly, Figure 1 shows a dendrogram of the real RDF resource southampton-ac-uk-org that has the exact characteristics of an average resource, thus having 28 different RDF properties that form 7 groups at a height of 0.1, 5 groups at a height of 0.2, and 4 groups at a height of 0.3. The diagram gives the impression of a clearly structured resource, as many properties are already grouped together at a height of 0 and the properties seem to have quite similar co-occurrence counts.

In contrast, Figure 2 depicts a dendrogram of synthetically generated resource (simulation number 473,494 of 1,000,000) that shows the average characteristics of simulated, small heterogeneous resources - 20 properties, 20 groups at h=0.1, 16 at h=0.2, 9 at h=0.3. The lack of structure can be deduced from the high number of groups at lower heights, individually consisting of less properties (usually max. 2 properties per

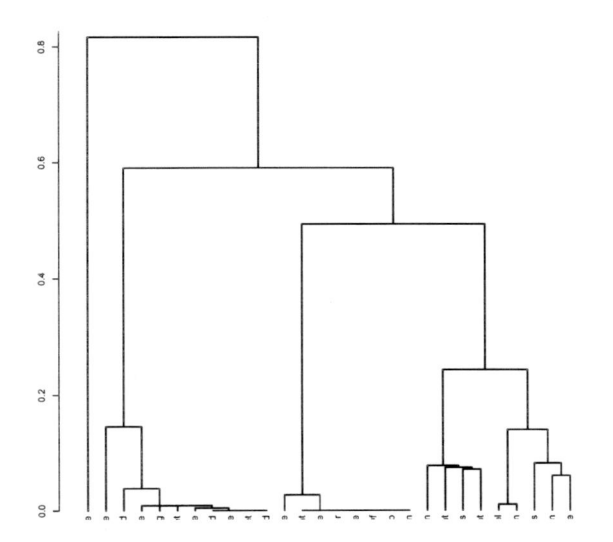

Fig. 1. A typical dendrogram of a real-world RDF resource: Many joins at lower (< 0.2) heights, indicating a high number of co-occurrences for these properties. Few joins above heights > 0.3, an high maximum height of 0.8 or above.

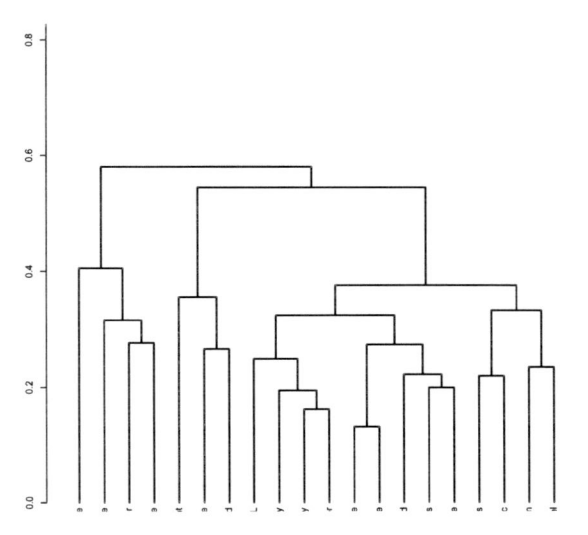

Fig. 2. A typical dendrogram of a synthetically generated heterogeneous RDF resource: Joins are evenly distributed between heights of 0.1 to 0.5, almost no joins at lower (< 0.2) heights, a low maximum height of < 0.6.

group at h=0.2). In addition, the lower maximum dendrogram height indicates that the properties are mutually less differentiable. As expected, the number of groups found in a cluster analysis is proportional to the number of unique properties the resource has. Resources with an RDF property count up to nine show on average 3 ± 2.4 groups at a height of 0.1. Resources with more properties, e.g. 70-79 distinct RDF properties, have 11 groups $\pm$ 2.63 at this height. This observation can be approximated by the rule of thumb "the more properties, the more groups". Though, resources with 60 to 69 properties contain the most groups of all at a height of 0.1, 15.67 ± 4 groups.

Figure 3 visualises the observed proportionality between the number of properties and the groups they form: it compares the ratio between the number of groups at a height of 0.1 with the number of unique RDF properties a resource has in total for all involved analyses. Almost all ratios are below 4/5 and the average ratio about 3/8, while, in contrast, the simulated heterogeneous resources both have ratios of nearly 1/1.

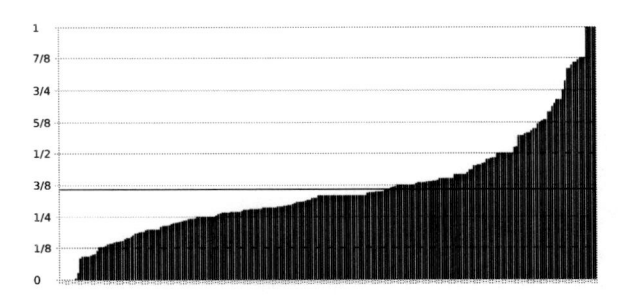

Fig. 3. Ratio of the number of properties and the number of cluster groups at h=0.1 for all analysed RDF datasets.

V. DISCUSSION

Only about half of the data on datahub.io is open, the majority of the rest bears legal uncertainty for application developers using it. Openness varies with the data formats: Excel is a very common format, but is usually not open. RDF is the third most common format, and is usually open. Accordingly, data on datahub.io is 53% Open Data, 15% Linked Data and about 11 % Linked *and* Open Data. However, of these RDF-based resources, 33% are non-existing downloads and nearly 20% are inaccessible due to parser errors. As a consequence of this distribution, RDF-only data integration approaches would not reach about 85% of the data that is out there. This fact underlines the necessity that data integration solutions support a whole spectrum of different formats.

Real data format quantities are almost evenly distributed across the scale of the 5-star rating model, despite for 2-stars data, usually represented by Microsoft Excel files which are often not openly licensed. However, the star rating in the 5-star model is proportional to the number of page views a resource gets: The more stars, the more page views. It seems that RDF is data-consumer friendly.

For a portal that conceptually only distributes URLs to resources and not the resources itself, having up-to-date meta data is essential - especially when considering the Link Rot phenomenon [6]. Unfortunately, a vast majority of meta data is never updated after it has been published. This might contribute to the 33% missing downloads mentioned above.

The cluster analysis revealed that RDF resources show clearly more characteristics of homogeneous data than of heterogeneous data. Almost all of the 251 dendrograms contain structures in form of properties that more or less exclusively co-exist with certain other properties [14].

So, even if it is not a constraint of the format, real-world RDF triples constitute somewhat differentiable entities that might fit in tabular structures as well as in graph-like ones. The cluster groups might give an approximate hint regarding the number of attributes each entity has: taking the average 28 properties and the 8 groups at h=0.1, and the 5 groups at h=0.2 into consideration, an entity of them would statistically consist of 4-6 properties.

VI. RELATED WORK

The LODstats project [23] collects similar statistics, but is limited to Linked Data only. The original setup is also quite different: this field study is implemented on an average laptop, while [23] work with Hadoop. They evaluated more RDF resources, nevertheless, similarities are noticeable: As found here, `rdf:type` and `rdfs:label` are frequently used RDF properties. Moreover, the proportion of "problematic" resources is comparable, c.f. [24].

[2] have introduced a clustering approach to automatically partitioning an RDF dataset with the aim of size-reduction. The methodology thereby involved a bisimulation, while in this paper the counts of co-occurrences of RDF properties are used. Thus, [2] finds subgraphs, consisting of clusters of similar subjects, while the work presented here finds clusters of related subjects.

The Roomba project [4] provides a similar analysis software for CKAN like introduced here. While the present work operates on meta data to provide a big picture on all data, Roomba probes all datasets to detect the mimetype.

VII. CONCLUSION

This field study provides a means to perform a reality check on what the term Linked and Open Data means, in practice, for the commonly known data portal datahub.io. It shows that real Linked *and* Open Data, ergo 4+-star data, is quite rare, while ordinary Office formats like Excel are twice as common. Next to technical aspects, datasets often do not possess a clear license, and thus, clear terms of use. This leaves a huge uncertainty for developers who want to build applications based on this data. RDF data, if available, does not seem to rely on OWL properties on a broad scale. After all, large amounts of data at datahub.io seem to be of tabular nature, independent from the fact if the actual format demands it (Spreadsheets and CSVs) or or not (RDF).

As mentioned, this work has two limitations: Firstly, while the meta data analysis was based on the entire data library of datahub.io, an in-depth analysis was only conducted for RDF resources with a page-view on this portal larger than 0. Secondly, in some cases, the system used for evaluating did not have enough computing power to load certain RDF resources.

Future work could address both these restrictions, possibly with a Big Data infrastructure, as suggested in [23]. Porting involved analysis tools like LODprobe on Map-Reduce-based jobs has been found to be feasible. Accordingly, in addition, also other CKAN-based data repositories could be analysed in this matter, too.

VIII. ACKNOWLEDGEMENTS

The authors want to thank Werner Helm and Adrian Schmitt from the Competence Center Stochastics & Operations Research (CCSOR) of the University of Applied Sciences Darmstadt for consulting in the statistical foundation of this work.

REFERENCES

[1] Complete-linkage clustering, Sept. 2014. Page Version ID: 625941679.
[2] A. Alzogbi and G. Lausen. Similar structures inside rdf-graphs. In C. Bizer, T. Heath, T. Berners-Lee, M. Hausenblas, and S. Auer, editors, *LDOW*, volume 996 of *CEUR Workshop Proceedings*. CEUR-WS.org, 2013.
[3] Apache POI. Apache POI - the Java API for Microsoft Documents, 2014. Last access 2015-06-08.
[4] A. Assaf, A. Sénart, and R. Troncy. Roomba: automatic validation, correction and generation of dataset metadata, 05 2015.
[5] T. Berners-Lee. Linked Data. Webpage, June 2006.
[6] M. Ceglowski. Remembrance of Links Past (Pinboard Blog), 05 2011.
[7] Datahub.io. New York Times - Linked Open Data - People (SKOS) - the Datahub, September 2010. Last access 2015-06-02.
[8] Datahub.io. About - the Datahub, 6 2015. Last access 2015-06-11.
[9] J. Edelstein, L. Galla, C. Li-Madeo, J. Marden, A. Rhonemus, and N. Whysel. Linked Open Data for Cultural Heritage: Evolution of an Information Technology. 2013.
[10] J. C. Gower. A General Coefficient of Similarity and Some of Its Properties. *Biometrics*, 27(4):857–871, Dec. 1971.
[11] T. Heuss. CKANStats datahub.io Cluster Analyses - github.com/heussd/CKANstats/blob/master/datahub.io/clusteranalysis.csv (last accessed 2016-02-26), 2015.
[12] T. Heuss. CKANStats datahub.io Dataset Meta Data - github.com/heussd/CKANstats/blob/master/datahub.io/datahub.io.csv (last accessed 2015-06-10), 2015.
[13] T. Heuss. CKANStats datahub.io Linked Data Download Meta Data - github.com/heussd/CKANstats/blob/master/datahub.io/all_ld_rdf_res _tracking_sum.csv (last accessed 2015-06-02), 2015.
[14] T. Heuss. CKANStats datahub.io RDF Dendrograms - github.com/heussd/CKANstats/tree/master/datahub.io/png (last accessed 2015-06-09), 2015.
[15] T. Heuss. CKANStats Repository - github.com/heussd/CKANstats (last accessed 2015-06-09), 2015.
[16] T. Heuss. LODprobe Source Repository - github.com/heussd/lodprobe (last accessed 2015-06-02), 2015.
[17] A. Isaac, W. Waites, J. Young, and M. Zeng. Library linked data incubator group: Datasets, value vocabularies, and metadata element sets. Technical report, W3C Incubator Group Report, 2005.
[18] M. Morsey, J. Lehmann, S. Auer, and A.-C. N. Ngomo. DBpedia SPARQL Benchmark – Performance Assessment with Real Queries on Real Data. In L. Aroyo, C. Welty, H. Alani, J. Taylor, A. Bernstein, L. Kagal, N. Noy, and E. Blomqvist, editors, *The Semantic Web – ISWC 2011*, number 7031 in Lecture Notes in Computer Science, pages 454–469. Springer Berlin Heidelberg, Jan. 2011.
[19] Open Knowledge Foundation. API guide — CKAN 2.4a documentation, 2013. Last access 2015-05-24.
[20] Open Knowledge Foundation. Page View Tracking — CKAN Data Management System Documentation 2.1a documentation, 2013. Last access 2015-05-24.
[21] Open Knowledge Foundation. User guide — CKAN 2.4a documentation, 2013. Last access 2015-05-24.
[22] Richard Cyganiak. lod-cloud/datahub2void - GitHub, 9 2014. Last access 2014-09-21.
[23] S. Stadtmüller, A. Harth, and M. Grobelnik. Accessing Information About Linked Data Vocabularies with vocab.cc. In J. Li, G. Qi, D. Zhao, W. Nejdl, and H.-T. Zheng, editors, *Semantic Web and Web Science*, Springer Proceedings in Complexity, pages 391–396. Springer New York, Jan. 2013.
[24] Webpage. LODStats - 9960 datasets, 6 2015. Last access 2015-06-09.

QoE Enhancements in IEEE 802.11e EDCA for Video Transmission through Selective Queueing

Najwan Khambari, Bogdan Ghita, David Lancaster, Lingfen Sun
School of Computing, Electronics and Mathematics
Plymouth University
Plymouth, United Kingdom
najwan@utem.edu.my, {bogdan.ghita, david.lancaster, L.Sun}@plymouth.ac.uk

Abstract—This paper proposes a set of performance enhancements techniques aiming to improve the perceived performance of video transmission across the IEEE 802.11e network. The proposed mechanism preserves the video Quality of Experience (QoE) by protecting the I-Frames transmitted as part of the Group of Pictures (GoP) during queue congestion. The method is evaluated using the NS-3 simulator with the Evalvid module and the results demonstrate the video flows will have better Peak Signal to Noise ratio (PSNR) and less video frame drops compared to the original IEEE 802.11e queueing.

Keywords—IEEE 802.11e; EDCA; QoE; NS-3; Evalvid

I. INTRODUCTION

Wireless Local Area network (WLAN) has been in strong and growing demand since the early 1990s [1][2][3] and remains the preferred network access while being widely used [4]. This is due to the low deployment costs, a variety of features, and ease of setup that provides an excellent platform for generic data transfer. As the network becomes more popular, the network load has become a critical issue. WLAN, which was originally designed and responsible to carry Best Effort (BE) services are now being used to carry heavy, real-time and multimedia traffic especially video.

Since the mid-2000s, the demand for video services over the Internet has increased significantly [5]. At the same time, the popularity of the Internet led to integrating video communications into the BE packet networks. Recent statistics showed a sharp increase of wireless video streaming, with wireless access likely to progressively replace wired networks. In 2010, [6] projected that 69% of the mobile traffic are accounted for video traffic. Meanwhile in 2011, [7] reported that video accounts for half of the total Internet traffic and projected that to increase by 2016. These predictions were confirmed in 2014, with users now spending more time watching video on a smartphone in 2014 compared to the previous year (2013) by 19.06% [8]. In 2015, [9] issued a Visual Networking Index (VNI) and predicted increase in video traffic across the Internet from 64% in 2014 to 80% by 2019. An increase of traffic from wireless and mobile devices was also predicted where it will represent 66% of IP traffic by 2019 compared to 46% in 2014.

Transmitting video traffic over dynamic environment such as wireless networks remains a challenging issue in spite of the progress made through the IEEE 802.11e framework and the associated research. Since WLANs are now heavily used to stream multimedia traffic, relying on QoS parameters is no longer sufficient.

In order to evaluate the user-perceived quality, looking to parameters beyond QoS is now vital. Thus, the term of Quality of Experience (QoE) has been introduced to expand the evaluation from the measurement of end-to-end performance at the services level to the impact these parameters have on the users' perception of the transmitted video. This new approach is required in order to define performance measurement while considering the subjective nature of the users [10].

II. RELATED WORKS

In order to fully understand the current state of the art in the area of wireless video QoE, this section will provide an overview of the video encoding process, the wireless queueing, and the efforts made to combine the two concepts in a communication architecture.

A. MPEG4 Group of Pictures (GoP)

MPEG-4 was developed mainly for storing and delivering multimedia content over the Internet [11]. MPEG-4 streams consist of three types of frames, namely I, P, and B, transmitted in a structure called Group of Pictures (GoP).

Fig. 1. The structure of an MPEG-4 Group of Picture

The I-Frames are independent of the rest of the stream, as they do not depend on other frames to allow decoding of the video stream. Meanwhile P-Frames and B-Frames only contain video information updates compared to the I-Frames. Because of their content, P-Frames and B-Frames have smaller sizes in comparison with I-Frames; they are also depending on the content of the I-Frame in order to allow the encoding of the video at the receiver.

B. IEEE 802.11e EDCA

Throughout the years, a lot of effort had been made to enhance the performance of the legacy IEEE 802.11 network. In spite of its benefits, the original IEEE 802.11 standard specification did include a number of inherent challenges including supporting QoS for video traffic. To address this issue, IEEE amended the original IEEE 802.11 and formed Task Group E. This group was assigned to enhance the IEEE 802.11 MAC to expand support for applications with QoS requirements. This resulted to a new amendment known as the IEEE 802.11e.

The IEEE 802.11e amendment introduced two new channel coordination functions: HCF Controlled Channel Access (HCCA) and Enhanced Distributed Channel Access (EDCA). HCCA is based on polling where the Access Point (AP) polls each Mobile Station (MS) to check whether it wants to send any data. In contrast, EDCA is a contention based channel coordination function that requires each MS to compete for accessing the wireless media.

Functionally, EDCA is derived from the legacy Distributed Coordination Function (DCF) of IEEE 802.11, with several enhancements. Four new different Access Categories (AC) namely the AC3, AC2, AC1 and AC0 were introduced, where they were intended to refine the granularity of the queue, based on the traffic priority. AC3 is reserved for voice stream (AC_VO), AC2 for video (AC_VI), AC1 for best effort traffic (AC_BE) and AC0 for background traffic (AC_BK). The priority ranks from the highest to the lowest, respectively. These streams will be treated differently in the EDCA mechanism. In this paper, focus was given on this particular feature where we further refine the AC_VI queue to manage the video traffic better.

The introduction of IEEE 802.11e EDCA has significantly improved the QoS provision for wireless network [12][13] by offering differentiated performance between AC. EDCA has been purposely designed to be selective towards the high priority AC.

However, several issues still need to be addressed before EDCA can really support QoS as well as QoE for video traffic. Multiple ACs in the queue lead to individual ACs competing with each other and can cause internal collision. Meanwhile, the current standard treats all video the same regardless of the content type while no fine prioritization has been given towards the different type of video frames.

C. Previous Works

Over the years, significant amount of work has been done to improve the performance of video traffic in the IEEE 802.11e EDCA.

Several papers improve the video transmission performance by adjusting the parameters of the IEEE 802.11e EDCA mechanism such as the Contention Window (CW), Transmission Opportunity (TXOP) and the Arbitrary Inter-frame Space (AIFS). These alterations reduce the waiting time to access the wireless media for the high priority traffic, but do not exploit the significance of specific traffic type such as video that needs an adaptive treatment due to the nature of its variability in data rates. For example, [14] aimed to enhance the QoS level in EDCA to for medical video communication in order to provide the required medical-grade QoS of various medical applications and ensure accurate visualization of the patient condition. By considering two metrics (packet delay and ratio of late/ receive packets), the AIFS were adjusted to improve network performance.

Rather than enhancements focused on the 802.11 standards, several papers considered a cross-layer approach, individually tagging packets according to their priority level and offering appropriate preference and fairness. As a result, queueing systems may identify the types of the video packets and treat them selectively. The authors of [15] proposed a new static mapping where I-Frame is mapped to AC_VI while P- and B-Frames are mapped to AC_BE and AC_BK respectively. Through this technique, I-Frames are given the highest priority and this prevents them from being dropped whenever the queue is congested. However when the video traffic load is light, channeling P- and B-Frames to AC_BE and AC_BK causes unnecessary delay for the video flow.

An alternative approach was used in [16] by introducing dynamic video frame mapping. The mapping is based on the significance of the video data and the traffic load. In video traffic, problems will arise when there is a sudden burst of video packets where the queue will suddenly be congested. Packets that are incoming toward the queue will have high probability to be dropped. Through this dynamic mapping, any incoming video packet will be channeled to AC_BE or AC_BK if AC_VI is full and video traffic will not interfere with the AC_VO, the highest priority AC. The evaluation tests indicate that the proposed mechanism increases the PSNR for video traffic by 8.11% to 11.80%.

Also in the context of cross layer approaches, [17] introduced a design to ensure better QoE for H.264 with Scalable Video Coding (SVC) video. The proposed mechanism involves three layers - APP, MAC and PHY. The APP and PHY layers are made aware of each other's condition. The receiver will send ACK to indicate whether packets were received correctly. Based on the ACK records, online QoS-QoE mapping was proposed. The PHY layer adapts to provide unequal error protection for each video layer based on the proposed mapping. Meanwhile, the APP layer is updated on the buffer starvation of the channel by the PHY and adjusts its rates accordingly. The simulation scenarios indicate that the architecture successfully avoids buffer starvation while handling channel and buffer fluctuations to achieve a 30% increase in video capacity. However in this experiment, only SVC videos were considered and the exact wireless network technology was not mentioned.

Adaptive Mapping Mechanism (AMM) was introduced in [18], based on the earlier work from [16]. It proposes a number of enhancements, allowing AMM to check the congestion level of all the voice, video, best effort and background queues before assigning video packets to the other queues. The main reason for the enhancement is to stop the video traffic from monopolizing the access control for the station. The study also introduces differentiated queuing depending on frame type, with I-Frames assigned to the highest AC priority, AC_VO and, depending on the mapping control module, P-Frames assigned to AC_VO or AC_VI and B-Frames assigned to AC_VI or AC_BE. Through simulation, the AMM proved to have less packet loss ratio, especially compared to EDCA.

Most of the previous study suggested and agreed that for video transmission, it is important to protect the I-Frames from being dropped. Channeling I-Frames to AC_VO increased the I-Frame's priority. However, P- and B-Frames will still have the same old priority. This means, although the I-Frame arrives first at the receiver, it still needs to wait for the consecutive P and B-Frames to be reconstructed to a video. This will cause delay especially in a scenario where the network is loaded with voice traffic (P and B-Frames needs to give way to the voice traffic). And if the I-Frame does not wait for the P and B-Frames, bandwidth has been wasted to transport the unused P and B-Frames to the receiver.

III. PROPOSED SCHEME

The I-Frame is the most important frame in the GoP of an MPEG-4 video, therefore protecting the I-Frame ensures a high probability of the video quality being preserved. In this paper, focus is given in a scenario where the AC_VI queue is congested. This can occur especially when there is a sudden increase in video flow or when the network traffic is highly loaded.

In this scenario, incoming packets carrying I-Frame information are due to be queued but are dropped due to the queue being full. This is undesirable because the following P- and B-Frames will carry unusable video information, given the I-Frame needed to reconstruct the video is lost. The follow-up P and B frames will not only congest the queue but will also contribute to bandwidth congestion as they do not serve any purpose.

Given the above scenario, the objective of the proposed scheme is to protect the I-Frames from being dropped by discarding the B-Frames from the AC_VI queue during congestion. In a preliminary experiment conducted, we have discovered that B-Frame packets can be dropped or discarded to a certain level without notably affecting the PSNR.

In the proposed mechanism, *MPEG-4 Frame Manager (MFM)*, packets with P- and B-Frame information (Pkt_P and Pkt_B) are queued using the default EDCA queuing mechanism *(DefaultQueue)*, but packets carrying I-Frame information (Pkt_I), are treated differently by going through a two-step queue testing. First is the AC_VI congestion level. If the AC_VI queue is not full, Pkt_I will be queued as usual using *DefaultQueue*. However if the AC_VI queue is full, the second queue testing will take place, which is to check whether there is a Pkt_B of that particular video flow available in the AC_VI to be removed. If it is positive, the Pkt_B will be removed from the queue and will be replaced by the incoming Pkt_I. The mechanism flow chart can be shown as in Fig. 2.

IV. NETWORK SIMULATION SETUP

A simulation study based on NS-3.22 was conducted to test the *MFM* mechanism against *DefaultQueue*. The network scenario is in a wireless infrastructure mode where it consists of four MS and an AP. However, only one sender and one receiver are involved during the course of data transmission. The wireless links use IEEE 802.11e (QoS enabled) and every station is within each other's coverage which means no hidden terminal is involved. Meanwhile, the request to Send/ Clear to Send (RTS/ CTS) mechanism is disabled to minimize the number of control packets involved.

The experiment was conducted using the publicly available video sequence "highway.yuv" [19]. This video was selected because it contains 2000 frames and will most probably cause queue congestion. This is important because the proposed mechanism is intended to address the issue of video queue congestion. The video is in a CIF format with a resolution of 352 x 288.

Evalvid [20] was imported into the NS-3 simulator to simulate real video frames transmission across the simulation scenario. Several other tools were also used for the simulation such as ETMP4, FFMPEG and PSNR to encode/ decode and evaluate the video quality used in the simulation. The video used in this experiment is encoded with a GoP size of 9.

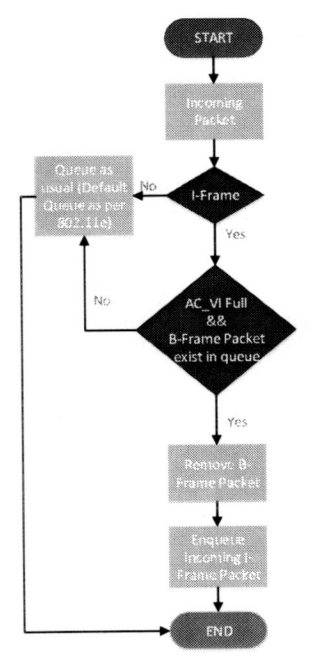

Fig. 2. The flow chart of *MFM* mechanism

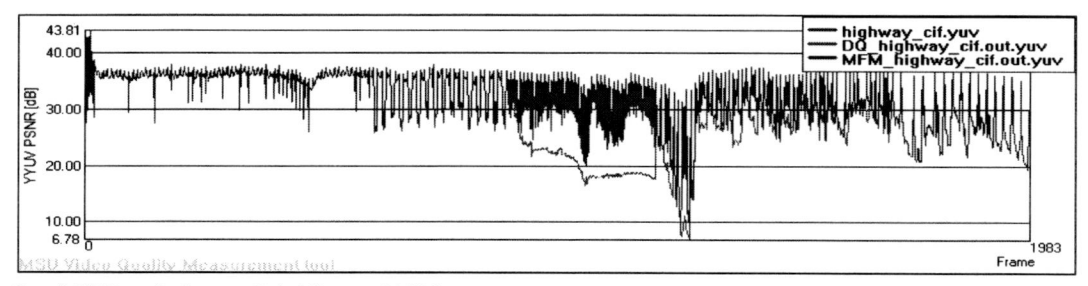

Fig. 3. Overall PSNR overlay between *DefaultQueue* and *MFM*

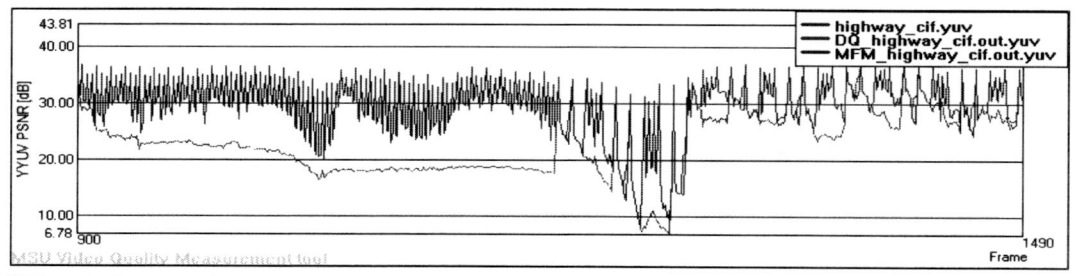

Fig. 4. PSNR overlay between DefaultQueue and MFM for the frames 900-1490.

V. RESULTS AND FINDINGS

Following the simulations, the video streams collected at the receiver are evaluated in terms of metrics analysis and visual comparison between the proposed queueing mechanism and the default queueing mechanism of the IEEE 802.11e. As part of the objective evaluation, Peak Signal to Noise Ratio (PSNR) and Structural Similarity (SSIM) were run against the video at the receiver's end to evaluate the quality. In addition, frame loss was also considered to evaluate the effectiveness of *MFM* in preventing I-Frame packets from being dropped.

A. Metrics analysis

Fig. 3 and Fig. 4 present the PSNR of the reconstructed video stream, following transmission using the default queue of IEEE 802.11e (red) and the proposed *MFM* method (blue). Fig. 3 presents the measured values over the entire video, while Fig. 4 expands on the frame 900 – 1490 interval, which included the most dynamic sequence and therefore was most affected by the encountered congestion loss.

During the course of Frame 900 to 1490, the queue has been congested which has been reflected by the PSNR readings. At this specific range, the proposed mechanism has been activated. Most of the I-Frames that were dropped in the IEEE 802.11e default queueing mechanism are now being recovered in *MFM*. While the PSNR and SSIM reading for *DefaultQueue* has dropped significantly to 23.03 and 0.69 respectively, MFM had a far better PSNR and SSIM reading of 29.20 and 0.84. This is shown as in TABLE I.

TABLE I. OVERAL RESULTS OF THE VIDEO QUALITY AND FRAME LOSS BETWEEN QUEUEDEFAULT AND *MFM*

Mechanism	PSNR Overall	PSNR Specific	SSIM Overall	SSIM Specific	Frame loss (%) I	P	B
DefaultQueue	29.52	23.03	0.82	0.69	36.04	33.63	44.14
MFM	31.43	29.20	0.86	0.84	9.01	33.63	61.56

In terms of frame loss, *MFM* had significantly improved the probability of I-Frame being dropped where only 9% of I-Frames were loss compared to 36.04% as in *DefaultQueue*.

B. Visual Comparison

Fig. 5 presents a visual comparison of the video quality for three different frames. The quality of video delivered using *MFM* significantly improved the video quality in comparison to *DefaultQueue*.

VI. CONCLUSION AND FUTURE WORK

This paper proposes a selective queuing method that enhances the performance of MPEG-4 video transmission in the IEEE 802.11e environment. The mechanism proposed preemptively drops B-Frame packets in the queue during congestion in order to prioritize the I-Frame packets. The validation experiments demonstrated that the proposed mechanism has the ability to provide enhancements in video transmission and thus offers better video QoE in the IEEE 802.11e.

This is a work in progress where in the future development, the proposed system would be able to differentiate the content of the video in a multiple video flow environment and

DefaultQueue	MFM
DefaultQueue	MFM
DefaultQueue	MFM

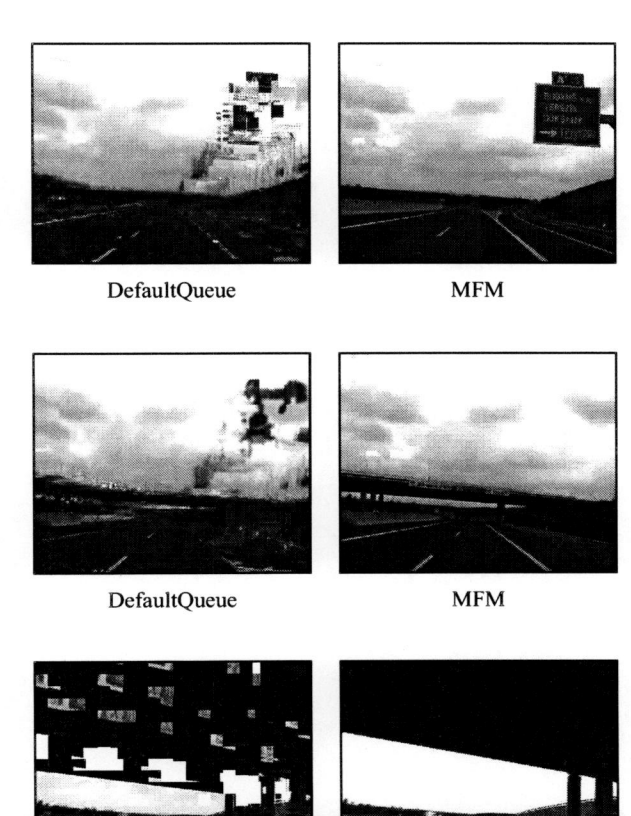

Fig. 5. Visual comparison of the reconstructed video at the receiver's end

prioritize the video frames accordingly. Meanwhile, PSNR is currently being used as the metric to compare the effectiveness of the proposed scheme. Although it is not the most ideal metric to be used to compare QoE, it provides a simple benchmark to compare the effectiveness of the proposed scheme. In the future, subjective metrics such as Mean Opinion Score (MOS) will be taken into account to provide a more realistic result as to the effectiveness of the proposed scheme.

ACKNOWLEDGMENT

This project is part of a PhD research currently being carried out at Centre for Security, Communications and Network Research (CSCAN), Plymouth University, U.K. The deepest gratitude and thanks to Universiti Teknikal Malaysia Melaka (UTeM) and the Malaysian Ministry of Higher Education for funding this PhD research.

REFERENCES

[1] R. Braden, D. Clark, and S. Shenker, "Integrated Services in the Internet Architecture: an Overview," 1994. [Online]. Available: https://tools.ietf.org/html/rfc1633.

[2] A. Khan, L. Sun, and E. Ifeachor, "Content Clustering Based Video Quality Prediction Model for MPEG4 Video Streaming over Wireless Networks," *J. Multimed.*, vol. 4, no. 4, pp. 228–239, Jun. 2009.

[3] M. Arabi, B. Ghita, and X. Wang, "Improving Fairness in Ad Hoc Networks through Collision Rate Control," in *International Network Conference*, 2010, pp. 51–59.

[4] K. Kosek-Szott, M. Natkaniec, S. Szott, A. Krasilov, A. Lyakhov, A. Safonov, and I. Tinnirello, "What's new for QoS in IEEE 802.11?," *IEEE Netw.*, 2013.

[5] V. Vassiliou, P. Antoniou, I. Giannakou, and A. Pitsillides, "Requirements for the Transmission of Streaming Video in Mobile Wireless Networks," in *International Conference on Artificial Neural Network*, 2006, pp. 528–537.

[6] M. Stanley, "Internet Trends," 2010.

[7] Cisco, "Cisco Visual Networking Index: Global Mobile Data Traffic Forecast Update, 2010–2015," 2011.

[8] Nielsen, "The Total Audience Report," 2014.

[9] Cisco, "Cisco Visual Networking Index: Forecast and Methodology, 2014 – 2019," 2015.

[10] R. Jain, "Media vision - Experience isn't only screen deep," *IEEE Multimed.*, vol.10, no. 1, pp. 80–81, Jan. 2003.

[11] S. Lingfen, M. Is-Haka, J. Emmanuel, and I. Emmanuel, *Guide to Voice and Video over IP*. Springer, 2013.

[12] A. Anitha and J. Jayakumari, "PERFORMANCE ANALYSIS OF WLAN UNDER VARIABLE NUMBER OF NODES USING THE ADJUSTABLE PARAMETERS IN EDCA," *J. Theor. Appl. Inf. Technol.*, vol. 60, no. 2, pp. 351–357, 2014.

[13] A. Abu-khadrah, Z. Zakaria, M. Othman, and U. Teknikal, "Evaluate QOS parameters for VOIP using IEEE 802.11 (DCF) and IEEE 802.11e (EDCA)," *Aust. J. Basic Appl. Sci.*, vol. 8, no. January, pp. 265–272, 2014.

[14] S. Son, K. Park, and E. Park, "Adaptive tuning of IEEE 802.11e EDCA for medical-grade QoS," in *2013 Fifth International Conference on Ubiquitous and Future Networks (ICUFN)*, 2013, no. 2, pp. 650–651.

[15] A. Ksentini, M. Naimi, and A. Gueroui, "Toward an improvement of H.264 video transmission over IEEE 802.11e through a cross-layer architecture," *IEEE Commun. Mag.*, vol.44, no. 1, pp. 107–114, Jan. 2006.

[16] C.-H. Lin, C.-K. Shieh, C.-H. Ke, N. K. Chilamkurti, and S. Zeadally, "An Adaptive Cross-Layer Mapping Algorithm for MPEG-4 Video Transmission over IEEE 802.11e WLAN," *Telecommun. Syst.*, vol. 42, no. 3–4,

pp. 223–234, Jul. 2009.

[17] A. Abdel Khalek, C. Caramanis, and R. W. Heath, "A Cross-Layer Design for Perceptual Optimization Of H.264/SVC with Unequal Error Protection," *IEEE J. Sel. Areas Commun.*, vol. 30, no. 7, pp. 1157–1171, Aug. 2012.

[18] X. X.-W. Yao, W. Wang, S. Yang, Y. Cen, X. X.-W. Yao, T. Pan, and J. Camp, "IPB-frame Adaptive Mapping Mechanism for Video Transmission over IEEE 802.11e WLANs," *ACM SIGCOMM Comput. Commun. Rev.*, vol. 44, no. 2, pp. 5–12, Apr. 2014.

[19] "YUV QCIF reference videos (lossless H.264 encoded)." [Online]. Available: http://www2.tkn.tu-berlin.de/research/evalvid/qcif.html. [Accessed: 15-Feb-2016].

[20] J. Klaue, B. Rathke, and A. Wolisz, "EvalVid - A Framework for Video Transmission and Quality Evaluation," in *International Conference on Modelling Techniques and Tools for Computer Performance Evaluation*, 2003, no. September.

Low Complexity Channel Estimation Method for IEEE 802.11p Vehicle Communications

Chi-Min Li
Dep. of Communications, Navigation and Control Engineering,
National Taiwan Ocean University, Taiwan

Feng-Ming Wu
Dep. of Communications, Navigation and Control Engineering,
National Taiwan Ocean University, Taiwan

Abstract—Modern Intelligent Transportation System (ITS) uses the wireless communication technologies to increase the traffic safety and the transportation efficiency. However, the doppler effect and the multipath fading problems severely attenuate the received signal in the vehicle communication environments. Therefore, channel estimation is a critical issue should be solved properly to improve the Bit Error Rate (BER) performance at the receiver. Basically, ITS adopted the IEEE802.11p standard as its protocol and it defines the preamble with a specific format to conduct the channel estimation. Besides, four pilot subcarriers transmitted along with the Orthogonal Frequency Division Multiplexing (OFDM) system can also be used during the channel estimation. In this paper, a low computational complexity channel estimation method is proposed for the IEEE802.11p vehicle communications. The proposed method belongs to the frequency domain channel estimation and uses the preamble and pilot subcarriers defined in IEEE802.11p for the initial estimation and the time-varying adjustment for the channel. The method has the low-complexity advantage and a satisfactory BER performance compared with the related Cyclic Prefix (CP) based channel estimation method.

Keywords—Channel Estimation; IEEE802.11p; OFDM

I. INTRODUCTION

Intelligent Transportation System (ITS) is a smart system that integrates the telecommunication, information, electronics technologies, and traffic management to efficiently manipulate public transportation in many modern metropolises. It adopts the mobile communication techniques to increase the traffic and the transportation efficiency in many applications such as the vehicle-to-vehicle communications (V2V) and the vehicle-to-road communications (V2R). For both the V2V and V2R communications, the signal transmitted at the Transmitter (Tx) will suffer the severe channel distortion due to the doppler effect and the multipath fading channel. To decode the transmitted symbols correctly, Receiver (Rx) has to conduct the channel estimation properly to improve the Bit Error Rate (BER) performance for further information manipulation.

ITS has adopted the IEEE802.11p standard as its protocol [1]. Besides, IEEE 802.11p also known as the Wireless Access in the Vehicular Environment (WAVE) can be applied in the Dedicated Short Range Communications (DSRC). Basically, IEEEE 802.11p is an Orthogonal Frequency Division Multiplexing (OFDM) system with the frequency band from 5.850GHz to 5.925GHz. The data rate can up to 3Mbps to 27Mbps within the coverage 300m to 1000m. Six data channels and one control channel have been defined in the IEEE 802.11p. Each channel consists of 64 sub-carriers within the 10MHz frequency band. In fact, 802.11p is an extension from the commercial IEEE 802.11a Wi-Fi system. However, the Guard Interval (GI) for the 802.11p is twice as the IEEE 802.11a that can be very helpful to avoid the Inter-symbol Interference (ISI) for the multipath vehicular communication environments. Table.1 lists the comparisons between the 802.11a and the 802.11p systems.

Table.1 Comparisons of the IEEE 802.11a and IEEE802.11p

Parameters	IEEE802.11a	IEEE802.11p	Changes
Bit rate (Mbit/s)	6,9,12,18,24,36,48,54	3,4,5,6,9,12,18,24,27	Half
Modulation mode	BPSK, QPSK, 16QAM, 64QAM	BPSK, QPSK, 16QAM, 64QAM	No change
Code rate	1/2, 2/3, 3/4	1/2, 2/3, 3/4	No change
Number of subcarriers	52	52	No change
Guard Time	0.8μs	1.6μs	Double
Symbol duration	4μs	8μs	Double
FFT period	3.2μs	6.4μs	Double
Preamble duration	3.2μs	6.4μs	Double
Subcarrier spacing	0.3125 MHz	0.15625 MHz	Half

In the literatures, many channel estimation for an OFDM system have been proposed to conduct the channel compensation at the Rx. Channel estimation can be achieved in the frequency domain or in the time domain [2]. The frequency domain estimations include the Inverse Fast Fourier Transform (IFFT) [3] and the Minimized Mean Square Error (MMSE) method [4] while the Finite and Infinite Length MMSE estimation [5] and the Linear Interpolation estimation [5] can be performed in the time domain [6].

In IEEE 802.11p, a pre-defined preamble with specific format has been defined to conduct the channel estimation (Fig.1). Besides, four pilot subcarriers transmitted along with the OFDM system can also be used during the channel estimation. In this paper, a low complexity channel estimation method based on the Correlation Invariant (CI) assumption within two successive training preambles is proposed for the IEEE802.11p vehicle communications. The proposed method belongs to the frequency domain channel estimation and uses the preamble and pilot subcarriers for the initial estimation and the time-varying adjustment for the channel. The paper is organized as follows, Section II describes a similar time domain Cyclic Prefix-based (CP) channel estimations and the proposed CI scheme in detail. Performance analysis of the proposed CI method and the CP-based method are evaluated in

Section III. Finally, some conclusions for this paper are summarized in Section IV.

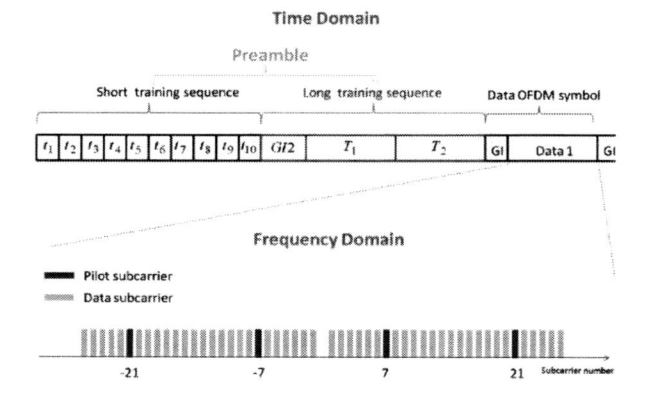

Fig.1 IEEE802.11p Preamble and Data Format

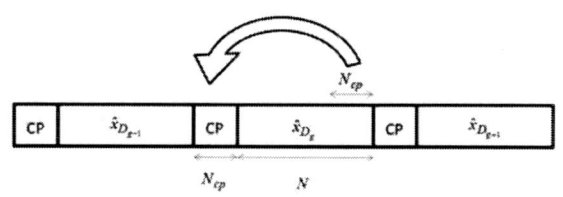

Fig.3 Illustration of the CP-based Channel Estimation

II. METHODS DESCRIPTIONS

In this section, the time domain Cyclic-Prefix (CP) based channel estimation and the proposed CI channel estimation methods are presented. Both methods use the preamble in time domain to conduct the channel estimation for the initial prediction. Then, the CP-based method adopts the duplicated feature of the CP with the tail sequences in OFDM symbols while the proposed CI method uses the correlation invariant assumption to complete the channel estimation (Fig.2).

Eq.(1) is the N-point Discrete Fourier Transform (DFT) of the received symbol, where N is the number of subcarrier for the OFDM system. Besides, if the channel frequency response can be estimated via the preamble of the previous OFDM, the estimated transmitted symbol can be determined as

$$\hat{x}_{D_g}[n] = \frac{1}{N}\sum_{n=0}^{N-1}\hat{X}_{D_g}(k)e^{\frac{2\pi jkn}{N}} \quad (2)$$

$$\hat{X}_{D_g}(k) = \frac{Y_{D_g}(k)}{\hat{H}_{D_{g-1}}(k)} \quad (3)$$

Where $\hat{H}_{D_{g-1}}(k)$ is the estimated channel at the previous time $g-1$. After determining the transmitted symbols, Rx has to reconstruct a $N_{cp} \times N_{cp}$ matrix M_{cp_g} shown in Eq.(3) and uses Eq.(4), Eq.(5) to complete the frequency response estimation of the channel $\hat{H}_{D_g}(k)$. Note that usually a zero-padding step is carried out in Eq.(5), N_{cp} is the length of sample for the inserted CP and y_{cp_g} denotes the received signal for the CP at time g.

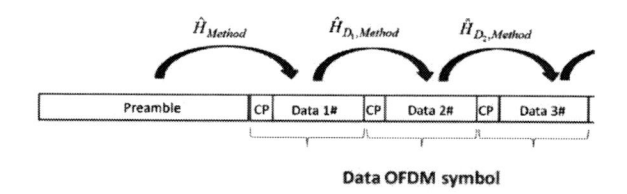

Fig.2 Channel Estimation Scheme for the CP-based and the Proposed CI Method

A. Cyclic-Prefix (CP) based Channel Estimation [5]

To avoid the Inter-Symbol Interference (ISI) due to the wireless transmission, OFDM system has to insert a Guard Interval (GI) at the beginning of each OFDM symbol before transmission. Usually, the GI can be the Cyclic-Prefix (CP) of the OFDM to avoid the ISI distortion (Fig.3).

Let the received OFDM symbol at time g be y_{D_g}, the corresponding frequency response of the received symbol can be expressed as

$$Y_{D_g}(k) = \sum_{n=0}^{N-1} y_{D_g}[n]e^{-\frac{2\pi jkn}{N}} \quad (1)$$

$$M_{cp_g} = \begin{bmatrix} \hat{x}_{D_g}[N-N_{cp}] & \hat{x}_{D_{g-1}}[N] & \hat{x}_{D_{g-1}}[N-1] & \cdots & \cdots & \hat{x}_{D_{g-1}}[N-(N_{cp}+1)] \\ \hat{x}_{D_g}[N-N_{cp}-1] & \hat{x}_{D_g}[N-N_{cp}] & \hat{x}_{D_{g-1}}[N] & & & \hat{x}_{D_{g-1}}[N-(N_{cp}+2)] \\ \vdots & & \hat{x}_{D_g}[N-N_{cp}-1] & \hat{x}_{D_g}[N-N_{cp}] & & \vdots \\ \hat{x}_{D_g}[N-2] & \vdots & & \hat{x}_{D_g}[N-N_{cp}-1] & \ddots & \hat{x}_{D_{g-1}}[N-1] \\ \hat{x}_{D_g}[N-1] & \hat{x}_{D_g}[N-2] & \vdots & & \ddots & \hat{x}_{D_{g-1}}[N] \\ \hat{x}_{D_g}[N] & \hat{x}_{D_g}[N-1] & \hat{x}_{D_g}[N-2] & \cdots & \cdots & \hat{x}_{D_g}[N-N_{cp}] \end{bmatrix}_{N_{cp} \times N_{cp}} \quad (3)$$

$$\hat{h}_{D_g} = (M_{cp_g}{}^H M_{cp_g})^{-1} M_{cp_g}{}^H y_{cp_g} \quad (4)$$

$$\hat{h}'_{D_g} = [\hat{h}_{D_g}{}^T \; 0_{N-N_{cp}}]$$

$$\hat{H}_{D_g} = \sum_{n=0}^{N-1} \hat{h}'_{D_g} e^{-\frac{2\pi j}{N}kn} \quad (5)$$

B. Proposed Correlation Invariant (CI) Channel Estimation Method

The main concern of the CP-based channel estimation is that there will be an error propagation problem of the estimated transmitted symbols to cause the estimated channel response inaccurately. This comes from the fact that the generated M_{cp_g} matrix has to take the estimated OFDM symbols into consideration. Once these estimated OFDM symbols are in errors, it will greatly degrade the final channel estimation accuracy. And this problem will become more and more seriously if the number of the OFDM symbols between two successive preambles is increasing. Another drawback for this method is the intensive computational complexity required due to the inverse matrix calculation in Eq.(4).

In most of the OFDM systems, after sending the preamble to conduct the initial channel estimation, some pilot sub-carriers are transmitted along with the OFDM data symbol afterward. For example, Long Term Evolution (LTE) and IEEE 802.11a Wi-Fi systems have the Reference Signal (RS) or pilot sub-carriers transmitted with the OFDM symbols. It is the same for the IEEE802.11p vehicular system. Therefore, it is reasonable and intuitively that after the preamble conducts the initial channel estimation and synchronization, the following RS or pilot sub-carriers can help to mitigate the varying timing characteristic of the multi-path fading channel.

Fundamental to the proposed method is the assumption that the correlations between the data sub-carriers with respect to the nearest pilot sub-carrier are unchanged during the two successive preambles. The validity of this assumption comes from the fact that the coherent time of the wireless channel is proportional to the inverse of the maximum of the Doppler shift [7]. For example, if there is a high speed rail train with 300 km/hr speed, the maximum Doppler shift is 1.611 KHz in 5.8GHz carrier and the coherent time of such scenario is 0.62 msec approximately. In this 0.62msec interval, the fading or the frequency response of the channel can be regarded as invariant or highly correlated.

The proposed channel estimation method is conducted within the coherent time of the considered channel. The preamble is used for the initial channel estimation and calculates the correlation coefficients between the pilot sub-carriers with the nearby data sub-carriers via Eq.(6).

$$C_k = \frac{\hat{H}_k \hat{H}_p^{'}}{|\hat{H}_p|^2} \quad (6)$$

In Eq.(6), p and k denote the index of the pilot and its nearby data-subcarriers. Then, Rx uses the pilot to estimate the exact frequency responses during the transmission of the OFDM symbols at these pilot sub-carriers and predict the response for the data sub-carriers with the help of the correlation coefficients via Eq.(7).

$$\hat{H}_{CI}(k) = C_k \times H_p \quad (7)$$

An example based on the IEEE 802.11p OFDM system can be depicted as Fig.4. The pilot sub-carriers are located at the -21, -7, 7, 21 sub-carriers. First of all, using the preamble to estimate the whole channel frequency response and calculate the correlation coefficients for the pilot sub-carrier with its nearby data sub-carriers enclosed in the dashed region. Then, Rx uses the pilots during the following OFDM data symbol to estimate the exact frequency response at these pilot sub-carriers, and predicts the response via Eq.(7) at the data sub-carriers according to the correlation estimated at the preamble.

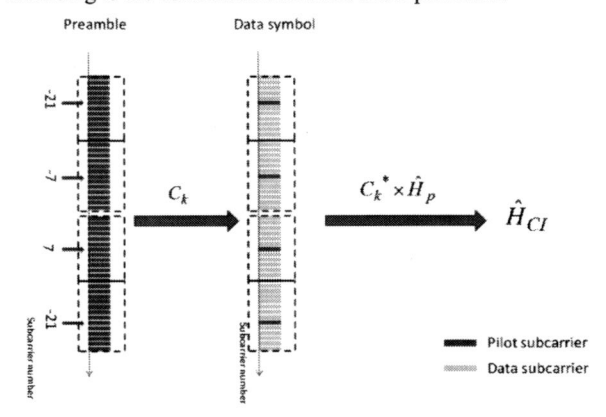

Fig.4 Illustration of the Proposed CI Channel Estimation

III. SIMULATION RESULTS

In this section, BER performance analysis of the proposed CI method and the CP-based method are evaluated under the time-invariant and time-varying fading channels. Table.2 lists the simulation parameter. It can be noted that with these parameters, the channel can be assumed highly correlated within 0.62 msec which proportional to 155 OFDM symbols duration. The channel model in this simulation is provided by Table.3 [5]. Besides, computational complexity of the proposed method is also provided.

Table.2 Simulation Parameters

Parameters	Value
Number of multipath (L)	8
Modulation	QPSK
Number of Subcarrier(N)	52
Carrier Frequency	5.8GHz
Speed of the Mobile	0, 300km/hr
Guard Time	0.8μs
Symbol duration	4μs
FFT period	3.2μs
Preamble duration	3.2μs
Subcarrier spacing	0.3125 MHz

Table.3 Channel Model [5]

Tap	Delay (ns)	Power (dB)
1	0	0, Rician, K=3.3 dB
2	100	-9.3
3	200	-14.0
4	300	-18.0
5	400	-19.4
6	500	-24.9
7	600	-27.5
8	700	-29.8

A. BER Analysis

Fig.5 and Fig.6 are the BER performance for the CP-based and the proposed CI channel estimation methods under the time-invariant multipath fading channel in Table.3. The number of the OFDM data symbols between two successive preambles changes from 2 to 32. In Fig.5, it is clear that the CP-based method has the serious error propagation method that will degrade the accuracy of the estimated channel and cause the BER performance to be very poor if the number of the OFDM symbols between two successive preamble is increasing. However, in Fig.6, we can note that if the channel condition is highly correlated within two successive preambles, the proposed CI method outperforms the CP-based method and has almost the same performance regardless the number of the OFDM data symbols. Fig.7 is the case if the speed of the mobile is 300Km/hr, and the number of the OFDM symbols between two successive preambles is 2. It shows that even in time-varying fading channel, the proposed method still has a better performance than the CP-based method.

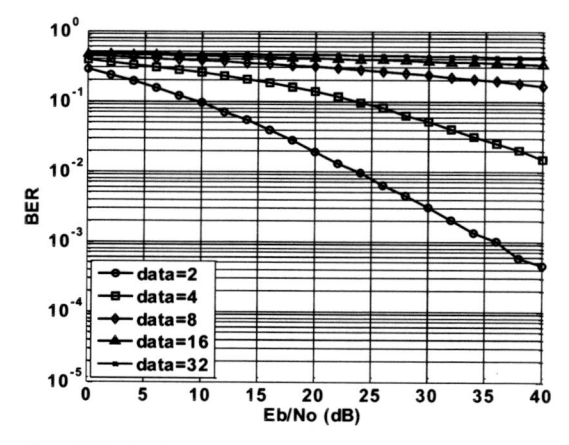

Fig.5 BER Performance of the CP-based Channel Estimation

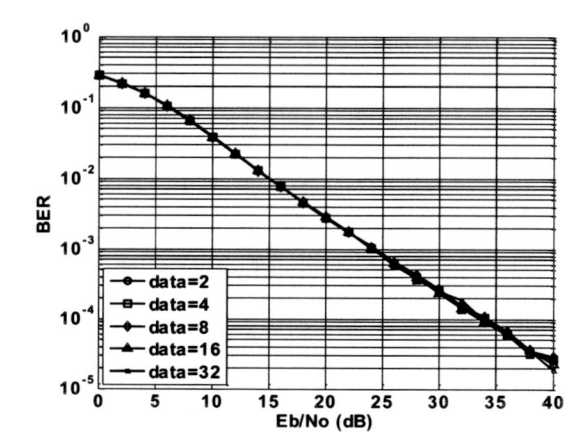

Fig.6 BER Performance of the Proposed CI Channel Estimation

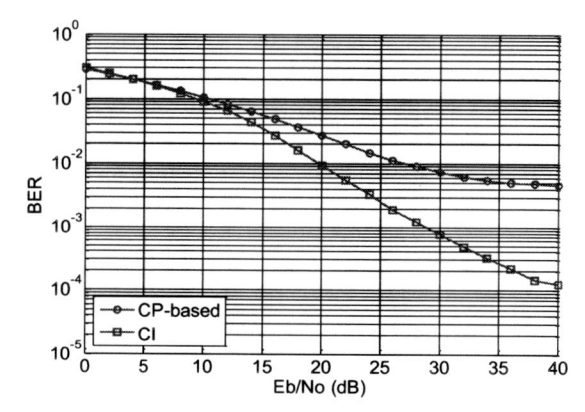

Fig.7 BER Comparison of the Proposed CI and CP-based Method (Mobile Speed=300Km/hr)

B. Complexity Analysis

The main contribution of the proposed method is the low computational complexity advantage. Since that the procedure of the CP-based method follows from Eq.(1) to Eq.(5), define C^{FFT} be the computation complexity to conduct the N-point DFT, G is the number of OFDM symbols between two successive preambles, N_{cp} is the number of sample for the inserted CP and N_u is the number of sub-carriers except the null sub-carriers. Assume also the computation complexity for the product and summation are the same, the CP-based method requires approximately $G(3 \times C^{FFT} + 4N_{cp}^3 + 3/2(N_{cp}^2 + N_{cp}) + N + 1)$ computations while the proposed CI method requires only $3N_u + G(C^{FFT} + N_u)$ in computations for the channel estimation within two successive preambles. Take the IEEE802.11p for example, the number of total sub-carriers is $N = 64$, the number of sample for CP is $N_{cp} = 16$, the number of sub-carriers except the null sub-carriers is $N_u = 52$, and $C^{FFT} \approx N\log_2 N = 384$, if $G = 4$, the proposed CI method requires only less than 6% compared with the CP-based method that is a huge reduction in the computation complexity.

IV. CONCLUSIONS

In this paper, a low complexity channel estimation method is proposed for the IEEE802.11p vehicle communications. The proposed method belongs to the frequency domain channel estimation and uses the preamble and pilot subcarriers for the initial estimation and the time-varying adjustment for the channel. Compared with the relative CP-based method, the method has the low-complexity advantage and the good BER performance. It requires only less than 6% computational complexity compared with the CP-based method. Since all these calculations can be easily conducted at the Rx, the proposed method can be easily and efficiently applied to the channel estimation for vehicle communications.

REFERENCES

[1] IEEE Standard for Information technology-- Local and metropolitan area networks-- Specific requirements-- Part 11: Wireless LAN Medium Access Control (MAC) and Physical Layer (PHY) Specifications Amendment 6: Wireless Access in Vehicular Environments,"IEEE Std 802.11p-2010 (Amendment to IEEE Std 802.11-2007 as amended by IEEE Std 802.11k-2008, IEEE Std 802.11r-2008, IEEE Std 802.11y-2008, IEEE Std 802.11n-2009, and IEEE Std 802.11w-2009), July 15 2010, pp.1,51,.

[2] Supplement to IEEE Standard for Information Technology - Telecommunications and Information Exchange Between Systems - Local and Metropolitan Area Networks - Specific Requirements. Part 11: Wireless LAN Medium Access Control (MAC) and Physical Layer (PHY) Specifications: High-Speed Physical Layer in the 5 GHz Band," IEEE Std 802.11a-1999 , 1999.

[3] Fernandez, J.A., Stancil, D.D., Fan Bai , "Dynamic channel equalization for IEEE 802.11p waveforms in the vehicle-to-vehicle channel", 2010 48th Annual Conf. on Communication, Control, and Computing, Allerton, Sept. 29 2010-Oct. 1 2010, pp.542-551.

[4] Chi-Sheng Lin, Jia-Chin Lin, "Improved time-domain channel estimation techniques in IEEE 802.11p environments," 2010 7th International Sym. on Communication Systems Networks and Digital Signal Processing (CSNDSP),pp.437,442, 21-23.

[5] Syafei, W.A., Nishijo, K., Nagao, Y., Kurosaki, M., Ochi, H., "Adaptive Channel Estimation using Cyclic Prefix for Single Carrier Wireless System with FDE," 10th International Conf. on Advanced Communication Technology, Feb. 2008, vol.2, no., pp.1032,1035, 17-20.

[6] Chi-Min Li, Feng-Ming Wu, "A Modified Time Domain Least Square Channel Estimation for the Vehicular Communications. Lecture Notes in Computer Science, LNCS 9502, pp.285-293. Dec, 2015

[7] Wireless Communications, Principle and Practice, 2nd Edition, T. S. Rappaport, Prentice Hall, 2002

A Framework for OpenFlow-like Policy-based Routing in Hybrid Software Defined Networks

Anshuman Mishra*, Deven Bansod[†], K Haribabu[‡]
*Dept. of Electrical and Electronics Engineering
[†][‡]Dept. of Computer Science and Information Systems
Birla Institute of Technology and Science, Pilani, India
{f2012074*, f2012316[†], khari[‡]}@pilani.bits-pilani.ac.in

Abstract—Software Defined Networks (SDNs) provide a centralized view and allow extensive programmability of the network. They separate the control and data planes opening up immense scope in developing low cost control and management applications to operate the network. Yet, network administrators are ambivalent to revamp their entire network hardware to bring in SDN-compatible switches. This leads to the need for developing models for gradual adaptation of SDN technology. In this paper, we present a framework which allows for policy implementations based on all OpenFlow version 1.4 specified match fields, over legacy Layer 3 devices. This would enable the legacy networks to reap the benefits of SDN in an incremental, controlled and consistent manner.

Keywords—Software Defined Networks, Hybrid SDN, Policy Framework, Legacy Devices, OpenFlow

I. INTRODUCTION

Software Defined Networks (SDNs) extend a centralized control of the entire network to the network administrator. This enables easy configuration of network policies and security measures in order to manage the traffic in the network. Improved visibility of the network leads to a substantial reduction in operational costs and allows for rapid and more dynamic provisioning of resources. It also offers faster recovery from link failures and makes traffic engineering much simpler. Separation of the control and data planes provides an abstraction, opening up possibilities for development of control applications to manage the network.

Despite the manifest benefits that SDN has to offer, network administrators are ambivalent towards upgrading their entire network architecture to incorporate SDN-enabled devices. The transition to SDN requires investment in new hardware along with remodeling of organisational structure to adapt to a new form of network management and application development. These impediments are the reason that the adaptation of SDN technology is meagre at best.

The need of the hour is a model which could provide SDN-like control over the network, without the need to completely revamp the entire network hardware. Vissicchio, et al. [1] have identified the research challenges and opportunities in such hybrid networks. They illustrate how SDN promises to simplify the design, operation and control of networks. At the same time they elucidate various challenges involved, such as incremental deployment, robustness and scalability that hinder full scale deployment of SDN.

In this paper, we present a framework which enables management of network traffic through the addition of some SDN-enabled switches alongside the existing legacy devices. The model provides an interface to implement SDN-like policies based on the OpenFlow [2] version 1.4 supported match fields, over the legacy devices. Each subnet within the network is required to be connected to at least one SDN compatible switch which in turn links it to the legacy Layer 3 network, though multiple subnets can connect to a single SDN-enabled switch. The SDN switch provides a gateway to monitor, control and modify the packets flowing in and out of the directly-connected subnet(s).

Even in very large networks with IP ranges analogous to class A (before CIDR), a vast pool of IP addresses remains *unused* from the perspective of the network (see Table I). Our idea aims to exploit this abundance of unused IP addresses available in the network in order to implement SDN-like policies without the need to fully upgrade the network to support SDN.

The paper is divided into the following sections: Section II reviews some existing literature relevant to the deployment of SDN and hybrid SDN networks. Section III presents the design of our model and outlines the algorithms used in the controller modules. Section IV describes the experimental setup and some policy implementation examples using the model. Section V concludes the discussion and explores the scope for future work.

II. RELATED WORK

Several efforts have been made to facilitate the transition from legacy networks to pure SDN networks. Lu et al. proposed HybNet [3] as an abstraction layer on top of a centralized controller and non-SDN switches so that it can coordinate the communication between them. Panopticon [4] provides a software solution to determine the optimal locations for adding SDN compatible devices to achieve a network wide control in hybrid networks. ClosedFlow [5] utilizes the functionalities of proprietary devices to implement OpenFlow-like control using routers which support features like Access Control Lists (ACLs) and route-maps. The implementation is limited to devices which support the given functionalities. Further, it focuses only on emulating the basic required aspects of OpenFlow and does not provide for policy implementation based on all OpenFlow supported fields. A layer-2 solution

Telekinesis was developed by Jin, et al. [6] but it failed to provide a generalisation for a similar implementation over layer 3. In this paper, we present a framework which allows for network wide SDN-like control over Layer 3 devices and supporting policies based on all OpenFlow version 1.4 specified match fields.

III. DESIGN

Deriving inspiration from the prior work done in this field, we propose an interface through which SDN-like control can be exercised in a hybrid SDN network. It supports policy implementations of various forms, providing extensive control and programmability of the network. The framework also allows for traffic engineering applications to work over it with a degree of delay incurred in updating the routing and flow tables.

Majority of routing protocols in legacy networks are constrained to work based on matching destination IP prefixes only. This leaves the network administrators with little flexibility to modulate network traffic based on any other criterion. To resolve this constraint, we make use of limited number of SDN compatible switches to match policy requirements. These policies are mapped onto a new set of destination IP addresses chosen from the pool of unused (free) IP addresses [See Table I for number of Free IPs available]. Simultaneously, static routes are installed in the legacy L3 devices along the path taken by the packets matching the policy using a custom driver script. The rest of the routing happens through the legacy network, which is able to route the traffic based on this new destination IP address. Finally, before reaching the destination subnet, another SDN switch maps the destination IP back to the original destination IP address of the packet. The flow entries for mapping (in the SDN switch at the source subnet) and reverse mapping (in the SDN switch at the destination subnet) are installed at the same time.

A. Model

We model the mapping of destination IPs onto the range of free/unused IPs in terms of the *limiting factors* that these mappings would bring in. A *policy path* is defined as the path which a packet would follow if it matches a certain policy. This path would be a collection of legacy routers and two SDN switches. It would start at the SDN switch directly connected to the source subnet and end at the SDN switch directly connected to the destination subnet.

Assumptions:
A.1 Topology requirements : Every subnet is connected to router(s) / L3 devices through at least 1 SDN switch.
A.2 Hybrid network before the introduction of any custom policy is functioning correctly.
A.3 The controller is aware of the details of the entire network topology.

$$\sum_{k=1}^{N} p^k = P_{total} \quad (1)$$

$$\forall k \in S, H_{src}^k + E_{non-map}^k + \sum_{i=1}^{p_k} H_{dest}^i \leq F_{max} \quad (2)$$

TABLE I: Statistics of reserved and available IPs

Statistics of reserved and available IPs		
Reserved Block address	**Address Count**	**Reference**
10.0.0.0/8	16,777,216	RFC 1918 [7]
100.64.0.0/10	4,194,304	RFC 6598 [8]
127.0.0.0/8	16,777,216	RFC 990 [9]
169.254.0.0/16	65,536	RFC 3927 [10]
172.16.0.0/12	1,048,576	RFC 1918 [7]
192.0.0.0/24	256	RFC 5736 [11]
192.0.2.0/24	256	RFC 5737 [12]
192.88.99.0/24	256	RFC 3068 [13]
192.168.0.0/16	65,536	RFC 1918 [7]
198.18.0.0/15	131,072	RFC 2544 [14]
198.51.100.0/24	256	RFC 5737 [12]
203.0.113.0/24	256	RFC 5737 [12]
224.0.0.0/40	268,435,456	RFC 5771 [15]
240.0.0.0/4	268,435,455	RFC 6890 [16]
255.255.255.255/32	1	RFC 6890 [16]
Total Reserved	**592,708,864**	–
Class A	**16,777,216**	–
Total Unavailable	**609,486,070**	–
Available for Re-map use	**3,685,481,226**	*Free IPs*

$$\forall j \in L, R_{def}^j + R_{IP-clashes}^j + p^j \leq T_{max} \quad (3)$$

$$\sum_{k=1}^{M} H_{dst}^k \leq U_{max} \quad (4)$$

where

- p^k - Number of policies at source SDN switch k
- P_{total} - Total number of Policies in the network from any source to any destination
- N - Number of new SDN switches, synonymous to number of subnets in the network as per the assumption A.1
- S - Set of SDN switches (refer to assumption A.1)
- H_{src}^k - Number of IPs in the subnet directly connected to the kth SDN switch
- $E_{non-map}^k$ - Number of flow entries not used for IP mapping in the kth SDN switch
- H_{dest}^i - Number of IPs in the destination subnet of the ith policy
- F_{max} - Maximal number of flow-entry tuples that can be added in an SDN switch
- L - Set of legacy routers/L3 devices in the core of the network, where we want to implement the policies
- R_{def}^j - Number of routes present in the routing table of the jth router/ L3 device for legacy functioning of the network
- $R_{IP-clashes}^j$ - Number of routes present in the routing table of the jth router/ L3 device for mappings that handle IP clashes
- p^j - Number of policy paths through j[th] legacy router
- T_{max} - Maximal number of IPv4 routes that can be added in a router in L
- M - Total number of unique paths in the network from any source to any destination
- H_{dst}^k - Number of IPs in the destination subnet of the kth path

- U_{max} - Maximum count of Free/unused IPs available in the network

Equation 1 adds up the number of policies implemented on each subnet as source to get the total number of policies currently implemented in the entire network.

Equation 2 deals with the limits on size of flow tables in the SDN switches. It involves H_{src}^{k} which is the number of entries required for reverse mapping the changed destination IP to the host IP at the destination SDN switch, $E_{non-map}^{k}$ and the summation of number of IP addresses in all the destination subnets for which unique policy paths have been defined from source S^k. The sum of these terms constitutes the total number of flows required in the SDN switches for the implementation of the policies and thus, should be less than the flow table size F_{max}. This sets a limit on the maximum number of policies which can be implemented concurrently in the network.

Similarly, **Equation 3** deals with limits imposed due to the size of routing tables in the L3 devices. It states that for every legacy router/L3 switch in the network, the sum of normal routes, routes required to resolve for Internet IP clash (refer to Section III-C) and number of policy paths passing through any given router should be less than its supported routing table size T_{max}.

Equation 4 suggests that the total IPs used for mapping, summed over all the policies implemented should be always less than the total available IPs (U_{max}).

As per the free IP address statistics presented in Table I, it is clear that even for Class A networks, the number of free IP addresses available would easily exceed the number of IP addresses required for the mapping process in a practical scenario. Moreover, the routing table size (T_{max}) is generally around 500K - 1M for a standard Cisco router [17]. Thus, even under an assumption that the legacy routes already occupy 50% of the routing tables, the size of routing tables would not pose much of a limit on the number of paths through a given router (p^j).

The number of different policy paths that an administrator can specify from a source subnet would realistically be limited only by the size of the flow table in the SDN switches. The general size of flow table is assumed to be dependent on the switch. The widely used Open vSwitch [18] supports about 500K - 1M flow entries while NoviFlow 2122 [19](an OpenFlow enabled hardware switch) supports around 125K-1M.

The equations only present constraints imposed on the total number of policies which can be concurrently implemented through the proposed framework. The terms can be viewed in a generic quantitative manner and evaluating exact values for the terms is not necessary for the implementation of the framework.

B. Controller Modules

For the implementation of the model on a network, the controller runs a few modules:

- **IP Range Allocator** :- This module manages the available IP pool, deciding which IP ranges should be allocated in order to minimize the number of IP clashes. It makes use of the network statistics from the NetStats Aggregator (discussed later) for optimal allocation.

- **Policy Translator** :- This module performs the actual mapping of a new policy to a corresponding range of IP addresses. It first verifies if the requested policy path is consistent, has all links in up state and does not contain a loop. The IP range allocated is directly mapped onto the destination subnet in order to reduce the number of flows required at the destination SDN switch.

- **Twin-flow pusher** :- After the mapping is done, this module installs flows in SDN switches at the source (for mapping) as well as the destination subnet (for reverse mapping). Along with modification of the destination IP address, the module also modifies the destination MAC address to that of the first router/L3 device in the policy path (similar to when a host sends a packet to its default gateway).

- **Legacy Route Modulator** :- The legacy devices in the network would not be aware of routing details for the new mapped IPs. This module generates static routes and installs them into the routers on the desired policy path to be implemented. The routes are configured by remote access using Telnet [20] or SSH [21]. The process can be automated using custom drivers.

- **NetStats Aggregator** :- This module periodically polls the SDN switches to get the number of matches for flows. It provides statistics to analyse patterns in the network traffic.

Algorithm 1 Twin Flow Pusher algorithm

procedure TWINFLOWPUSHER (S_{src}, S_{dest}, MatchConditions)

In SDN switch connected to subnet dst,
add entries to map IPs of map to dst.

In SDN switch connected to subnet src,
add entries to map IPs of dst to map,
with appropriate MatchConditions.

return;
end procedure

Algorithm 2 Legacy route Modulator

procedure LEGACYROUTERMODULATOR (P, M)
P_{rev} = reverse of P
for each router $R \in P_{rev}$ **do**
install static routes
to match the prefix of subnet M,
add entries to map IPs of dst to map,
and appropriate next hop to next router in P_{rev}.
end for

return;
end procedure

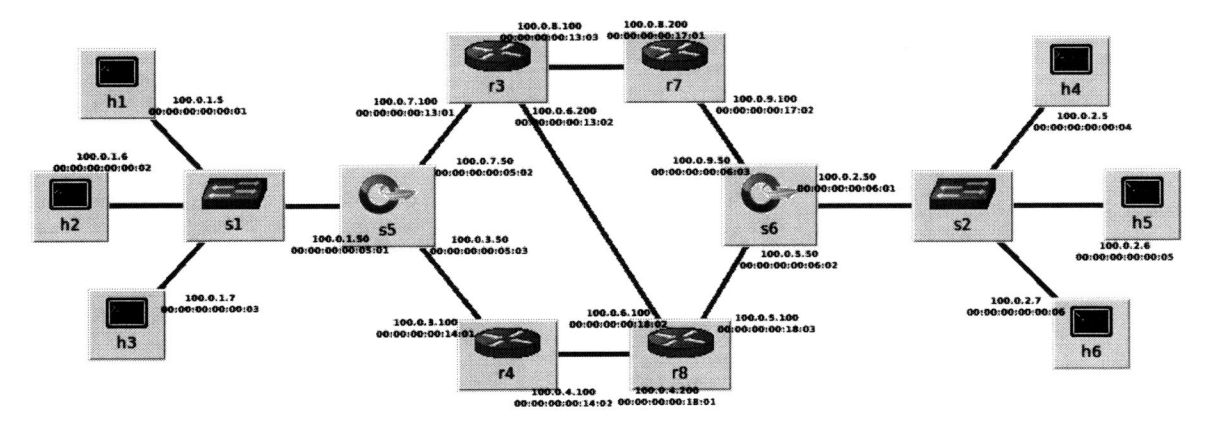

Fig. 1: Example Topology

Algorithm 3 Policy Translator algorithm
---

procedure POLICYTRANSLATOR (U, D, Src, Dst, Match-Conditions, P)

    Divide the List of free IPs U
    into subnets (based on size of Dst subnet)
    which can be used to map policies to.

    Sort these subnets in descending order
    based on usage statistics data D.

    Choose the subnet which has
    shown lowest Internet IP traffic.

    Remove this subnet from list U.
    Call this subnet as M.

    call LegacyRouterModulator(P, M);
    call TwinPushFlow(M, Src, Dst, MatchConditions);

    return;
end procedure

The inter-relation of the controller modules is explained in the following section.

C. IP Mapping

Whenever a new policy is to be installed in the network, a set of IP addresses from the unused IP address pool is needed to map the policy onto. The policy would be stated as certain match conditions which when satisfied would route the packet through a specified policy path P. The Policy Translator module in the controller carries out this function of creating a one-to-one mapping of an IP range onto the destination subnet of the policy. For a destination subnet such as xxx.xxx.xxx.0/24, the module would pick up an IP address range of the form xxx.xxx.xxx.0/24 from the free IP pool and directly map the entries. This direct mapping enables us to reduce the number of flow entries required for reverse-mapping at the destination SDN switch. The controller would add a simple flow at the destination SDN switch, which matches the destination IP based on a wildcard of the form 0.0.0.255 and the ingress port and then resets the destination IP accordingly. This reduces the number of flows required for all reverse mappings to the order of number of hosts in the destination subnet.

The Policy Translator module calls the Legacy Route Modulator module before the Twin Flow Pusher module in order to retain consistency of routes in the network. The routes are added in reverse order on the path so that the source SDN switch where the destination IP is mapped, is updated at the end. Thus, the policies are implemented through a transactional interface in an *all-or-nothing* manner based on a principle similar to the controller implementation in Software Transactional Networking (STN) by Canini, et al. [22]. If any inconsistencies are encountered while setting up routes for a policy, all the changes made would be rolled back.

Each IP mapping will also require static routes to be added into the legacy routers on policy path P so that the legacy network is able to route the new IP range as desired. The Policy Translator would reuse IP addresses in order to map different policies which use the same policy path. This optimizes the number of static routes required in the legacy routers.

The controller can be configured to listen to SNMP traps sent out from the routers in the network in order to learn about any failures in the network. In such an event, the controller can simply perform a complete roll back by removing all the entries in the SDN switches and the legacy devices.

D. Internet IP Address Clash

The inherent problem with mapping IPs is that even these free IP addresses could possibly be associated with some host outside the entire network (For ex. a Web Server outside the network). Now, if traffic needs to be sent to such an IP address, we might end up with a clash. Our network might be configured to map a certain policy onto this IP address while unaware that this packet (intended for an external host) is not to be considered under the policy. The legacy network would thus end up routing the packet based on static routes configured as per the policy and thus would route the packet incorrectly.

A proposed solution is to dynamically map these IPs. A packet intended to be sent outside of the network can be easily identified at the source SDN switch. A simple flow would be installed to send such packets to the controller. These flows would be installed at the same time when the flows for the conflicting policy would be installed in the SDN switch. Once the controller receives such packets, it creates a temporary map onto IP addresses from the free IP pool. Flows and static routes are added and the traffic is then routed based on this temporary mapping. Unlike policy mappings, these mappings would have an associated time to live and would be flushed if not matched for a certain time. The flushed IPs are then returned to the free IP pool.

The IP range allocator/reallocator module in the controller would analyse the traffic and optimize the allocation of IP ranges in order to avoid such IP clashes. The time-to-live of the temporary mappings can also be modulated in order to achieve a balance between delay in transmission and excessive use of IPs from the free IP pool for such temporary maps.

IV. Experimental Setup and Examples

We deploy a custom topology in mininet [23] using 6 hosts (divided as 2 subnets), 4 legacy routers R3, R4, R7 and R8. According to assumption A.1, both the subnets have a SDN switch on the path to their individual gateway router. (See Figure 1)

Components of the topology:
- Hosts - h1 to h6
  - Subnet 1 - h1 to h3 (100.0.1.0/24)
  - Subnet 2 - h4 to h6 (100.0.2.0/24)
- Legacy L2 switches - s1 and s2
- Legacy L3 switches/ routers - r3, r4, r7 and r8
- SDN-enabled switches - s5 and s6
- Controller C1 (not depicted in Figure 1) is connected out-of-band to s5 and s6

Policy Implementations:

Example 1:

All traffic with source as subnet 1, destination as subnet 2 and destination TCP port as 23 (Telnet) should follow a path P1 as s5 → r3 → r8 → s6 before reaching intended host on subnet 2

Flow entries in S5 (for mapping):
- `priority=10, ip, nw_src=100.0.1.0/24, nw_dst=100.0.2.5, tcp_dst=23 actions = mod_dl_dst=00:00:00:00:13:01, mod_nw_dst=1.0.0.5, output:1`
- `priority=10, ip, nw_src=100.0.1.0/24, nw_dst=100.0.2.6, tcp_dst=23 actions = mod_dl_dst=00:00:00:00:13:01, mod_nw_dst=1.0.0.6, output:1`
- `priority=10, ip, nw_src=100.0.1.0/24, nw_dst=100.0.2.7, tcp_dst=23 actions = mod_dl_dst=00:00:00:00:13:01, mod_nw_dst=1.0.0.7, output:1`
- `priority=11, ip, nw_src=100.0.1.0/24, nw_dst=1.0.0.0/24, actions=send_to_controller`

Flow entries in S6 (for reverse mapping):
- `priority=10, nw_dst=0.0.0.5/0.0.0.255, in_port=2 actions = mod_dl_dst=00:00:00:00:00:04, mod_nw_dst=100.0.2.5, output:1`
- `priority=10, nw_dst=0.0.0.6/0.0.0.255, in_port=2 actions = mod_dl_dst=00:00:00:00:00:05, mod_nw_dst=100.0.2.6, output:1`
- `priority=10, nw_dst=0.0.0.7/0.0.0.255, in_port=2 actions = mod_dl_dst=00:00:00:00:00:06, mod_nw_dst=100.0.2.7, output:1`

Static routes in R3:
- match 1.0.0.0/24 via 100.0.6.100 dev r3-eth2

Static routes in R8:
- match 1.0.0.0/24 via 100.0.5.50 dev r8-eth3

Example 2:

Now, if later on, administrator decides to have all TCP port 20 (FTP) traffic to follow a path P3 as s5 → r3 → r8 → s6 before reaching intended host on subnet 2.

The controller checks if this exact path is already being mapped to some IPs and finds that we are already mapping the exact same path for some other policy (Example 1), so decides not to map this policy to newer ranges but rather uses the same IP mapping without any changes required to the static routes in legacy L3 devices/routers on the way and just installs the flow-entries to map to same IPs.

Flow entries in S5 (for mapping):
- `priority=10, ip, nw_src=100.0.1.0/24, nw_dst=100.0.2.5, tcp_dst=23 actions= mod_dl_dst=00:00:00:00:13:01, mod_nw_dst=1.0.0.5, output:1`
- `priority=10, ip, nw_src=100.0.1.0/24, nw_dst=100.0.2.6, tcp_dst=23, actions= mod_dl_dst=00:00:00:00:13:01, mod_nw_dst=1.0.0.6, output:1`
- `priority=10, ip, nw_src=100.0.1.0/24, nw_dst=100.0.2.7, tcp_dst=23 actions= mod_dl_dst=00:00:00:00:13:01, mod_nw_dst=1.0.0.7, output:1`

The reverse mapping entries in S6 would not be required as we have already installed the reverse mapping entries while setting up the policy in Example 1.

V. Conclusion and Future Work

In this paper, we introduced a framework for the network administrators to implement network policies, by mapping those policies to the IP addresses which are unused inside the network. The test runs in Section IV show that we are able to implement policy-based routing in legacy routers supporting all other OpenFlow version 1.4 match fields (a total of 41), in addition to the destination IP address.

Through the tests, we have shown the examples of policies implemented through our model, though there is a need to study the impact of these mappings and reverse-mappings and interaction of controller with the legacy routers on a large network in terms of latencies introduced due to the increase in control traffic, delays due to the Internet IP clash problem and so on.

As pointed in Section III-D, the mapped IP might clash with an actual IP address in the Internet. Though we have suggested a way to handle these clashes to provide a consistency in the network, this workaround introduces its own delays. There is scope to find a way to optimize the allocation of IP addresses for mapping in order to minimize the number of clashes.

Currently, a major constraint in the IP allocation procedure is that every policy requires us to add as many flow entries in the SDN switch as there are hosts in its directly connected subnet. There is scope to implement filtering methods on the policies in order to remove redundancies within them.

Though the maximum number of policies that can be implemented in the network is realistically limited only by the flow-table size in SDN switches, use of IPv6 address space (only if the network hardware has support for IPv6) instead of IPv4 address space, would provide for a larger free IP pool availability and the idea can be explored in the future.

References

[1] S. Vissicchio, L. Vanbever, and O. Bonaventure, "Opportunities and research challenges of hybrid software defined networks," vol. 44, no. 2, pp. 70–75. [Online]. Available: http://doi.acm.org/10.1145/2602204.2602216

[2] N. McKeown, T. Anderson, H. Balakrishnan, G. Parulkar, L. Peterson, J. Rexford, S. Shenker, and J. Turner, "Openflow: Enabling innovation in campus networks," *SIGCOMM Comput. Commun. Rev.*, vol. 38, no. 2, pp. 69–74, Mar. 2008. [Online]. Available: http://doi.acm.org/10.1145/1355734.1355746

[3] H. Lu, N. Arora, H. Zhang, C. Lumezanu, J. Rhee, and G. Jiang, "Hybnet: Network manager for a hybrid network infrastructure," in *Proceedings of the Industrial Track of the 13th ACM/IFIP/USENIX International Middleware Conference*. ACM, p. 6. [Online]. Available: http://dl.acm.org/citation.cfm?id=2541602

[4] D. Levin, M. Canini, S. Schmid, F. Schaffert, A. Feldmann, and others, "Panopticon: Reaping the benefits of incremental sdn deployment in enterprise networks," in *USENIX ATC*. [Online]. Available: https://www.usenix.org/system/files/conference/atc14/atc14-paper-levin.pdf

[5] R. Hand and E. Keller, "ClosedFlow: openflow-like control over proprietary devices." ACM Press, pp. 7–12. [Online]. Available: http://dl.acm.org/citation.cfm?doid=2620728.2620738

[6] C. Jin, C. Lumezanu, Q. Xu, Z.-L. Zhang, and G. Jiang, "Telekinesis: controlling legacy switch routing with OpenFlow in hybrid networks." ACM Press, pp. 1–7. [Online]. Available: http://dl.acm.org/citation.cfm?doid=2774993.2775013

[7] Y. Rekhter, R. G. Moskowitz, D. Karrenberg, G. J. de Groot, and E. Lear, "Address allocation for private internets," Internet Requests for Comments, RFC Editor, BCP 5, February 1996, http://www.rfc-editor.org/rfc/rfc1918.txt. [Online]. Available: http://www.rfc-editor.org/rfc/rfc1918.txt

[8] J. Weil, V. Kuarsingh, C. Donley, C. Liljenstolpe, and M. Azinger, "Iana-reserved ipv4 prefix for shared address space," Internet Requests for Comments, RFC Editor, BCP 153, April 2012, http://www.rfc-editor.org/rfc/rfc6598.txt. [Online]. Available: http://www.rfc-editor.org/rfc/rfc6598.txt

[9] J. Reynolds and J. Postel, "Assigned numbers," Internet Requests for Comments, RFC Editor, RFC 990, November 1986.

[10] S. Cheshire, B. Aboba, and E. Guttman, "Dynamic configuration of ipv4 link-local addresses," Internet Requests for Comments, RFC Editor, RFC 3927, May 2005.

[11] G. Huston, M. Cotton, and L. Vegoda, "Iana ipv4 special purpose address registry," Internet Requests for Comments, RFC Editor, RFC 5736, January 2010.

[12] J. Arkko, M. Cotton, and L. Vegoda, "Ipv4 address blocks reserved for documentation," Internet Requests for Comments, RFC Editor, RFC 5737, January 2010.

[13] C. Huitema, "An anycast prefix for 6to4 relay routers," Internet Requests for Comments, RFC Editor, RFC 3068, June 2001.

[14] S. Bradner and J. McQuaid, "Benchmarking methodology for network interconnect devices," Internet Requests for Comments, RFC Editor, RFC 2544, March 1999, http://www.rfc-editor.org/rfc/rfc2544.txt. [Online]. Available: http://www.rfc-editor.org/rfc/rfc2544.txt

[15] M. Cotton, L. Vegoda, and D. Meyer, "Iana guidelines for ipv4 multicast address assignments," Internet Requests for Comments, RFC Editor, BCP 51, March 2010.

[16] M. Cotton, L. Vegoda, R. Bonica, and B. Haberman, "Special-purpose ip address registries," Internet Requests for Comments, RFC Editor, BCP 153, April 2013, http://www.rfc-editor.org/rfc/rfc6890.txt. [Online]. Available: http://www.rfc-editor.org/rfc/rfc6890.txt

[17] "CAT 6500 and 7600 Series Routers and Switches," http://www.cisco.com/c/en/us/support/docs/switches/catalyst-6500-series-switches/117712-problemsolution-cat6500-00.html/.

[18] "Open vSwitch," http://openvswitch.org/.

[19] "NoviSwitch," http://noviflow.com/products/noviswitch/.

[20] J. Postel and J. Reynolds, "Telnet protocol specification," Internet Requests for Comments, RFC Editor, STD 8, May 1983, http://www.rfc-editor.org/rfc/rfc854.txt. [Online]. Available: http://www.rfc-editor.org/rfc/rfc854.txt

[21] T. Ylonen and C. Lonvick, "The secure shell (ssh) protocol architecture," Internet Requests for Comments, RFC Editor, RFC 4251, January 2006, http://www.rfc-editor.org/rfc/rfc4251.txt. [Online]. Available: http://www.rfc-editor.org/rfc/rfc4251.txt

[22] M. Canini, D. De Cicco, P. Kuznetsov, D. Levin, S. Schmid, S. Vissicchio, and others, "STN: A robust and distributed SDN control plane." [Online]. Available: https://www.usenix.org/sites/default/files/ons2014-poster-canini.pdf

[23] "Mininet," http://mininet.org/.

A View of WSN-facilitating Application's Design and a Cloud Infrastructure in Academic Environment and Research

Alexander Novinskiy
Fb2, Informatik und Ingenieurwissenschaften
Frankfurt University of Applied Sciences
Frankfurt am Main, Hessen
Email: a.novinskiy@fb2.fra-uas.de

Abstract— This paper presents a view of seamless integration of Wireless Sensor Networks and server-side applications working with sensor data. The aim of this paper is to show a vector toward organizing a flexible and scalable platform for educational and research institutions or small organizations which demand privately running "Internet of Things" solutions when having restricted computational resources.

I. Introduction

During the recent years the area of Internet of Things has arisen and gained increasing attention. Being facilitated by the use of multiple wireless network protocols such as ZigBee, Bluetooth, wirelessHART and sensor technologies IoT is gradually penetrating into humans lives. The interconnection of two concepts, Internet of Things and Wireless Sensor Networks, made them almost interchangeable. Wireless Sensor Networks significantly differ from traditional networks. First, communication goes via radio based signal exchange. Therefore, concepts such as operational frequency, number of channels available, range and power consumption go into the first plan when designing or choosing appropriate hardware solutions for your network. The need to operate long in the autonomous mode imposes multiple restrictions to hardware. First of all it must be power efficient. That led to the dramatical degradation of computational capabilities compared to nodes of traditional networks with permanent power supply. Having that limited computational power WSN-nodes are being designed to be able to read sensor data, transmit and receive signals via wireless networks. Most of the computationally intensive tasks such as statistical analysis, numerical data processing, decision making routines moved to the regular networks. That made engineers think about the architectural design of wsn-driven applications. Having omitted basic client/server approach developers and researchers came to the use of publish/subscribe architecture. This approach allowed software developers to integrated as many WSNs and applications as they needed into a single communicational system, thus, increasing scalability and simplifying development process. Nevertheless, economical needs made researchers and software developers seek for a better way of resources utilization and scalability possibilities, higher level of informational security and easier ways of software deployment. It has been 10 years since the concept of Cloud Computing had come into life and brought significant opportunities for developers and end-users. This paper covers how cloud computing core technologies and publish/subscribe communicational protocols make a suitable platform for Internet of Things solutions.

II. Problem definition

Due to the gaining popularity and promising prospects of the Internet of Things concept many organizations, companies and universities work in this area to deliver prototypes and/or complete solutions for home automation [1], weather monitoring, human behaviour recognition, motion tracking and many other areas of human life. Nevertheless, research institutions and universities have to deal with highly restricted financial, infrastructural and therefore computational resources. Being supported by highly volatile teams consisting of students, research assistants and simply enthusiasts these institutions deal with a great variety of approaches toward architectural design which are no longer supported after the lifespan of a project has come to its end. In order to manage risks caused by these specifics universities and research institutions need to be able to utilize available computational resources at its maximum and offer a simple and unified approach toward software design which would facilitate both software modules communication and seamless integration of WSNs with server-side business logic.

III. Communicational System Design

A. Naive approach

As long as most data processing jobs take place on the server side due to restrictive nature of devices comprising WSNs it has become a major issue to find out a way to organize data exchange between sensor nodes and server-side applications. Since most WSN solutions are being driven by network protocols different from those facilitated by the TCP/IP protocol stack such as Wi-Fi the concept of a gateway arose. Gateways are devices which establish communication between different media and network protocols. In the most straight-forward approach a gateway establishes a direct connection with a server-side application and exchange data via a TCP/IP socket. Server side applications accept incoming data and store it in databases.

Nevertheless, as the amount of projects increases this approach shows its major disadvantages. Server-side applications and corresponding clients are strongly coupled. Having established a socket connection server-side applications bind themself to a certain port number. In this case replication of the server would require significant administrative efforts. Furthermore, real-time data access is being provided for a single application only. Could we need to add an alternative business logic to process the same data in real-time we might have to multicast these data among different server-side applications. That would make software development process more tangled and intolerant to architectural changes.

The use of databases on the other hand would destroy advantages of real-time communication which is crucial for many applications.

B. Publish/subscribe-based approach

The scale of distributed systems has dramatically increased with the development of Internet and networks in general. The publish/subscribe communicational model is dedicated to provide a very loosely coupled form of interaction for entities of distributed systems. The idea is that subscribers can register their interest in a particular event or a pattern of events, when publishers generate events on a software bus or an event manager [2], which are being asynchronously propagated to subscribers according to their interest. Many industrial systems and research prototypes support this style of interaction. Regardless the great variety of these systems all of them aim to achieve time, space, and synchronization decoupling of subscribers and publishers.

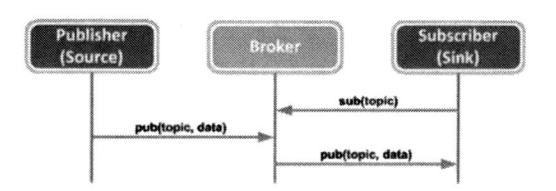

Fig. 1. Publish/Subscribe architecture

Communicational parties do not need to actively participate in data exchange. In fact, publishers can send their data even when subscribers are disconnected. And on the contrary, if a publisher has disconnected after the message was sent, corresponding subscribers will get notified about the event and perhaps about the disconnection of the publisher. This property is called time decoupling - something that we can not achieve with pure client/server architecture. Synchronization decoupling means that publishers are not blocked when generating an event and subscribers can get asynchronously notified while performing some concurrent activity. Moreover, participants of interaction do not have to know each other.

This is called space decoupling which is achieved by the use of communicational middleware - a service responsible for messages redistribution.

By removing all unnecessary dependencies between communicational parties we can increase overall scalability of our systems. More information about publish/subscribe communicational paradigm can be found in the article "Many faces of publish/subscribe" [3].

Nevertheless, an IoT facilitating feasible publish/subscribe system should meet following requirements.

- It should be lightweight in order to intercommunicate with tiny devices comprising WSNs.
- It should be reliable, but yet rapidly operating.
- It should be simple to learn and to use and yet be extendable. Rapid prototyping requires low entry costs for developers, but there must be room for improvements.
- It should be supported by a wide community of software developers from different application areas.
- It should provide security mechanisms such as authentication of clients and prevention of unauthorized access to published data.
- It should be scalable to support high scale deployment.

C. MQTT

MQTT stands for Message Queue Telemetry Transport and is a "light weight" application layer communicational protocol based on publish/subscribe model. Even though, there is a great variety of publish/subscribe model implementations, MQTT is definitely one of those which hold many of properties desired by IoT developers [4] [5].

The MQTT protocol relies on communicational middleware called a message broker, which is responsible for orchestration of communicational flows. MQTT has a modification for smart sensor networks called MQTT-SN or MQTT-S [6]. It introduces a concept of a gateway - a framework which, when used, is responsible for data transfer between a smart sensor network and a message broker. It is usually being located on a physical gateway which is traditionally represented as a tiny device interconnecting different media and protocols.

MQTT supports basic end-to-end quality of service. The simplest one is the QoS level 0. It offers the best effort service where a message is either delivered once or not at all. Retransmission or delivery acknowledgement is not defined. QoS level 1 ensures delivery of a message but the message can be delivered more then once due to retransmission. QoS level 2 is the highest one and it ensures messages are being delivered exactly once.

MQTT supports username/password authentication and is capable of authorizing users to provide specified access rights to published data. Furthermore, MQTT clients can still transmit encrypted payload via SSH/TLS tunnels or by means of custom encryption [7].

MQTT is easy to use. It provides "CONNECT" function to connect to a message broker, "PUBLISH" function to publish sensor data or user controls, and "SUBSCRIBE" function to register clients interest in certain data. Yet, many broker implementations provide plugins and APIs to extend the default behaviour.

Some MQTT brokers support bridging - direct broker-to-broker connections, which makes scaling easier and provides higher level of flexibility.

IV. CLOUD INFRASTRUCTURE

A. Motivation

There are multiple reasons to make use of "clouds" in research projects and prototyping tasks. Among them are lower cost of entry, reduced risk of IT infrastructure failure, higher Return On Investment (ROI), quick responses to changes on demand, rapid deployment, increased security, and ability to focus on the core business of an organization [8]. By making use of cloud environment one can increase efficiency of resources utilization in comparison with the bare metal deployment. It can be achieved via the core cloud-comprising technology called virtualisation. Rather then having only one bare metal machine we can have several virtual ones with a certain amount of allocated resources. Moreover, we can save significant amount of administrative efforts as long as cloud infrastructure supports high level of automation.

B. General cloud architecture

A cloud infrastructure can be created based on computer clusters with the help of special orchestrating software. OpenStack and Ecalyptus are examples of such systems.

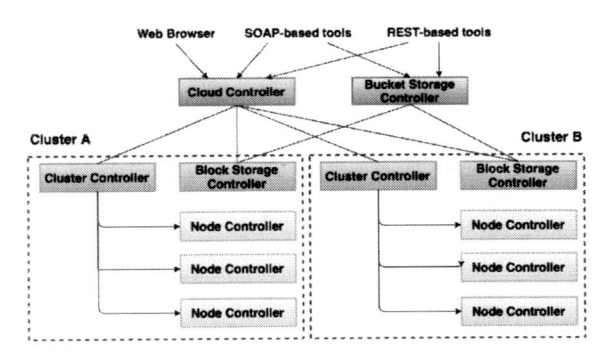

Fig. 2. Eucalyptus architectural layers and advanced setup according to Z. Pantic et al. [8]

A conventional cloud computing orchestration software system contains modules to elicit resources usage statistics, manage virtual instances, control available storage and provide a user interface. Cloud computing system of that level is called an Infrastructure as a Service and it aims to provide isolated computational resources on demand.

1) Node controller: This module is responsible for "instances" - virtual machines with operational systems on them. Each node with a node controller installed may have zero, one or many simultaneously running instances with possible different OS on them. Node Controllers communicate with the hyper-visor running on the node, host operational system and with the corresponding Cluster Controller. It gathers data about utilization of available resources and about instances running on that node. [8]

2) Cluster controller: This module gathers information about nodes, resources available on them and about running instances by communicating with corresponding Node Controllers. It also communicates with the Cloud Controller propagating information about NCs to it, receiving requests for deploying instances, and deciding about where they should be put. It is also responsible for virtual networks available to instances.

3) Block level storage controller: Instances on the cluster level may need to get access to storage volumes just as any OS be it deployed on the bare-metal or inside of virtual machine requires storage devices to keep its files and programs on it. A conventional IaaS platform is supposed to encapsulate block level storage access as an abstraction from actual storage devices. Eucalyptus does it via ATA over Ethernet (AoE) or Internet SCSI (iSCSI) protocol to mount virtual storage devices. [8]

4) Bucket-based storage controller: This module is responsible for managing a put/get storage model (create and delete buckets, create objects, put or get those objects from buckets). [8]. This kind of service is being used to keep machine images and snapshots.

5) Cloud Controller: This is the top level service module and is an entry point to the cloud. It provisions both end-user and administrator web interfaces. All the relevant information about the cloud including the amount of available resources and running instances is collected here. Based on this information a Cloud Controller arbitrates available resources, dispatching the load to clusters.

6) Network organization: There are several ways how network infrastructure can be organized for a cloud. The simplest but not the safest option is to put all machines to the public network as shown on Fig. 3. Nevertheless, this approach imposes some inconveniences such as the need for more public IP's as well as for additional security measures to protect publicly available nodes.

The alternative network configuration assumes that we have a public network with all the internet facing services, and a private network with internal services such as Node Controller and Block Level Storage Controller. Having set up firewalls both on the public and private networks entry points we can organize a so called demilitarized zone (DMZ). [9]

C. Deployment on limited amount of resources

Nevertheless, the actual network scheme significantly depends on the amount of machines available to build a network. In the ideal case we would have hundreds of computers distributed over different network broadcast domains, comprising a huge data centre with a vast cloudy infrastructure. In this case the deployment scheme would be approximately like depicted in Fig. 2.

Unfortunately, small organization and/or research groups with limited budgets can not afford large scale data centres.

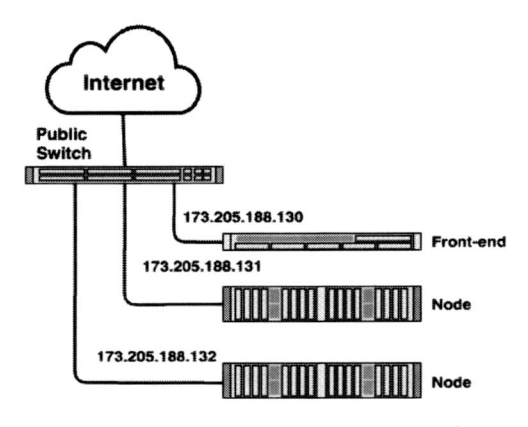

Fig. 3. Nodes connected directly to the public network according to Z. Pantic et al. [8]

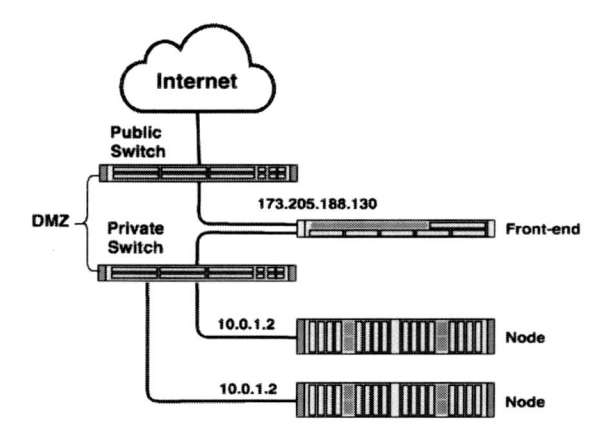

Fig. 4. Nodes on the private subnet, front-end on the public according to Z. Pantic et al. [8]according to Z. Pantic et al. [8]

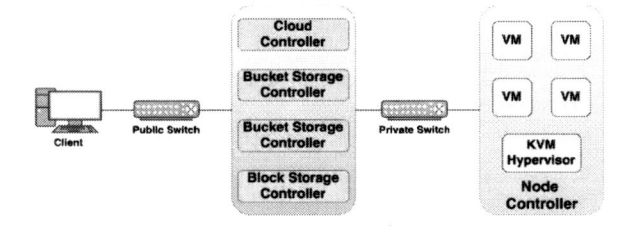

Fig. 5. Minimal set up according to Z. Pantic et al. [8]

In this case we should consider deployment of cloud infrastructure on limited amount of resources. Theoretically, all necessary services can be located on a single machine. But it is highly recommended having at least two machines to isolate computationally intensive services such as NCs from those, which are responsible mostly for monitoring and scheduling. There are also security considerations which dictate to split those services (See Fig. 5).

D. Linux Containers

Linux containers is a novel technology based on the Linux kernel addition called **cgroups**. Cgroups kernel module is responsible for managing resources for groups of processes. This allowed to make products which are capable of creating lightweigh Linux virtual machines. Linux Containers (LXC) provide operating-system-level virtualisation which is characterized by having multiple user-spaces when sharing a single kernel-space. By eliminating the necessity of having multiple kernels booted simultaneously, LXC provides better productivity, [10] [11] [12] achieves higher density level when multiple Linux containers are deployed.

Linux containers gave birth to many different products such as LXD and Docker. LXD is a Linux containers management tool which is capable of controlling multiple container instances. Docker is also based on cgroups but it doesn't let users to change its configuration. Once created it can not be modified and therefore can not serve as a virtual machine. Instead, Docker serves as an applications wrapper and facilitates rapid deployment of software.

One of the most powerful and promising feature of LXC and other products based on it is the Software Defined Networking (SDN) [13] which makes it possible to connect different containers into a single network regardless of where they are located [14].

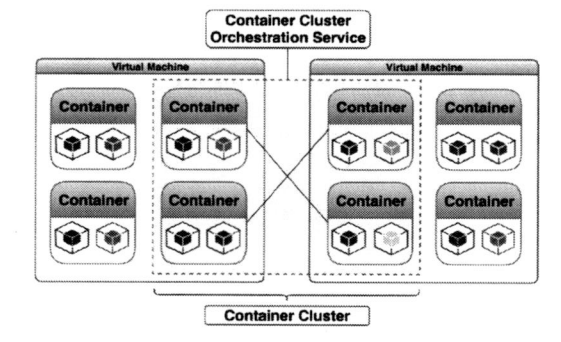

Fig. 6. Container Cluster Organization

This functionality makes it possible to consider a variety of communicational system architectures, characterized by message broker placement.

One of the obvious options is to place a message broker at the highest level on one of the internet facing servers. This broker would be publicly available to all clients and would be able to create a global communicational middleware. There are certain pitfalls related to this approach. High availability level might cause security and reliability issues. Clients which by chance might have gotten authentication credentials which they must not possess could gain access to data they would have not normally been authenticated for. For security sensitive applications such as processing medical data it can be a serious issue. Nevertheless, this approach can be suitable for less critical applications and therefore shall be considered as a simple way of organizing communicational infrastructure. When used, one should plan a broker scaling strategy either by means of bridging or via third party software such as load-balancers and distributed message brokers like Apache Kafka.

Another option of organizing communicational systems is to place a message broker onto a subnetwork level or inside a demilitarized zone (see Figure 4) protected by an internet facing firewall. This configuration would create a private communicational system for services located inside a corresponding subnetwork.

The third option is to let users place message brokers inside their virtual machines, Linux containers (LXCs) and application wrappers such as Docker. This highly adjustable approach would let developers achieve the highest level of privacy for their communicational flows. Moreover by placing a custom message broker developers would be able to extend brokers default functionality on demand.

There are also examples when mixed approaches may take place. The concept of computational pipelines may need up to three brokers installed on different levels in order to be fully implemented.

V. PIPELINES

Most WSN and IoT applications are data centric. It means they make use of existing network- and computing infrastructure to collect, transfer, process and store data about real world. Data processing jobs can be generalized in a form of data transforms. Each transform modifies incoming data according to some business logic. Transforms may be chained together to make a pipeline. A similar concept has been used by Google in their public cloud solution [15].

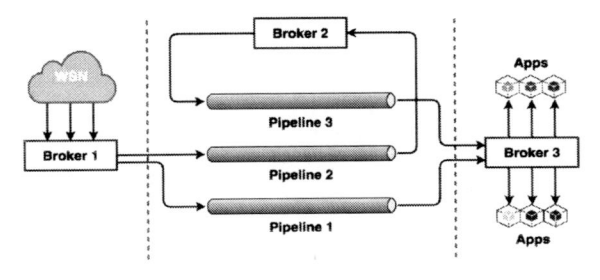

Fig. 7. Pipelines

In computer science a pipeline is a set of data processing elements connected together so that an output of one element can be an input of another. Having implemented a set of standard routines such as getting a mean value, generating distributions, transforming data from one format to another, generating key-pairs for data elements, calculating hash-values, ciphering and/or deciphering incoming data, one can build a sequential chain of transformations or make them work in parallel.

There are multiple ways of organizing such functionality, but there is a need in a simple and yet flexible design for small organizations, universities, research institutions and groups.

On Figure 7 there is a pipelines design pattern depicted. In this case each data processing job is represented as a running instance of a routine and/or executable, which performs a simple transformation.

In this case brokers 1, 2 and 3 act as middleware between the outside world represented by WSNs, data transforms, and user applications. Even though the same functionality could be implemented having only one broker which might be feasible for some very tiny data aggregating centres or for data-centric software prototyping, having three brokers helps organize logical isolation of system components and apply different security rules on every level.

```
public interface DataTransform{
  DataSourceDescriptor ←
     getOutputDataDescriptor();
  void setInputDataDescriptor(←
     DataSourceDescriptor);
  void setTParameterList(TParameterList);
  void addParameter(TParameter);
  void cleanTParameterList();
  void run();
  void stop();
}
```

Listing 1. DataTransform Class

A certain SDK is needed in order to build and manage pipelines. A core element of such SDK can be represented as an abstract class or an interface containing descriptions of major methods necessary to operate with data transforms. Listing 1 shows an example of such interface which defines core methods to manage data transforms such as

- *void setInputDataDescriptor(**DataSourceDescriptor**)* to define a subscription topic and user credentials to get authorized access to input data,
- ***DataSourceDescriptor*** *getOutputDataDescriptor()* to get a corresponding data object for published data,
- *void setTParameterList(**TParameterList**)* to define a set of parameters for the corresponding data transformation routine be it a software module or an instance of an executable,
- *void run()* and *void stop()* to start and terminate data transformation routines.

In the Listing 2 there is an example of a common data transform use case. First, two classes, MeanValue and NormalDistribution, are being declared as an implementation of DataTransform interface. The corresponding objects are being created. Second, a pipeline is built by binding MeanValue output with NormalDistribution input via a corresponding topic name and under common user credentials represented as a DataSourceDescriptor object. When the pipeline is built, both transformations comprising it are started in the order opposite to how they are connected. This is required in order to avoid data losses. I.e. NormalDistribution transform shall start listening for incoming data before MeanValue transform begins publishing them.

```
//create a Mean Value transformation
class MeanValue implements DataTransform{
...
}
//create a Normal Distribution ↵
    transformation
class NormalDistribution implements ↵
    DataTransform{
...
}
//create an input values source descriptor
DataSourceDescriptor mySensorVal = new ↵
    DataSourceDescriptor(username,password,↵
    topicname);
...
//create a Mean Value transform object
DataTransform meanVal = new MeanValue();
meanVal.addParameter("-samplesize 50")
meanVal.setInputDataDescriptor(sensorVal);
...
//create a Normal Distribution transform ↵
    object and link it with the MeanValue ↵
    transform
DataTransform normalDist = new ↵
    NormalDistribution();
normalDist.addParameter("-stdDev 1.5");
normalDist.setInputDataDescriptor(meanVal.↵
    getOutputDataDescriptor());
...
//launch both transforms
normalDist.run();
meanVal.run();
...
//stop both transforms
meanVal.stop();
normalDist.stop();
```

Listing 2. Pipeline Use-Case

Simplicity of the presented architecture favours rapid development and deployment, encourages small teams and individual enthusiasts to contribute to its state, and facilitates data centric IoT projects with useful tools and infrastructure.

VI. CONCLUSION

In reply to multiple challenges encountered during IoT and WSN related projects an analysis of modern technologies which can be leveraged to boost effectiveness of computational resources' utilization and developers productivity has been made. There has been discovered what modern data-centric communicational protocols, such as publish/subscribe-based MQTT, offer in order to provide higher decoupling level for applications working with sensor data in real-time.

Having multiple projects of different levels of complexity and duration we were also looking toward an optimal solution for rapid software prototyping and deployment. Our aim was to utilize existing limited hardware and network infrastructure in such way, that multiple software developers and researchers could make use of isolated environment to safely manage their data and run their prototypes independently from other participants. It was concluded that a minimal cloud infrastructure can provide this level of comfort when solving a number of other problems such as rapid scaling up and down when demanded, providing appropriate security level, and automation of administrative tasks.

Also, a concept of computational pipelines as a chain of data transform has been presented. It was concluded that a corresponding SDK might be required to manage pipelines and data transforms as well as data flows between them. A simple implementation and usage example have been presented in order to show suggested simplicity of pipelines and to demonstrate how such SDK could be implemented.

These means are supposed to facilitate rapid prototyping, development and deployment of private IoT solutions.

REFERENCES

[1] X. Li, L. Nie, S. Chen, D. Zhan, and X. Xu, "An iot service framework for smart home: Case study on hem," in *2015 IEEE International Conference on Mobile Services*, June 2015, pp. 438–445.

[2] D. Ajitomi, H. Kawazoe, K. Minami, and N. Esaka, "A cost-effective method to keep availability of many cloud-connected devices," in *2015 IEEE 8th International Conference on Cloud Computing*, June 2015, pp. 1–8.

[3] P. T. Eugster, P. A. Felber, R. Guerraoui, and A.-M. Kermarrec, "The many faces of publish/subscribe," *ACM Comput. Surv.*, vol. 35, no. 2, pp. 114–131, Jun. 2003. [Online]. Available: http://doi.acm.org/10.1145/857076.857078

[4] J. L. Espinosa-Aranda, N. Vallez, C. Sanchez-Bueno, D. Aguado-Araujo, G. Bueno, and O. Deniz, "Pulga, a tiny open-source mqtt broker for flexible and secure iot deployments," in *Communications and Network Security (CNS), 2015 IEEE Conference on*, Sept 2015, pp. 690–694.

[5] A. Antoni, M. Marjanovi, P. Skoir, and I. P. arko, "Comparison of the cupus middleware and mqtt protocol for smart city services," in *Telecommunications (ConTEL), 2015 13th International Conference on*, July 2015, pp. 1–8.

[6] U. Hunkeler, H. L. Truong, and A. Stanford-Clark, "Mqtt-s - a publish/subscribe protocol for wireless sensor networks," in *Communication Systems Software and Middleware and Workshops, 2008. COMSWARE 2008. 3rd International Conference on*, Jan 2008, pp. 791–798.

[7] D. Lee and N. Park, "Security through authentication infrastructure in open maritime cloud," in *2016 International Conference on Platform Technology and Service (PlatCon)*, Feb 2016, pp. 1–2.

[8] Z. Pantic and M. A. Babar, "Guidelines for building a private cloud infrastructure," IT University of Copenhagen, Tech. Rep. TR-2012-153, 2012.

[9] A. Babar and B. Ramsey, "Tutorial: Building secure and scalable private cloud infrastructure with open stack," in *Enterprise Distributed Object Computing Workshop (EDOCW), 2015 IEEE 19th International*, Sept 2015, pp. 166–166.

[10] W. Felter, A. Ferreira, R. Rajamony, and J. Rubio, "An updated performance comparison of virtual machines and linux containers," in *Performance Analysis of Systems and Software (ISPASS), 2015 IEEE International Symposium on*, March 2015, pp. 171–172.

[11] A. M. Joy, "Performance comparison between linux containers and virtual machines," in *Computer Engineering and Applications (ICACEA), 2015 International Conference on Advances in*, March 2015, pp. 342–346.

[12] M. G. Xavier, M. V. Neves, F. D. Rossi, T. C. Ferreto, T. Lange, and C. A. F. D. Rose, "Performance evaluation of container-based virtualization for high performance computing environments," in *2013 21st Euromicro International Conference on Parallel, Distributed, and Network-Based Processing*, Feb 2013, pp. 233–240.

[13] C. Costache, O. Machidon, A. Mladin, F. Sandu, and R. Bocu, "Software-defined networking of linux containers," in *2014 RoEduNet Conference 13th Edition: Networking in Education and Research Joint Event RENAM 8th Conference*, Sept 2014, pp. 1–4.

[14] M. Hausenblas, *Docker Networking and Service Discovery*. 1005 Gravenstein Highway North, Sebastopol, CA 95472: OReilly Media, Inc., 2016.

[15] (2016) Dataflow programming model. [Online]. Available: https://cloud.google.com/dataflow/model/programming-model

Bitcoin Network Measurements for Simulation Validation and Parameterisation

Muntadher Fadhil; Gareth Owen; Mo Adda
University of Portsmouth, Buckingham Building, Portsmouth, United Kingdom
{Muntadher.sallal; Gareth.owen; Mo.Adda}@port.ac.uk

Abstract— Bitcoin is gaining increasing popularity nowadays, even though the crypto-currencies field has plenty of digital currencies that have emerged before the adoption of Bitcoin idea. Bitcoin is a decentralized digital currency which relies on set of miners to maintain a distributed public ledger and peer-to-peer network to broadcast transactions. In this paper, we analyse how transaction validation is achieved by the transaction propagation round trip and how transaction dissemination throughout the network can lead to inconsistencies in the view of the current transactions ledger by different nodes. We then measure the transaction propagation delay in the real Bitcoin network and how it is affected by the number of nodes and network topology. This measurement enables a precise validation of any simulation model of the Bitcoin network. Large-scale measurements of the real Bitcoin network are performed in this paper. This will provide an opportunity to parameterise any model of the Bitcoin system accurately.

Keywords—Bitcoin ; Propagation delay ;Simulation Validation

I. INTRODUCTION

Bitcoin is a decentralized peer-to-peer electronic currency that allows online payments between two parties without any form of central authority [1]. The system was proposed in 2008 by Satoshi Nakamoto and deployed as a payment system in January 2009 [2], [3]. Bitcoin relies on a cryptographic protocol that operates on top of the Bitcoin peer-to-peer network. The user's identity in Bitcoin is represented by a public key as opposed to their name or other identifiable information [4]. Furthermore, Bitcoin is also the name of the currency that this network enables where, one Bitcoin (BTC) has an equivalent value in British pounds (GBP).

Bitcoin is considered as a reliable currency which allows global transactions to be processed as fast as local ones. In addition, it offers a public history of all transactions that have ever been processed. It also introduces such new payment strategies, such as micropayment, contract, and escrow transactions.

Bitcoin follows a distributed trust mechanism which relies on distributed validation and tracking of transactions. Based on this mechanism, a Bitcoin transaction has to be broadcasted to all nodes within the network to reach a consensus about which transactions are valid. The consensus is recorded in a publicly distributed ledger which is shared by the entire network.

As Transactions are validated against the public ledger, inconsistency in the replicas of ledger is unavoidable. This introduces uncertainty about the validity of a given transaction which may lead to an attacker being able to spend a Bitcoin twice.

In this work, we present measurements of the transaction propagation delay as well as measurements of the real Bitcoin network. These measurements are important to validate and parameterise any simulation model of Bitcoin network. We further analyse transaction validation in the Bitcoin network and how the consistency of the public ledger is affected by transaction propagation.

The paper is organised as follows: Section II focuses on giving an overview of the Bitcoin system and briefly describing the Bitcoin networking aspects. In Section III, we discuss in details the information propagation in the Bitcoin network and analyse the double spending attack which is caused by the transaction propagation delay. In addition, related work in measuring and analysing Bitcoin information propagation and in modelling approaches to avoid double spending attacks will be outlined. In Section IV, measurements of the transaction propagation delay as well as measurements of the real Bitcoin network parameters will be presented. In Section V, we conclude the paper and discuss the future work.

II. BACKGROUND

In this section we provide a general overview of the Bitcoin system. We focus on the Bitcoin protocol by discussing the basic operation of the Bitcoin network and how the globally consistent state is achieved. We then give a brief description of the relevant aspects of Bitcoin which are block chain and the network structure.

A. The Bitcoin protocol

The Bitcoin protocol is built on the basis of creation and distribution of public record of all the Bitcoins in the system. This record considers each entry as a transaction by which the transfer of virtual currency is accomplished. Each transaction consists of inputs and outputs. A transaction's output which indicates the new owner of the transferred Bitcoins, will be referenced as inputs in future transactions to create new output/outputs [5]. Transactions are formed as a directed graph which helps when giving constants about transaction record.

Each transaction input should have a digital signature that unlocks the previous transactions' output. This signature is created only by the user who possesses an appropriate private key. This ensures that Bitcoins can only be spent by their owners. In addition, the sum of the values of the inputs should be equal to or greater than the sum of all outputs.

B. Block Chain

Block chain is simply the ledger of all transactions, grouped into blocks. Every block is linked with previous blocks by including the unique hash of the previous block in its header. The first block in the block chain is known as the genesis block and it has no references to previous blocks. A branch is a path in the block chain which starts from a leaf block to the genesis block [6]. Block chain technology is deemed as the most important invention in the field of cryptography and security of decentralised networks, because it allows an immutable record of all transactions to be created, such that it is resistant to modification from the most resourceful attackers. Block chain is publicly visible and allows nodes within the network to agree to be confident about the transfer of money between users [7],[8]. Any valid transactions disseminated in the Bitcoin network are collected in a block by miners. After that, this block requires a degree of computational effort before it will be accepted by other nodes as valid. A group of nodes known as miners provide this effort when they solve the computational problem, and for which they are rewarded with a small number of Bitcoins. The solution to the problem is easy to verify but difficult to calculate and as such the solution can be considered a proof of work (POW) [6]. Blocks are chained together, and thus, modifying a block becomes exponentially harder with the passage of time, as all subsequent blocks must also modified[9].

C. Bitcoin peer-to-peer network

In the Bitcoin network, as shown in Fig.1, each peer connects randomly with other peers over a TCP channel [10]. Each node maintains a list of IPs of peers that the node established connections with. For the purpose of making denial of service impractical, just the valid transactions and blocks are propagated, whereas invalid transactions and blocks are discarded. Furthermore, Bitcoin network achieves a reputation protocol by which each node maintains a penalty score for every connection. Once a node receives a corrupted message from a particular connection of its connections, it increases the penalty score of the connection and bans the misbehaving IP when the score reaches the value of 100. Bitcoin network nodes are classified into two groups. Servers which can accept incoming connections and those which can't (clients), because

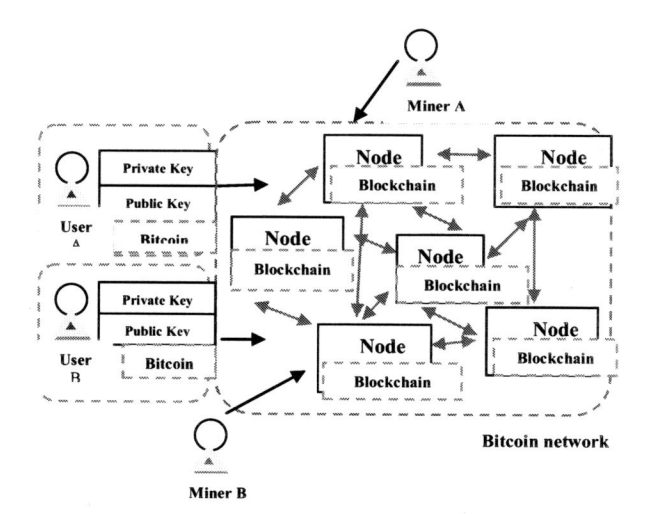

Figure 1: The structure of the Bitcoin network

they are behind NAT or firewall. Peers in the Bitcoin network maintains up to 8 outgoing connections and accept up to 117 incoming connections. Bitcoin peer stays connected to the 8 outgoing connections until it is restarted, whereas connections will be replaced if any of the outgoing connections drop [10].

III. INFORMATION PROPAGATION AND RELATED WORKS

There are two types of information that are propagated in the Bitcoin network: Transactions and Blocks. Transactions are responsible for transferring values, whereas blocks are used to ensure a chronological ordering of transactions across all nodes in the Bitcoin network and also form part of the ledger [11]. To broadcast a transaction, a user simply connects to a number of peers within the network and sends it to them. Each peer maintains history of forwarded transactions for each connection and if it has not seen that transaction before then it will rebroadcast it to all of its peers [12]. In the following, we discuss how the Bitcoin transaction propagation affects the synchronization of the public ledger and the role inconsistency of the public ledger plays in making double spending attack achievable. Finally, we close this section by highlighting related work on measuring, analysing, and speeding up Bitcoins transaction propagation.

A. Transaction propagation

Bitcoin uses a gossip-like protocol to broadcast information throughout the network [7]. Therefore, transactions are not forwarded directly in order to avoid sending a transaction to a node that already received it from other nodes. Instead, a node announces to its neighbour nodes about the transaction availability once the transaction has been verified. As shown in Fig.2, transactions are disseminated through the network using a protocol, which includes propagating two types of messages, an INV message and a GETDATA message.

When a node receives a transaction from one of its neighbours, it sends an INV message containing the hash of the transaction to all of its peers. When a node receives an INV, it checks whether the hash of a transaction has been seen before. If it has not been seen before, the node will request the transaction by sending a GETDATA message. In terms of receiving a GETDATA message, a node responds by sending the transaction's data.

An INV message is not propagated to all of the connected peers at the same time, instead, every 100ms it is sent to a random selected peer of all connected peers. Therefore, the required time for forwarding the INV message relies on the number of connected nodes [13]. Due to the above broadcasting scenario, a delay in transaction propagation happens, and this delay combines between time which takes to validate the transaction and propagate it. Essentially, propagation delay pertains to many issues in the Bitcoin due to the inconsistency of the public ledger which comes up with the opportunity for an attacker to abuse the network consensus. Specifically, inconsistency in the public ledger will induce the dishonest nodes to disturb the confirmation operation of a valid transaction by broadcasting a conflicting transaction with the same amount of coin during the period of confirmation, in which the valid transaction waits to be added to the block chain. This type of attack is called double spending attack in which the attacker attempts to spend the same transaction output more than once.

Double spending attacks happen when an attacker creates two transactions (T_A and T_M) with the same input (same source of Bitcoin) and different outputs (different recipients, suppose we have two transactions, T_A will go to the majority of peers and T_M will go to the vendor). We can consider the double spending attack as successful when T_A is confirmed before T_M. This means the majority of peers accept T_A while the vendor accepts just T_M. This will lead to the acceptability of T_A by subsequent blocks as an original transaction and the vender can not redeem the T_M because it is considered as an invalid transaction because it is trying to spend money which has already been spent [14].

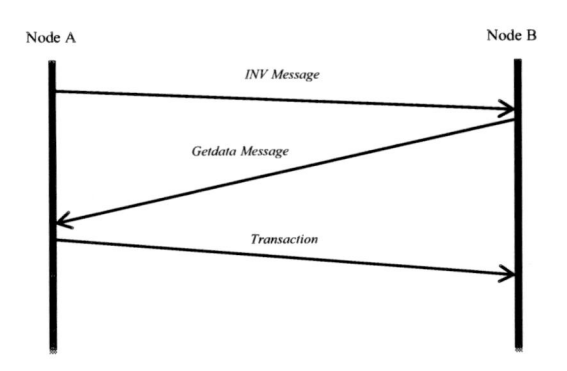

Figure 2: Transaction propagation protocol between Nodes A and B

The second scenario of double spending is when an attacker secretly mines a branch which includes, the transaction that returns the payment to himself, while disseminating the merchant's transaction [15]. The attacker will not broadcast this branch until the merchant's transaction gets confirmed. In this scenario, the merchant is going to be confident about the transaction and then he will consider delivering the product. Furthermore, the attacker has to be sure that the secret branch is longer than the public branch, so if necessary, continue extending the secret branch. Finally, an attacker broadcasts the secret branch when he confirms that the secret branch is longer than the public one. Typically, this is computationally expensive, requiring the attacker to control 50% of the computing available in the network.

B. Related works

Most previous analytical studies of the Bitcoin network have presented measurements of the network that are linked to the information propagation delay. Recent [11] research has shown that the number of nodes in the Bitcoin network and the structure of overlay network have a great impact on transaction propagation time. Their results showed that the transaction propagation time is improved by reducing the number of nodes from 6000 to 2000. Furthermore, their results demonstrated that the overlay topology of the Bitcoin network, which is not geographically localised, offers inefficient transaction propagation time. Transaction propagation delay in real Bitcoin network has been measured in [13],[16] by developing a Bitcoin client that tracks how transactions are disseminated through the network by listening for INV messages.However, previous propagation delay measurements do not represent the real propagation delay as it does not indicate the exact time by which peers announce transactions.

The probability of double spending attack in fast payments, have been measured in the previous research through analytical models, based on measurements in real Bitcoin network [12]. In terms of avoiding double spending attack, [17] introduced some counter-measures to avoid double spending attacks and proposed a prototype system, which is applied in vending machines. The main idea of this system is to set a server that will observe the transaction. When transaction propagation reaches over 40 nodes, the server will give a signal, which means that the transaction has been confirmed. Unfortunately, this solution is limited because the attacker's transaction could still be propagated to the majority of nodes.

In [18] a new protocol has been proposed which tackles the problem of inconsistency in the public ledger by reducing the information propagation time. This solution claims that the information propagation could be pipelined instead of waiting to receive the transaction. In other words, any node can immediately forward an invitation message (INV Message) that includes a list of hashes of available transactions, rather than waiting for receiving transactions. Another change has been proposed in the same theory. This change increases the geographical connectivity in Bitcoin network in order to offer faster information propagation. However, this theory reduces the propagation delay with a very low rate because the transaction still needs to visit the all nodes in the Bitcoin network. Additionally, the transaction verification time still remains inefficient due to the size of the public ledger.

A model for faster transaction propagation has been presented in [19] by considering some modifications in the transaction dissemination protocol. The core idea of this model is that when nodes receive a transaction, they check whether this transaction has been seen before in their pool. In case the transaction has not been seen before, they add the transaction to their pool and forward it to the other nodes. Otherwise, they directly forward the transaction to other neighbours without adding it to their pool. This scenario allows the fake transaction to be received by the node that issues the original transaction.

IV. BITCOIN PARAMETERS MEASUREMENT :

Large scale parameters of real Bitcoin network are difficult to predict, therefore, some certainty is required before any simulation model of Bitcoin system would be implemented. To this purpose, we provide accurate measurements of different parameters of the real Bitcoin network. In the following subsections, the measurement of transaction propagation as well as large scale measurements of real Bitcoin network will be presented. Propagation delay is very important for the validation of simulation measurements as many aspects of the Bitcoin network such as network topology, clients' behaviour, and processing delay affect it. By offering these measurments, validation of any Bitcoin simulation model would be possible through comparing the propagation delay measurements that will be collected from the Bitcoin simulator to the same measurements that have been collected in this experiment. Also the real Bitcoin network measurements are essential to parametrize any model of Bitcoin.

A. TRANSACTION PROPAGATION MEASUREMENT

In this section, we investigate how fast a transaction propagates in the Bitcoin network and how this is impacted by the number of nodes. A transaction propagation delay was measured in the prior research by setup a Bitcoin client which keeps listening for INV messages. However, we present a novel methodology by which the transaction propagation delay is accurately measured as the measurements are indicated when peers receive transactions. Experiment methodology and results are presented in the following subsections.

1) Experiment description and methodology
To measure the propagation delay, the Bitcoin protocol was implemented and used to establish connections to many points in the network, in order to measure the time that a transaction takes to reach each point. Specifically, we first implemented a measuring node, which behaves exactly like a normal node with the following functionalities. The measuring node connects to 14 reachable peers in the network. Furthermore, it

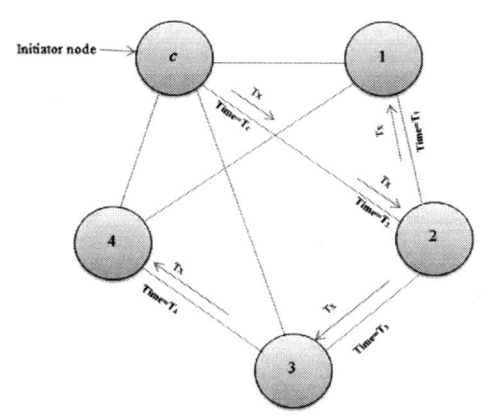

Figure 3: Illustration of propagation experimental setup

is able to create a valid transaction and send it to one peer of its connections, and then it tracks the transaction in order to record the time by which each peer of its connections announces the transaction. To measure how fast a transaction is exchanged between the connected nodes, we calculated the time by which the transaction is propagated by our measuring node and reached each node of our measuring nodes connections. Specifically, suppose a client c has connections (1,2 ,3,...., n), c propagates a transaction at time T_c, and it is received by its connected nodes at different times $(T_1, T_2, T_3, ..., T_n)$ as illustrated in Fig.3. The time differences between the first transaction propagation and subsequent receptions of the transaction by connected nodes were calculated ($\Delta t_{c,1}$,...., $\Delta t_{c,n}$) according to Eq.1:

$$\Delta t_{c,n} = T_n - T_c \qquad (1)$$

In order to get accurate measurements, the timing information was collected by running the experiment 1000 times as errors such as loss of connection and data corruption, are expected to happen in case of dealing with real network. At each run, the measuring node is randomly connected to 14 nodes. The timing information contains the hash of the transaction, the announcing nodes IP, transaction confirmation time and a local time stamp, which represents propagation time once the transaction was received.

2) Results
The propagation measurements from this experiment are shown in Fig.4. The number of connected nodes represents the sequence of the random nodes that the measuring node connects with at each run. Fig 4 indicates that during the first 13 seconds, transaction has been propagated faster and 6 nodes received it with low variance of delays. It should be noted that the transaction propagation delays is dramatically increased over nodes (9,10,14) which means that the transaction has been received by these nodes with significantly larger variances of delays. Obviously, these results reveal that

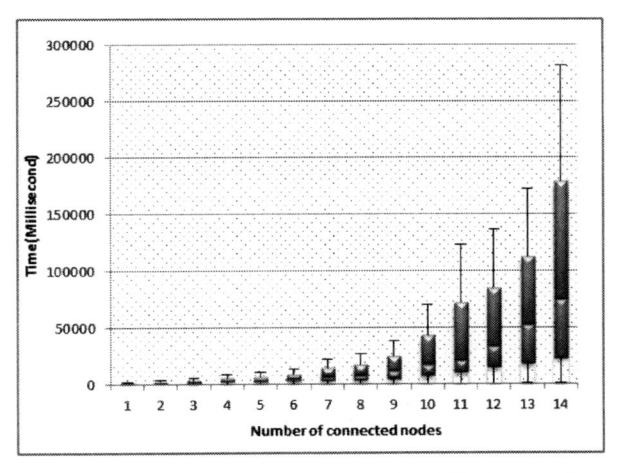

Figure 4: Transaction propagation time in real Bitcoin network

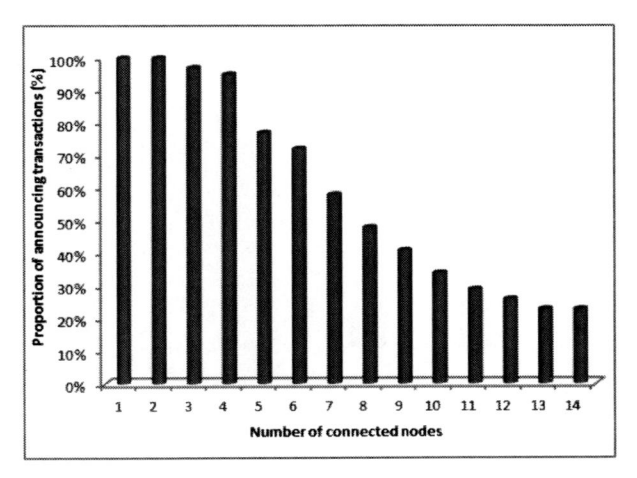

Figure 5: Proportion of each node announced the transaction

the propagation delay negatively corresponds with the number of nodes, as the total duration of subsequent announcements of the transaction by the remaining nodes increases with larger numbers of connected nodes. This happened due to each node being connected to large segments of the network, while the connected nodes were not geographically localized. On the other hand, transaction verification at each node affects trickling transaction to the remaining nodes. However, there are possible ways that can improve information propagation in the Bitcoin network which in turn would reduce the probability of double spending attacks. Reducing the noncompulsory hops in that the transaction passes through in conjunction with increasing the locality of connectivity are considered as a possible scenario that would achieve significantly faster information propagation. This can be achieved by applying a clustering theory by which the Bitcoin network nodes are fully partitioned into clusters depend on its geographical location. To evaluate any clustering theory based on improving information propagation, major changes are required to the Bitcoin protocol which would have to be accepted by the Bitcoin community. Therefore, Bitcoin model which behaves as close as real Bitcoin network is required. Both clustering theory and Bitcoin model are considered as our future work.

Surprisingly, we noticed that not all of the connected nodes received the transaction except rare cases in which all the 14 connected nodes announced the transaction. Fig.6 shows proportions of announcing transactions for each node. Each proportion was calculated over 1000 runs. Nodes 1, 2, 3 and 4 are almost announced transactions within proportions between 90-100. The proportion dramatically declined at node 5 and continued to go down to reach 23 at node 14. This pointed to the issue caused by network partitions in which the network is divided into two or more partitions due to network outages or link failure, so that no information flow between partitions is possible. Network partitions are more likely to happen within the network topology, which is not geographically localized. However, network partitions can be done by an attacker to impair main Bitcoin functions. We leave a further analysis of this issue as future work.

B. Bitcoin network measurements

In this section, we present the measurements of two Bitcoin network parameters which are number of the reachable nodes and link latencies between peers. These parameters are considered as the most influential parameters in the Bitcoin network due to their direct impact on the information propagation delay in the network. Therefore, these parameters are important to parameterise any model of Bitcoin accurately. For this purpose, Bitcoin client was implemented and used to crawl the entire Bitcoin network through establishing connections to all reachable peers in the Bitcoin network. Every five minutes the snapshot of IP addresses of all reachable peers was published by the developed crawler. We discovered that the crawler learned 313676 IP addresses but was only able to connect to 5378 peers. This indicates that the Bitcoin network size is presently around 5400 nodes.

Fig 6 shows the distribution of latencies in the real Bitcoin network. The crawler was connected to around 5000 network peers and observing a total of 20,000 ping/pong messages. It should be noted that the measured distribution only represents the latency between our crawler and other peers in the network.

As these measurements have a direct impact on the information propagation time, it is necessitated to perform these measurements when any model of Bitcoin is built. Though, attaching the measured distribution to the model would give an accurate estimate of the time delay that is taken by a transaction to reach different peers in the network.

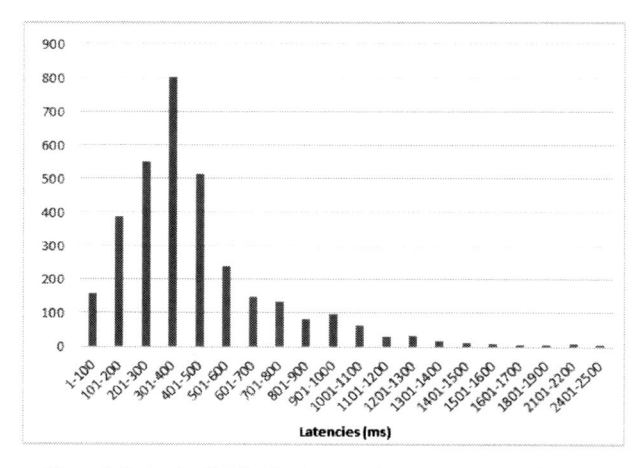

Figure 6: Latencies distribution between the measurement node and other peers

V. CONCLUSION

A brief background of Bitcoin system and block chain technology was presented in this paper. In addition, we analysed the information propagation in the real Bitcoin network. We have also discussed how propagation delay could affect the security by offering an opportunity to double spend the same coins, thereby abusing the consistency of the public ledger. Furthermore, previous studies to analyse and measure the information propagation delay were explained briefly.

In order to offer an opportunity to validate and parameterise any model of Bitcoin network, different kinds of measurements have been presented in this paper. We implemented a novel methodology to measure the transaction propagation delay in real Bitcoin network. Our measurements show that the transaction propagation time is significantly affected by the number of the connected nodes and the network topology which is not geographically localised. In addition, partitions in the connection graph are actively detected. Finally, the size of the Bitcoin network and distribution of latencies between nodes are accurately measured in this paper.

Future work:
The future work will be to examine clustering as a mechanism to improve the propagation delay. Our proposed approach claims that the fully Bitcoin network nodes could be partitioned into clusters depend on geographical location. Each node will be included in a cluster that correlates to its geographical location. We claim that giving rise to the locality of connectivity can affect the information dissemination by reducing the noncompulsory hops that the transaction passes through, so that, on other hand, this could minimize the propagation delay.

VI. REFERENCES

[1] Nakamoto, S. (2009). Bitcoin: A peer-to-peer electronic cash system. Retrieved from http://www.bitcoin.org/bitcoin.pdf.

[2] Ron, D., & Shamir, A. (2013). Quantitative analysis of the full bitcoin transaction graph. In Financia Cryptography and Data Security (pp. 6–24). Springer.

[3] Moore, T., & Christin, N. (2013). Beware the middleman: Empirical analysis of Bitcoin-exchange risk. In Financial Cryptography and Data Security (Vol. 7859, pp. 25–33). Springer.

[4] Biryukov, A., Khovratovich, D., & Pustogarov, I. (2014). Deanonymisation of clients in Bitcoin P2P network. arXiv Preprint arXiv:1405.7418.

[5] Heilman, E., Kendler, A., Zohar, A., & Goldberg, S. (2015). Eclipse Attacks on Bitcoin's Peer-to-Peer Network. In: 24th USENIX Security Symposium(USENIX Security 15), Washington, D.C., USENIX Association.

[6] Androulaki, E., Karame, G. O., Roeschlin, M., Scherer, T., & Capkun, S. (2013). Evaluating user privacy in bitcoin. In Financial Cryptography and Data Security (pp. 34–51). Springer.

[7] Ober, M., Katzenbeisser, S., & Hamacher, K. (2013). Structure and Anonymity of the Bitcoin Transaction Graph. Future Internet, 5(2), 237–250. doi:10.3390/fi5020237.

[8] Koshy, P., Koshy, D., & Mcdaniel, P. (2014). An analysis of anonymity in bitcoin using p2p network traffic. In Proceedings of FinancialCryptography and Data Security (FC'14). Springer.

[9] Barber, S., Boyen, X., Shi, E., & Uzun, E. (2012). Bitter to better— how to make bitcoin a better currency. In Financial cryptography and data security (pp. 399–414). Springer.

[10] Biryukov, A., Khovratovich, D., & Pustogarov, I. (2014). Deanonymisation of clients in Bitcoin P2P network. arXiv Preprint arXiv:1405.7418.

[11] Miller, A., & Jansen, R. Shadow-Bitcoin: Scalable simulation via direct execution of multithreaded applications. IACR Cryptology ePrint Archive 2015 (2015), 469.

[12] Karame, G. O., Androulaki, E., & Capkun, S. (2012). Two Bitcoins at the Price of One? Double- Spending Attacks on Fast Payments in Bitcoin. IACR Cryptology ePrint Archive, 2012, 248.

[13] Neudecker, T., Andelfinger, P., & Hartenstein, H. (2015). A simulation model for analysis of attacks on the Bitcoin peer-to-peer network. In Integrated Network Management (IM), 2015 IFIP/IEEE International Symposium on (pp. 1327-1332). IEEE.

[14] Karame, G. O., Androulaki, E., & Capkun, S. (2012). Two Bitcoins at the Price of One? Double- Spending Attacks on Fast Payments in Bitcoin. IACR Cryptology ePrint Archive, 2012, 248.

[15] Rosenfeld, M. (2014). Analysis of Hashrate-Based Double Spending, 13. Cryptography and Security. Retrieved from http://arxiv.org/abs/1402.2009.

[16] Decker, C., & Wattenhofer, R. (2013, September). Information propagation in the bitcoin network. In Peer-to-Peer Computing (P2P), 2013 IEEE Thirteenth International Conference on (pp. 1-10). IEEE.

[17] Bamert, T., Decker, C., Elsen, L., Wattenhofer, R., & Welten, S. (2013). Have a snack, pay with Bitcoins. IEEE P2P 2013 Proceedings, 1–5. doi:10.1109/P2P.2013.6688717.

[18] Stathakopoulou, C.(2015).A faster Bitcoin network. Tech. rep., ETH, Zurich,. SemesterThesis, supervised by Decker.C and Wattenhofer.R.

[19] Karame, G. O., Androulaki, E., Roeschlin, M., Gervais, A., & Èapkun, S. (2015). Misbehavior in Bitcoin: A Study of Double-Spending and Accountability. ACM Transactions on Information and System Security (TISSEC), 18(1), 2.

P2P-based M2M Community Applications

Michael Steinheimer[1,3], Ulrich Trick[1], Woldemar Fuhrmann[2], and Bogdan Ghita[3]

[1]Research Group for Telecommunication Networks, Frankfurt University of Applied Sciences, Frankfurt/M., Germany
[2]Department for Computer Science, University of Applied Sciences Darmstadt, Darmstadt, Germany
[3]Centre for Security, Communications and Network Research, University of Plymouth, Plymouth, UK
steinheimer@e-technik.org, trick@e-technik.org, w.fuhrmann@fbi.h-da.de, bogdan.ghita@plymouth.ac.uk

Abstract—This publication presents a novel concept for decentralised service and application provision in a Peer-to-Peer (P2P) connected Machine-To-Machine (M2M) network based on community mechanisms. Several execution environments are introduced and evaluated. Requirements are defined to achieve application/ service provision in M2M application fields. This publication also introduces an application, consisting of several services, for building surveillance, realised via the presented concept of P2P based application provision in M2M networks.

Keywords—Service/Application Provision; P2P; M2M

I. INTRODUCTION

In previous publication a concept for decentralised service provision by end-users has been presented.[4] The aim of the concept described in that publication is to enable end-users (previous service consumer) to take the role of a service provider and offer services for other end-users and corporations. The end-users can be networked to provide cooperative services, consisting of several identical or different services, realised by individual end-users. These services can be aggregated/ composed and can be consumed by central corporations or other customers. The approach of provision services by end-users and consummation of these services by end-users is defined as "horizontal service provision" (illustrated in Fig. 1). The approaches of service provision by end-users (individual or cooperative) which are consumed by central corporations or other end-users are defined as "bottom-up service provision" (illustrated in Fig. 2).

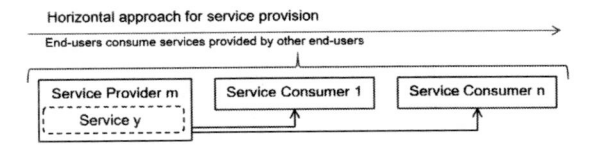

Fig. 1. Horizontal approach for service provisioning

Until now, service provision followed the centralised approach (central service provider which provides services to the end-user). The presented concept changes the relationship from service provider to service consumer which can be described as bottom-up service relationship (end-user jointly offers a service that can be used by central corporation) or as a horizontal service relationship (end-user offer services to other end-users). The described concept is realised by M2M. For this a framework has been defined, that realises service/ application provision using SIP-based P2P networking, so that no central appliances for realisation are required. Furthermore the concept includes social networking approaches, by forming communities and sub-communities for establishing the P2P network and networking the participants corresponding to their interests, geographical locations as well as different application field etc. Through the described concept, in addition of service/ application provision in end-user domain, also service/ application provision in M2M application field becomes possible, whereby M2M devices also are considered as peers.

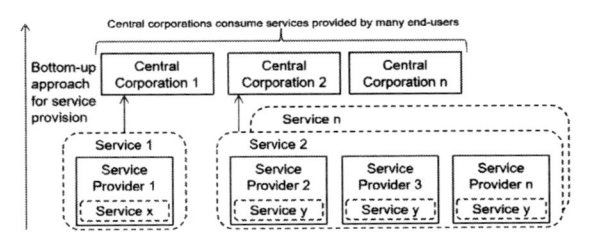

Fig. 2. Bottom-up approach for service provisioning

This publication specifies the concept more detailed to provide community applications which are not covered (and not focused) by the ETSI M2M standard. The presented concept defines a novel framework for application provision, based on M2M Systems.

The service/ application provision in M2M, according to the presented concept, can be separated in two main categories: 1. Autonomous service provision (compare Fig. 1). Here peers provide a service which is consumed by other peers on the same hierarchical level. 2. Cooperative service provision (illustrated in Fig. 3). Here many peers provide a service which is consumed by other peers on same or higher hierarchical level. In case of service aggregation peers e.g. provide a joint service by simultaneously offering the same service. In case of service composition, peers provide a joint service by offering different services.

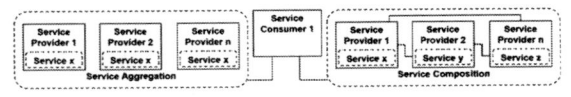

Fig. 3. Cooperative service Provisioning

II. TERMS AND DEFINITIONS OF SERVICE PROVISION IN M2M

In order to clarify how an application in M2M context is structured, definitions of [5, 6, 7] are used to classify and separate service and application in context of application/ service provision in M2M (illustrated in Fig. 4). It illustrates that an application consists of one or more underlying services that are combined (i.e. aggregated or composed) and, if required, exchange information. The services are realised by one or more service components, which form the building blocks of services. The service components itself are realised via several software applications executed on several execution environments.

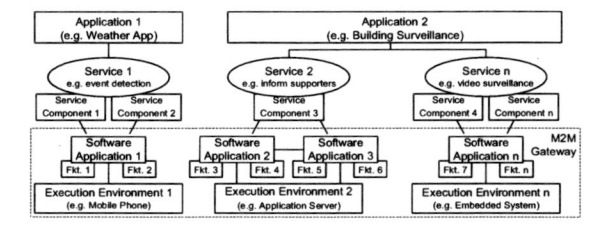

Fig. 4. Classification of Service and Application

A service as well as an application can be realised on technical or non-technical principles (i.e. it can be provided using technical devices, e.g. computers, or by a human, e.g. personal assistance services). To distinguish the kind of services and applications, if necessary they are indicated as technical service/ application or non-technical service/ application. General indication of both is service/ application.

In the presented concept of P2P based application provision in M2M, definition of service and application follows the definition illustrated in Fig. 4. Same as for service and application, peers can be technical devices or humans (if applicable supported by technical devices). To distinguish the kind of peer, if necessary, it is indicated as technical peer or non-technical peer. General indication of both is peer. Peers are able to provide services. The service is executed on the execution environment of the specific device or, in case of a non-technical service, provided by the personal execution of the human service provider (if applicable supported by a device providing a technical service, e.g. a Smartphone).

Based on references [8, 9, 10, 11] M2M is defined as follows: Machine-to-Machine communications (M2M) "refer to physical telecommunication based interconnection for data exchange between two ETSI M2M compliant entities, like: device, gateways and network infrastructure"[8] M2M area network provides "physically and MAC layer connectivity between different M2M devices connected to the same M2M area network or allowing an M2M device to gain access to a public network via […] a gateway."[10] "M2M Applications: are respectively Device Application (DA), Gateway Application (GA) and Network Application (NA)."[9] "M2M Applications […] run the service logic […]."[8] In general [8] defines an application as an "entity (typically in software) designed to perform specific tasks on behalf of /in order to help a user to operate for a specific goal." "M2M Application Service Provider: is an entity (e.g. a company) that provides M2M Application Services in the M2M System to the end user."[8] „M2M value-added services are not services at the M2M application level. The M2M value-added services relate to the data communication services themselves, not to the application in the M2M device and M2M server. Examples of M2M value-added services are: QoS and priority differentiation; charging and subscription management; device management; connection monitoring; fraud control; secure connections."[10] This statement is substantiated by [11] who summarises that despite all networking and communication abilities all M2M applications focus on optimisation of collaboration of M2M devices based on M2M applications within a defined, separated overall process, often using a M2M service platform.[11] According to ETSI the end user operates M2M Application Services (provided by M2M Application Service Provider, i.e. companies). This especially means that the end user (according to the ETSI standard of M2M) does not create and provide services as well as is a different role separated from the M2M Application Service Provider. In summary this means that up to this point only a framework is defined for provision of M2M Network Applications and no framework for application provision on end users domain has been defined yet.

III. EXECUTION ENVIRONMENTS FOR SERVICES/ APPLICATIONS

Currently several concepts for hosting services/ applications exists. Well-known approaches of service/ application provision are central server approach (using servers, hosting the applications on central locations in the network) and Cloud Computing approach. Next to this approaches two new architectural approaches for hosting services and applications came up: Edge and Fog Computing.

"Edge computing is all about pushing processing for certain data intensive, remotely isolated applications away from the core of the data center to the outer edges of the network where all the interactions are happening and the actual processing needs to take place."[12] Mobile-edge Computing is a part of Edge Computing which "provides IT and cloud-computing capabilities within the Radio Access Network (RAN) in close proximity to mobile subscribers."[13] "Mobile-edge Computing can be seen as a cloud server running at the edge of a mobile network and performing specific tasks that could not be achieved with traditional network infrastructure. Machine-to-Machine gateway and control functions are one example […]."[13] The second new approach of hosting services and applications is Fog Computing, which "is a highly virtualized platform that provides compute, storage, and networking services between end devices […], typically, but not exclusively located at the edge of network."[14] Also [15] describes, that virtualisation plays a big role in Fog Computing and „the Fog enables user devices to become the virtualisation platform themselves". "In the fog, both the network and the services running on top of it can be deployed on demand in a fog of [..] devices."[15] In [15] Fog Computing is defined as „a scenario where a huge number of heterogeneous (wireless and sometimes autonomous) ubiquitous and decentralised devices communicate and potentially cooperate among them and with the network to perform storage and processing tasks without the intervention of third parties. These tasks can be for supporting basic network functions or new services and applications that run in a sandboxed environment. Users leasing part of their devices to host these services get incentives for doing so". Fog Computing is defined according to [14] as "a platform to deliver […] services and applications at the edge of the network".

The main intention of Edge and Fog Computing is to support network services, reduce the load in the core network, enlarge the Quality of Service for the customers, provide storage as well as perform distributed computing tasks. Considering the definition of Cloud Computing and application provision using centralised server approach as well as the definitions of Edge and Fog Computing acc. to [12, 13, 14, 15], Fig. 5 illustrates the execution environments of services/ applications according to the several approaches.

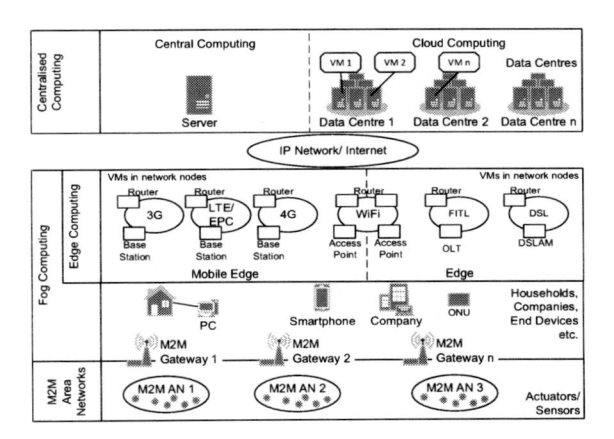

Fig. 5. Execution Environments of Services and Applications

Edge Computing is realised in the infrastructure provided by the network operator (i.e. access networks or devices located close to the customers, e.g. services executed in base stations). This eliminates service provision by end-users in the edge. Fog computing also is executed in same infrastructure and, in addition, more close to the customer (e.g. in IADs) and extended by virtualisation concepts. Edge computing can only be operated by the network operators because no one else has access to the network equipment located in the access network. Fog computing also requires the existence of central corporations for coordination of the distributed computing tasks as well as the management and arrangement of the virtualised services executed in devices next to the customers. Despite Fog Computing offers the possibility for service execution next to the customer, end-users service provision is still not integrated due to missing access to the infrastructure of the Fog Computing provider.

Combining the concept of P2P based service/ application provision by end-users with Fog Computing aspects of virtualisation and service execution next to end-users, by enabling the platforms next to the end-users for execution of services provided by the end-users, with possibility of information exchange between end-users devices, forms a novel concept for provision of M2M services and enables end-users to participate in application provision on end-users domain.

IV. P2P BASED SERVICE/ APPLICATION PROVISION IN M2M

The following chapter describes a solution for P2P based service provision in M2M. First a framework is introduced to provide a solution for service provision in M2M networks. Afterwards the requirements are defined to achieve application/ service provisioning in M2M application fields. This chapter closes with a description of the communication between the involved parties and an evaluation of the presented approach regarding existing execution environments (described in chapter III).

Previous publications, e.g. [1, 2, 3] describe that existing research and development activities for optimisation of Smart Homes and Smart Grids do not consider service provisioning, networking and decentralised optimisation via information exchange. Therefore, a solution is presented in [1, 2, 3], oriented at the personal needs of users, to offer cost-efficient energy management, according to users personal needs, and integration within their house automation as well as combined with multimedia communication. Also the interaction between households is included to exchange information regarding the local energy production and consumption. This information is used for joint, independent and decentralised energy optimisation. The principles and architectures of the proposed framework for provision of services and optimisation possibilities in Smart Grids are presented in [1, 2]. The Concept is mainly based on a Service Management Framework (SMF), consisting of a Service Delivery Platform (SDP) and a Service Creation Environment (SCE), see [3], which is installed in the local households. The SCE brings the functionality to design and configure value-added services graphically, according to the personal needs of the users, to monitor and control actuators, sensors and devices in user households. The SDP is used to provide a solution for service provision, service control and service management and serves as a runtime environment for the generated services. SCE and SDP in combination allow easy service design by the customer, as well as local controlling/ management of energy producers and devices (energy consumer) in Smart Homes. With that solution the optimisation of energy consumption e.g. by optimal load distribution is possible.

The presented concept include the clustering of households for more effective optimisation because of independent optimisation of individual households does not automatically lead to optimisation of the local or distribution grid. The concept is totally based on decentralised approaches to avoid central instances in the infrastructure. In order to provide the aggregation of households, the SMFs of individual households are connected using a SIP-based peer-to-peer (P2P) network as introduced in [16]. To solve issues for networking, avoid legal restrictions, optimisation, missing mechanisms to form the P2P network or the fact that user aim different goals for optimisation (e.g. cost reduction, obtain only "green energy", most benefit for energy supply) the P2P networking approach was extended by community mechanism (see [1, 2, 3]). The community-based approach forms a new comfortable way to join a network of peers, whereby the connection of peers is done by joining the users to a social network. Using IP-based information exchange guarantees the applicability by everyone that has access to the Internet. Therefore the realisation is possible with minimal costs. Inside that Energy-Community not only the single customer goals are considered, the goal is to reach a benefit for every participant in the community. In addition the participants can form sub-communities to address common shared interests (e.g. energy saving, cost reduction, obtain only "green energy").

References [1, 2, 3] present the principles of the proposed framework for creation, provisioning and optimisation of services in Smart Homes and Smart Grids. Also the architecture of the implementation of the proposed solution is described. As exemplary service the optimisation of the energy consumption in single and clustered Smart Homes is outlined that forms a novel solution for optimisation in Smart Grids. This described framework demonstrates that service provisioning and joint optimisation by end-users can be implemented in an application field that hadn't addressed those topics yet.

The novel concept of a P2P-connected community offers many advantages and can be applied in various sectors of M2M to form intelligent environments. The SMF is the main component of the solution in provision and consummation of M2M services by connecting service providers and service consumers, using an overall solution for information exchange. All peers, providing services and applications, are associated in a M2M community. The M2M community is the mechanism to form the P2P network and avoid legal restrictions. The M2M community forms a social network of peers. Various sub-communities are used to address different application fields, interests, geographical locations etc. Fig. 6 illustrates the collocation of M2M Community, sub-communities and applications based on the classification of service and application illustrated in Fig. 4. Existing infrastructure (IP network and devices, e.g. IAD or smartphone) can be used to provide different kind of services in different application field with same and cost efficient hardware (e.g. Smartphone). Fig. 6 illustrates the overall architecture of execution environments for applications/ services, where the community and the sub-communities are integrated. The overall goal is to provide a concept for application/ service provisioning in M2M application field and to provide this applications/ services using P2P mechanisms without central instances.

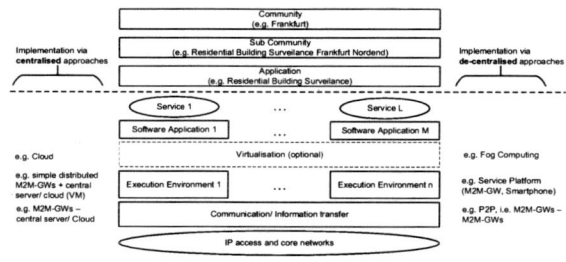

Fig. 6. Collocation of M2M Community, Sub-Communities, Applications

The networking enables the participating peers to provide a service that can be consumed by others. Especially the cooperative service provisioning is considered in the concept (e.g. to provide services consumed by central corporations).

The overall goal can be separated in the goals "joint service provisioning" and "autonomous service provisioning". Joint service provision is separated into service aggregation (provide a joint service by simultaneously offering the same service) and service composition (provide a joint service by offering different services).

M2M is a special field of networked devices with special requirements and limitation for available data storage, processing power, bandwidth etc. For application/ service provision and consummation in M2M, according to the presented concept, following requirements have been defined: Possibility for service provision (incl. cooperative service provision) by end-users using existing resources (e.g. IAD or mobile phone); autonomous service provision; decentralised mechanism for service description/ registration by devices and people; unified communication of service provider and consumer; management of constraints for services (e.g. temporal and local availability). Requirements according networking and resources: Integrated multimedia communication (and other IT services) to services and service platform; minimal hardware requirements for decentralised service execution; networking of service provider and service consumer for decentralised communication and cooperative service provision; estimable Quality of Service (QoS) in dependence of service; avoidance of central instances for (joint) service provision; efficient usage of limited resources (available data storage, processing power, network connectivity); determinability and predictability of network capabilities (bandwidth, availability, latency); flexible, scalable, and robust self-organised network; solutions must address scalability, robustness, openness, and flexibility.

For satisfying the requirement of integrated multimedia communication, the communication unit of the SMF provides an interface for Next Generation Network conform multimedia communication which also offers total communication possibility between the peers. The communication between the peers is realised based on IP-technology (via Internet/ NGNs) which is todays and future standard in network communication. Also IPv6 offers a large scalability for addressing devices. The information exchange between the peers and the connection of the peers is based on the Session Initiation Protocol (SIP)[17]. The communication protocol SIP is a standardised, widely adopted communication protocol for signalling in Internet/ NGNs. SIP provides standardised functionality for information exchanged based on the subscribe/ notify principle. In addition for messages exchange between the peers, SIP is also used for further communication e.g. via audio/ video call, IM. This allows the communication of service consumers and service providers for detailed coordination of service usage (e.g. personal consultations, etc.). Also SIP has standardised functionality for transport of XML-data and mechanisms for reliable communication, realised in OSI Application Layer that offers the functionality to act in heterogeneous networks. SIP has already integrated control functionalities for point-to-point/ multicast connections and provides many features that can be advantageously used for the connection of peers and the exchange of information. Advantageous functionalities of SIP are: The globally defined SIP address (SIP URI) for users that allows location-independent availability via unique identifiers; Location Service functionality for worldwide localisation of users over the Internet (including mobile users); Presence functionality to request information regarding the availability of users; Event Notification Framework[19] that "enables SIP entities to subscribe to specific events occurring on other SIP entities."[11] and Instant Messaging[20] that can be used "to carry short text messages in a simple way from one SIP entity to another."[11] In addition SIP provides existing security functionalities, described in [17]. Furthermore Interactive Connectivity Establishment (ICE)[18] can be used to traverse a Network Address and Port Translation (NAPT) gateway or a Firewall.

TABLE I. EVALUATION OF EXECUTION ENVIRONMENTS

Advantages/ Dis-advantages reg. single M2M Application	Centr.	Cloud	Fog Computing Edge		P2P
Costs	-	o	+	+	+
Short time to market	-	+	+	+	+
Demand for energy	-	+	+	+	+
Large flexibility	-	+	-	+	+
High availability reg. platform breakdown	o	+	o	o	+
Privacy	-	-	-	+	+
Ability of end-users for service provision	o	o	-	+	+
Scalability	-	+	o	+	+
M2M Gateway integrated	-	-	-	+	+
Support of sensor networks with high amount of nodes	-	-	o	+	+
Virtualisation possible	-	+	+	+	-
Distributed data storage	-	o	-	+	+
Independence of network/ platform operator	-	-	-	-	+
Avoidance of central instances	-	-	-	+	+
Automated (optimised) networking	-	o	-	o	+
Corporate application provision by cooperation of end-users	+	+	-	-	+
Community approach is realisable	+	+	-	-	+

V. EVALUATION OF APPROACHES FOR APPLICATION PROVISION

TABLE I illustrates an extract of an evaluation for M2M application provision regarding the approaches introduced in chapter III (central server approach, Cloud Computing, Edge/ Fog Computing and application provision according to the proposed P2P approach). Especially the topics "Independence of network/ platform operator", "Automated (optimised) networking", "Corporate application provision by cooperation of end-users" and "Community approach is realisable" shows the advantages of P2P based application provision as. The positive evaluation of the P2P approach is illustrated once more when evaluations are not carried out respect a single M2M application, but considers multiple applications.

VI. APPLICATION EXAMPLE

In the following the application "P2P Building Surveillance" is described with the basic functionality of building surveillance. The application observes certain buildings if defined events occur in the building (e.g. fire or intrusion detection) and informs the corresponding supporter (peers) about this event. The application is realised by a sub-community for building surveillance with P2P interconnected participants. The aim of that sub-community is to assist each other for surveillance of certain buildings. The specialty of this application, as same as for the complete approach, is that no central corporation for application provision are required.The application consists of in total seven different services which are composed to realise the application and provided by the different peers (e.g. executed inside of a Smart Home platform or a mobile phone). All services can be executed independently and in particular provided directly by different peers, located at different locations in the network (i.e. that it is possible that all peers are connected via separated access networks to the core network). For information of the supporter (offering the non-technical service of building monitoring) two different variants exist. Variant 1: Supporting peers register at service 1 with indication of kind of event, specific building ID, and their corresponding contact information. Service 1 generates a list of supporters which are responsible for a specific event occurred in a specific building (or many buildings, e.g. fire brigade). The supporters also report their current availability status and geographical locations continuously to service 2. Service 2 manages the availability information as well as the geographical locations of supporters and responses location and availability information of supporter, if requested. If a supporting peer should be informed about an event, then a SIP NOTIFY message is sent to it (Fig. 7, step 10). Variant 2: Supporters don't report their current availability and location information. If the support is required they receive a SIP SUBSCRIBE message and response with a SIP NOTIFY message about acceptance (Fig. 7, step 10). Service 3 records sensor data (e.g. smoke detector or intrusion detection sensor) and forwards the sensor value for requested sensor ID to service 4 (incl. destination address contained in request. Sensors transmit sensor values periodically or at state changes to service 3. Service 4 transmits requested sensor values to the contact destination contained in the request. Service 5 receives the current sensor values of a specific building and evaluates if an event has occurred. This service can be configured for self-contained request of sensor values at service 3 or advices same service to transmit the sensor value to a specific destination address. If this service detects an event, it generates a notification event. Service 6 specifies which supporter should be notified. This service receives an alarm event as well as building ID and determines (using service 1) the supporter which should be notified, depending on its availability and location information (using service 2). If supporter is available, the service returns the contact information as well as event occurred. Service 7 contacts the supporter about occurred events in monitored buildings, including information regarding event and location of building, either by sending a SIP SUBSCRIBE or by sending a SIP NOTIFY. Fig. 7 shows the combination of the services described above for realisation of the application for building surveillance.

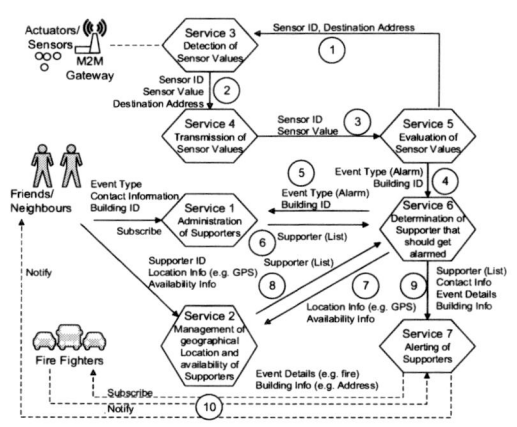

Fig. 7. Service Interaction of Application „P2P Building Surveillance"

VII. CONCLUSION

This publication presented a novel concept of service/ application provision in M2M and defines a so far missing framework using SIP-based P2P networks with communities. This concept offers new possibilities for applications, realised by several peers, independent of central appliances or corporations. Especially the concept of cooperative service provision enables new application fields. Requirements have been defined to realise service/ application provision in M2M. Definition and classification of software application/ service and applications in M2M as well as classification of execution environments of services and applications offers detailed indexing and evaluation of several approaches for service/ application provision. Based on this the evaluation of approaches for service/ application provision has indicated that the concept of P2P-based service/ application provision has explicit advantages compared with the other approaches, especially when combining the presented concept with elements of Fog Computing. The presented application "P2P Building Surveillance" clarifies the concept and illustrates exemplarily which new application fields can be addressed by the concept, without utilisation of central appliances or corporations. Using the existing IP network infrastructure (Internet or NGNs) and devices (e.g. IADs or Smartphones) enables the realisation of M2M applications without additional hardware.

REFERENCES

[1] M. Steinheimer, U. Trick, W. Fuhrmann, B. Ghita, "Load reduction in distribution networks through P2P networked energy-community", Proc. of Fifth International Conference on Internet Technologies & Applications (ITA 13), Wrexham, Wales, UK, September 2013

[2] M. Steinheimer, U. Trick, W. Fuhrmann, B. Ghita, "P2P-based community concept for M2M Applications", Proc. of Second International Conference on Future Generation Communication Technologies (FGCT 2013), London, UK, December 2013

[3] M. Steinheimer, U. Trick, P. Ruhrig, R. Tönjes, M. Fischer, D. Hölker, "SIP-basierte P2P-Vernetzung in einer Energie-Community", ITG-Fachbericht 242: Mobilkommunikation, VDE Verlag GmbH, Osnabrück, Germany, ISBN: 978-3-8007-3516-7, ISSN: 0932-6022, pp. 64, Mai 2013

[4] M. Steinheimer, U. Trick, W. Fuhrmann, B. Ghita, "P2P based service provisioning in M2M networks", Proc. of Sixth International Conference on Internet Technologies & Applications (ITA 15), Wrexham, Wales, UK, September 2015

[5] ITU-T Y.101 (2000), Recommendation, "Global Information Infrastructure terminology: Terms and definitions", ITU

[6] ISO IEC 20000-1:2011 (2011) "Part 1: Service management system requirements", IEEE

[7] ITIL V3.1.24 (2007) "Glossary of Terms, Definitions and Acronyms", ITIL

[8] ETSI TR 102 725, V1.1.1, 2013-06: Technical Report, "Machine-to-Machine communications (M2M); Definitions", ETSI TISPAN

[9] TS 102 690: Machine-to-Machine communications (M2M); Functional architecture, V.2.1.1. ETSI, October 2013

[10] Boswarthick, David; Elloumi, Omar; Hersent, Olivier: M2M Communications – A Systems Approach. Wiles; 2012

[11] Trick, Ulrich and Weber, Frank (2015), "SIP und Telekommunikationsnetze", De Greuyter, Berlin, Germany, ISBN: 978-3-486-77853-3

[12] LeClair 2014, http://insights.wired.com/profiles/blogs/the-edge-of-computing-it-s-not-all-about-the-cloud#axzz3rC9fmJ23, The Edge of Computing_It_is_Not_All_About_the_Cloud.pdf, posted by Dave LeClair on July 22, 2014, Last visited 2015-11-11

[13] ETSI 2014, Mobile-Edge Computing–Introductory Technical White Paper, https://portal.etsi.org/Portals/0/TBpages/MEC/Docs/Mobile-edge_Computing_-_Introductory_Technical_White_Paper_V1%2018-09-14.pdf, Mobile-edge_Computing_-_Introductory_Technical_White_Paper_V1 18-09-14.pdf

[14] Bonomi 2012, "Fog Computing and Its Role in the Internet of Things", ACM, p13.pdf, http://conferences.sigcomm.org/sigcomm/2012/paper/mcc/p13.pdf

[15] Vaquero 2014, "Finding your Way in the Fog: Towards a Comprehensive Definition of Fog Computing", ACM SIGCOMM, 0000000-0000003.pdf

[16] A. Lehmann, W. Fuhrmann, U. Trick, B. Ghita, "New possibilities for the provision of value-added services in SIP-based peer-to-peer networks", Proc. of SEIN (Symposium on Security, E-learning, Internet and Networking), University of Wrexham, UK, November 2008

[17] IETF (The Internet Engineering Task Force), Request For Comments (RFC) 3261, "SIP: Session Initiation Protocol", June 2002

[18] IETF (The Internet Engineering Task Force), Request For Comments (RFC) 5245, "Interactive Connectivity Establishment (ICE): A Protocol for Network Address Translator (NAT) Traversal for Offer/Answer Protocols", April 2010

[19] IETF (The Internet Engineering Task Force), Request For Comments (RFC) 3265, "Session Initiation Protocol (SIP) Specific Event Notification", June 2002

[20] IETF (The Internet Engineering Task Force), Request For Comments (RFC) 3428, "Session Initiation Protocol (SIP) Extension for Instant Messaging", December 2002

Identity-as-a-Service (IDaaS): a Missing Gap for Moving Enterprise Applications in Inter-Cloud

Tri Hoang Vo
Deutsche Telekom
Berlin, Germany
Tri.Vo-Hoang@telekom.de

Woldemar Fuhrmann
University of Applied Sciences Darmstadt
Darmstadt, Germany
w.fuhrmann@fbi.h-da.de

Klaus-Peter Fischer-Hellmann
Digamma GmbH
Darmstadt, Germany
K.P.Fischer-Hellmann@digamma.de

Abstract—Migration of existing enterprise applications to the Cloud requires heavy adaptation effort in individual architectural components of the applications. Existing work has focused on migrating the whole application or a particular component to the Cloud with functional and non-functional aspects. However, none of them has focused so far on the adaptation of web service security. Towards this goal, we focus on the adaptation of web service security for migrating applications from local hosting to the Cloud, and for moving applications in Inter-Cloud environment. Identity-as-a-service (IDaaS) decouples web service security from the business logic as a manageable resource during the life cycle of an application in the Cloud environment. On the other hand, IDaaS provides identity roaming for Cloud users to access multiple service providers on demand, but also preserve user's privacy. IDaaS coordinates automated trust negotiation between Cloud users, who want to enforce their data privacy, and service providers, who have heterogeneous security policy in federated security domains. In this paper, we first introduce IDaaS with scenarios and new requirements in comparison to traditional Identity Management systems, and propose a brief model for IDaaS.

Keywords—identity as a service; federated identity management; inter-cloud; identity roaming; attribute-based access control; privacy-aware access control

I. INTRODUCTION

In a local hosting environment, traditional applications have their own implementation for authentication and authorization. One local application has n user accounts. The management process of user identities associated with different levels of access control gave birth to Identity Management (IDM). In Cloud computing, enterprise applications come from federated security domains; provide themselves as a Service Provider (SP) and cooperate with each other. From the beginning, they might adapt their local IDM with one another manually. However as time goes by, their applications migrate to another Cloud provider, or their partner service de-provisioning from the current Cloud provider, so they need to synchronize and grant new access controls upon each change. In such a dynamic provisioning environment on the Cloud, enterprise applications may prefer outsourcing their security implementation to a third party central service [1]. In this case, their security can be strengthened by a specialized provider and reduce their cost.

A traditional authorization system is Role Based Access Control (RBAC), whereby access control depends on the role of an entity after it authenticates to the system. Developers of the application also tend to hardcoding the authorization logics into the source code of the program and only these developers can understand it. Authorization hardcoding is in contrast to a policy-based approach, in which administrators can manage different rules and dynamically changed interpreted logic without modifying the underlying implementation [2]. Without policy-based approach, it is a big obstacle for applications to be portable on the Clouds, because developers have to adapt source code to various security domains with different security policies.

The Attribute Based Access Control (ABAC) is a policy-based approach for fine-grained authorization because access control in this approach does not require identifying the entity as a whole, but depends on its attributes, for example: "A user can buy a specific DVD if he is an adult". XACML (eXtensible Access Control Markup Language) [3] is a standard policy language and supports ABAC. A reference architecture includes four main components: Policy Decision Point (PDP) evaluates access request against the security policies, Policy Enforcement Points (PEP) enforces authorization decision from PDP, Policy Information Point (PIP) stores and collects missing user attributes in the request, and Policy Administration Point (PAP) administrates the policy. Gartner predicts: "By 2020, 70% of all businesses will use ABAC as the dominant mechanism to protect critical assets" [4]. This is the reason why we focus on IDM not only for the traditional RBAC, but also for ABAC. Existing work adapted functional components of applications to the Cloud environment [5]. The adaptation for authentication and authorization has security challenges and needs more research.

From the user's perspective, users may have multiple identities with public and private profiles in the Internet. They may prefer to access multiple SPs in federated security domains, but also preserve their privacy. When users do not store their personal identities in a local machine, but in an SP in the Cloud, they may be interested in questions such as where their data are stored actually, how secure it is, who can access it except themselves. Even if SPs specified their privacy policies, we cannot guarantee that they will follow their policies and will not transfer user data to another party. If users cannot trust any third parties to hold their data, they might prefer to trust themselves. In a user-centric approach, users actively decide which identity credentials they want to exchange with which SPs. They can selectively disclose a minimal attribute set [6] or hide their identities by using anonymous credentials in transactions with SPs [7] [8].

However, user-centric approach has a limitation for the users themselves because it overloads the IDM tasks to the user's decision in every transaction. Moreover, anonymous credentials require SPs to accept it and to develop an adaptation. But most SPs, who select an Identity Provider (IdP) based on how much information they can collect from the user [9], are not likely to support anonymous credentials.

OASIS Identity in the Cloud TC [10] mentioned Identity-as-a-Service (IDaaS) as an approach to identity management in which an entity (individual or organization) relies on special service provider's functionalities that allows the entity to perform an electronic transaction, which requires identity data managed by this provider. Since the definition is non-standard and coarse, in the following paper we revisit the requirements of a traditional IDM system by Kim Cameron [11] and specify which requirements are still missing in Cloud computing. An IDM system is much likely to succeed when it benefits to all parties, including users, SPs and IdP [9]. This is our goal to propose such a model for IDaaS.

In the first place, we will start with scenarios and analyze missing requirements of IDaaS in section II and III, respectively. In section IV, we will propose a draft model of IDaaS: how it should look, and whether the given model could be successful, based on lessons learned from failures of IDM system in the past. In the end, we will summarize related work that helped us to understand and to propose the draft model.

II. MOTIVATING SCENARIOS

IBM's Cloud Computing Reference Architecture [12] defines three main roles in any cloud computing environment: a service creator develops a service running on one or more platforms, a Cloud provider who runs those services on demand, and Cloud consumers or end users who consume these services. Based on these roles, we define the following scenarios. A Cloud provider, for example Amazon WS, opens a Software (or Platform) as a service business market place. Service creators register two SPs in the repository: An office service for multiple users to corporate their daily work and a storage service for saving data. The following issues come up very often:

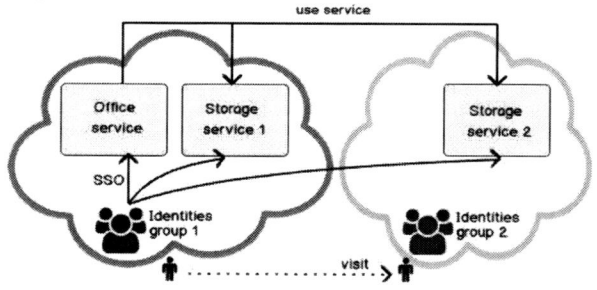

Fig. 1. User visits another Cloud in distant location

1) Dynamic Single-Sign-On (SSO): The Cloud provider already has a number of users, who agreed on a set of policies for data privacy. They signed the contracts and provided their billing information. Fig. 1 shows an end user who uses the two Cloud services. Without Single-Sign-On support, he has to use two different credentials: one credential to download his data from the storage service locally and another one to re-upload the data to the office service, although the two services reside on the same Cloud provider. On the other hand, the office service comes from a local environment. It has its own user accounts and security policies. The office service might offer its local users to SSO to other Cloud services. In traditional IDM, tenant administrator pre-configures IdP manually as trust parties to verify user's authentication request and issue authentication token for users to SSO to multiple relying services. Problems may occur when privacy policies of Cloud users and the security policies of relying services conflict with each other.

2) Dynamic service binding: The Cloud provider may have a statistic report about the business market place. The report may indicate that most users, who use the office service, also use the storage service. Based on such a statistic report, the creator of the office service might want to cooperate with the storage service as its persistent backend. The current solution in IDM provides an IdP to issue credentials for each relying services to trust and authorize access control. However, relying services have to configure their implementation manually. As an independent software vendor (ISV), the service creator may have designed his application to run on multiple platforms and may refuse fixed bindings to any web services. The statistic report is only true in the current business marketplace, but in another market, the office service might cooperate with a different storage service.

3) Identities roaming: A user uses an interactive application like online playing game and moves to geographically distant locations (another city, country or continent) temporally. Due to long distance implying many intermediate nodes at different sites, a query transaction to the database may take 200 ms or even longer to complete. Therefore, access control may have a downgrade in performance if the PDP and PIP of his home provider are far from the PEP of the application. In best practice, mobile users authenticate to an endpoint closest to their location and exchange a symmetric key before they may access to further resources in the data center of an application [10]. As a result, user attributes may be temporally migrated to the visitor provider closest to the user location. The visitor Cloud provider may host another instance of the same distributed application but the user has no billing contracts with this provider. As a citizen who works for a government in Europe, for instance, he may not disclose his personal information in country C according to the EU Data Protection Directive [13]. This scenario raises a question how we can protect user privacy but satisfy access control to an SP, which belongs to different federated security domains.

III. IDAAS REQUIREMENTS

By learning from the failure of IDM systems like Microsoft's Passport in the past, Kim Cameron pointed out "*the seven laws of Identity*" to build a successful IDM system [11]. Briefly, an IDM system has to reveal least user information with the user's consent to limited parties, which necessarily participate in the transaction. It has to support both private and public profiles for an entity. It should not limit users to only one Identity Provider, but support interoperability between them so that users can easily switch between pseudonymous identities, and provides users with a simple, consistent experience through multiple technologies. Our scenarios given in section II emphasized that Cloud is a dynamic environment, whereby applications provision and de-provision frequently; users change their locations and access multiple SPs from federated security domains. Therefore, we should extend the requirements of traditional IDM as follows:

1) Control the life cycle of Authentication and Authorization Infrastructure (AAI): Since the SPs may hesitate to change their implementations in order to adapt to diverse hosting environments, IDaaS can support the adaptation of SPs by defining service components for authentication and authorization. It decouples AAI from the business logic of the application. The security service components should have well-defined configurable templates with interfaces and parameters like with the concept of Service Component Architecture (SCA) [14] such that values can be entered at the time the service is provisioned to the Cloud. The lifecycle of such security components should be well defined and orchestrated automatically together with the lifecycle of the Cloud application.

2) Scalability: A new deployed application should not affect any running applications already existing on the platform; otherwise, any changes would require a huge cascading refresh of all tenants on the platform.

3) Automated trust negotiation: Traditional IDM system requires administrators to pre-configure the IdP to trust the authority of a partner service manually. IDaaS can support handshakes between parties so that no information is revealed, until the negotiation process completes and all parties can start their business transactions.

4) Privacy protection for identity roaming: IDaaS can support users in the identity-roaming scenario by protecting their identities with privacy-aware access control. Traditional IDM is missing a mechanism to protect user data when it is temporally roaming to a new location.

5) Performance: XACML has a limitation in performance [15]. For each user request to a resource, PEP has to interact with its PDP to ask for authorization decision, and PDP further queries user attributes from PIP for taking decision. If user attributes are stored in external location or distributed in federated domains, PIP has latency to collect and synchronize user attributes. As a result, authorization decision has a delay for each user request to a resource, or fails to take decision when external resource is not available. Therefore, we should keep user identities (in PIP), access control policies (in PDP), and policy enforcement point (PEP) for an authorization request of an application closed to each other. An Identity Server typically enables caching for policies and user attributes, and also enables user provisioning from external resource to local IDM system [16].

The first two requirements support the adaptation of application to the Cloud for *dynamic SSO, service-binding* scenarios. The later three requirements support *identity roaming in federated domains* scenarios.

IV. IDAAS PROPOSED MODEL

A. Trust model

The dynamic provisioning of SPs on a Cloud platform requires dynamic trust establishments between several parties: Trusts between Cloud users and SPs in the same or in different Cloud providers. Trust establishment should take advantages of exiting trust relationships. For instance, users and SPs have signed contracts with their Cloud provider, so they built bilateral direct trusts: users trust Cloud provider to administrate and provide lawful SPs and protect their data according to the user's privacy policy description, SPs trust their Cloud provider to provide natural users and accountable for their actions with a billing system. Fig. 2 shows a home provider with bilateral trust and a visitor provider with which users and SPs have no contracts.

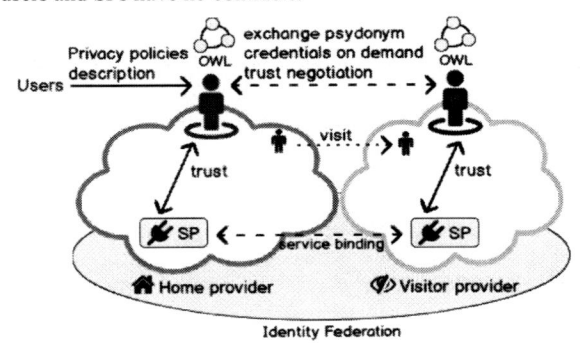

Fig. 2. IDaaS trust model

From the user's perspective, IDaaS of the home provider (home IDaaS) should be a central place to collect all user attributes (due to the bilateral trust). It includes user basic information when the users registered on the business market place (e.g., name, age), billing information (e.g., PayPal account), and contact information (e.g., mobile number). The home IDaaS can also collect positive attributes from one SP (according to the user's privacy policies), for instances reviews and ratings. If user data are distributed within all service members and are collected just in time for access control, the performance may degrade depending on the data distribution grades in multiple external resources. Moreover, if the users have no direct contracts with the SPs, the SPs have no right to collect all user attributes.

From the perspective of SPs, home IDaaS is the only party that SPs can trust and contact for handling requests. Automated trust negotiation between users and an SP in the same local domain as well as between federated domains is the responsibility of home IDaaS and not of the SPs themselves. SPs should only concentrate on developing and providing their business services.

B. IDaaS components

Fig. 3 shows several components of the IDaaS with separation of duty. We reuse the reference architecture XACML and add additional functionalities to satisfy our requirements in section III:

1) Policy Enforcement Point: This plugin intercepts authentication request and handle authorization for the SP. When the SPs are provisioned to a Cloud platform, PEP is a configurable module depending on adaptive information from a deployment process of the Cloud provider's orchestration engine.

2) Policy Decision Point: Ideally, IDaaS can support SP's designers by giving them an inference mechanism to analyze and derive any elements related to Security Policy from an existing implementation during the pre-configuration phase of the service. Security policy should be derived semi- or fully-automatically and published in a uniform way (by using XACML privacy policy profile [17]) to a central service of the Cloud provider to facilitate automated trust negotiation with other partner services in the Cloud.

3) Policy Information Point: PIP in the reference architecture of XACML provides user information for PDP to make decisions. In IDaaS, this component also handles identity roaming between IDaaS in different security domains. Fig. 3 shows that PIP can be an external service, whereby a set of users signed the contract with, but independently from the Cloud provider.

4) Policy Administration Point: Is an endpoint (not shown in Fig. 3) to provide functionalities for operators of tenant application to review the derived policies in (2) and configure on demand.

5) Orchestration engine: Is the central service of a home Cloud provider, to orchestrate the life cycle of AAI in the provider (described next in section C).

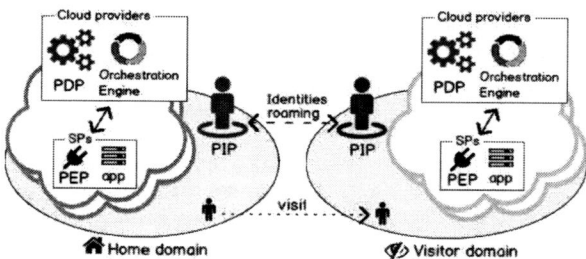

Fig. 3. IDaaS components

C. Control the life cycle of AAI

Enterprise Architecture Management (EAM) defines the guidelines, design principles, and evolution paths for enterprise IT [18]. However, no generally accepted model to denote enterprise architectures has evolved yet. Most enterprise applications have no clear picture about their topology. The more complex the system, the more effort and error-proneness is involved in adaptation upon topology changes [5].

Topology and Orchestration Specification for Cloud Applications (TOSCA) [19] is recently well-known as the upcoming standard to describe topology for Cloud applications [20]. TOSCA describes each component in the application by deriving from a *node type* (with specific *properties* and *interfaces*). Components connect to each other through *relationships* (with *requirements*, and *capabilities*). A *plan* describes the management lifecycle of service creation and termination. When developers describe an application's topology in TOSCA, they can deploy the application to any platforms that support a TOSCA orchestration engine.

The concept of AAI separates the security implementation from the web services so developers can focus on implementation of business logic only. So far, TOSCA does not have elements to describe the notation for WS-Security component. XACML does not have elements to describe the parameters and interfaces of a PEP. Therefore, we will consider extending (or inheriting) TOSCA elements for describing the PEP, PDP and PIP modules. For instance, PEP can have special *properties*, (e.g., public/private keys, identity service endpoint) and *interfaces*, (e.g., interface to update service policy and publish local user attributes in the scope of the application, or interface to retrieve updates from a deployment process to establish trust with an entity). In short, a Cloud provider orchestration engine can setup, update and clean up configurable WS-Security components during the life cycle of an application until the application terminates its contract to a Cloud provider.

D. Identity Roaming

OECD stated eight privacy guidelines that every IDM should follow [21]. Briefly, the collection of personal data should be lawful under the consent of users and with a specified purpose for which they are used. The purpose for data collection has a time limit (from the time to collect data to the time to fulfill the purpose). For later use, personal data should not be disclosed for other purposes than the ones they have been collected for, as well as are to be protected from unauthorized access and modification. In addition, users have the right to control their data.

User identities are roaming to another party for the purpose of authentication and authorization to an SP in a visitor domain. We consider these guidelines in a visitor domain as follows. Due to the *"use limitation principle"*, the roaming data should not be visible to any entity except for the PDP in the visitor IDaaS, for which purpose the data is collected. For instance, system administrators cannot read roaming data from the database in plain text. After the purpose is fulfilled, due to the *"purpose specification principle"*, the roaming data should be deleted or self-destroyed.

Moreover, in our proposed model, only the home IDaaS knows the real user behind the transaction for billing purposes. The visitor IDaaS as well as the SP in the visitor domains will only know a pseudonym userid and the identifier of the home IDaaS where the pseudonym was issued, so they can send requests for payment to the home IDaaS. This is particularly similar to roaming mobile networks where the visitor network contains neither all user information of the visiting mobile in his network nor the secret authentication key to identify this mobile.

In comparison to the pseudonym system *Idemix* [7], we have a more relaxed level of protection because it cannot protect user privacy when the home and the visitor IDaaS, or the home IDaaS and an SP cooperate with each other to reveal the user identity. Here the home IDaaS may play the roles as credential issuer, revocation authority, and credential inspector when something goes wrong. The computation resource is moved from the user client to a high performance server in his home IDaaS.

However, the OECD privacy guidelines cannot protect user data from a system that steals personal data unlawfully (by programmatically implementing an interceptor to dump unencrypted data from the memory of the authorization service and transfer it to a third party).

V. Related Work & Discussion

In the following section we first summarize design patterns of AAI collected from [22] [23] and point out which pattern fits our needs.

1) Isolated IDM: Because a third party can be an untrusted host and target to correlation attacks, this design does not reply on a Trusted Third Party (TTP) for issuing and verifying credentials. Work in [24] gives user the possibilities to issue his encrypted credentials and give them to SPs. The SPs can then evaluate the predicate of the given encrypted credentials by contacting multi-party computing. It does not mention how the users can prove that he really possesses his attributes, because without a TTP, the user can only self-assert his attributes. The major limitation of such approach is scalability when the number of users and SPs increase.

2) Circle of Trust (CoT): This pattern requires all SPs completely trusting each other to exchange information about their subjects in operational agreements and to exchange data in business agreements. As a result, users may authenticate to an IdP of one SP and consume all other services in this CoT. However, user attributes are exchanged between all services in a domain of trust with no filtering and protections. An existing implementation of this pattern is Liberty ID-FF [25].

3) Centralized IDM: In contrast to the CoT, this pattern centralizes the administration of identity. A central IdP is responsible for storing and providing identity to SPs within a security domain. Microsoft Passport is an example of this pattern, which failed in the past because it violates the rule justifiable parties of the "seven laws of Identity" [26].

4) Identity Federation: This pattern concerns identities across multiple security domains. A unique IdP manages local identities in one security domain and a user may have multiple local identities with some SPs. A SP from domain 1 forms a federation with a SP from domain 2 by developing offline-operating agreement. Identity of a user may have various presentations in different domains and a federated identity may be gathered from all domains to consolidate in one place.

Either a central service collects federated attributed about a user from all federated members as in [1] [27], or an SP actively queries local identities and transfers all attributes from domain 1 to his peer service in domain 2 as in [22].

GEYSERS, an EU project described in [28], allows e-research users and groups to provision dynamic infrastructure in IaaS provider. It uses Enterprise Service Bus (ESB) and WS-Trust to provide trust binding between services. This solution perfectly fits in academic research projects and Federated Cloud when services volunteer to use the same framework implementation. Notice that we do not consider ESB a solution for IDaaS, because there are no global standard concepts or implementations for ESB. ESB vendors define their own messaging encapsulation differently and it is not mandatory for all IDaaS providers to use the same vendor implementation. Our focus is Inter-Cloud computing targeting general Cloud services that straightforward interact with each other with no tight binding in vendor implementation.

5) User-centric: This IDM involves users as a man in the middle to retrieve credentials from an IdP and selectively decide which credentials to exchange to SPs. Thus, the users avoid direct contact between Identity Provider and SPs. Idemix [29] [30] [7] introduced an approach for a user to hide his identity by using pseudonym and anonymous credentials in transactions with SPs. User first obtains credentials from an issuing organization. Based on the issued credential he can use his secret master key to generate any pseudonyms and subset of credentials to show in following transactions with SPs that trust the issuing organization. The issuing organization does not need to be available during the transactions between users and SPs. Even if the issuing organization and the SPs cooperate with each other, they cannot link all transactions together to reveal the identity of the user. Based on Idemix, ABC4Trust [31] provided a language framework for attributes based credentials. It defines an XML schema to present pseudonym, anonymous credentials, service policy, and demonstrate an integration with standard protocols like WS-Trust, SAML [32].

Discussion: Using Inter-Cloud taxonomy [33], we think *Federated Cloud* fits the CoT pattern because Cloud providers volunteer to share their resources and academic research projects may get the most benefits from it. On the other hand, *Multi-Cloud* fits *Identity Federation* because this concerns multiple security domains of independent vendors and demands transfer of attributes between domains. A *User-centric* approach, however, delegates the Identity Management tasks to the users. The *"seven laws of Identity"* stated that human and PC is the weakest link compared to the links between PC, SPs and Identity Providers. Therefore, the human link is the major target of Identity theft [26]. ABC4Trust might need to outsource some management tasks to IDaaS, but still provides the basic features such as selective disclosure of attributes and pseudonym. ABC4Trust may also lack support from SPs. In this case, an orchestration engine of IDaaS in our research to adapt SPs to the Cloud may be very helpful. None of the existing work supports an orchestration engine to adapt and control the AAI of SPs to an existing Cloud platform, the privacy protection for identity roaming, as well as automated trust negotiation.

VI. SUMMARY AND FUTURE WORK

In this paper, we first collected scenarios, new requirements of IDaaS in addition to a traditional IDM and proposed a draft model for IDaaS. We mention our future works as follows:

1) We will extend TOSCA specification language to describe a model for IDaaS components (PIP, PDP and PEP) as plugin modules of Cloud applications.

2) According to the privacy guidelines principles, we may develop a mechanism to protect the identity roaming against identity theft by making them available to the authorization service only on user demand.

The separation of PIP as an external service has a benefit to take advantages of existing identity providers to establish trust between users and Cloud providers. The most attractive identity providers are mobile network operators, since they already have mobile users, who are willing to access multiple SPs on a Cloud provider. These operators also have signing contracts for mobile roaming with each other, so they can easily adapt to IDaaS for identity roaming and billing system. In future work, we will consider automated trust negotiation between IDaaS based on existing trust between mobile network operators.

REFERENCES

[1] C. Schläger, M. Sojer, B. Muschall, and G. Pernul, "Attribute-Based Authentication and Authorisation Infrastructures for E-Commerce Providers," in *E-Commerce and Web Technologies SE - 14*, vol. 4082, K. Bauknecht, B. Pröll, and H. Werthner, Eds. Springer Berlin Heidelberg, 2006, pp. 132–141.

[2] Wikipedia contributors, "Policy-based management," *Wikipedia, The Free Encyclopedia*, 2016. [Online]. Available: https://en.wikipedia.org/w/index.php?title=Policy-based_management&oldid=700392159. [Accessed: 18-Jan-2016].

[3] "eXtensible Access Control Markup Language (XACML) Version 3.0," *OASIS Standard*, 2013. [Online]. Available: http://docs.oasis-open.org/xacml/3.0/xacml-3.0-core-spec-os-en.html.

[4] R. Wagner, "Identity and Access Management 2020," *ISSA J.*, 2014.

[5] V. Andrikopoulos, T. Binz, F. Leymann, and S. Strauch, "How to adapt applications for the Cloud environment," *Computing*, vol. 95, no. 6, pp. 493–535, Dec. 2012.

[6] A. Nanda and M. B. Jones, "Identity selector interoperability profile v1. 5," *Microsoft Corporation*, 2008. [Online]. Available: http://download.microsoft.com/download/1/1/a/11ac6505-e4c0-.

[7] J. Camenisch and E. Van Herreweghen, "Design and implementation of the idemix anonymous credential system," *9th ACM Conf. Comput. Commun. Secur. CCS 02*, p. 21, 2002.

[8] D. B. Skillicorn and M. Hussain, "Personas: Beyond Identity Protection by Information Control A Report to the Privacy Commissioner of Canada," *Identities*, no. April, 2009.

[9] S. Landau and T. Moore, "Economic tussles in federated identity management," *First Monday*, vol. 17, no. 10, 2012.

[10] "Identity in the Cloud Use Cases Version 1.0," *OASIS Committee Note 01*, 2012. [Online]. Available: http://docs.oasis-open.org/id-cloud/IDCloud-usecases/v1.0/cn01/IDCloud-usecases-v1.0-cn01.html.

[11] K. Cameron, "The Laws of Identity," 2005. [Online]. Available: http://www.identityblog.com/?p=352/#lawsofiden_topic3.

[12] M. Behrendt, "IBM Cloud Computing Reference Architecture," *Open Group submission*, 2011. [Online]. Available: http://www.opengroup.org/cloudcomputing/uploads/40/23840/CCRA.I BMSubmission.02282011.doc.

[13] F. H. Cate, "The EU Data Protection Directive, Information Privacy, and the Public Interest," *80 Iowa Law Rev. 431*, p. 646, 1995.

[14] M. Edwards, "Service Component Architecture Specification (SCA)," *OASIS Standard*, 2007. [Online]. Available: http://www.oasis-opencsa.org/sca.

[15] G. Gebel, "Authorization Performance Myth Busting," 2010. [Online]. Available: http://analyzingidentity.com/2010/04/30/authorization-performance-myth-busting/. [Accessed: 30-Apr-2010].

[16] S. Gnaniah, "Improving XACML PDP Performance with Caching Techniques," *WSO2 Identity Server 5.1.0 Documentation*, 2015. [Online]. Available: http://docs.wso2.com/.

[17] "XACML v3.0 Privacy Policy Profile Version 1.0.," *OASIS Committee Specification 02*, 2015. [Online]. Available: http://docs.oasis-open.org/xacml/3.0/privacy/v1.0/xacml-3.0-privacy-v1.0.html.

[18] R. Winter and R. Fischer, "Essential Layers, Artifacts, and Dependencies of Enterprise Architecture," in *2006 10th IEEE International Enterprise Distributed Object Computing Conference Workshops (EDOCW'06)*, 2006, pp. 30–30.

[19] "Topology and Orchestration Specification for Cloud Applications Version 1.0," *OASIS Standard*, 2013. [Online]. Available: http://docs.oasis-open.org/tosca/TOSCA/v1.0/TOSCA-v1.0.html.

[20] T. Binz, U. Breitenbücher, O. Kopp, and F. Leymann, "TOSCA: Portable Automated Deployment and Management of Cloud Applications," in *Advanced Web Services SE - 22*, A. Bouguettaya, Q. Z. Sheng, and F. Daniel, Eds. Springer New York, 2014, pp. 527–549.

[21] "Guidelines on the protection of privacy and transborder flows of personal data," *OECD*, 1980. [Online]. Available: http://www.oecd.org/document/18/0,3343,en_2649_34255_1815186_1_1_1_1,00.html.

[22] N. Delessy, E. B. Fernandez, and M. M. Larrondo-Petrie, "A Pattern Language for Identity Management," *Comput. Glob. Inf. Technol. 2007. ICCGI 2007. Int. Multi-Conference*, pp. 31–31, 2007.

[23] U. Habiba, R. Masood, M. Shibli, and M. Niazi, "Cloud identity management security issues & solutions: a taxonomy," *Complex Adapt. Syst. Model.*, vol. 2, no. 1, pp. 1–37, 2014.

[24] R. Ranchal, B. Bhargava, L. Ben Othmane, L. Lilien, A. Kim, M. Kang, and M. Linderman, "Protection of Identity Information in Cloud Computing without Trusted Third Party," in *2010 29th IEEE Symposium on Reliable Distributed Systems*, 2010, pp. 368–372.

[25] "Liberty Alliance project." [Online]. Available: http://www.projectliberty.org.

[26] D. Chadwick, "Federated Identity Management," in *Foundations of Security Analysis and Design V SE - 3*, vol. 5705, A. Aldini, G. Barthe, and R. Gorrieri, Eds. Springer Berlin Heidelberg, 2009, pp. 96–120.

[27] C. Schläger, T. Nowey, and J. a. Montenegro, "A reference model for authentication and authorisation infrastructures respecting privacy and flexibility in b2c eCommerce," *Proc. - First Int. Conf. Availability, Reliab. Secur. ARES 2006*, vol. 2006, pp. 709–716, 2006.

[28] Y. Demchenko, C. Ngo, C. de Laat, D. Lopez, A. Morales, and J. García-Espín, "Security Infrastructure for Dynamically Provisioned Cloud Infrastructure Services," in *Privacy and Security for Cloud Computing SE - 5*, S. Pearson and G. Yee, Eds. Springer London, 2013, pp. 167–210.

[29] D. Chaum, "Security without identification: transaction systems to make big brother obsolete," *Commun. ACM*, vol. 28, no. 10, pp. 1030–1044, 1985.

[30] J. Camenisch and A. Lysyanskaya, "An Efficient System for Non-transferable Anonymous Credentials with Optional Anonymity Revocation.," *Adv. Cryptol. - EUROCRYPT 2001, Int. Conf. Theory Appl. Cryptogr. Tech. Innsbruck, Austria, May 6-10, 2001*, vol. 2045, pp. 93–118, 2001.

[31] K. Rannenberg, J. Camenisch, and S. Ahmad, *Attribute-based Credentials for Trust*. Springer, 2015.

[32] S. Cantor and I. Kemp, "Assertions and protocols for the oasis security assertion markup language," *OASIS Stand. (March ...*, no. March, pp. 1–86, 2005.

[33] N. Grozev and R. Buyya, "Inter-Cloud architectures and application brokering: Taxonomy and survey," *Softw. - Pract. Exp.*, vol. 44, no. 3, pp. 369–390, 2014.

Efficient Test Case Derivation from Statecharts-Based Models

Patrick Wacht[1,3], Ulrich Trick[1], Woldemar Fuhrmann[2], and Bogdan Ghita[3]

[1]Research Group for Telecommunication Networks, Frankfurt University of Applied Sciences, Frankfurt, Germany

[2]Department of Computer Science, University of Applied Sciences Darmstadt, Darmstadt, Germany

[3]Centre for Security, Communications, and Network Research, Plymouth University, Plymouth, United Kingdom
wacht@e-technik.org, trick@e-technik.org, w.fuhrmann@fbi.h-da.de, bogdan.ghita@plymouth.ac.uk

Abstract—**This paper presents important aspects of a novel framework for the automated functional testing of value-added telecommunication services. Besides the introduction of a new approach to model the potential behaviour of a service by means of the Statecharts notation, the paper describes an efficient test case derivation algorithm.**

Keywords—automated functional testing; test case generation; test framework; value-added services

I. INTRODUCTION

The demand for advanced value-added services in the telecommunication domain has increased enormously over the last years. This fact is a major challenge especially for service providers who have to provide a fast transition from concept to market product and have to offer low prices for their products to satisfy their customers. In order to face these challenges, service providers have integrated Service Creation Environments (SCE) to allow their developers to rapidly create new and individual value-added services and bring them to market. However, relying on the quality of the SCEs and the skills of the developers to create value-added services is not sufficient to provide the services in best quality. Therefore, a novel test framework is required to enable consequent testing of value-added services before the deployment and provisioning. Then, service providers are able to assure their customers of a proper execution of the delivered value-added services and that they perform according to the specified requirements.

In literature, most testing approaches and frameworks follow a model-based strategy [1]. Here, a formal model of the implementation to be tested is created from which subsequently test cases are derived. Most popular models for the purpose of model-based testing are based on Finite State Machines (FSM), Extended Finite State Machines (EFSM) and sometimes Statecharts. Unfortunately, the existing approaches such as [2] and [3] often lack an efficient automated test case derivation method. In fact, the approaches either lead to an enormous amount of generated test cases because of the increasing complexity of the underlying formal model, or the test case derivation leads to infeasible path results. Here, the generated test paths can never be evaluated because the described behaviour never takes place. Finally, the approaches often lack flexibility regarding the test case generation method. Although different coverage criteria are offered, the structure of the formal models usually contains static.

In this paper, we propose a new method for test case derivation and generation based on a Statechart-based formal model notation. The method is embedded within the architecture of a novel framework for testing value-added telecommunication services, the Test Creation Framework (TCF). The Statecharts-based formal model in the approach is automatically generated based on a semi-formal requirements specification and is comprised of a number of reusable test modules. The approach supports different coverage criteria and considers the infeasible path issue.

The remainder of this paper is structured as follows: the following section 2 introduces the architecture of the mentioned TCF. Section 3 introduces the selected modelling notation of the formal model and illustrates how the reusable test modules are described. Afterwards, section 4 discusses the method to derive abstract test cases from the Statecharts-based models.

II. TEST CREATION FRAMEWORK ARCHITECTURE

This section provides an overview of the architecture of the novel Test Creation Framework (TCF) for the testing of value-added telecommunication services.

Fig. 1 illustrates the architecture components as well as the workflow of the methodology starting with the test developer who can access the Test Modules Environment (TME) and the Test Framework User Terminal (TFUT).

The TME enables the test developer to create, modify or erase so-called reusable test modules which are based on a modelling notation (Statecharts) and describe typical service characteristics such as sequences of multimedia protocols like SIP (Session Initiation Protocol) or HTTP (Hypertext Transfer Protocol). The test modules usually define a protocol-specific behaviour of a certain use case, e.g. the sending of an instant message by using SIP, and cover both standard behavior as well as possible alternative behavior. The reusable test modules are stored persistently in a specific database, the Test Modules Repository (TMR). Furthermore, a reusable test module generally contains test data templates which are stored separately within the Test Data Pool (TDP). The databases are separated because the existing test data templates can be used for diverse reusable test modules.

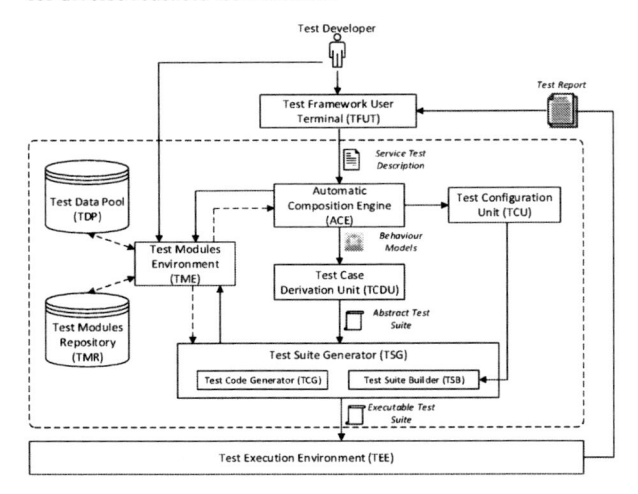

Fig. 1. Test Creation Framework architecture

Via the TFUT, the test developer can specify instances of a novel sort of specification or rather service description language which is named Service Test Description (STD). Once defined by a test developer, the STD triggers a fully automated process which results in the execution of generated test cases against the considered value-added service. In principle, the STD comprises elements of test specifications and service specifications. Furthermore, it contains architectural definitions describing the participating roles involved in the consumption of a value-added service and their relationships as well as dynamic behavioural definitions specifying use-case related requirements. The specification of the behavior is performed by means of an applied pi-calculus approach [4]. The overall structure of the STD has already been published in [5].

On the basis of an STD instance, the Automatic Composition Engine generates Behaviour Models, complete formal models based on Statecharts notation which describe the desired possible behaviour of the specified value-added service. The process includes the automated selection of identified reusable test modules and their composition to more complex models as well as the automated instantiation of test data templates. As a result, the ACE generates one Behaviour Model for each specified requirement within the STD instance. This enables a direct mapping from specified requirements to the formal model and automatically, a mapping from requirements to test cases.

The Test Case Derivation Unit (TCDU) includes a test case finder which uses an algorithm and follows selected coverage criteria to enable the derivation of abstract test cases from the Behaviour Models. Depending on the selected coverage criteria and the selected reusable test modules, the amount of test cases differs significantly. The output of the TCDU is an abstract test suite which includes abstract test cases for each Behaviour Model.

The Test Suite Generator (TSG) creates a valid and executable test suite that can be imported into a TTCN-3 (Testing and Test Control Notation version 3) test execution environment. To achieve this, the abstract test cases have to be translated into TTCN-3 test cases by means of the Test Code Generator. The Test Suite Builder will enhance the TTCN-3 code with specific test modules and includes also the configuration of TTCN-3 codecs and adapters. Furthermore, the Test Suite Builder includes the TTCN-3 compilations as well as the Java compilation in order to generate an executable test suite.

The final step of the framework's underlying methodology takes place within the Test Execution Environment (TEE). Here, the generated executable test suite will be loaded and subsequently executed against the System Under Test (SUT), the value-added service. After all test cases have been executed, a test report is generated which includes information about successful and failed test cases.

This paper is mainly concerned with the TMR (see section 3) and the TCDU (see section 4).

III. MODELLING SERVICE BEHAVIOUR FOR THE PURPOSE OF TESTING

To generate appropriate functional test cases, a formal modelling notation needs to be selected that enables a behavioural description of a value-added telecommunication service.

A. *Requirements on a modelling notation*

The ETSI standard [1] lists the following general requirements that have to be fulfilled by potential modelling notations for model-based testing approaches:

- The notation shall be based on unambiguous operational semantics.
- The notation shall support diverse simple data types such as boolean, integer and character strings.
- The notation shall support user-defined abstract data types.
- The notation shall support basic control structures like variables, assignments and conditional statements.
- The notation shall support advanced control constructs such as loops.

Considering these general requirements, the ETSI standard [1] discusses that modelling notations for the specification of behaviour are limited to rule-based notations (such as EFSMs and abstract state machines), process-oriented notations (such as the Business Process Execution Language (BPEL)) and Statecharts [6]. If the properties of value-added services are taken into consideration, further specific requirements have to be met by the modelling notation:

- The notation shall allow the definition of reusable test modules.

- The notation shall enable the composition of reusable test modules.
- The notation shall support the description of concurrent behaviour.
- The notation shall support temporal logic (e.g. timer integration).
- The notation shall deliver a standardised formal description.

Based on these stated requirements, Statecharts were selected as modelling notation. First, Statecharts explicitly support modularity through the defined concept of hierarchical states. Within such a hierarchical state, the behaviour of reusable test modules can be specified. Second, the syntax of Statecharts is very similar to EFSM-based approaches. This aspect allows to include new transitions between reusable test modules and therefore enables compositions. Third, Statecharts support concurrency through so-called concurrent hierarchical states (so-called AND-states). Within such a concurrent hierarchical state, it can be more than one state executing simultaneously. This is a very important aspect for value-added services as they are running within concurrent environments. Fourth, the support for timers is provided as soon as a state is reached within a Statecharts model. Finally, the fifth requirement is met by Statecharts because of the existence of the State Chart extensible Markup Language (SCXML) [7], a formal language which has been defined as World Wide Web Consortium (W3C) recommendation.

To sum up, the Statecharts modelling notation meets all the stated specific requirements. Rule-based notations have not been taken into consideration because they do not support concurrency and they generally do not provide an existing standardised formal description. Process-oriented notations lack a concept for the composition of reusable test modules.

B. Principles of modelling potential service behaviour

As Statecharts have been selected as foundation for the description, the principles of modelling potential service behaviour have to be determined in the approach. The authors suggest a novel concept of modelling behaviour with a formal model which includes both system-specific and test-specific artefacts. The concept has been derived from the transaction user (TU) which is the fourth and topmost layer of the Session Initiation Protocol (SIP) [8] structure. In the context of the SIP protocol, the TU contains both User Agent Client (UAC) and User Agent Server (UAS) core. According to [8], a "core designates the functions specific to a particular type of SIP entity". Therefore, the TU is either able to send requests and receive responses through UAC or receive requests and send responses through UAS. In the context of this test modelling approach, the TU is part of the SUT and it is enhanced by further client-based and server-based cores. Although the TU concept has been taken from the SIP standard, also cores of other protocols that are dedicated to the Open Systems Interconnection Model (OSI) application layer can be applied. Having access to a set of client-based and server-based cores, the TU can act as a mediator between available client and server cores and is therefore able to control the service logic without having any information about the internal information of a value-added service. A generalised example of the TU acting as mediator between a server core of a not specified "Protocol A" and a client core of a not specified "Protocol B" is illustrated in Fig. 2.

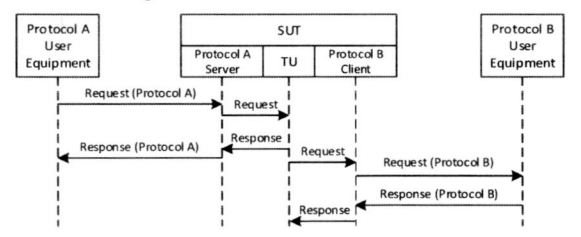

Fig. 2. Transaction user as mediator between client and server cores

The scenario shows that the TU as part of the SUT is informed about any incoming protocol message by the specified cores. It is also able to initiate messages through the cores. Based on this generic example, a Statecharts-based model can be defined to describe the behaviour. Such a model consists of states and transitions. Each transition can contain events and actions. In fact, the events as well as actions in the Statecharts notation are represented by protocol messages (both requests and responses). Fig. 3 shows the Statecharts model describing the behaviour illustrated in Fig. 2.

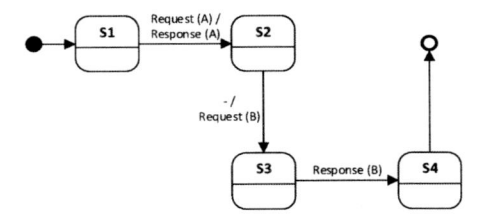

Fig. 3. Example simple Statecharts model

The focus of interest regarding the notation are the participating cores and the transactions they manage. An event within the Statecharts notation means that a certain core, which is part of the SUT, receives a message. If it is a server-based core, the received message is always a request type (see Fig. 3, message "Request (A)"). Otherwise, if it is a client-based core, the received message is always a response type (see Fig. 3, message "Response (B)"). So, an event in the Statecharts notation always refers to an input the SUT has to process. In contrast, the actions refer to the reactions of the SUT through the corresponding cores (see Fig. 3, messages "Response (A)" and "Request (B)").

C. Reusable test modules

The recent example illustrated behaviour of generic protocols. For the concrete OSI application layer protocol SIP, two so-called reusable test modules have been derived for the server core, SIP UAS non-INVITE and SIP UAS INVITE. For the client core, there are also two, SIP UAC non-INVITE and SIP UAC INVITE. The "INVITE"-specific reusable test modules refer to transactions that include the initiation of a call using the INVITE method of the SIP protocol. All other SIP methods (such as BYE, CANCEL and MESSAGE) are handled by the "non-INVITE" reusable test modules. In the following Fig. 4, the SIP UAS non-INVITE reusable test module is displayed as an example.

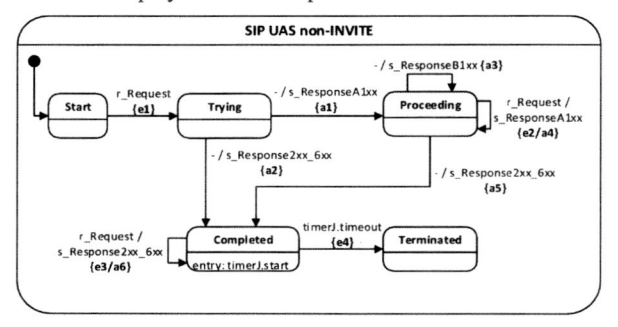

Fig. 4. Statecharts model of SIP UAS non-INVITE reusable test module

The entry point into the reusable test module is the "Start" state which contains a transition to the state "Trying" which holds the event "r_Request". Here, the "r" prefix is an abbreviation for "received" and refers to the SUT that actually receives a message by this statement. Once in the "Trying" state, there are two valid optional paths that can be taken, either to the "Proceeding" state with the "s_ResponseA1xx" action or to the "Completed" state with the "s_Response2xx_6xx" action. Both actions contain the prefix "s" for "send", which states that the SUT actually sends the message back to the initiator of the "r_Request" message. The alternative paths describe the potential behaviour of the SUT (the value-added service). It could happen that based on the "r_Request", the SUT directly acknowledged with a "200 OK" response by performing the action "s_Response2xx_6xx". Here, the range of status codes from 200 until 699 can be selected by means of the Service Test Description [5]. Alternatively, the SUT first sends a provisional response "s_ResponseA1xx" (status codes from 100 until 199) and afterwards sends a "s_Response2xx_6xx", which is also the action determined in the transition that has "Proceeding" as source and "Completed" as destination state. As soon as the "Completed" state is reached, the "timerJ" is started and its timeout is expected. The reaching of the state "Terminated" after the timeout denotes the end of the transaction. Besides the straight paths within the behaviour description, there are also three self-transitions defined that describe specific recurring behaviour that could take place.

Based on the specified behaviour in the SIP UAS non-INVITE reusable test module, test cases can be later on derived by a specific test case derivation algorithm. In general, this algorithm will be performed on the resulting behaviour models, which are compositions of several reusable test modules.

IV. TEST CASE DERIVATION

The test case derivation from formal models is widely discussed in literature (such as in [9], [10], and [11]). Generally, so-called structural coverage criteria are applied for transition-based models such as Statecharts.

A. Selection of a proper structural coverage criteria

Depending on the selected structural coverage criteria, a test case generator automatically generates a set of test paths within the model from an initial state to the end state. A selection of possible structural coverage criteria has been specified in [12] and is illustrated in the following Fig. 5.

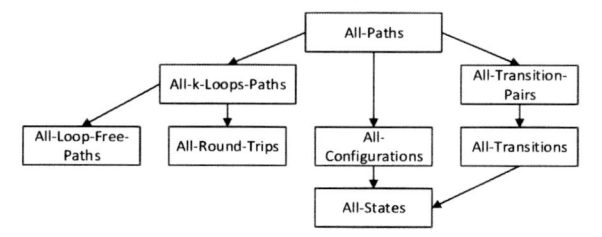

Fig. 5. Hierarchy of structural coverage criteria

The diagram shows the strongest structural coverage criterion at the top and weaker ones in a lower level. The arrow between the criteria illustrates that every test suite satisfying criterion c_1 (arrow source) subsumes another criterion c_2 (arrow destination). The meaning of the diverse structural coverage criteria is as described in [10] [12] [13]:

- *All-States* – Every defined state within a given model is visited at least once.
- *All-Transitions* – Every transition of the model must be traversed at least once.
- *All-Transition-Pairs* – Every pair of adjacent transitions in the model must be traversed at least once.
- *All-Configurations* – A configuration is a set of concurrently active states. This criterion requires that all configurations of the model's states are visited.
- *All-Round-Trips* – This criterion requires a test case for each loop in the model and that it only has to iterate once around the loop.
- *All-k-Loops-Paths* – Every path that contains at most two repetitions of one configuration has to be traversed at least once. This requires all the loop-free paths within the model to be visited at least once and additionally, all the paths that loop once.
- *All-Loop-Free-Paths* – Every path free of loops has to be traversed at least once. A path is loop-free if it does not contain any repetitions.
- *All-Paths* – This coverage is satisfied as soon as all paths of the model are traversed at least once.

The selection of a proper structural coverage criteria depends on the underlying formal model. If the model contains many alternative branches and also loops, the All-Paths-based criteria (such as All-Paths, All-k-Loops-Paths and All-Loop-Free-Paths) lead to an infinite number of test paths. In fact, the underlying models applied in this approach can contain quite a lot of branches and self-transitions (see Fig. 4). The All-Paths-based criteria cannot be applied here. Alternatively, the structural coverage criterion All-Round-Trips can be satisfied with a linear number of test cases. It has been selected as coverage criterion because in comparison to standard structural coverage criteria such as All-Transitions and All-States, it is able to detect faults more thoroughly. Furthermore, it is recommended in literature by [9], [13] and [14] for model-based testing approaches.

B. Representation of test cases in proposed approach

Although a proper structural coverage criterion has been selected, the properties of value-added telecommunication services have to be taken into consideration. Of course, it would be possible to apply the All-Round-Trip structural coverage criterion on the Statechart-based notation, but most of the derived abstract test cases will run results in an inconclusive verdict as soon as they have been made executable. This has to do with the fact that resulting from the coverage criterion, linear test cases are derived consisting of a linear sequence of events and actions. In principle, this aspect is not well suited for testing of a value-added service that is supposed to operate within a reactive environment. It might be possible that a value-added service responds to a stimuli triggered by the test execution environment in a valid but unexpected way. To exemplify the issue, a standard Three-Way-Handshake for the SIP protocol is considered [8]. The test execution environment sends an INVITE request in order to establish a session to a value-added service. The linear test cases that this behaviour relies on first expects a provisional message (e.g. "100 Trying") from the SUT and afterwards a successful "200 OK" response. Now the SUT, after having sent the expected "100 Trying" message, sends another provisional message (e.g. "180 Ringing"). Although this behaviour is allowed as an option, the test system compares the incoming "180 Ringing" with the expected "200 OK" message and will come to the conclusion that the response does not match. Accordingly, the test case will fail or will be evaluated as inconclusive. The problem of this test case derivation strategy is that the linear test cases do not describe multiple expected output states. However, the concept of the applied Statecharts notation, having the messages that the SUT expects as events and the ones it potentially sends as actions, allows a different representation of test cases than in the standard linear form. In fact, a test case derived from a Statecharts-based model can also be presented as a directed graph $G = (V, E)$, where V is a set of vertices and E is a set of edges and where each edge is a pair of vertices. Especially in a directed graph, an edge is an ordered pair of two vertices (u,v) with the edge pointing from u to v. Contrary to linear representations of test cases, a graph is able to determine branches. So, any given vertex $v_i \in V$ can theoretically have an infinite number of outgoing edges. However, according to the test case representation, there is a restriction defined. A vertex $v_i \in V$ can only have more than one outgoing edge if it specifies an action and not an event. This has to do with the fact that within the proposed approach, events can be definitely predicted whereas actions cannot.

C. Exemplified test case derivation from Statecharts models

The principle of test case derivation will be exemplified by means of the SIP UAC non-INVITE and the SIP UAS non-INVITE reusable test modules. In the following Fig. 6, the SIP UAC non-INVITE behavioural description is illustrated with a special identification of the transitions (e.g. "{a1}").

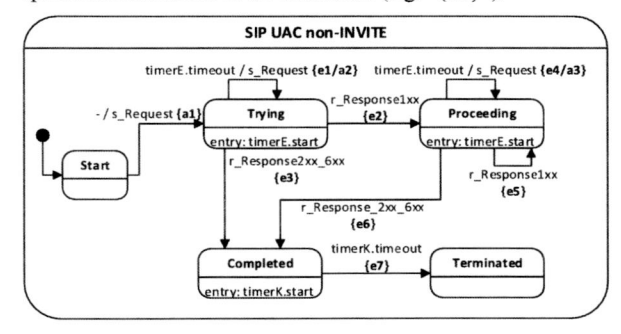

Fig. 6. Statecharts model of SIP UAC non-INVITE reusable test module

In principle, the All-Round-Trips algorithm includes the All-Transitions algorithm without loops and adds one further test case for each occurring loop within the model. Based on the behavioural description, the following five test cases can be derived (see Fig. 7).

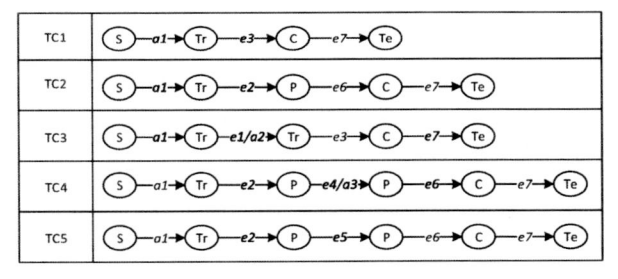

Fig. 7. Test case derivation from SIP UAC non-INVITE

The state names within Fig. 6 have been abbreviated in Fig. 7 ("Start" to "S", "Trying" to Tr", "Proceeding" to "P", "Completed" to "C" and "Terminated" to "Te"). "TC1" and "TC2" in Fig. 7 are based on the All-Transitions criteria without loops. Both test cases describe a standard behaviour of a SIP request being sent from the SUT to the participating entities. The other three test cases "TC3", "TC4" and "TC5" refer back to the three loops or rather self-transitions that are part of the behavioural description of the SIP UAC non-INVITE reusable test module. As it is a client core-based reusable test module, the SUT acts as a trigger by sending the initial request. The test execution environment will react based on the request and will send the appropriate responses the SUT has to deal with. The perspective changes if a server core-based reusable test module is applied. Then, the graph-based test case descriptions with branches become relevant. In the following Fig. 8, the test case derivation algorithm is applied to the SIP UAS non-INVITE reusable test module (see Fig. 4) which leads to three test cases.

All three test cases start the same way describing an event "e1" received by the SUT. Afterwards, the SUT can act in two different ways either by first sending a provisional response (action "a1") or a terminating response (action "a2"). This branch illustrates why a graph-based test description is required. It cannot be predicted whether the SUT responds with "a1" or "a2", but it is obvious that both responses represent valid behaviour. A further action "a3" describes a provisional response which can be retransmitted a not specified number of times. Therefore, a self-loop is included in all three test cases.

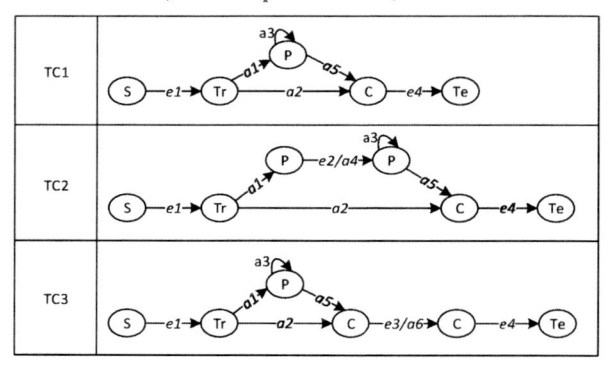

Fig. 8. Test case derivation from SIP UAS non-INVITE

To sum up, the proposed approach enables an efficient test derivation method by applying the All-Round-Trip structural coverage criteria. It offers significantly better coverage than the weaker standard coverage criteria All-Transitions and All-States without the disadvantage of generating an infinite number of test cases. Furthermore, because of the introduced graph-based test case structure, there are no possible infeasible path results. Even if some paths within a test case are not reached, the execution can still be evaluated as "pass". However, this is only valid if optional paths are included. Finally, the proposed approach also supports further flexibility regarding the structure of the reusable test modules. Theoretically, it is possible to manipulate the Statecharts-based models describing recurring behaviour. An example would be to erase the "Proceeding" state of the SIP UAC non-INVITE and the SIP UAS non-INVITE reusable test modules. Then, the provisional messages are not considered anymore. For certain behaviour this can be a useful feature (such as in instant messaging, where provisional messages are not used).

V. CONCLUSION

In this paper, we have introduced parts of a novel framework for the automated functional testing of value-added telecommunication services. As the approach includes a model-based testing process, the requirements on an appropriate modelling notation have been stated and the Statecharts notation has been selected after evaluation. Furthermore, we developed a new principle of modelling behaviour with Statecharts. Through their server and client cores, recurring behaviour of application layer protocols can be specified for further usage. Finally, an efficient way to derive abstract test cases from the models has been demonstrated.

Further papers to be published will focus on the missing aspects of the proposed TCF, such as the relevance of the Service Test Description within the process as well as the transformation of the derived abstract test cases into executable TTCN-3 test cases.

REFERENCES

[1] ES 202 951: "Methods for Testing and Specification (MTS); Model-Based Testing (MBT); Requirements for Modelling Notations", ETSI Standard, 2011.

[2] P. Wacht, T. Eichelmann, A. Lehmann, and U. Trick, "A new Approach to design graphically functional Tests for Communication Services", Proc. 4th IEEE International Conference on New Technologies, Mobility and Security (NTMS 2011), IEEE press, Feb. 2011, pp. 1-5, doi:10.1109/NTMS.2011.5721068.

[3] J. Ernits, A. Kull, K. Raiend, and J. Vain, "Generating TTCN-3 Test Cases from EFSM Models of Reactive Software using Model Checking", Proc. 36th Jahrestagung der Gesellschaft für Informatik e.V. (INFORMATIK 2006), GI, Oct. 2006, Vol. 94, pp. 241-248.

[4] R. Milner, J. Parrow, and D. Walker, "A calculus for mobile processes", Information and Computation, Elsevier, 1992, Vol. 100, Issue 1, pp.1-40.

[5] P. Wacht, U. Trick, W. Fuhrmann, and B. Ghita, "A new Service Description for Communication Services as Basis for automated functional Testing", Proc. 2nd IEEE International Conference on Future Generation Communication Technology (FGCT 2013), IEEE press, Dec. 2013, pp. 59-64, doi:10.1109/FGCT.2013.6767211.

[6] D. Harel and M. Politi, "Modeling Reactive Systems with Statecharts: The Statemate Approach (Software Development)", McGraw-Hill Inc., 1998, New York, USA, ISBN: 978-0-070-26205-8.

[7] W3C, "State Chart XML (SCXML): State Machine Notation for Control Abstraction", W3C Recommendation, 2015.

[8] IETF RFC 3261: "SIP: Session Initiation Protocol", Request For Comments, IETF, 2002.

[9] M. Utting and B. Legeard, "Practical Model-Based Testing: A Tools Approach", Morgan Kaufmann Publishers Inc., 2007, San Francisco, USA, ISBN: 978-0-1237-2501-1.

[10] P. Ammann and J. Offutt, "Introduction to Software Testing", Cambridge University Press, Cambridge, 2008, UK, ISBN: 978-0.521-88038-1.

[11] L.H. Tahat, B. Vaysburg, B. Korel, and A.J. Bader, "Requirement-based automated black-box test generation", Proc. 25th Annual International Computer Software and Applications Conference (COMPSAC 2001), IEEE press, Oct. 2001, pp. 489-495, doi:10.1109/CMPSAC.2001.960658.

[12] S. Haschemi, "Model transformations to satisfy all-configurations-transitions on statecharts", Proc. 6th International Workshop on Model-Driven Engineering (MoDeVVa 2009), ACM press, Oct. 2009, doi:10.1145/1656485.1656490.

[13] R. Binder, "Testing Object-Oriented Systems: Models, Patterns, and Tools", Addison-Wesley, 1999, Boston, USA, ISBN: 0-201-80938-9.

[14] G. Antoniol, L.C. Briand, M. Di Penta, and Y. Labiche, "A case study using the round-trip strategy for state-based class testing", Proc. 13th International Symposium on Software Reliability Engineering (ISSRE 2002), IEEE press, Nov. 2002, pp. 269-279, doi:10.1109/ISSRE.2002.1173268

Chapter 2

Posters

Deploying Contextual Computing in a Campus Setting

Fabio Aversente, David Klein, Schekeb Sultani, Dmitri Vronski, Jörg Schäfer
Department of Computer Science
Frankfurt University of Applied Sciences
Frankfurt am Main, Germany
Email: {faversente, d.klein, schekeb.sultani, dmitri.vronski, jschaefer}@fb2.fra-uas.de

Abstract—Location Based Services (LBS) are regarded as a major constituent of contextual computing. However, deploying LBS for indoor localization remains still a largely unsolved problem, in particular if practical considerations like, e.g., effortless calibration are taken into account. In our work we analyze challenges in a university environment characterized by hundreds of access points deployed and by heterogeneous mobile handsets of unknown technical specifications and quality. We developed an open architecture to deploy LBS on a campus and integrate them with other services and useful applications to support campus life.

Index Terms—Location Based Services, Indoor Localization, Contextual Computing, Architecture, Mobile

I. INTRODUCTION

A. Contextual Computing

The vision of contextual computing has been around more than two decades and with the ubiquitous availability of connected smartphones and similar devices it is slowly becoming reality. According to the vision of Marc Weiser "The best computer is a quiet, invisible servant" [1], the contextual information should be obtained automatically with no or minimal user interaction. The goal is to use different contexts (e.g., location, time, ID) to improve forecasts and context-sensitive services. One particularly important aspect of contextual computing is the awareness of a user's location. In this paper we describe practical aspects of deploying an infrastructure for contextual location awareness in a university's campus setting for indoor environments.

B. Indoor Localization Overview

For an overview on indoor localization based on WiFi, we refer to [2]. In general, techniques either make use of triangulation based on a theoretical propagation model or on scene-analysis, i.e., fingerprinting. Although propagation models look attractive from first principles, the lack of a good theoretical foundation for indoor radio propagation yields less than optimal results in the field. Henceforth, most applications use fingerprinting, where the signal is matched (testing phase) to previously recorded signals (training phase) with some probabilistic model. One of the earliest such systems is the Horus system, see [3], for a general overview of probabilistic techniques see, e.g., [4]. With these techniques one can achieve localization accuracy of 2-3 meters and 95% room classification (depending on the room topology) in areas of high coverage of WiFi signals, i.e., with many accessible access points for fingerprinting, see [2] and [5]. The disadvantage of these methods is the relatively high effort for the training phase which requires a careful measurement that needs to be recalibrated whenever a change of the topology happens. Furthermore, in practical applications the testing data is usually generated by a different handset than the ones used for training which further complicates the analysis and reduces the accuracy. Our approach tries to minimize these efforts by choosing robust classification techniques [5] and generating training data (semi-) automatically with the help of crowdsourcing, see Section II-C1.

II. OFFERED SERVICES

A. MoCa and CoCo Project

In 2012 at Frankfurt University of Applied Sciences the project MoCa (Mobile Campus Applications) was launched. Its mission is to provide personalized, context-sensitive services to students (and university staff) based on individual and role-based requirements. To provide context information for many services such as lecture and seminar support, an indoor localization service was developed as a core component of the MoCa infrastructure. Among the services voting applications (see, e.g., Section IV-A) or social network services such as "find-my-buddy" applications (see, e.g., Section IV-B) are supported. One of the key requirements of the project is (close-to) zero maintenance efforts for the operations of this service due to resource constraints. Henceforth, any time-consuming efforts such as, e.g., expensive calibration must be avoided and we rather try to make use of crowdsourcing techniques to facilitate the data generation (training) process. For a comprehensive overview of the MoCa vision we refer to [6]. In 2015 the Project Contextual Computing (CoCo) was launched to investigate how contextual information could be used to develop intelligent personalized applications. The main focus was initially on indoor localization techniques. It is currently investigated how to improve the accuracy and/or performance of the existing localization approach developed by the MoCa Project. To achieve the goals of contextual computing, we need to aggregate data from several sources. As the project aims to enhance the campus life at Frankfurt University of Applied Sciences, the data can be broadly categorized as data related to the students' studies, location based data and general campus related data. For this purpose, machine learning methods such as particle filters [7] are applied and data from different sensors are fused.

B. Student Lifecycle Management

As the most relevant information for students using the services relate to their studies, namely their courses, grades, and general information about the university, the project integrates with the Digital Campus (DC) application of the university. The DC project is based on the Student Lifecycle Management (SLCM) system from SAP and provides a portal for students to keep track of their studies. It also allows the retrieval of information required for the organization of the program, e.g., the timetables and room occupations. For further background information we refer to [8].

C. Location Based Services (LBS)

To avoid unnecessary distractions we aim to filter the presented data to only currently relevant services. Besides the user's identity, one of the main indicators for relevance is the user's current location. To provide personalized services to students, distinct services could be available in specific rooms at predefined times only. Thus the applications need to be able to depend on the user's location as they aim to provide a good user experience in the spirit of Marc Weiser [1]. The main source of location information is currently based on WiFi fingerprinting. For a detailed discussion of the used approach we refer to [5].

1) Calibration: The procedure to collect the signal strength values for the initial calibration (described in [5]) was very thorough, involving for example geodetic surveys, and thus very time consuming. While this level of accuracy was necessary for the development and validation of the used techniques, performing similar measurements across the whole campus is not feasible.

An additional issue is that the set of access points is in constant flux as access points are frequently replaced, moved, and new ones installed without or with little notice. Recalibrating the system therefore has to be reasonably simple and autonomous, e.g., via constant recalibration based on some form of crowdsourced data. To this end, the SmartClick application (described in Section IV-A) enables the collection of crowdsourced data in a natural and non-intrusive manner.

2) Extensibility: Our research group aims to refine the localization accuracy and therefore actively participates and supports research to improve the classification results. A recently concluded project attempted to use sensors built into modern smartphones to devise additional approaches to determine the location in a building. In [9] magnetometers were used to measure magnetic field vectors. These provide patterns which allow to calculate the position of the device inside the building. The first results look promising and are currently investigated as part of the project CoCo.

D. External Services

In addition to the services mentioned above we want to provide additional information relevant to the campus life. Many of these are not under control of the universities IT department, contain semi- or even unstructured data, and henceforth different techniques to integrate them into the ecosystem (e.g., web scraping) have to be used. A popular example is the menu of the refectory on the campus, which naturally is of interest for students, see Section IV-C.

III. ARCHITECTURE AND INFRASTRUCTURE

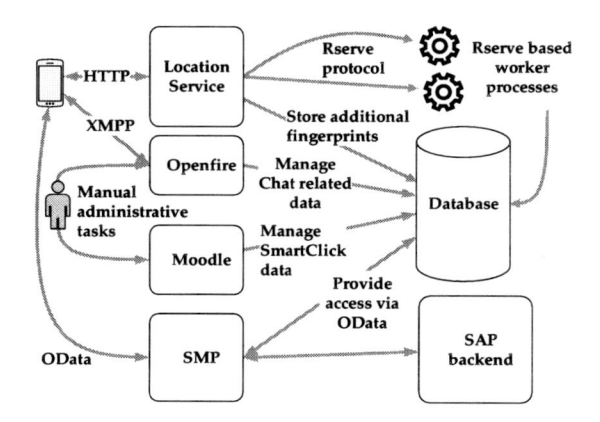

Fig. 1. Moca Architecture – Interaction between components

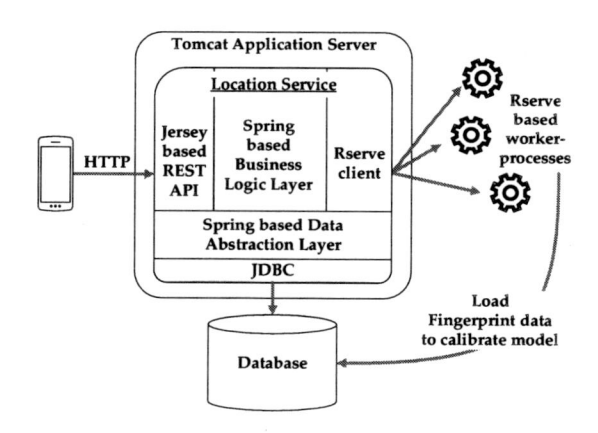

Fig. 2. Location Service – Design Overview

A core ingredient of the MoCa infrastructure is the SAP Mobile Platform (SAP Mobile Platform SDK V. 3.10, SAP Mobile Platform Server V. 3.0.10.0 and Apache Cordova V. 5.1.1), representing the foundation for our mobile applications. In addition we also maintain several specialized services, which provide specific features for (planned) applications.

For all services other than the SAP Mobile Platform we follow an open source and open protocol strategy. For example, the Location Service which performs the fingerprint classification, is build with Java and R, see below. Another example is the chat functionality of the *SmartBuddy* application

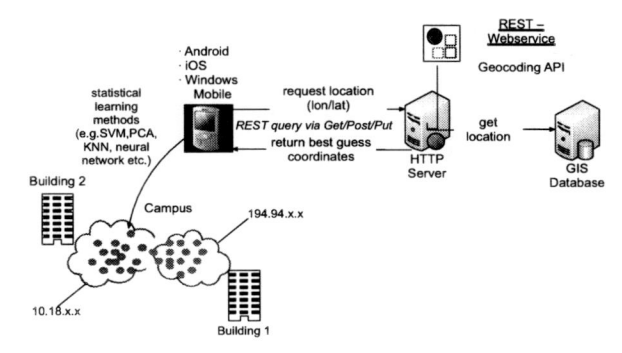

Fig. 3. The localization process

see Section IV. The chat is based on the *Extensible Messaging and Presence Protocol* (XMPP) provided by OpenFire.

Figures 1 and 2 provide an overview on MoCa's overall architecture and design. The details of the data-flow requesting the current position are depicted in Figure 3.

A. SAP Mobile Platform

To make the DC data available to students on their mobile devices, SAP offers the SAP Mobile Platform (SMP) providing the following services:

1) Model driven data access to SAP backend of DC
2) Model driven data access to other backends
3) Model driven data transformation
4) Device registration
5) User authentication and authorization
6) App provisioning

On the server side, SMP offers an unified interface for the SAP based backend infrastructure. We make use of a web service access to the room management service provided by the DC which provides data such as a lecture to room (and lecturer) mapping for each semester. This association is then used by other services such as, e.g., the *SmartClick* Application, see Section IV-A below. Clients can leverage *Open Data Protocol* (OData) based RESTful web services to retrieve and publish information. As OData is an open standard [10] and based on regular HTTP, it is a good fit to our use case.

To develop mobile applications interacting with SMP, we make use of their support for Apache Cordova based Hybrid Web Container applications. These provide a runtime which manages application updates, provisioning, user management, etc.

On top of the SMP runtime mobile applications are developed using web technologies, i.e., JavaScript, and HTML5. This allows us to minimize native developments and therefore helps to develop mostly platform independent applications, available on devices running iOS, Android, Windows Phone and BlackBerry. This reduces the development – and more importantly – the operations costs. Henceforth, the SMP architecture [11] and our development approach [12] allow us to support all major mobile platforms in an efficient manner.

However, for certain services access to device specific interfaces is required. For example, we need to access the WiFi radio to scan for available access points. In order to support this requirement, we developed a native library and exposed it to the Web Container. Thus, native, device- or OS-specific development is minimized and confined.

In addition to the mobile platforms, it is also easily possible to test and deploy the SMP based application as a website. When running in the browser it is of course impossible to make use of native libraries and some of the more advanced SMP runtime features. Nonetheless, the major functionality can be seamlessly tested in this manner.

Overall, due to using the SAP SMP framework, we are able to develop applications targeting all major mobile operating systems while keeping platform specific code to an absolute minimum. Platform specific testing is obviously still required and inherent restrictions make complete feature parity impossible. It nevertheless allows us to keep a unified release schedule, while offering applications with mostly identical feature sets and user interfaces.

B. Location Service

As it is not feasible to perform the classification locally on the user's phone, we chose a centralized approach. This minimizes the work done on the client device and thus optimizes its battery usage. It also avoids the need to distribute and update the data sets required to perform the calculations.

We therefore decided to make the Location Service available through a stateless REST service. To decouple it from the largely unrelated SAP infrastructure, we decided to provide a simple REST web service instead of making it available via OData and SMP.

This has several advantages for us. It allows students to access the service for arbitrary projects, without having to get familiar with OData. The service can also be made available to a wider audience via ad-hoc services, e.g., to use it during external events, like a conference.

The model used to classify the fingerprints and the surrounding functionality is implemented in R. This choice is based on the advantages of an interpreted language suitable for agile methodologies in a research context and the immense popularity of the R language and its ecosystem. With "more than 2 million users" [13] and several thousand open source packages maintained by the community [14], R offers support for most machine learning and data analysis tasks.

In addition, R offers straightforward interoperability with other languages, mainly via bindings for native, performance optimized libraries implementing the underlying functionality. This offsets most performance losses that incur from using R instead of a compiled language like, e.g., C++ or Fortran.

Communication between the REST web service and the R application is realized with the help of Rserve. It acts as a server, making the R process available to clients, allowing them to remotely execute R commands and retrieve the results. Rserve was originally introduced in [15] and is widely used, e.g., in products like SAP HANA [16].

This approach allows us to have a simple Java based REST web service acting as the front-end. It maintains a list of established connections to Rserve processes and forwards requests to said worker processes which perform the actual classification.

As Rserve communicates over TCP/IP, worker nodes can be distributed across several servers. This allows us to distribute the computationally expensive operations across several machines while keeping the overall architecture simple. Using the stateless REST web service as a front-end thus allows us to adjust the number of worker nodes according to user demand without service interruptions for the clients. This also allows us to seamlessly change the underlying calculations, e.g., to refine the classification algorithm, without changes to client applications.

To determine their current location, clients send WiFi fingerprints to our service. Said fingerprints contain information about all access points in range, namely their *basic service set identification* (BSSID), *service set identification* (SSID) as well as the measured *signal strength* (RSS) values. In addition to performing the classification, the service stores the fingerprint data and calculated location. No personal information is recorded whatsoever, i.e., the usage of the service is anonymous.

As long as the installed access points only change gradually, e.g., broken ones are replaced instead of abrupt, larger changes (say, all access points are upgraded to newer hardware), we should be able to continuously recalibrate the system based on the growing data set. This allows us to automatically recognize and incorporate changes in the WiFi infrastructure and adjust the model accordingly. This also avoids the manual recalibration of the system. In the past 24 months the university has replaced roughly 30% of its access points in the computer science building. Although the system was not fully deployed in its current stage at the time, the system could be operated as if it was already automated and we could verify that it would cope with the changes without loosing accuracy. As described in [5], our systems using Support Vector Machines (SVM) for classification yields an average classification error of better than 95% and a mean error of less than 2.5 – 3.0 meters which is compatible with best results published in the literature, see [5] for details.

To further improve localization accuracy, state dependent methods can help, i.e., methods that do not just analyze the current signals but rather the history of sensor and location data. Sequential Monte Carlo methods such as particle filtering enable to solve the otherwise intractable bayesian filter recursions. An example of a simulation is shown in Figure 4. It depicts a random walk of a potential user of our system, where the dots on the connected line depict the walk and the free (blue) dots represent the particles. The particles approximating the actual user position are clustered close to the right position, i.e., close to ground truth. The errors are comparable to the results obtained via SVM described in the previous section, however, particle filters can fuse other sensor data in a more meaningful manner. Research is currently in progress to further improve the localization accuracy. One approach is to use the log-normal shadowing model which represents the signal strength decrease dependent on the distance.

Another approach is to assess the viability of using the strength of the magnetic field vector of the earth's magnetic field as well as data from other (inertial) sensors (accelerometer, gyroscope) and combine this information with WiFi signals.

Recently [17] it was shown that combining (inertial) sensors with WiFi data using sensor fusion with Kalman filters can further improve WiFi accuracy by as much as 0.5 meters. Thus, for the future we plan to combine this approach with our existing WiFi based location techniques using SVM and particle filters.

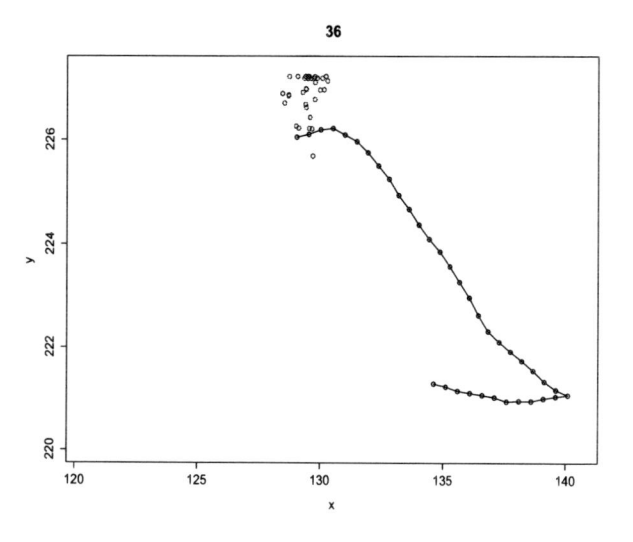

Fig. 4. Particle Filter

IV. APPLICATIONS

A. SmartClick

SmartClick is an audience response system (ARS) developed for classroom usage. It helps lecturers to keep track of how well students understand the study material at hand by taking short surveys during the lectures.

By incorporating contextual information, we aim to minimize the overhead caused by using non specialized hardware, namely the students' smartphones, as responders. The application uses the current date, time, and the users location to automatically determine which lecture the user currently attends. This allows us to only display questions relevant to the student. The automatic preselection minimizes the user interaction required to participate in the quiz and consequentially its duration. Results are available both in the mobile application (Fig. 5a) and on the courses website. The mobile application also allows to correct wrong localization results by manually selecting a room. The corrected data point can then be sent back to

(a) SmartClick (b) SmartMensa

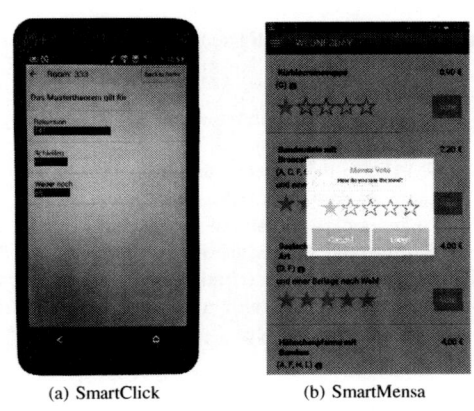

Fig. 5. SmartClick and SmartMensa App

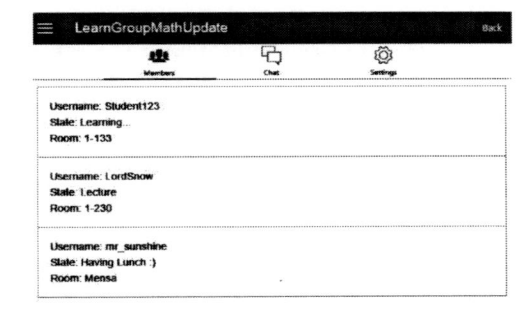

Fig. 6. SmartBuddy App – The current locations of your friends

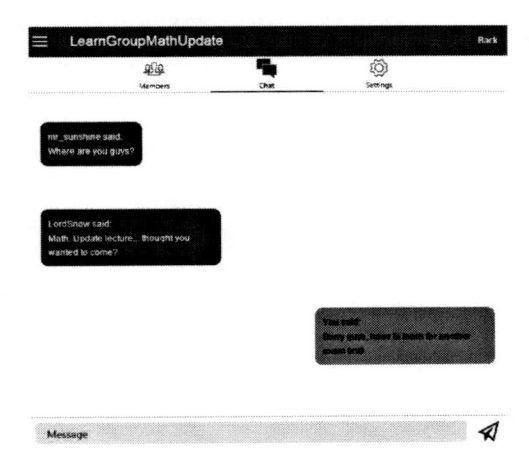

Fig. 7. SmartBuddy App – Chat functionality

the server, allowing us to crowdsource the collection of new measurements.

SmartClick also provides a web interface. Lecturers use the website to create and maintain questions while students can access results of already concluded polls, allowing them to revisit past topics. The web interface is implemented as a plugin for the Moodle [18] learning platform. Moodle is a widely used online learning platform, providing access to course related information and materials over the Internet. Integrating our application into the e-learning platform ensures that the course specific information (e.g., time, location, start date, and end date) used by our system is available and up to date, avoiding any manual maintenance. This also applies to user account management. All students as well as staff members are registered on the Moodle platform and use it to sign up for lectures they attend. As a plugin, our application automatically uses the course and user information already maintained in Moodle as well as its security infrastructure. This architecture additionally ensures that potential users are already familiar with the application and its user interface.

Integrating parts of our infrastructure into existing and widely used systems, here the online learning platform, helps with minimizing the effort required to introduce as well as to maintain an audience response system in classroom settings.

B. SmartBuddy

SmartBuddy (Figures 6 and 7) is a "find-my-buddy" application locating "buddies" automatically on the campus. Aimed at students, it helps to organize study groups and keeping in touch with other students without the necessity to exchange personal information (e.g., mobile phone number, email address). Students need to create an account to use the application. Once logged in they can create and join groups. To offer more privacy, groups can be password protected. Existing members then have to explicitly invite interested users by sharing the secret password allowing to join the group. Each group has an associated chat room. As the applications intends to facilitate studying in groups, it also allows users to share their current location. This can be used by study groups, helping with the coordination of (spontaneous) encounters on the campus.

C. SmartMensa

SmartMensa is an application for students and staff who intend to eat at the university refectory. It displays the current menu, together with recommendations. The ratings are crowdsourced, collected from other users who use the application (Fig. 5b) to anonymously rate the food.

Whilst mainly intended for fun, it serves as an opportunity to experiment with and test the infrastructure. It is useful for all people frequenting the campus. It therefore also helps to bring more users into our application ecosystem and to generate additional feedback.

V. OPERATIONS

The Location Service went live in early 2015. During the operations period, several changes to the access point infrastructure took place. Figure 8 shows the results of cross validating the data of six selected handsets partitioned into 15 randomly chosen subsets for training and validation versus training data of 60 combinations of only two handsets and tested against a third one. The statistical aggregates of the error measures as described in [5] are depicted in Table I. As one concludes from the tabular data, using only two handsets yields a much worse median classification error as compared to training data with 6 handsets. Furthermore, the variance as depicted in Figure 8 is *much* higher and renders some tests practically useless (median error bigger than 50%). This demonstrates one of the practical difficulties in training the system. In our case the major contribution to the data being worse than the one collected in [5] stems from two particular devices that show very different RSS characteristics compared to the others. We found empirically that training with at least half a dozen devices from different OEMs is advisable to avoid strong dependency on single device types. Recently we have started to use crowdsourcing to collect enough data from a large set of mobiles, thus helping to mitigate device dependency on a continuous basis.

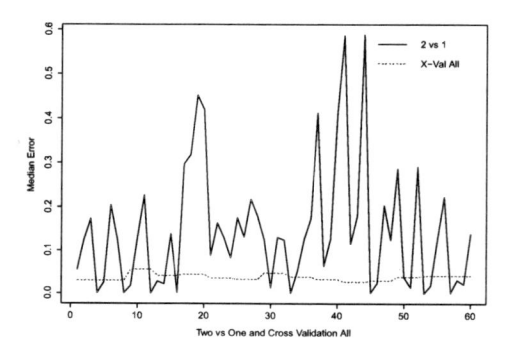

Fig. 8. Two vs. One and Cross Validation

TABLE I
PERFORMANCE – TWO VS. ONE AND CROSS VALIDATION ALL

	median(e)	max(e)	median(m)	min(p)	min(r)	min(f)
2 vs 1	0.145	0.177	NA	0.694	0.446	0.626
Cross-Val	0.038	0.052	NA	0.857	0.744	0.835

As we expand the coverage of the rooms, we noticed another phenomenon, namely the incorrect classification of rooms between different *floors*, see, e.g., the confusion matrix, Table II mixing rooms 131 (first floor) and 401 (fourth floor). This could be the result of the open architecture of the computer science building (e.g., atrium, and galleries). These type of errors are

TABLE II
CONFUSION MATRIX

	129	130	131	234	235	332	333	401
129	33	0	0	0	0	0	0	0
130	1	38	1	0	0	0	0	0
131	0	0	40	0	0	0	0	0
234	0	0	0	31	0	0	0	0
235	0	0	0	0	25	0	0	0
332	0	0	0	0	0	45	0	0
333	1	0	0	0	0	4	44	0
401	0	0	7	0	0	0	0	75

easily taken care of by state-based machine learning techniques such as particle filters investigated in the CoCo project.

VI. CONCLUSION

We have demonstrated the feasibility of SMP for agile development and integrating contextual services via REST. We have also shown the practical feasibility of a location based service to support campus services with room accuracy.

For future research we intend to further improve accuracy by better algorithms and sensor fusion. Furthermore, in addition we will integrate sensor data from other sources to improve contextual computing and will make use of reality-mining techniques to improve services.

REFERENCES

[1] M. Weiser, "The computer for the 21st century," *Scientific American*, vol. 265, no. 3, pp. 94–104, September 1991.
[2] H. Liu, H. Darabi, P. Banerjee, and J. Liu, "Survey of wireless indoor positioning techniques and systems," *Trans. Sys. Man Cyber Part C*, vol. 37, no. 6, pp. 1067–1080, Nov. 2007. [Online]. Available: http://dx.doi.org/10.1109/TSMCC.2007.905750
[3] M. Youssef and A. Agrawala, "The horus wlan location determination system," in *Proceedings of the 3rd International Conference on Mobile Systems, Applications, and Services*, ser. MobiSys '05. New York, NY, USA: ACM, 2005, pp. 205–218. [Online]. Available: http://doi.acm.org/10.1145/1067170.1067193
[4] P. Kontkanen, P. Myllymaki, T. Roos, H. Tirri, K. Valtonen, and H. Wettig, "Topics in probabilistic location estimation in wireless networks," in *Proc. 15th IEEE Int. Symposium on Personal, Indoor and Mobile Radio Communications*. Barcelona, Spain: IEEE Press, 2004. [Online]. Available: http://cosco.hiit.fi/Articles/pimrc2004.pdf
[5] J. Schäfer, "Practical Concerns of Implementing Machine Learning Algorithms for W-LAN Location Fingerprinting," in *Ultra Modern Telecommunications and Control Systems and Workshops (ICUMT), 2014 6th International Congress on*, Oct 2014, pp. 310–317.
[6] B. Jaser, "Design and set-up of an architecture for the development of a framework for location-based, mobile campus applications," Master Thesis, FH-Frankfurt, Jan. 2014.
[7] M. Arulampalam, S. Maskell, N. Gordon, and T. Clapp, "A tutorial on particle filters for online nonlinear/non-gaussian bayesian tracking," *Signal Processing, IEEE Transactions on*, vol. 50, no. 2, pp. 174–188, Feb 2002.
[8] C. T. Ulrich Schrader, *Best Practice to IT : erste Erfahrungen aus dem Projekt Digitaler Campus*. DHI Deutsches Hochschul-Institut, 2012, vol. Schriftenreihe Hochschulen im Fokus, no. 5.
[9] A. Steinbrecher, "Indoor localization using magnetic field vectors," Master's thesis, Frankfurt University of Applied Sciences, June 2015.
[10] OData Technical Committee. OASIS open data protocol (OData) TC. Accessed May 17, 2016. [Online]. Available: https://www.oasis-open.org/committees/odata/
[11] *SAP Mobile Platform Version 2.3 – Architecture*, 2013, accessed May 17, 2016. [Online]. Available: http://scn.sap.com/docs/DOC-42440
[12] *Sybase Unwired Platform 2.1.x Development Paradigm White Paper*, 2012, accessed May 17, 2016. [Online]. Available: http://scn.sap.com/docs/DOC-30196
[13] Revolution Analytics, "The R community," accessed May 17, 2016. [Online]. Available: http://www.revolutionanalytics.com/r-community
[14] C. R. Maintainers, "The comprehensive R archive network," accessed May 17, 2016. [Online]. Available: https://cran.r-project.org/
[15] S. Urbanek, "Rserve – a fast way to provide R functionality to applications," in *Proceedings of the 3rd International Workshop on Distributed Statistical Computing (DSC 2003)*, 2003.
[16] *SAP HANA R Integration Guide*, 1st ed., May 2015, accessed May 17, 2016. [Online]. Available: http://scn.sap.com/docs/DOC-60314
[17] C. Bianucci, "Enhancement of wifi positioning with a low-cost inertial measurement unit," Master Thesis, Frankfurt University of Applied Sciences, Jan. 2016.
[18] Moodle Docs 3.0. Accessed May 17, 2016. [Online]. Available: https://docs.moodle.org/30/en/Main_page

Assay of Multipath TCP for Session Continuity in Distributed Mobility Management

Dawood M[1,2], Fuhrmann W[1,2], Ghita BV[2]

[1]Faculty of Computer Science, University of Applied Sciences Darmstadt, Germany
woldemar.fuhrmann@h-da.de

[2]Centre for Security, Communications and Network Research (CSCAN),
Plymouth University, Plymouth, PL4 8AA, United Kingdom
e-mail: {muhammad.dawood, bogdan.ghita}@plymouth.ac.uk

Abstract—The evolution of wireless access networks flat IP architecture implies a key-role for IP mobility management in providing the ubiquitous always-on network access services. In particular the connection-oriented transport services requires an optimized routing by gateway relocation during the user's mobility. This paper proposes distributed co-located mobility and IP anchors in the core network to solve the problem of unnecessary long routes and delay. Session continuity in connection with user mobility also require for a single connection to be capable of using multiple network paths, the proposed architecture applied Multipath TCP (MPTCP) functions for the simultaneous exchange of IP traffic through the transient use of multiple distributed IP anchors. We describe the important call control flows being exchanged across the various network elements of the proposed architecture due to mobility of mobile nodes. It also provides an evaluation of MPTCP enabled IP mobility to show how it can be systematically exploited to gain session continuity.

Keywords—Distributed Mobility Management; IP Mobility; Distributed Anchors; Multiple PDN connections; Multipath TCP;

I. INTRODUCTION

The continuous improvement to the radio access networks (RAN) architecture is becoming increasingly important to support the performance requirements for the ubiquitous wireless connections. More and more people see their handheld devices as an annex of their workspace while on move. Support mobility is one of the major challenges in vehicular networks for intelligent transportation systems (ITS) applications supporting, infotainment (information and entertainment), road safety and traffic efficiency through vehicle-to-vehicle (V2V) and vehicle-to-infrastructure (V2I) communications. Some of ITS applications particularly need to be continuously connected to internet. In addition vehicular communications have some unique features, in terms of generation patterns, delivery requirements, communication primitives, and spatial scope. These growing demand of wireless communication with user mobility for Service continuity implies enabling seamless IP mobility as an integral implementation of ubiquitous wireless access.

There are ongoing attempts to provide IP mobility management, such as Mobile IPv6 (MIPv6) [1], Dual Stack MIPv6 (DSMIPv6) [2], Proxy MIPv6 [3] and GPRS tunneling protocol [4]. Global reachability and session continuity is enabled by introducing an entity located at the home network of the Mobile Node (MN) which anchors the permanent IP address. When the MN is away from its home network, the MN acquires a temporal IP address from the visited network and informs the home IP anchor about its current location. Depending on the mobility management approach (client or network based) the traffic between MN and home IP anchor is redirected by bi-directional tunnel between the corresponding nodes.

Several limitations of these centralized mobility management approaches have been identified when compared to the always-on network access service requirements of seamless mobility. With centralized network architectures, incoming user traffic will always need to go first to the home network and then to the corresponding service node, adding unnecessary delay and wasting resources. Since the mobile node (MN) use the single address anchored at central IP gateway, the traffic always traverses the central anchor, leading to paths that are in general longer than the direct one between the MN and its corresponding node. This poses excessive traffic concentration on a single gateway element and possibly un-optimized routing leading in turn higher latency. Centralized solutions are probable to have reliability problem, as the central entity is potentially a single point of failure. Central IP mobility anchor have to deal with higher user traffic simultaneously, thus need to have enough processing and routing capabilities implies several scalability and network design problems [5].

To cope with these issues: we followed the concept of distributed mobility management (DMM) in contrast to centralized anchors in a hierarchical model. There are number of design approaches that can be considered to extend and apply on distribution of mobility functions, the Access, the Remote and the core IP anchoring by terminals [6]. In this paper, to limit the potentially huge design space and the envisioned research towards a common core network architecture we focus mainly on provision of IP session continuity that can be realized by distribution of GWs within current 3GPP core network architecture. Figure 1 shows the reference architecture of distributed Serving Gateway (S-GW)

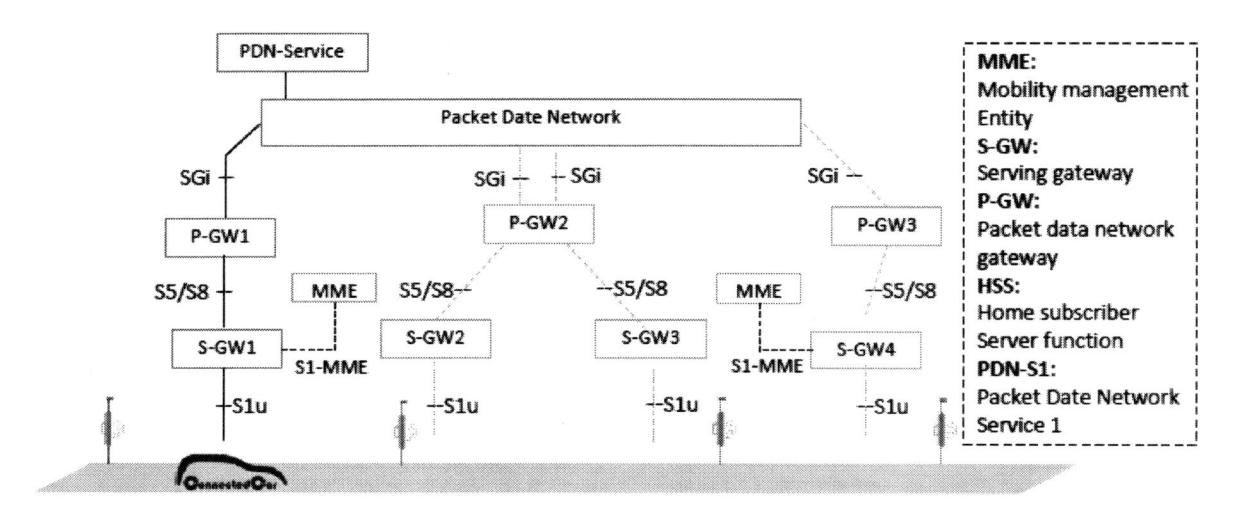

Figure 1: Baseline architecture for distributed mobility management.

and Packet Data network Gateway (P-GW), a common IP-based core network to provide MNs seamless mobility and service continuity. The basic idea is to select and re-locate when necessary P-GWs that are topologically/geographically close to the MN.

Among other considerations different types of future ITS applications require multiple different dimensions of distributing the IP flows with respect to their mobility management needs [6]. Some applications (e.g., instant messengers) can deal with IP address changes on their own. Such applications detect a host's IP address change and notify their corresponding nodes of the new IP address. Flows used by certain server application (e.g., in-vehicle camera serving remote system) require a fixed IP address allocation on its local end so that the incoming connections can find the server application at a published IP address. Some floating car data (FCD) applications (e.g., environmental monitoring sensors) do not need a fixed IP address, as they are the originator of the communication. They can choose any available IP address as the source address for communication. However, certain applications for transmissions of information collected by vehicles, from internal and external sensors to remote management servers require that the IP address changes does not interrupt an ongoing IP session. Furthermore, some flows need neither a fixed IP address nor IP session continuity.

In order to address these particular challenges associated with distribution of mobility functions, in this paper we intend to make the following contributions:

- Propose a MPTCP-based DMM architecture with distributed co-located S-GW and P-GW in the core network to solve the problem of unnecessary long routes and delay.
- Describe how MPTCP guarantee session continuity during GW relocation without the use of bi-directional tunnels between the source and target GWs, avoiding signaling overhead.
- Explore how MPTCP-based DMM can help for the exchange of IP traffic through the use of distributed P-GWs and select the right one for use in the following cases. i) The MN acts as a server and requires a static IP address for incoming IP flows. Static anchoring at the home P-GW will be required. ii) No fixed IP address, i.e. the MN acts as client, but IP session continuity: No static anchoring at the home P-GW will be required. iii) No fixed IP address and no IP session continuity: no static anchoring at the home P-GW will be required
- Evaluate whether an MPTCP-based solution can indeed support seamless mobility for MNs and significantly reduce signaling and delay compared to tunnel and routing based approaches and identify the research directions.

The rest of this paper is organized as follows. The paper first gives an overview of different approaches introduced by different standards that can be relevant, extended or applied for DMM. We then proceed with an MPTCP-based solution for distribution of mobility anchors and gateway functions and describe proposed architecture. In the next section we present important call control flows being exchanged across the various network elements of the proposed architecture for session continuity. The last section provides an evaluation of the concept and concludes the paper.

II. RELATED WORK

In this section we provide an overview of current IP mobility management initiatives with in IETF and 3GPP and their extensions that are complement to distributed anchoring. Based on IP mobility protocols such as MIPv6, PMIPv6 and GTP there are two main approaches for distributed GWs anchoring client-based approach and network-based approach.

A. Client-based IP Mobility management

In client based mobility management approach (MIPv6), session continuity is enabled by an entity called Home Agent (HA) which anchors the permanent IP address used by the MN, called the Home Address (HoA). As MN moves away from its home network, it acquires a temporal IP address from the visited network called Care of Address (CoA). The HA is responsible to maintain the MN's HoA and redirect traffic to and from the MN's current location. Following the proposal of distributing the anchoring IETF specified some extensions to MIPv6 [7]. As shown in figure 2, multiple HAs are deployed at the edge of access network. The MN initially attaches to the distributed anchor HA/AR1 and configures the IPv6 address HoA1 to communicate with a correspondent PDN-Service. If MN moves to new HA/AR2, the MN have to keep bind home (while maintaining the reachability for those IP addresses that are still in use by active communications) address and configure the locally-anchored address to start new communications which is actually playing the role of care-of address in these bindings. Session continuity is guaranteed by the use of bi-directional tunnels between the MN and each one of the home agents anchoring in-use addresses.

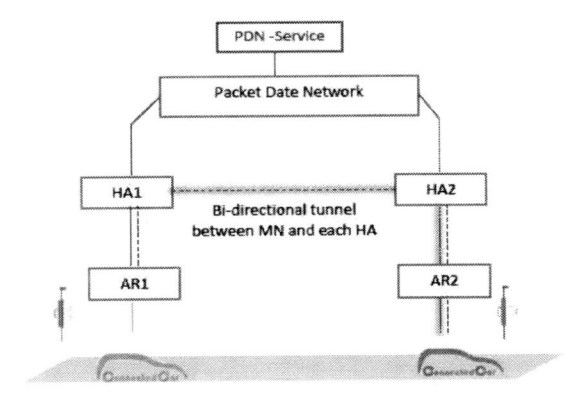

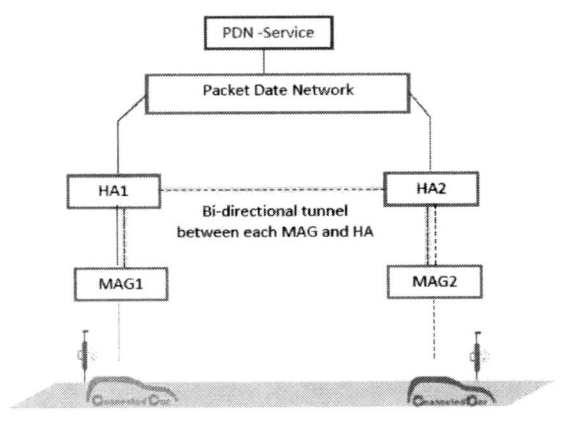

Figure 2: Client-based Distributed IP Mobility Management

This approach requires additional intelligence on the mobile node side, as it has to manage multiple addresses simultaneously, select the right one to use for each communication, keep track of those addresses which need mobility support, and perform the required maintenance operations (i.e., binding signaling and tunneling) [8].

B. Network-based IP Mobility management

With network-based approach such as in PMIPv6 as well as the GTP, mobility management is provided without involvement of mobile users. Movement detection and signaling functionalities are performed through a network functional entity. Referred as Mobile Access Gateway (MAG)/ S-GW in IETF/3GPP context respectively. An example of the operation of a generic network-based DMM solution is shown in Figure 3. Mobility anchors are moved to the edge of the access network thus anchoring and routing the local traffic for a given user. Furthermore whether the control plane and the data plane are tightly coupled or not, there are two sub variants of network based solutions fully and partially distributed. In a fully distributed model and using the PMIv6 terminology each access router implements both control and data plane functions and for each user the access router could behave as a local mobility anchor. In a partially distributed model, data plane and control plane are separated and only the data plane is distributed [9]. In this sense, the operations are similar to 3GPP networks where the control plane is managed by the Mobility Management Entity (MME) and the data plane by the S-GW and P-GW.

Figure 3: Network-based Distributed IP mobility management.

C. Multipath TCP

The IP mobility management through the use of multiple distributed IP anchors implies a key role involvement of transport layer protocols to enables simultaneous exchange of IP traffic flows. MPTCP is an ongoing effort within IETF to support multipath operation, a set of extensions to enables a regular TCP connection to use multiple different IP addresses and interfaces [10]. In the mobility context, when MN moves

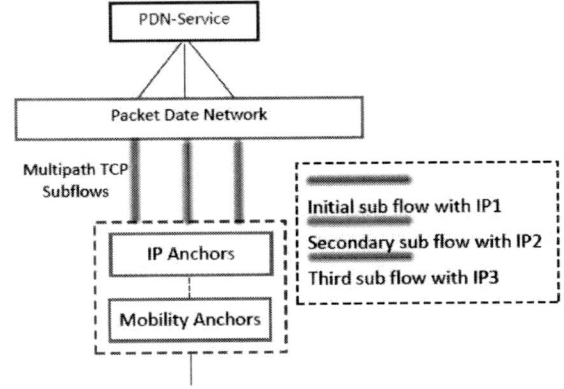

Figure 4: Multipath TCP multipath operations.

from one point of attachment (in 3GPP terminology P-GW) to another i.e., it receives or configures a new IP address through new network attachment. MPTCP enable multiple IP addresses

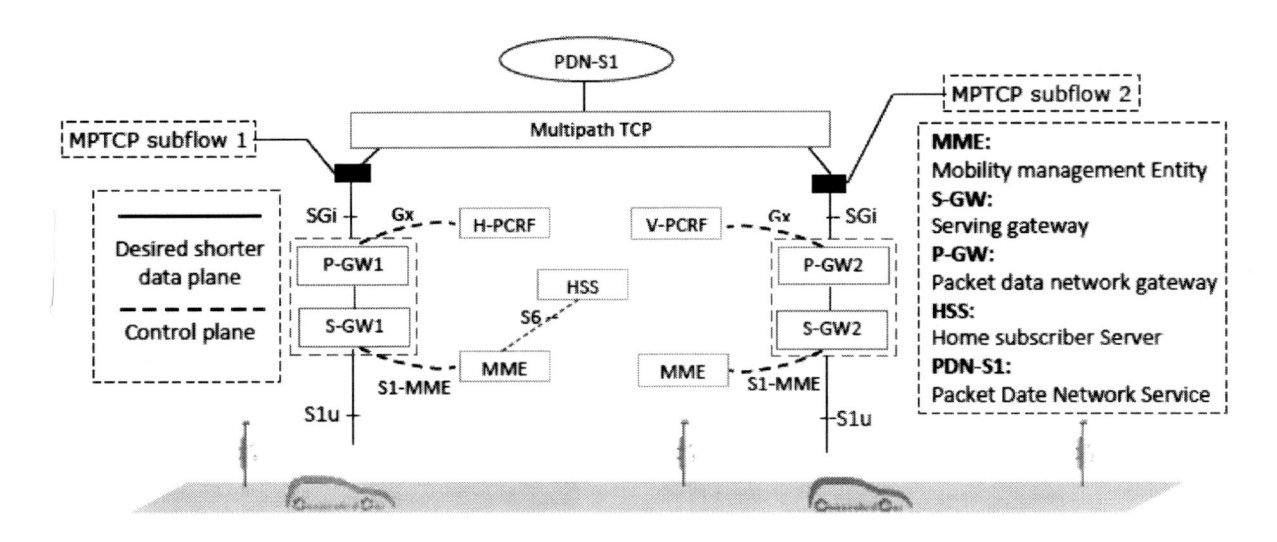

Figure 5: Proposed mobility management with distributed flat IP architecture.

by adding subflows. Each sub-flow behaves as a separate regular TCP connection inside the network. Subflows can be added and removed at any point of time, in any MPTCP ongoing communication, with the help of ADD_ADDR option and REMOVE_ADDR option for any interface [10]. To maintain the ongoing communication MPTCP support "make before break" method and uses MP-PRIO option to specify any subflow as backup mode. In Fig. 4, in the mobility scenario, With the MN have multiple IP addresses so in this case MPTCP can create multiple subflows and the MN is connected to Packet Data Network (PDN) service. Defined by MPPRIO option MPTCP support different flow modes, in the single-path mode only one TCP sub-flow is used at any time or using all subflows simultaneously between two communication nodes or uses only a subset of subflows for transmission of data packets.

III. PROPOSED ARCHITECTURE

To fully appreciate the particular issues identified above; this paper proposes distribution of mobility anchors and gateway functions to select P-GW that is topologically/geographically close to the MN. We proposed twofold IP mobility management, at the core network we adopt distributed co-located S-GW and P-GW to solve the problems of unnecessary long routes and delays and at the transport layer applied the Multipath TCP functions that enables the use of multiple IP addresses. Figure 5 illustrate the proposed architecture, MN is connected to PDN-Service1 (ITS Application) with co-located S-GW and P-GW, with established MPTCP connection of MPTCP capable MN and PDN-Service1 and will be able to synchronize the user traffic using different IP addresses.

In the following we describe the important call control flows being exchanged across the various network elements of the proposed architecture to show how it can be systematically exploited to gain benefits:

A. Multiple PDN connections enablement

Followed by 3GPP initial attach procedures [11] (attach request/response, identification, S-GW assignment, create session request/response and EPS bearer setup), after the Attach Accept message, the MN has obtained a PDN address and MN can then sends uplink data towards the eNodeB which will be tunneled to S-GW and P-GW. The first step of multiple PDN enablement is to establish MPTCP connection. Figure 6 shows the signaling diagram illustrating an expression of proposed architecture to establish initial MPTCP subflow, with implied MPTCP capable MN and PDN-Service1, MN initiates an initial subflow through S-GW1 onto P-GW1 with its IP address and sends SYN segment to PDN-Service1. This SYN segment may include different options most particularly MP-JOIN option that declares MN is capable of MPTCP and wish to add subflow on this particular connection. Amid to three way handshake PDN-Service1 replies with SYN+ACK segment. MPTCP use unique identifier called Token to make a subflows global to link with other subflows. MN add its token within SYN segment which is local identifier inside the MPTCP connection and PDN-Service1 provide its own token. In this way the need for the maintaining a tunnel between source and target anchors is not required to link different flows for session continuity. Furthermore considering the expected handover with MN mobility, The MME in cooperation with the S-GW1 and P-GW1 notify the needed support for GW relocation and keep the established PDN-Connection context.

B. GW Relocation

During the movement of MN several events occur (e.g., eNodeB handover over X2 interface, selection of relevant S-GW) that tag along with P-GW relocation and it must connect a set of appropriate GWs that are close to the MN as an additional MPTCP subflow. The MPTCP based signaling for GW relocation is shown in Figure 7. Typically MME

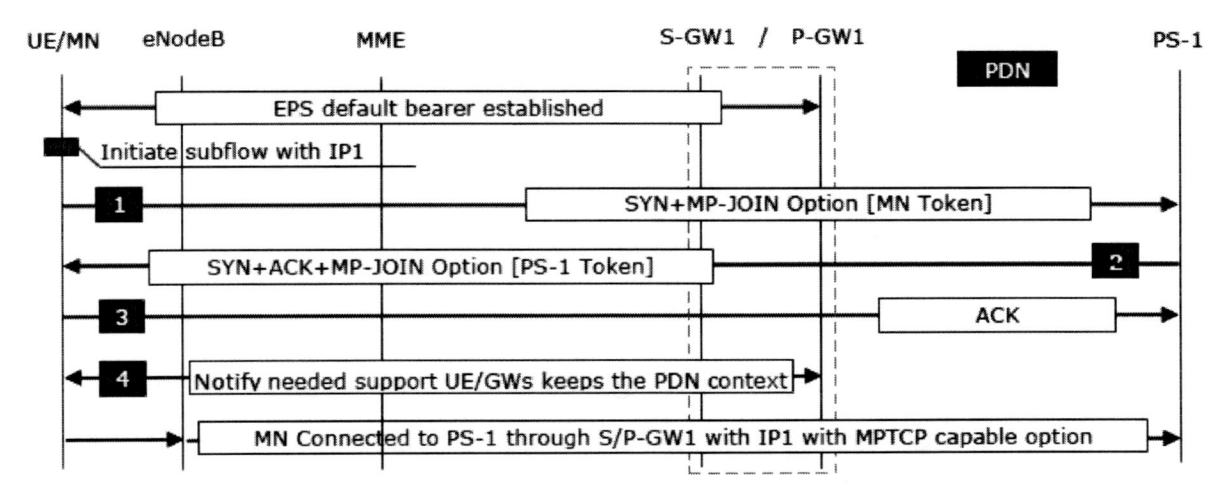

Figure 6: MPTCP connection establishment between MN and PDN-Service1 through S/P-GW1

implemented S/P-GW relocation with reactivation message during Tracking Area Update (TAU) when a MN is in idle mode. To ensure the continuity of active communication and to prevent MN from idle mode as conferred in [12], we take in to shift the relocation decision from MME to S-GW that triggered the GW relocation with create session request to new S-GW. The new S-GW sends a modify bearer request to new P-GW, Together with this procedure MN gets a new IP address (IP2) to be used in the MPTCP new subflow. Since the PDN context is maintained when handing over the MN as notified above, a great deal of signaling is avoided, As a result latency is greatly reduced since the rounds of communications in the EPC between network nodes such as updates with HSS, create session with S-GW/P-GW and perform Policy and Charging Rules Function (PCRF), no longer must be performed.

After the bearer modification, MN initiates new subflow in the same way the MP_CAPABLE handshake and sends SYN segment through S-GW2 onto P-GW2 with its new IP address to PDN-Service1. The new subflow needs to differ at least one of elements of four-tuples (MN IP address, PDN-S1 IP address, MN port and PDN-S1 port). With pre included local identifier (token) carried as an MP-JOIN option of SYN segment, both MN and PDN-S1 are linked to existing MPTCP connection. After the subflows has been established the PDN-Service1 will be able to synchronize the MN's traffic using different IP addresses distributed on MPTCP sub-flows. To provide reliable byte stream on different subflow MPTCP uses two levels of sequence numbers (Regular TCP sequence number and Data sequence number which is corresponds to each byte stream) and maintains one window flow control shared among all subflows relative to last acked data (Data Ack), In this way avoid any loss of inflight packets during the end-to-end state convergence. Packets not acknowledged by corresponding service are retransmitted by another subflow. The presented architecture proposes enhancements in default MPTCP scheduler [13] that decide and direct data to different subflows. The enhanced scheduler can manage different cases of IP flows. The data packets from service requiring static IP anchoring are directed to initial subflow, so the MN is enabled to keep the initially assigned IP address despite its location changes and where no static anchoring at the P-GW1 is required, the MN uses the new subflow for active communication, while maintaining the reachability for the IP address that is still in use.

C. Release connection with long route/delay

As soon communication is successfully established over new subflow, the subflow of long route/delay is set as backup with MP-PRIO option. The old P-GW checks the MN activity, as no traffic is carried in the initial subflow (during the timer interval) the P-GW starts the releases procedure for the removal of initial IP address from the PDN-S1 IP list. The MN could generate a FIN segment/RST flag to close a subflow. Unlike regular TCP that does not allow sending a RST while the connection is in a synchronized state [14], with MPTCP the RST only has the scope of subflow and only close the concerned subflow but not affect the remaining subflows. The release cause tag along the session management and perform the GW binding information update.

IV. CONCLUSIONS

In this paper we have presented improvements for distributed network connections to enable seamless IP mobility, novel perspective to maintain session continuity during the movement of MN that tag along GW relocation. The MPTCP protocol is used to remove the chains of IP preservation of current mobility management solutions, leading in turn seamless IP mobility. Distributed co-located S-GW/P-GW is adopted for optimal data paths, the transport path length between the corresponding nodes has thus dwindled significantly in the architecture presented. The proposed solution further comprises maintaining PDN context for GW relocation, the pictorial call control flows thus created has shown a significant decrease in signaling and delay compared to tunnel and routing based approaches of

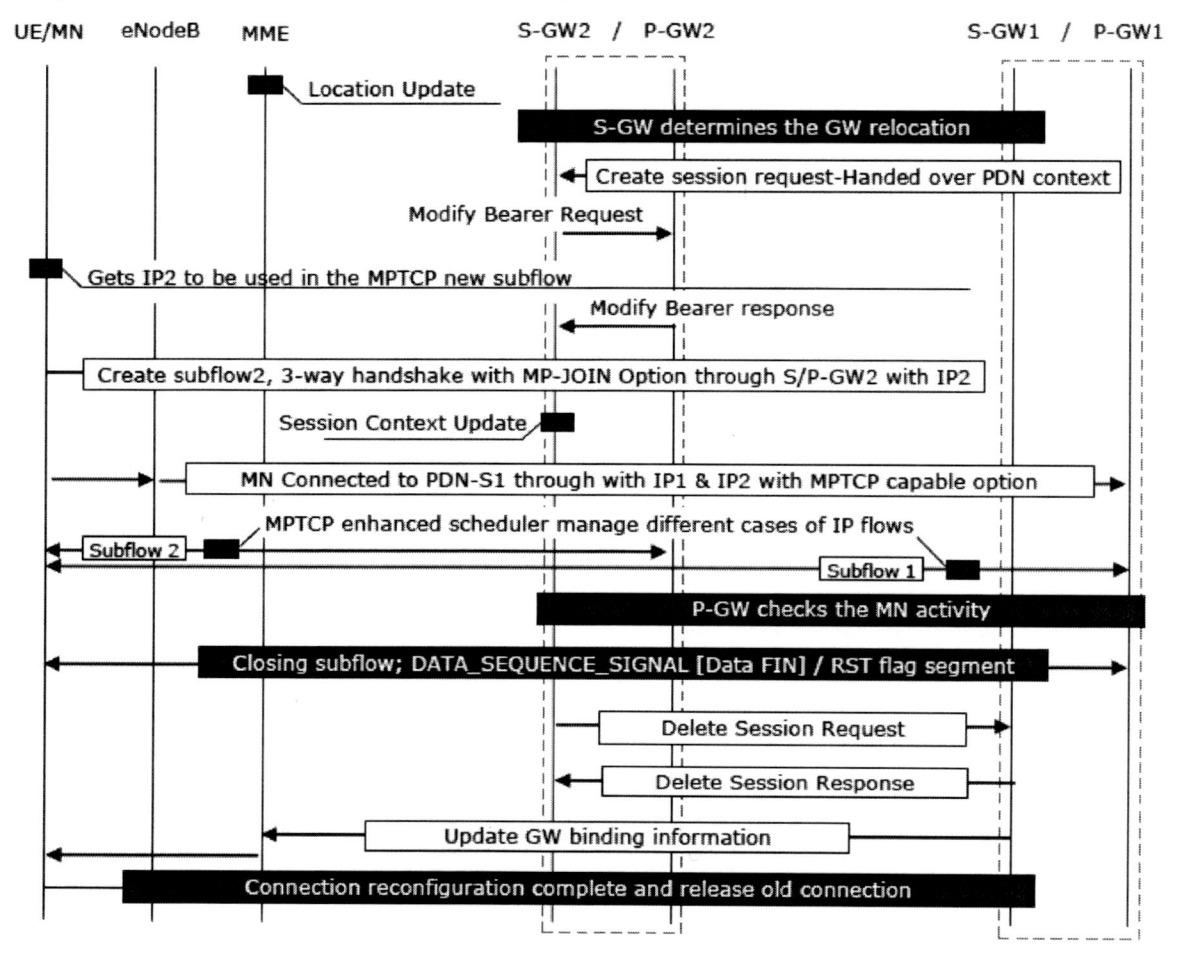

Figure 7: S-GW initiated Gateway relocation with location update.

distributed mobility management. MPTCP provides an overall umbrella and a longer evolution perspective of using simultaneously multiple network path, In future work we intend to enhance the MPTCP default scheduler to manage different types of IP flows and evaluate the proposed solution in an experimental setup in order to illustrate further system realization of the architecture presented.

References

[1] C. Perkins, D. Johnson, and J. Arkko, "Mobility Support in IPv6," RFC 6275, Internet Engineering Task Force, July 2011.

[2] H. Soliman, "Mobile IPv6 Support for Dual Stack Hosts and Routers," RFC 5555, IETF Network Working Group, June 2009

[3] S. Gundavelli, K. Leung, V. Devarapalli, K. Chowdhury, B. Patil "Proxy Mobile IPv6"., RFC 5213, Internet Engineering Task Force, August 2008.

[4] 3GPP, "Evolved General Packet Radio Service (GPRS) Tunnelling Protocol for Control plane (GTPv2-C)," 3GPP TS 29.274, Sept. 2011.

[5] H. Chan, D. Liu, P. Seite, H. Yokota, J. Korhonen, "Requirements for Distributed Mobility Management", RFC 7333, Internet Engineering Task Force, August 2014.

[6] A. Yegin, J. Park, K. Kweon, J. Lee, "Terminal-centric distribution and orchestration of IP mobility for 5G networks", IEEE Communications Magazine, vol. 52, November 2014, pp. 86-92

[7] A. Ford, C. Raiciu, M. Handley, O. Bonaventure, "TCP Extensions for multipath operation with multiple addresses", RFC 6824, IETF 2013.

[8] B. Sarikaya, "Distributed Mobile IPv6," Internet-Draft, IETF Network Working Group, Feb. 2012.

[9] Bernardos, Carlos Jesús, Antonio De la Oliva, and Fabio Giust. "A PMIPv6-based solution for distributed mobility management." (2013).

[10] A. Ford, C. Raiciu, M. Handley, O. Bonaventure, "TCP Extensions for multipath operation with multiple addresses", RFC 6824, IETF 2013.

[11] 3GPP TS 23.401 "TE Enhancements for Evolved Universal Terrestrial Radio Access Network access" V13.5.0 March 2016.

[12] W. Hahn, "3GPP Evolved Packet Core support for distributed mobility anchors: Control enhancements for GW relocation," ITS Telecommunications (ITST), 2011 11th International Conference on, St. Petersburg, 2011, pp. 264-267.

[13] S. Barré, , C. Paasch, O. Bonaventure. "Multipath TCP: from theory to practice." In NETWORKING 2011, pp. 444-457. Springer Berlin Heidelberg, 2011.

[14] O. Bonaventure, C. Paasch, G. Detal "Processing of RST segments by Multipath TCP," Internet-Draft, IETF Network Working Group, July. 2014

Algorithm for Generating Peer-to-Peer Overlay Graphs based on WebRTC Events

Christian von Harscher, Marco Schindler, Johannes Kinzig and Sergej Alekseev
Computer Science and Engineering
Frankfurt University of Applied Sciences
Frankfurt am Main, Germany
{harscher|mschindl|kinzig}@stud.fra-uas.de, alekseev@fb2.fra-uas.de

Abstract—The peer-to-peer paradigm is widely used in the distribution of data and documents and direct multimedia communications on the internet. The network nodes, which are concerned in a peer-to-peer network, create an infrastructure that provides and offers a desired functionality or application in a distributed manner. Upcoming communication standards, such as WebRTC, also enable a setup where web browsers can act as peer-to-peer nodes.

In this paper we present an algorithm for generating connection graphs of the peers based on WebRTC state events. The essential idea of the algorithm is to collect events, generated by changing a signaling and connection state of peers. The algorithm processes the collected events and generates a connection graph of the peers, which represent the overlay topology of the peer-to-peer application.

Additionally we present examples of collected events and corresponding connection graphs.

Index Terms—WebRTC, Finite State Machine, Graph, Algorithm

I. INTRODUCTION

Performance monitoring is an challenging aspect of system and service development, it is helpful by detecting and diagnosing performance issues and assists in maintaining a high availability. These days developing teams mainly take data-driven decisions, and these performance measurements play a major role in debugging.

WebRTC is a steadily evolving web communication standard, but it does not provide any interfaces or tools to monitor peer-to-peer overlay structures.

A WebRTC application creates RTCPeerConnection objects [3, sect. 4.3.3] to establish connections between peers. The state of a RTCPeerConnection is represented by three finite state machines: signaling, gathering and connection state machine [1]. Each peer generates an event by changing a signaling, gathering and connection state.

By gathering and storing these events and data it is possible to analyze WebRTC sessions. Since the evaluation of the entire data is a painstaking effort, this article describes the implementation of an algorithm that automatically evaluate these data by generating expressive connection graphs. This contains the representation of the events as a derived graph as well as statistical data of each client. The algorithm is also able to distinguish between the peer itself and the corresponding connections established to other peers, see fig. 1.

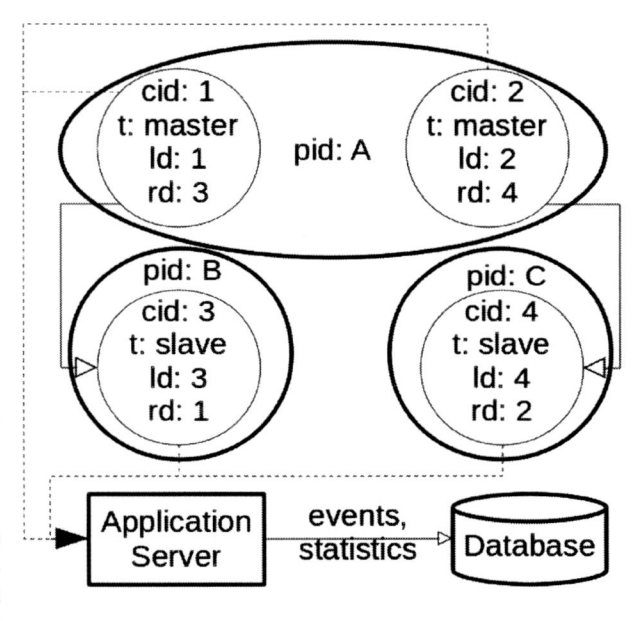

Fig. 1. System Overview, see III-A for details

II. RELATED WORKS

Monitoring the performance of P2P based WebRTC applications is a major aspect in system and service environments. Performance can be tracked, issues and non-stable connections can be identified and the diagnosis of these failures help to deliver a high quality of service and availability. Therefore the first step is to gather the WebRTC statistics. Proprietary and also open source frameworks exist for this purpose. One proprietary framework is named *callstats.io* [8] which allows the user to use the vendor's databases to store the WebRTC statistics. The statistics are then represented graphically showing the data rates, network latencies, number of succeeded and failed conferences. Additionally *callstats.io* allows the session users to provide subjective feedback about the call's quality. One drawback is that *callstats.io* is not able to show a graph giving information about the user's connection topology.

One open source method gathering the statistics is presented in [1]. Table I shows an extract of the database table for gathering the WebRTC statistics as presented in [1]. These statistics are important for measuring the general quality of a session. By looking closely at the table it becomes obvious that it is complicated to conclude the quality of a session just from looking at this table. This leads to the basic necessity to have a tool which is able to graphically interpret the gathered data. An algorithm for exactly this purpose is described in this paper.

There are libraries available that provide a way of generating graphs in form of diagrams out of structured information [4], [5] and [6]. This paper will not describe a new way of generating graphs but use Graphviz.

III. PROPOSED APPROACH

Basically we are providing an approach for automatically generating a graph structure out of the WebRTC statistics described in [1]. The general aim is to get a structured graph which can be displayed graphically to simplify the forthcoming analysis. Additionally the proposed algorithm can be used to transfer the graph into other data structures (e.g. XML, JSON) for further automated processing.

The following sections describe in more detail the dependency between the WebRTC events to generate the graph, as well as the first steps necessary to implement the algorithm.

A. Terminology and Definition

The system overview is provided in fig. 1. It shows the basic structure with three peers. The peer A is the session initiator which is connected to the peers B and C. The peer-id pid, connection-id cid, type t, local description ld and remote description rd are given. A peer can hold more than one RTCPeerConnection object. The type as well as the corresponding connection-id are defining the direction of a connection, shown as a line with an ending arrow to the slave peer. A connection with type master is always a outgoing connection, whereas a incoming connection is always represented through type slave. Local and remote description are extracted out of the Session Description Protocol (SDP) [7], used for the initialization of the connection.

B. Events Gathering

The event collection is realized by the *WebRTCStateAnalyzer* from [1]. This JavaScript library is used by the WebRTC Application. The client-side code is using the event listeners of the RTCPeerConnection to catch the events. An event E is defined as follows:

$$E(ts, pid, cid, ld, rd, t, l, Z_s) \qquad (1)$$

where ts is the timestamp and Z_s the state of an event. The timestamp is necessary to define the ordering of a queue of events Q:

$$\forall E \in Q : ts(E_n) < ts(E_{n+1}) \qquad (2)$$

The event listener l is needed for later analysis and is describing which function of the RTCPeerConnection fired the event. The state of the RTCPeerConnection object Z_s is given by $Z_s = (S, G, C)$ where S represents the signaling state machine, G the gathering state machine and C the connection state machine (fig. 4) of the RTCPeerConnection [1, Sec. III].

The actual acquisition of the events is done via a HTTP-POST request from the peer to the application server. After receiving the request the events are stored into a database. In addition statistical data is sent on each event. This data can be consolidated for displaying in the graph. This process and further analysis of the statistical data is described in [2].

C. Algorithm for Generation Connection Graphs

The algorithm creates a directed graph based on gathered raw events. The graph is defined as following:

$$G(N, T, r), r \in N \qquad (3)$$

where N are the nodes (peers), T are the transitions (connections) and r is the root peer called session initiator.

Listing 1 shows the main part of the algorithm taking the queue of events Q and returning the graph G as N, T, r (line 10). All events in Q are iterated and added to the node object N. Each peer with its connections is added once in line 3. The second iteration will loop through all of the node objects for extracting the connections and assigning the transitions. These both algorithms can be found in listings 2 and 3. Last steps to do are to extract all transitions into the transitions object T and finding the root node r. The root node is the node with no incoming transitions.

Listing 1
MAIN ALGORITHM FOR GENERATING THE GRAPH STRUCTURE

```
1   GENERATE_GRAPH(Q){
2     for(i = 0; i < sizeof(Q); i++){
3       N.add(Q[i].getPeer())
4     }
5     for(i = 0; i < sizeof(N); i++){
6       GET_CONNECTIONS(Q, &N[i]);
7       ASSIGN_TRANSITIONS(Q, &N[i]);
8     T = N.getAllTransitions()
9     r = N.getRootNode()
10    return N, T, r
11    }
12  }
```

Finding all connections of one node is done by the algorithm in listing 2. For this reason all events in Q need to be iterated. The connection id of the current event $Q[i]$ and the given node object n are compared. The connection type of n needs to be non-slave. After fulfilling these criteria the connection id cid can be added to the given node in line 5.

Listing 2
ALGORITHM FOR EXTRACTING THE CONNECTIONS

```
1   GET_CONNECTIONS(Q, *n){
2     for(i = 0; i < sizeof(Q); i++){
3       if(Q[i].getCid() == n.getCid()
4         && n.getType() != 'slave'){
5         n.addTransitionId(n.getCid())
6       }
7     }
8   }
```

148

TABLE I
DATABASE EXCERPT WITH WEBRTC RAW EVENTS (COLUMNS EXPLAINED IN III-A)

pid	cid	ld	rd	t	ts	l	S	G	C
18	2364	7938	7768	master	1445330422	oniceconnectionstatechange	stable	complete	connected
58	9854	7768	7938	slave	1445330422	oniceconnectionstatechange	stable	complete	connected
18	3230	3629	7845	master	1445330424	oniceconnectionstatechange	stable	complete	connected
67	3711	7845	3629	slave	1445330424	oniceconnectionstatechange	stable	complete	connected
[...]	[...]	[...]	[...]	[...]	[...]	[...]	[...]	[...]	[...]

The third part of the algorithm in listing 3 is the assignment of the transitions between two peers. A connection is defined by a connection id cid, a local description ld and a remote description rd. The descriptions give the exact information of which node is connected to which other node. The type t is defining the direction of a transition. In this case only the type master is considered so that the first parameter of *assignTransition()* is representing the master and the second parameter represents the slave side of the connection. The transition is directed from the master to the slave node. Additionally the events are treated with descending timestamps, see line 2. Last important thing to remark is that not all events in Q are carrying the local and remote description. To filter the events that are impractical for this use, the constraints in lines 3-5 are defined. The event listener l must be *oniceconnectionstatechange*, the signaling state machine $S \in Z_s$ must be in the state *stable* and the connection state machine $C \in Z_s$ must be in state *connected*. All other events could carry either only one of the descriptions or none of them. Once a transition is found it will be added to the node object in line 9. The local description is always the other peer's remote description and vice versa.

Listing 3
ALGORITHM FOR ASSIGNING THE TRANSITIONS BETWEEN NODES

```
1  ASSIGN_TRANSITIONS(Q, *n){
2   for(i = sizeof(Q); i > 0; i--){
3    if(Q[i].getListener() == '
        ↪ oniceconnectionstatechange'
4     && Q[i].getSig() == 'stable'
5     && Q[i].getCon() == 'connected'
6     && n.getType() == 'master'
7     && Q[i].getLDesc() == n.getRDesc()
8     && transitionNotYetFound()){
9      n.assignTransition(n.getLDesc(), Q[i].
        ↪ getLDesc())
10    }
11   }
12  }
```

D. Example

In this section the whole algorithm will be executed on basis of the presented raw events in table I. These events will be taken as input. The necessary filtering of the events by l, C and S described in III-C is already done. This makes it obvious that some of the events are missing in table I. A balanced tree topology with three nodes is used for the example graph.

After the first loop in line 4 of listing 1 all nodes are extracted:

$$\{18, 58, 67\} \quad (4)$$

The next step is to extract all connections based on the previously extracted nodes. To accomplish this the *GET_CONNECTIONS()* algorithm listing 2 is called. The resulting connections can be represented as:

$$\{(18, 2364), (18, 3230)\} \quad (5)$$

The first value represents the peer id pid and the second value represents the connection id cid. Based on these connections the transitions can be assigned by ASSIGN_TRANSITIONS (listing 3). This is the resulting structure containing the cid followed by the local description ld and remote description rd:

$$\{(2364, 7938, 7768), (3230, 3629, 7845)\} \quad (6)$$

Out of this structured data the graph G can be created:

$$G = (\{18, 58, 67\}, \{(18, 58), (18, 67)\}, 18) \quad (7)$$

E. Graph Representation

Now that the necessary graph structure is created by the algorithm it can be visualized in several ways. The fig. 2 represents a graph which is generated from the dot language in listing 4. This generated graph shows a simple representation. It is also possible to use labels for the node itself and its transitions to generated a more complex graph, see fig. 5. The labels include statistical information on the connections between nodes as well as the location of the nodes. Even further analysis can be done by converting the graph structure to other formats like JSON or XML.

Listing 4
EXAMPLE GRAPH IN DOT LANGUAGE

```
1  digraph G {
2   18 -> 58
3   18 -> 67
4  }
```

F. Exception handling

For the analysis and exception handling it is important to detect connecting and disconnecting peers. Fig. 3 shows the joining and leaving peers based on the time. For the forthcoming analysis the following interpretations can be done. Fig. 3 shows a session example where four intervals were identified.

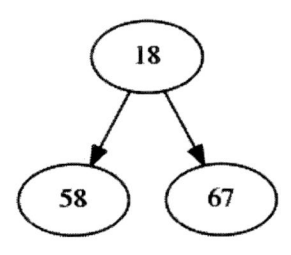

Fig. 2. Example graph with no additional details

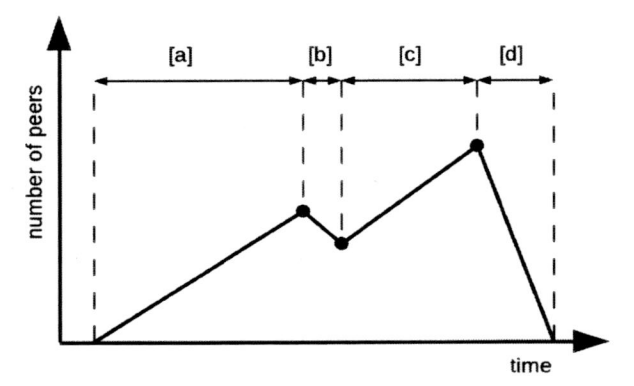

Fig. 3. Connections and disconnections based on time

Interval [a] begins with the opening of a session. Then the number of peers is increasing, the peers join the session. Interval [b] starts when the number of peers is decreasing for the first time. The first peer has disconnected. The reason for a disconnect can be caused by two incidents. Either the user has left the session on purpose or the connection became unstable and this lead to a disconnect. The second described scenario is the most important one for the analysis because it is necessary to distinguish between these two. When the users leaves the session on purpose this must not be shown as an error. When looking at Interval [c] it becomes obvious that the number of peers is increases again. Some peers are again joining the session. Interval [d] is the last identified section. In a short amount of time, the number of clients is decreasing until the number of peers equals zero. This means that the session has ended and every user has left the session.

The connection state machine in fig. 4 is one out of three finite state machines of the RTCPeerConnection. Combined these FSM are representing the status Z_s of a WebRTC connection. With this information it is possible to determine if the connection is successfully established, if there is no signaling or if the connection failed.

IV. RESULTS

It is now possible to extract a expressive graph out of the raw data collected in an WebRTC application. The output

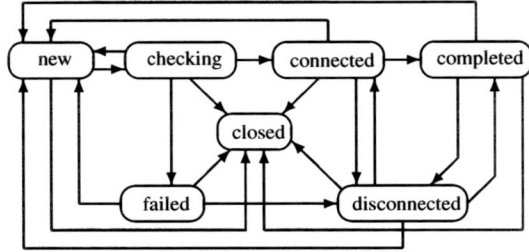

Fig. 4. Connection state machine

graph also contains statistical network data of each connection, determining the link quality. The choosen network statistics for this graph are consisting of the round trip time (RTT) and the send and lost packets between two peers. The algorithm also provides a possibility to evaluate the quality of service through checking of the state machines. There is a distinction between three different states: no signaling, no connection and success. An example graph, representing events and statistical data of three clients and the consequential connections, is shown in fig. 5.

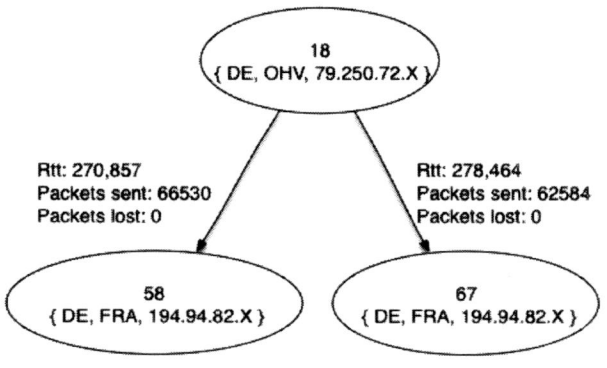

Fig. 5. Example graph with details

V. CONCLUSION

This article describes an algorithm for generating overlay graphs based on WebRTC state events.

This is a graphical solution to display the evaluation of single WebRTC sessions. Essential information such as the topology of a session or single connection states can be determined by looking at the derived graph.

REFERENCES

[1] S. Alekseev, C. von Harscher and M. Schindler, Finite State Machine based Flow Analysis for WebRTC Applications, Fourth International Conference on Innovative Computing Technology (IEEE INTECH), University of Bedfordshire, Luton, UK, 2014 http://ieeexplore.ieee.org/xpl/articleDetails.jsp?arnumber=6927739

[2] S. Alekseev, J. Schaefer, A New Algorithm for Construction of a P2P Multicast Hybrid Overlay Tree Based on Topological Distances, The Seventh International Conference on Networks and Communications, 2015

[3] Adam Bergkvist, Daniel C. Burnett, Cullen Jennings, Anant Narayanan, WebRTC 1.0: Real-time Communication Between Browsers, Working Draft 10 February 2015 *https://www.w3.org/TR/webrtc/*
[4] AT&T, Graphviz - Graph Visualization Software *http://www.graphviz.org/*
[5] Mathieu Bastian, Eduardo Ramos Ibaez, Mathieu Jacomy, et al., Gephi - The Open Graph Viz Platform *https://gephi.org/*
[6] Wolfram Research, Wolfram Mathematica *http://www.wolfram.com/mathematica/*
[7] M. Handley, V. Jacobson, C. Perkins, SDP: Session Description Protocol *https://tools.ietf.org/html/rfc4566*
[8] Nemu Dialogue Systems Oy, callstats.io, *callstats.io monitors and manages the performance of video calls in an WebRTC application.*, Helsinki, Finland, 01.2016.

SIP Automated Test Platform

Yagmur Kirkagac
Netas Telecommunication Corp.
Marmara University
Electrical and Electronics Engineering
Istanbul, Turkey
Email: yagmur@netas.com.tr

Serdar Simsek
Kocaeli University
Computer Engineering
Human Computer Interaction Lab.
Kocaeli, Turkey
Email: ssimsek@outlook.com

Demir Y. Yavas
Netas Telecommunication Corp.
Istanbul Technical University
Electrical and Electronics Engineering
Istanbul, Turkey
Email: demiry@netas.com.tr

Abstract—IP networks have been becoming more popular communication infrastructures due to the lower operational costs in recent years. Mainly, usage of IP networks in voice services, which is denominated by VoIP (Voice over IP), has made difference in telephony networks not only the way of the people's communications, but also telecommunication companies' and operators' solutions. In this scope, IMS (IP Multimedia Subsystems)/SIP (Session Initiation Protocol) networks have some challenges for testing processes. Testing and validation of SIP scenarios in IMS networks can be complex and time consuming due to the lots of different kind of scenarios with traditional manual methods. This paper aims to develop automated test environment for SIP messages. In this perspective, this system provides to manage SIPp-like XML (eXtensible Markup Language) scenario files, which is aimed to support IMS network nodes with GUI (Graphical User Interface). Automation of SIP signaling test environment is also implemented for plotting data automatically.

Keywords—SIP; SIPp; Automated Test Environment; GUI; VoIP; IMS

I. INTRODUCTION

IMS provides the voice transmission over IP to merge all networks for IP based communication. VoIP solutions also use SIP for session management [1], and RTP (Real-Time Transport Protocol) for multimedia transmissions [2]. SIP is one of the commonly used protocol for session management of video and voice transmissions in recent years.

Verification and validation tests are important part of the product development life cycle and can give an idea about the quality of the product. Testing can either be done manually or using an automated testing tool. Manual testing is extremely time-consuming and error-prone process. It is common expectation that automated testing saves resources and makes testing process more expedite, efficient and reliable. In addition, automated testing can be a part of CI (Continuous Integration). More generally, the correct and efficient mapping between requirements and test cases and full implementation of them might be time consuming and difficult to reach [3].

More specifically, testing SIP protocol has some challenges valid for both manual and automated testing approaches. Although the text based message format simplifies interpretation messages and message flows; when it is combined with rich feature set of SIP, dynamic behavior of certain message headers (such as "Via" and "Contact" headers), the large diversity of header field values, the testing becomes a complex and error-prone task. In detail, the header parameter interpretation may differ according to their precise location within a specific message flow [3].

In the case of sequentially invoked test cases for a specific user or service, a failure on a test case may lead the SUT (System Under Test) to inconsistent states that subsequent tests cases may also fail. This may cause difficulties on determining actual problems. In this context, the automated testing tools are needed to recover failure cases (such that sending CANCEL or BYE SIP messages in order to end the current session as depending on the phase of the session).

Support for RTP with the test tool is a valuable facility to be able to verify media path establishment and call scenarios including SIP-based media servers.

If a test tool supports protocols, such as HTTP (Hyper-Text Transfer Protocol), SOAP (Simple Object Access Protocol), to be used change the configuration of the SUT dynamically, it can be more effectively used in a automated test process.

On manual testing and during the test case development, CLI (Command Line Interface) might be challenging for testing process even if it has some advantages. CLI allows to experienced testers to get in contact with the system as quickly as possible. On the other hand, CLI has lots of problems for testers. Supporting GUI does not make only creating test cases easier but also providing accelerated and efficient testing time.

All these kind of issues with combining some others such as incorporating with the new additions to specifications and maintaining also the backward compatibility make providing a comprehensive test tool a challenging task.

In this paper, we presented a test tool and a test platform addressing these kind of challenges. The test tool supports SIPp-like XML-based scenarios, test cases covering test scenarios and test suites covering test cases. Supporting SIPp-like scenarios is selected to capitalize on habits of testers who have already known about SIPp [4]. Besides, properties provided by the SIPp approach are extended to provide complex call scenarios including multi-dialogs and nested transactions. The test platform provides sharing applied test structures through a database and reorganization between teams taking role at different testing phases such as compatibility testing, sanity testing, regression testing and acceptance testing, except performance tests which is not assumed for the tool. In this way, we plan to build a corpus of SIP messages containing a rich mix of requests and responses across different services. The presented tool supports sending media stream by using media files, and it can generate and recognize both inband and outband (RFC 2388) DTMF (Dual Tone Multi Frequency) tones through RTP streams [5].

The tool can simulate SIP client and SIP server behaviors including, but not limited to proxy server, B2BUA (Back-to-Back User Agent), registrar, SIP media server.

The proposed tool offers the utilization of powerful SIP test scenarios by using the proposed methodology which is explained in Section II. The technologies, used in our tool, are explained in Section III and supported graphical user interface is explained in Section IV.

II. METHODOLOGY

A. Testing Objectives

As testing is an integrated part of a product development, it is necessary to perform testing at any phase of the development life cycle for distinct objectives. Our tool and platform is aimed for *(i)* design phase tests (e.g. as an message injector), *(ii)* compatibility testing, *(iii)* sanity testing, *(iv)* regression testing, and *(v)* acceptance testing. It is planned to be used for reproducing of reported problems and collecting required debug information at customer sites. The tool is not assumed for performance tests. The tool can be used for manual testing as well as integrated with CI for automated real time tests.

B. High Level Design

The high level design of the tool is done by considering the following criteria:

Simplicity: The tool supports minimal menu options and configuration details for ease of use in user interface (UI) design. All test components are movable with drag and drop design mechanism. The tool is natural design considering human-machine interactions and user profiles. Testers can learn without experience the tool easily, and use the system quickly. New testers become productive in a short time.

Reusability: Our designed tool supports to reuse, change and improve all test components such as test messages, test scenarios, test cases to another test.

Portability: Our designed tool allows to run the same tests with another platforms which are another SIP enabled servers or clients with simple configuration changes like IP/userID.

Flexibility: All test components can adapt all processes without cause of any flow damages.

Collaboration: Our tool design encourages the sharing and collaboration. It allows to share test components with other testers easily. Testers can search test components not only in our created library but also other testers working areas.

The high level design components are listed below.

C. Design Components

1) User Login and Credentials: There are user login window for each tester to sign in. After the tester signing in, they do not have to memorize the script codes for functionalities which are founding in RFC. Also they do not have to re-write the codes over and over again. Testers can try the test scenarios with the constituted default test cases. Moreover, testers can add and/or save their specialized test scenarios into the system. In fact, they can edit or pull the pieces the scenarios. With this approach the testers can share their experiences about testing cases and improve their methods. Every user has a different account in order to accomplish those facts laying in previous sentences. Test message templates can be edited only by its creator. Otherwise, a clone is transferred to the user who is attempting to save. After the clone, the message will be appeared other users pool.

2) Standards/Specifications: The testing and developing process in VoIP technologies, is necessary to provide IETF (Internet Engineering Task Force) and 3GPP standards. Designed tool is supported by multiple protocols like SIP, RTP, SOAP, HTTP [6] and also is used in network transport protocol layers TCP, TLS/TCP or UDP [7].

3) Platform Independence: For platform independence, the tool is implemented by using Java and tested on Windows and Linux OSs.

4) Extendability for Multi-protocol Support: An event driven core mechanism is implemented as independent of protocol messages and flows. The event driven mechanism follows only events defined in the scenario flow such as message sending, message receiving and time expiry events. A new protocol definition can bind itself to the core mechanism to invoke and get events.

5) Multi-agent Support: As multi-agent support, the tool can form itself as a client or a server as depending on the first action in the scenario; e.g. if the first action is to send a request message, it considers a client behavior.

6) Mode of Operation: The tool considers three mode of operation on message processing. It parses messages according to SIP ABNF (Augmented Backus-Naur Form) grammar before sending through SIP transaction and dialog state machine by default. This is to prevent uncontrolled message structure and flow errors. The advanced mode controls only mistakes only message grammar before sending, but not transaction and dialog states. JAIN-SIP stack [8] is used for these purposes. The advanced mode uses only the message parser of JAIN-SIP stack. The more advanced mode does not perform any control on message structure and flow and it uses an internally developed stack. This is mode can be used to produce malformed messages for stress and robustness tests.

7) Test Scenarios Setup: All test scenarios are grouped under a specific functionality by specific users. Test scenarios lists can be grown by adding more scenarios from testers. Our designed tool does not need any configuration to setup for

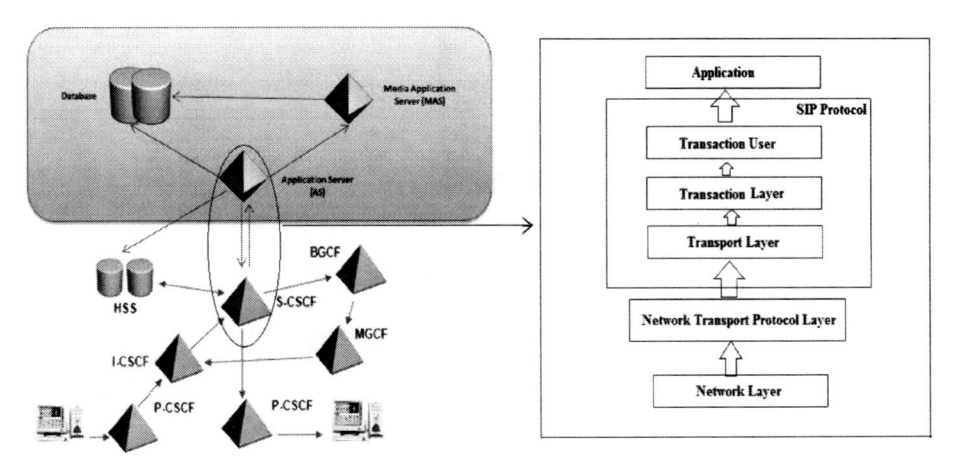

Fig. 1. SIP Protocol Stack in a Typical IMS Structure

test scenarios. User can use test scenarios only drag and drop method.

8) External Tools: Our designed tool does not need any additional tools for examining tests. It provides a log screen at the bottom of the window that testers can see messages and exceptions in this part of the tool. Packet analyzer tools like Wireshark still can be used for network troubleshooting.

9) Test Scripts: Basic test scripts are developed by in-house testers which are denominated by admin users in designed test tool. Other additional test scripts can be specified by other testers. Stress testing is more difficult without automated testing tool. Designed tool supports 5 testing types which are compatibility, sanity, regression and acceptance including stress testing automation [3].

10) Verification: Creating reliable and functional SIP signaling testing tool is quite challenging. There are lots of parameters which are depending on protocol failing (when deployed) even after testing process. Tool design should also provide verification with automatically. To explain the real-case example, call establishment stage can be failed in VoIP testing. Other testing tools do not give any information to indicate error. Testers spend a lot time for reproducing problem and identifying error. Designed tool detects any problem when the call signal is failed in the call process and inform the tester which stage is failed. By this means, testers can identify problems easily and fixing time also will decrease.

11) Test Case and Test Suite: Test cases consist of scenarios which defined a complete test case, such as grouping scenarios of originating and terminating agents in a test case which can be invoked at the same time from the same computer. For flexibility, scenarios in test case can be invoked at the same time or sequentially. Similarly, a group of test cases can be grouped into a *test suite* which can be correspond to a specific feature or functionality test. Our test suite is designed to run multiple test cases ordered one by one execution, or a group of test cases simultaneous.

12) User Friendliness: A well defined GUI (Graphical User Interface) is considered for user friendliness. The user can build a test scenario by drag and drop from the entire corpus provided by the test platform using a database. The GUI provides facilities for users to edit, re-configure, run tests and to collect results.

13) Graphical Display: The tool has a graphical interface providing operational management (OM) statistics for every monitored network element (NE). The graphical display is supported by OM data with a specific time interval. In addition, it plotting graphs with supports available data sets. Thus, testers not only can detect problems of OM data but also manage fault performance with using graphical display easily.

14) User Interface: The GUI software testing is promised to the graphical front-end meets with tool specifications. GUI software testing must provide not only cover all functionalities but also ensures that the GUI itself is fully tested.

III. TEST PLATFORM DESIGN TECHNOLOGIES

IMS network structure and SIP Stack structure considered for the tool is illustrated in Figure 1. The tool can be positioned as any SIP enabled node in the network such as SCSF, AS, SBC, SIP GW, SIP Clients [9]. JAIN-SIP and an internally developed stack are used in the SIP stack level. The internally developed stack is also used for RTP, HTTP and SOAP.

Designed tool is a desktop application for testers. High level design is required user-friendly design which is mentioned in

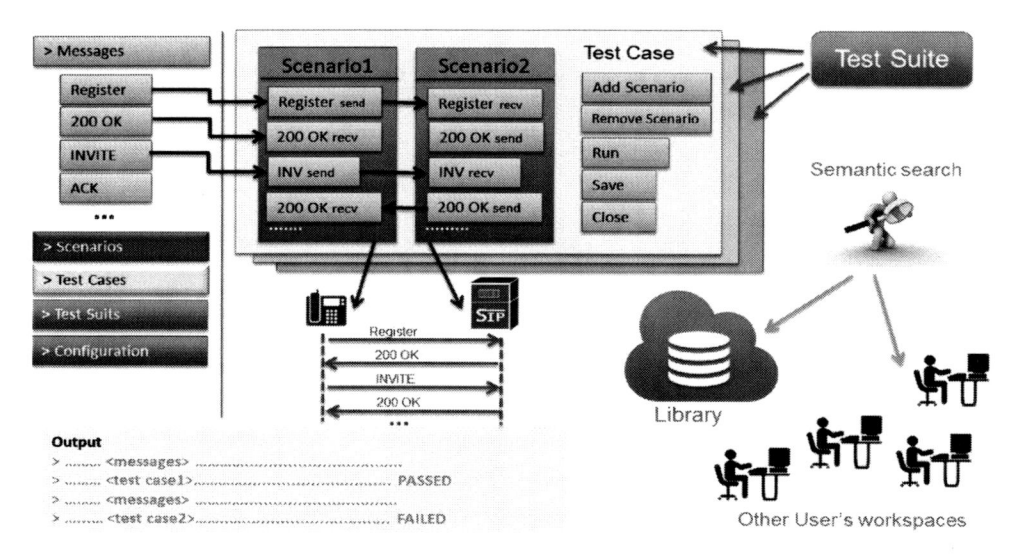

Fig. 2. Designed Tool Overall System Design

section II-C. It has been developed using JavaFX for building user-friendly GUI. It is developed with using Model-View-Controller(MVC) design pattern.

MVC design pattern has three types of objects. There are; model, view and controller. These objects can handle entity (data), boundary (presentation) and control (behavior). View and controller objects compose user interface. MVC model has useful advantages at runtime such as providing multiple views, synchronization of views and controllers. Designed tool is used to model object to operate and implement the logic. View model object is used to interact with testers. Control object is used to control the web applications.

The back-end software of the tool is implemented in Core Java. Database system is developed in LAMP (Linux + Apache + MySQL + PHP). LAMP server use script languages such as PHP, Perl, JSP or ASP. These are quite efficient for quick learning and deployment. Core Java objects are connected with relational database MySQL by using Java Database Connection. In this means, all parameters are placed in relational database MySQL.

Mapping is one of the most important part in designed tool. Mapping allows to the testers to map the test cases with users. In other work, our designed tool allows to semantic search in library or other users workspaces for test cases. Designed tool is supported Object Relational Mapping (ORM) design which is provided a framework for mapping an object oriented model design to relational database. ORM design is mostly used with Hibernate. We designed unique ORM framework design for mapping objects to relational database. Original ORM framework design was carried out in this tool.

Designed tool overall system schema is illustrated in Figure 2. Our tool supports multi-protocol (SIP-RTP-HTTP-SOAP) in the same scenario. Testers can search libraries and other users workspaces with semantic search method.

Race condition problems, which may not be reproducible in real time, can be created by the with extending test scenarios by adding timers.

IV. GRAPHICAL USER INTERFACE

The GUI has been developed in JavaFX for improving the user-interface experiences. User account is an important parameter which is provided sharing, utilization of scripts in designed tool, in that scope testers can learn and drive testing processes much more easier way. In this section, designed tool sample screens will be shown and will be given brief information.

The tool provides a user login screen. Testers create an account first. The tool allows to semantic search for test scenarios searching in our created library or other testers workspaces. Testers can define their SIP messages with filling special fields. Admin users can also share messages in the library as a template. Other testers can also add created test objects into the library as a template, after verifications. If testers do not share their test objects to the library, test objects can be visible on only themselves workspaces. However, our semantic search also allows to find test objects even testers do not share to the library. All test objects can use with cloning testers workspaces.

Template messages can be added another users pool. The user can change the messages and save specialized message to own pool without any changes in original template messages. We also implemented chat screen for providing a communication of testers about testing processes and templates. Figure 3

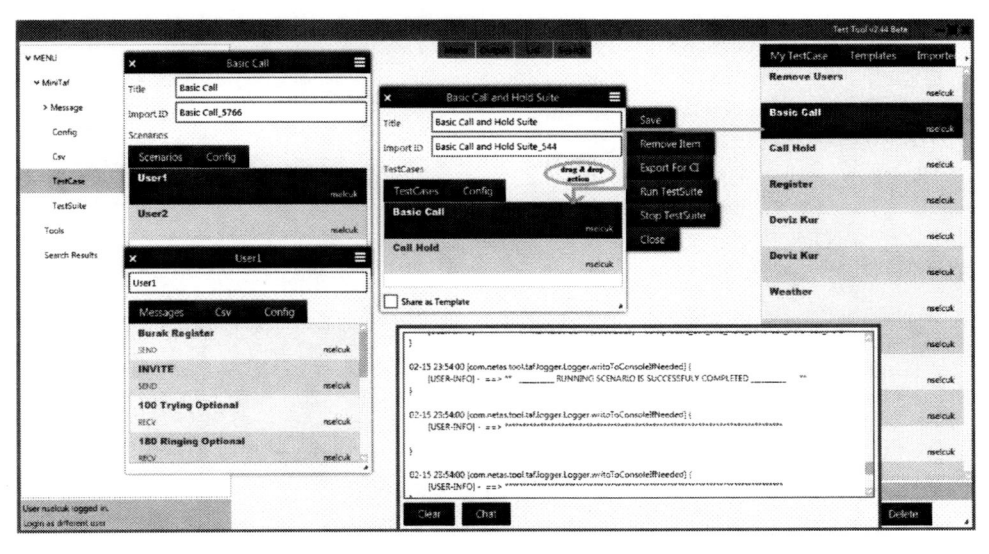

Fig. 3. Designed Test Environment Test Suite Example

shows our designed test environment which is supported with basic call and call hold test suite example.

The tool plotted graphics depends on customer data automatically for catalyzing the analysis. It also allows to add another features in graphics for making easier to comparisons and analyses. System can analyze two or more parameters in the same graph for making easier to comparison.

V. Conclusion

In this paper, we present our automated SIP testing tool and platform with solutions for SIP testing problems. These problems are solved with supporting multi-protocol structure, multi-platform computing methods, complex SIP call scenarios, user friendly and collaborative GUI design. All of our solutions consider not to change users's habits but simplify. For this reason, our tool design supports XML syntax which has already known by testers. Our designed Test Case and Test Suite structure can handle complex SIP call scenarios by running the organized more than one test scenarios sequentially. The tool supports protocols such as HTTP and SOAP for changing the configuration of the SUT during the tests, dynamically. The tool consists of an user-friendly GUI design. Drag and drop feature simplifies the usage and learning the tool. It plots graphs from data and runs the stored scenarios from the library which is shared other tester's scenarios pool. These are the advantages for the cases which have to be analyzed and tested immediately.

In the future works, our tool can be expanded for involving all IMS network protocols by adding features such as supporting Diameter protocol and RESTFUL services. In addition, we desire our tool behave as a traffic tool with supporting complex call scenarios.

Acknowledgment

This project has been supported by Netas Telecommunication Corporation.

References

[1] J. Rosenberg et al., SIP: Session Initiation Protocol, RFC 3261, June 2002.
[2] H. Schulzrinne, et al., RTP: A Transport Protocol for Real-Time Applications, RFC 3550, July 2003.
[3] D. Goncalves, A. Amaral, A. Costa, P. Sousa, "Towards Automated Test and Validation of SIP Solutions", Telecommunication Systems March 2016, Volume 61, Issue 3, pp. 579-590.
[4] SIPp development team, "SIPp - SIP performance Testing Tool" [online] Available: http://sipp.sourceforge.net/.
[5] L. Masinter, Returning Values from Forms: multipart/form-data, RFC 2388, August 1998.
[6] P. Subramanian, B. PG, "Convergence of Java EE and SIP in IMS AS", IP Multimedia Subsystem Architecture and Applications, Int. Conf., Bangalore, 2007, pp. 1-5.
[7] M. Ranganathan, O. Deruelle, D. Montgomery, "Testing SIP Call Flows Using XML Protocol Templates", TestCom'03 Proc. of the 15th IFIP Int. Conf. on Testing of Communicating systems, pp. 33-48
[8] The Source for Java Technology Collaboration, "JAIN-SIP Stack" [online] Available: https://jsip.java.net/.
[9] M. Poikselka and G. Mayer, "The IMS: IP Multimedia Concepts and Services", 3rd Ed., Wiley, 2009.

The Usage of Body Area Networks for Fall-Detection

Luigi La Blunda, Matthias Wagner
WSN & IoT Research Group
Frankfurt University of Applied Sciences
Frankfurt am Main, Germany
l.lablunda — mfwagner@fb2.fra-uas.de

Abstract—This paper presents an ongoing research analyzing existing fall-detection systems and developing a fully automated fall-detection system. The system is based on a Body Area Network (BAN), which is worn in form of a belt on the hip. To provide an accurate fall-detection five nodes continuously acquire data and the data exchange with the coordinator is done by ZigBee protocol. A sensor fusion algorithm on the coordinator determines the fall type sending a flag to an Android smart phone attached via Bluetooth. The Android Application contacts the emergency services. This architecture provides redundancy that is an important aspect of safety critical systems.

Keywords: Body Area Network, fall-detection, threshold-based method, reliability, safety, ZigBee

I. INTRODUCTION

The progress of medical care increases life expectancy leading to an ageing population. The probability of multiple falls rises for persons because of growing age and diseases (e.g. Dementia & Parkinson). Falls cause severe injuries that require long convalescence or restriction of mobility.

In accordance with the study "Das Unfallgeschehen bei Erwachsenen in Deutschland" of Robert Koch Institute [1] 53.7 % of accidents in the age group over 60 are caused by falls. Additionally elderly people are scared to fall again and this leads to reluctance to move, which causes decrease of muscle strength and uncertainty of movement. Another reason that causes falls of elderly people are diseases e.g. Parkinson and Dementia. Research has shown that Dementia-patients have a 20 times higher risk and Parkinson-patients a 10 times higher risk of falling than healthy people of the same age. Other main reasons for falls are gait disturbances, reduced sight and disturbance of equilibrium [2].

Jean-Eric-Lundy, founder of Vigilio TeleMedical [3], reported that annually more than 20 million people over the age of 65 in Europe fall and that is the main reason for traumatic based cases of death [4]. A fast assistance is in this case very important to save life, because after a fall the person may not be able to call for help because of unconsciousness.

A. Statement of the problem

In the case of a fall situation or unconsciousness a prompt and fully automated assistance is needed. A solution to guarantee this could be continuous monitoring of vital signs via a wearable sensor network that is called a Body Area Network (BAN). The Wireless Smart Sensor Network (WSN) consists of wearable medical sensors, which communicate with computer systems and is worn on the body so that the mobility of the person is not restricted (Figure 1: Principle of Body Area Networks).

Fig. 1. Principle of Body Area Networks

A special challenge for the realization of this kind of assistance system is a reliable fall recognition. The fall-detection system should be able to distinguish between activities of daily life (e.g. running, walking, jump), fall-like activities(e.g. quick sit-down upright/reclined) and real falls (e.g. forward fall, left/right fall). Another aspect that should be considered is the purchase price of the system, that means it should be affordable for medical insurance so that patients can be supported to get this assistance. Because of the importance regarding the fast support of fall victims the European Union promoted a project called Fallwatch and one result of this is the fall-detection system "VigiFall" developed by the company Vigilio TeleMedical [3] [4]. The problem of this solution is the high purchase price so that one important requirement for the thesis will be the development of a cheap and efficient solution.

II. CURRENT STATE OF RESEARCH

A. Vigi Fall [3] [4]

There are several approaches for fall-recognition which are available on the market. A solution which is already available is the above mentioned VigiFall system [3] [4], that consists of a sensor node that is worn by the person. This system should be able to detect a fall and contact fully automated the emergency services. The node communicates with infrared-motion sensors which are placed in the area and a central control unit. In the case that the person falls, the node sends a signal out. Thereby the motion sensors detect that there are no motions and they send a flag to the central control unit. With this incoming signal the control unit contacts fully automated the emergency services.

B. Igual et al. [5]

The scientific article of Igual et al. [5] is about fall-recognition and it gives an overview of several fall-detection systems. The paper presents context-aware systems and wearable systems that are used to detect falls.

Context-aware systems are placed in the environment, which means that sensors and actuators should be fixed in the area where the person is, so that falls can be detected. A context-aware system can be a video-based solution, which has the advantage that a person can have a reliable fall-detection with a prompt support. In spite of the accurate detection this solution has a disadvantage regarding privacy. People are monitored by camera and this is not well accepted by many. Additionally the high purchase price makes this not affordable for everyone and the system is not working outside the networked area, which is essential for detection.

The other category of fall-detection systems that was presented in this paper are wearable systems, which are worn on the body and are based on a Body Area Network (BAN, see Figure 1: Principle of Body Area Networks). This solution is able to detect falls independent from the environment compared to context-aware systems. Igual et al. [5] present systems that use the sensor combination of accelerometer and gyroscope and built-in systems, which represent the usage of the internal sensors of smart phones. The investigations of Igual et al. [5] illustrate that for context-aware systems the following techniques were used:

- Image processing + threshold based recognition
- Image processing + classification models

For wearable systems these techniques were used:
- Threshold based recognition
- Fall-detection based on machine learning

C. Li et al. [6]

Li et al. [6] demonstrate a solution regarding fall-detection based on Body Area Networks. The system consists of two nodes (Figure 2: System according to Li et al. [6]). These nodes are wearable microcontrollers, which have integrated the sensor combination of accelerometer and gyroscope and are placed on the chest (Node A) and on the thigh (Node B).

Li et al. [6] distinguish between two categories of motion sequences:

- Static postures

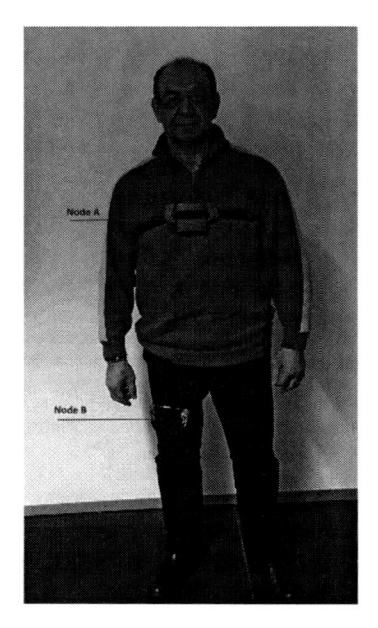

Fig. 2. System according to Li et al. [6]

  – standing, sitting, lying & bending
- Dynamic postures

  – Activities of daily life → walking, walk on stairs, sit, jump, lay down, run

  – Fall-like motions → quick sit-down upright, quick sit-down reclined

  – Flat surface falls → fall forward, fall backward, fall right, fall left

  – Inclined falls → fall on stairs

The following diagram illustrates the difference between static & dynamic postures. To avoid huge computational effort for the microcontroller a 3-Phases-Algorithm was developed to detect falls and is composed as follows:

- 1.Phase - Activity analysis → monitoring if person is in a static or dynamic position.

- 2.Phase - Position analysis → If static posture, check whether the actual position is lying position.

- 3.Phase - State transition analysis → If lying position, check whether this was intentional or unintentional. For this the previous 5 seconds of data are used to analyze it. Is this position unintentional the algorithm categorizes it as a fall.

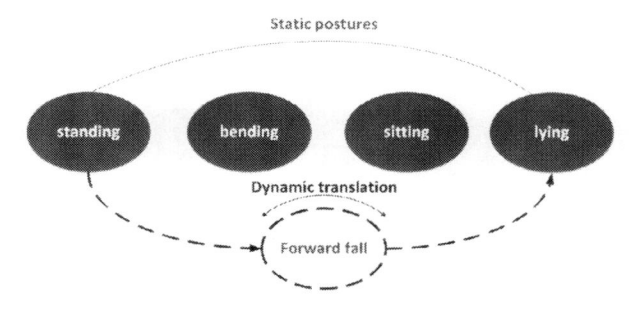

Fig. 3. Static & Dynamic postures by Li et al. [6]

The algorithm is a threshold-based solution, that means thresholds from the sensors are used in the different phases of the algorithm for classification. The test result shows a positive result with 91% of sensitivity on 70 measurements and 92% of accuracy on 72 measurements. The challenge of this proposed solution is that the algorithm has the difficulty in differentiating jumping into bed and falling against a wall with seated posture.

III. FURTHER RESEARCH

In this chapter we present the actual ongoing research and development regarding our fall-detection solution. The target of our research is to develop an fully automated fall-detection system in form of a belt that is able to allow a reliable detection of falls and in case of falls to contact the emergency services (Figure 4: Fall event escalation scheme). The following subsections describe the development path that includes the reproduction of the algorithm used by Li et al. [6], our proposed system architecture and the hardware that is used to realize the fall-detection belt.

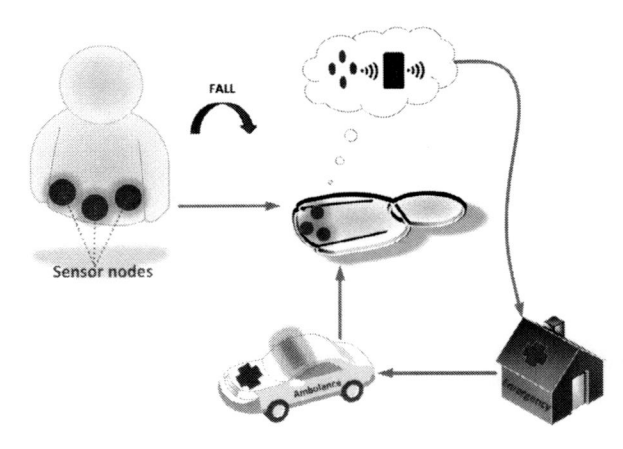

Fig. 4. Fall event escalation scheme

A. *Reproduction of Li et al. - Architecture [6]*

The first step of the development path is the reproduction of the fall-detection system proposed by Li et al. [6] which is based on a Body Area Network (BAN) that is composed of two wearable sensor nodes (see Figure 2: System according to Li et al. [6]). This BAN comprises two nodes which acquire continuously sensor data and send it via the ZigBee protocol to the coordinator (see Figure 5: BAN according to Li et al. [6]). After the development of this system a test protocol that

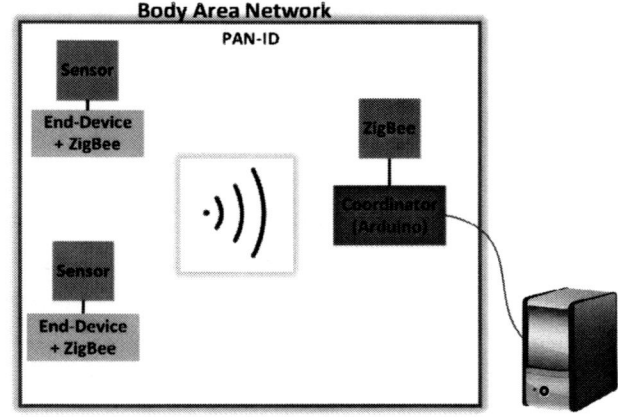

Fig. 5. BAN according to Li et al. [6]

is based on Li et al. [6] and Pannurat et al. [7] was created to reproduce several motions with test persons. The test protocol includes the movements that are stated in the chapter before. With this testing model we are able to detect the thresholds which categorize the different kind of motions. Important to know is, that the physical properties of a human e.g. body weight, body height and age can influence the measured values. For example when a person suffering from obesity is falling down, the impact value differs from the value of a thin body. Additionally it should be taken into consideration that simulated falls or other movements cannot correspond perfectly to a real fall, because persons form protective mechanisms to avoid injuries during the test. The tests are done with several test persons to have an overview about the different thresholds. The following measurements illustrate some motions from different persons that are represented from the acceleration and angular rate of both nodes (chest & thigh). From the measurements the different peak values are evident. When we consider the graph, which illustrates a long term measurement of the acceleration and angular rate magnitude of both nodes that are placed on the chest and thigh (see Figure 6: Person A - Rotation with fall-event) we can evaluate falls. For this we used the magnitude of the acceleration and angular rate how it is proposed by Li et al. [6] The magnitude is calculated by the formulae:

$$|\vec{a}| = \sqrt{a_x^2 + a_y^2 + a_z^2}$$
$$|\vec{\omega}| = \sqrt{\omega_x^2 + \omega_y^2 + \omega_z^2}$$

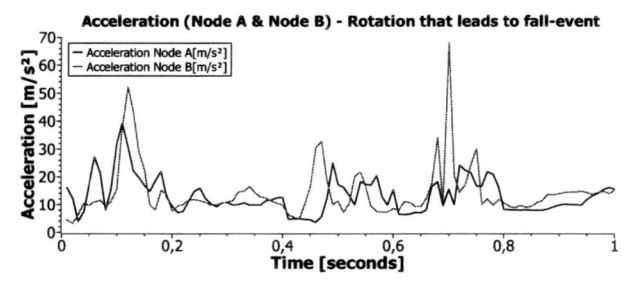

Fig. 6. Person A - Rotation with fall-event (Acceleration)

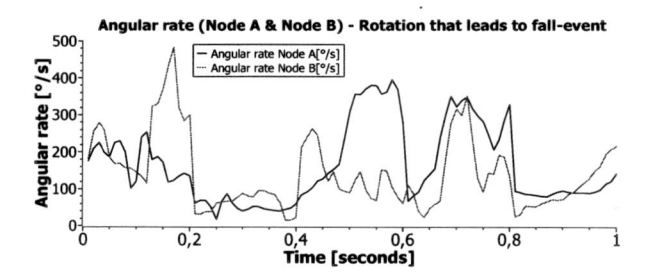

Fig. 7. Person A - Rotation with fall-event (Angular rate)

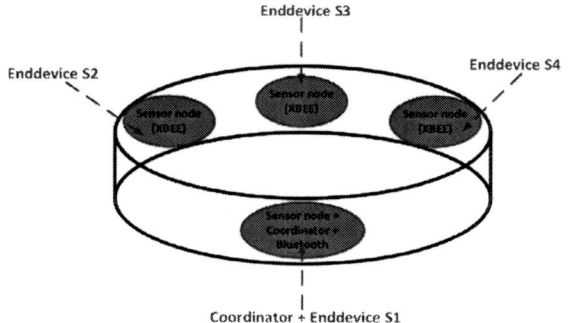

Fig. 8. Fall-detection belt

For example when we analyze the time window of 0.7 seconds a huge acceleration on the thigh (Node B) and a small acceleration on Node A is displayed. This means that the test person had the first impact with the thigh and because of this the acceleration of the chest was damped. The graph that displays the angular rate (see Figure 7: Person A - Rotation with fall-event (Angular rate)), shows at the same time, that the person did rotational move before and during the fall-event.

B. Fall-detection belt

After several tests were made with the Li et al. - Architecture [6] (see Figure 2: System according to Li et al. [6]), we built up a prototype in form of a belt that is worn on the hip (see Figure 9: Fall-detection belt). The proposed solution has the requirements to be reliable and build in a way that the patient has no restriction of movement. For these reasons we came up with a fall-detection system in form of a belt, which is worn on the hip and is composed of a five sensor node BAN. Each node contains an accelerometer and a gyroscope and communicates via ZigBee (see Figure 8: Fall-detection Belt). In the BAN four of the nodes are acting as end-devices and the other node as the coordinator. All four nodes acquire data continuously, monitor thresholds for different fall types and exchange the data with the coordinator. The proposed positioning of sensors in the belt facilitates this recognition in contrast to the system architecture used by Li et al. [6] (Figure 10: Three axis reference draft).

Fig. 9. Fall-detection belt

The idea is, that with this special positioning more precise fall characterization are achieved. The categorization is divided in two parts:

- Initial event → leads to subsequent event
- End event → end position which is a static posture e.g. lying on the floor

To have a comparison between the architecture of Li et al. [6] and our proposed solution we used the same test procedure used before to see how efficient the fall-detection belt can recognize falls.

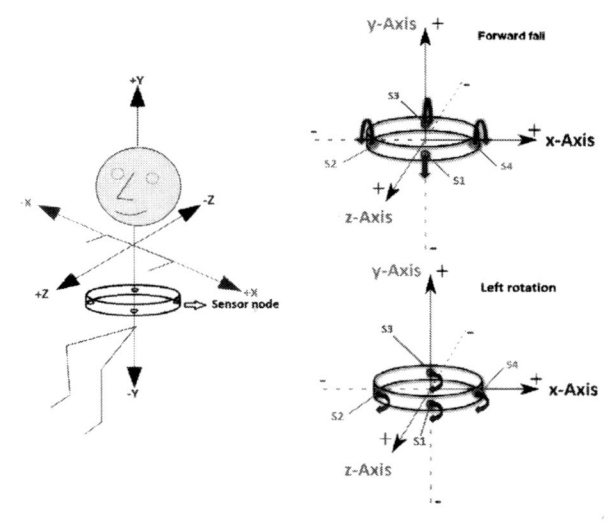

Proceedings of the Eleventh International Network Conference (INC 2016)

Fig. 10. Three axis reference draft

In this section some measurements of the belt-nodes are illustrated that represent a rotation that leads to a fall-event. Important to know is that for our solution we use the acceleration magnitude, that signalizes a fall and the single value of the axis x, y and z of the gyroscope to detect which kind of rotation was done by the person. How the following graphs display with this architecture we have more detailed information to rebuild the fall-event.

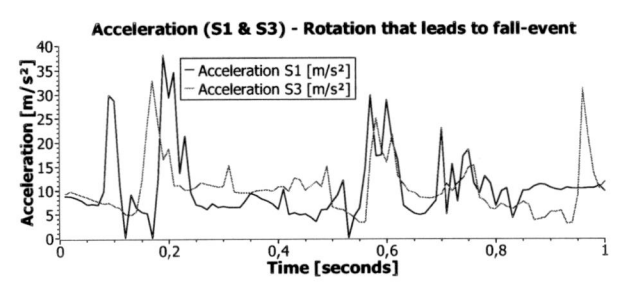

Fig. 11. Person A (S1+S3) - Rotation with fall-event (Acceleration)

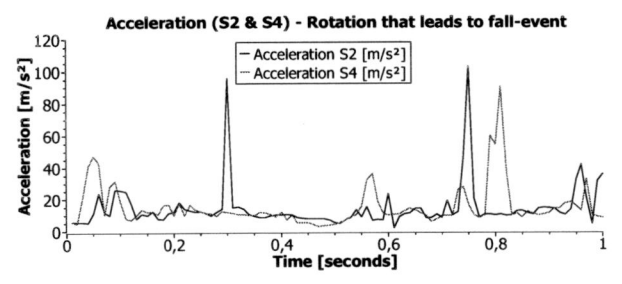

Fig. 12. Person A (S2+S4) - Rotation with fall-event (Acceleration)

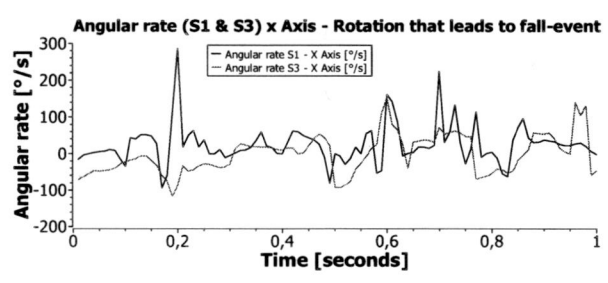

Fig. 13. Person A (S1+S3) - Rotation with fall-event x-Axis (Angular rate)

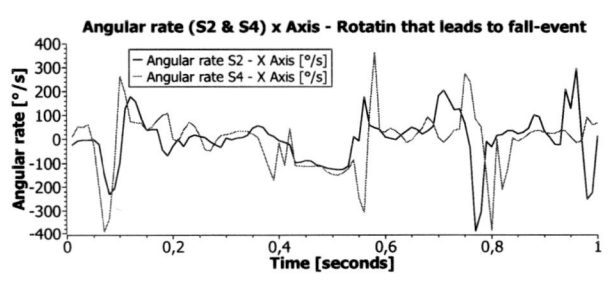

Fig. 14. Person A (S2+S4) - Rotation with fall-event x-Axis (Angular rate)

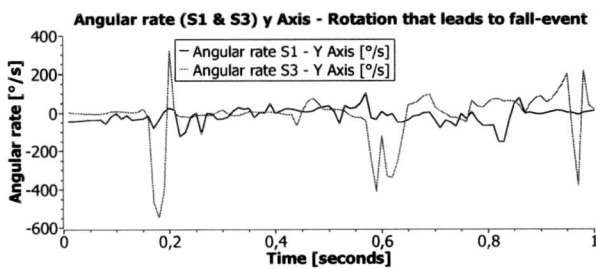

Fig. 15. Person A (S1+S3) - Rotation with fall-event y-Axis (Angular rate)

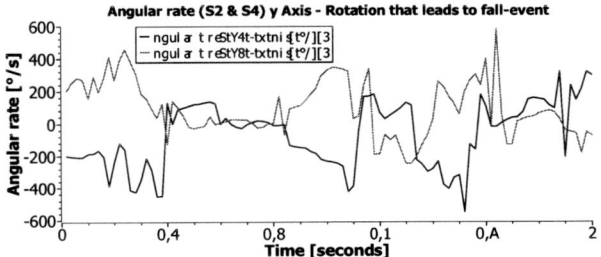

Fig. 16. Person A (S2+S4) - Rotation with fall-event y-Axis (Angular rate)

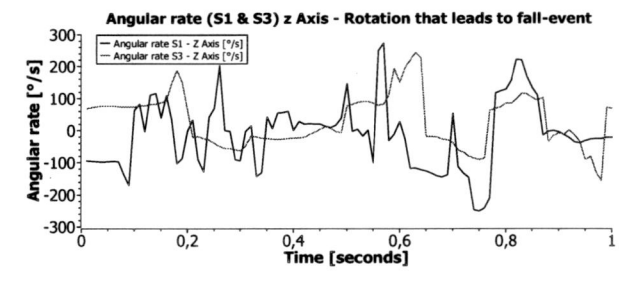

Fig. 17. Person A (S1+S3) - Rotation with fall-event z-Axis (Angular rate)

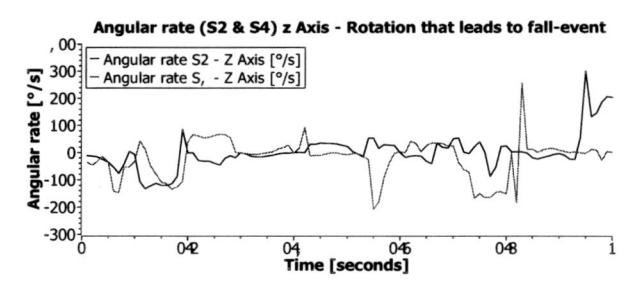

Fig. 18. Person A (S2+S4) - Rotation with fall-event z-Axis (Angular rate)

IV. FUTURE PROSPECT

The target of this ongoing research is to continue the development of this prototype. Especially we intend to improve the architecture with more powerful hardware. An idea is to place tiny sensors inside the belt and hard-wire these with the main-node (coordinator). For algorithmic performance reasons the used coordinator board should be replaced with a microcontroller, which is able to handle parallel running tasks. Additionally to elaborate the threshold-based approach a Complex Event Processing (CEP) algorithm proposed by Boubeta-Puig et al. [8] is investigated.

REFERENCES

[1] G. Varnaccia; A. Rommel and A- C. Saß, *Das Unfallgeschehen bei Erwachsenen in Deutschland: Gesundheitsberichterstattung des Bundes*, 2013: Robert Koch-Institut

[2] Neurologen und Psychiater im Netz, *Demenz-Kranke stürzen besonders häufig*, Online: http://www.neurologen-und-psychiater-im-netz.org/psychiatrie-psychosomatik-psychotherapie/news-archiv/meldungen/article/demenz-kranke-stuerzen-besonders-haeufig, 29 April 2011

[3] Vigilio ,*Vigilio S.A. - Vigilio S.A.Solutions*, Online: http://www.vigilio.fr, Access-Date (12 February 2016)

[4] M. Schaper, *EU fördert "Fallwatch", ein Erkennungssystem, das Senioren nach Stürzen schneller hilft*, Online: http://www.ots.at/presseaussendung/OTS_20130617_OTS0225/, 17 June 2013: OTS/SK

[5] R. Igual; C. Medrano; I. Plaza, *Challenges, issues and trends in fall detection systems*, 6 July 2013: BioMedical Engineering OnLine

[6] Q. Li; J.A. Stankovic; M.A. Hanson; A. T. Barth; J. Lach; G. Zhou, *Accurate, Fast Fall Detection Using Gyroscopes and Accelerometer-Derived Posture Information*, 3-5 June 2009: BSN 2009

[7] N. Pannurat; S. Thiemjarus; E. Nantajeewarawat, *Automatic Fall Monitoring*, 18 July 2014: Sensors 2014

[8] J. Boubeta-Puig; G. Ortiz; I. Medina-Bulo, *ModeL4CEP: Graphical domain-specific modeling languages for CEP domains and event patterns*, 2 July 2015: Experts Systems with Applications (42) 2015

Optimization of Wireless Disaster Network Through Network Virtualization

A. Lehmann, A. Paguem Tchinda, and U. Trick
Research Group for Telecommunication Networks
Frankfurt University of Applied Sciences
Frankfurt/Main, Germany
Email: {lehmann, paguem, trick}@e-technik.org

Abstract—Natural disasters reported to have occurred increased dramatically over the second half of the 20th century. Floods, earthquakes, tsunamis and storms have appeared worldwide with catastrophic consequences. Right after the catastrophic events, the demand for communication services explosively increases, while communication resources are often affected entirely or partially. Without a working communication infrastructure, the coordination among numerous disorganized helpers and rescue teams is impossible. This paper proposes a wireless disaster network that integrates network functions virtualization (NFV), which offers a large number of possibilities to optimize a disaster network, such as availability, reliability, cost-efficiency, scalability, lower power consumption, and adaptable network configuration and topology. Finally, the paper concludes with a future perspective of a distributed orchestration system for the proposed disaster network.

Keywords—Ad Hoc Networks; Disaster Networks; Network Functions Virtualization; Wireless Mesh Networks;

I. INTRODUCTION

In disaster situations, an operative communication infrastructure is essential, in order to rescue victims and organize, coordinate, and support rescue teams [1]. Existing communication infrastructures are often affected in case of disaster, so that the infrastructure is damaged in whole or part [2]. Consequently, the necessity occurs to develop a proper communication system. This system should be enabled to be established rapidly, easily, and cost-effectively in order to share information inside and with the disaster area constantly and robust. Moreover, a desirable system provides not only voice communication but also multimedia communication to support the rescue teams and helpers sufficiently [3]. Another crucial aspect within disaster networks are routing protocols and types of ad hoc networks, e.g. mobile ad hoc network (MANET) [4]. To overcome the challenges in disaster networks the concept of network functions virtualization (NFV) offers numerous new approaches to optimize availability, redundancy, reliability, reparability, recoverability, efficiency, and robustness of communication infrastructure in disaster situations. The main objective of this paper is to present a new approach to optimize disaster networks on basis of ad hoc networks with integrated NFV. Section 2 describes and summarizes challenges for ad hoc networks in disaster areas. Section 3 illustrates functions and architectures of MANET and wireless mesh network (WMN). Furthermore, a few ad hoc protocols are briefly shown. Section 4 illustrates different virtualization technologies and NFV. In addition, advantages and disadvantages are discussed under considerations of energy efficiency and performance. In section 5, an optimized wireless disaster network will be presented on basis of ad hoc technology, and finally conclusions and future perspectives are drawn in section 6.

II. CHALLENGES IN COMMUNICATION NETWORKS FOR DISASTER OPERATION

The impact of natural disasters on communication infrastructures leads to poor communication and coordination of disaster response workers and insufficient information. A working communication system is crucial to disaster response. Hence, a disaster network should be constructed rapidly to provide communication services in disaster areas. Due to the fact that a communication network is essential for disaster response, a large number of challenges arise. The following lists these challenges [5]-[8].

- **Popularity** – Common technologies, such as cell or smart phones should be utilized, because most people can use them. They are user friendly and easy to use. Furthermore, a sufficient amount of terminals should exist, which may be fulfilled by phones, notebooks and tablet PCs.

- **Usability** – To possess usability, a disaster network should provide task oriented communication services (e.g. push-to-talk), support mobility (e.g. small, light devices) and has adequate quality of service (QoS). Besides, the resources of disaster network should have long durability, which may be realized by rechargeable batteries. Therefore, efficient utilization of power is required.

- **Practicability** – The network should be constructed under limited budget as easy as possible within shortest time, also the equipment has to be easily accessible.

- **Capacity** – Support sufficient number of concurrent users and overcome traffic congestion.

- **Sustainability** – The communication network should operate until the public network is recovered and it should continually provide service, even if it is broken down, it should recover quickly.

- **Adaptability** – Cause of constantly changes due to aftershocks, fires and progress of disaster response, etc. the communication system should be adaptable and flexible.
- **Operability** – Operation, administration and maintenance (OAM) functions are needed to keep the system running, adjust network topology, and allocate bandwidth according to the requirements of the user groups, e.g. response workers.
- **Connectivity** – Communication among different user groups, such as rescue team members, headquarters and victims, has to be guaranteed, which represents inter and intra communication.
- **Security** – Security functions should protect the network, also against attackers. In addition, high reliability and availability is necessary.

Considering these challenges for different technologies that are known to be candidates for disaster networks the following conclusions can be drawn. Microwave radio relays and mobile satellite equipment, such as very small aperture terminal (VSAT), should be used for long range inter communication. These technologies including TETRA/TETRAPOL, which has very low bitrates, are specialized and not accessible for everyone. Cellular communications such as Long Term Evolution advanced (LTE-advanced) device-to-device mode also allows communication between two terminals [9]. A drawback of the device-to-device mode is that the terminals need the telecommunication infrastructure to start the communication. The infrastructure is responsible for detecting the candidates for ad hoc communication. This fact leads to a problem; in disaster scenarios, the deployed infrastructure can be damaged. Consequently, this technology is not always applicable [4]. Technologies such as Wi-Fi or Bluetooth are very common, free of charge, and many devices are equipped with transceivers for these technologies. Based on these technologies MANET and WMN can be established, which are relevant for ad hoc networks in disaster areas.

III. MOBILE AD HOC AND WIRELESS MESH NETWORKS

A MANET is an autonomous system of mobile routers connected by wireless links (see Fig. 1). The routers are free to move randomly and organize themselves arbitrarily; thus, the network's wireless topology may change rapidly and unpredictably. Such a network may operate in a standalone fashion, or may be connected to Internet [10].

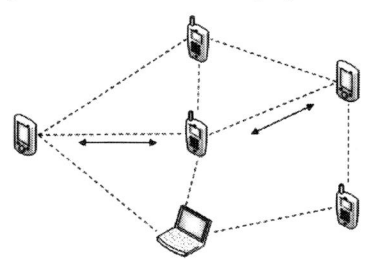

Fig. 1. Ad hoc network architecture

One special feature of a MANET is the capability of self-organizing and self-configuring. MANETs are so-called self-organized networks (SON), which offer a good load balancing and do not use centralized management. The main advantages of MANETs are saving of energy, scalability and robustness. Such a network can adapt its resources by the number of participants. The network's robustness and stability increases with the number of participants, because there will be more relays (senders/receivers).

A next step in evolution of wireless ad hoc networks are WMN, they are dynamically self-organized and self-configured. WMNs are comprised of two types of nodes: mesh routers and mesh clients. Other than conventional wireless router, the capability for gateway/bridge functions differs in additional routing functions to support mesh network. The architecture of WMNs can be classified into three types [11]:

- **Backbone** – The mesh routers/gateways form an infrastructure for clients and can be connected to various networks, e.g. Internet. Furthermore, the mesh routers have minimal mobility.
- **Client** – Client meshing provides peer-to-peer networks among client devices. In this type of architecture, client nodes constitute the actual network to perform end-user applications to customers.
- **Hybrid** – This architecture is the combination of backbone and client meshing, as shown in Fig. 2. Mesh clients can access the network through mesh routers and directly connect to other mesh clients. The backbone provides connectivity to other networks.

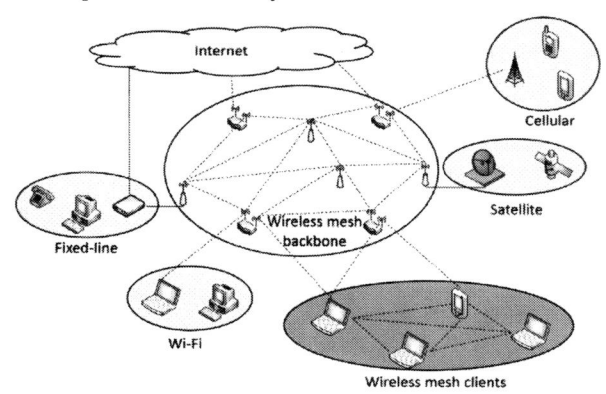

Fig. 2. Hybrid WMN architecture

Mobile ad hoc networks are multi-hop networks that utilize routing protocols. Numerous routing protocols have been introduced in recent years. The protocols can be classified into three groups – proactive, reactive, and hybrid (see Fig. 3). In proactive routing protocols, the routes to the destination are determined at the start up, and maintained by using a periodic route update process. In reactive protocols, routes are determined when they are required by the source using a route discovery process. Hybrid routing protocols combine the basic properties of the first two classes of protocols into one [12].

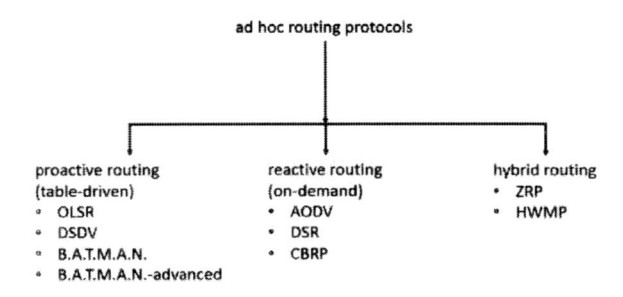

Fig. 3. Ad hoc routing protocols

In [13]-[16] several routing protocols for MANETs are evaluated in disaster scenarios. Further evaluations on routing protocols regarding performance analysis have been made in [17]-[20]. The results of these researches vary significantly. Some only evaluated reactive protocols, such as ad hoc on-demand distance vector (AODV), dynamic source routing (DSR) and cluster based routing protocol (CBRP). AODV and CBRP resulted as suitable protocols for disaster or emergency scenarios. Others evaluated proactive protocols such as optimized link state routing protocol (OLSR), better approach to mobile ad hoc networking (B.A.T.M.A.N.) and B.A.T.M.A.N.-advanced. The last-named routing protocol was highlighted to be a good candidate. Despite the results from numerous investigations, further research should be done. For instance, all shown protocols presented in Fig. 3 should be examined against each other under special consideration of disaster scenarios, performance and energy efficiency. Especially routing protocols such as B.A.T.M.A.N.-advanced and hybrid wireless mesh routing protocol (HWMP) should be focused on. These protocols work on the data link layer and offer a number of advantages.

- Support of IPv4 and IPv6
- Interface bonding, to increase reliability or throughput
- Network coding, to improve throughput, efficiency and scalability
- Faster roaming and simple configuration, MAC addresses are unique

Certainly, these protocols also have disadvantages such as overhead in data link layer and performance issues regarding to a large number of nodes. Based on top of the routing protocols further services can be provided, for example dynamic host configuration protocol (DHCP), virtual private network (VPN), network and port translation (NAPT) or voice over IP (VoIP). These network functions can be virtualized, managed and orchestrated by utilization of NFV. The benefit of utilizing NFV will be described in the next section.

IV. NETWORK VIRTUALIZATION

Some of the leading telecom operators initiated a new specification group for virtualization of network functions at European Telecommunications Standards Institute (ETSI) in 2012. Their aim is to transform the way network operators architect networks by evolving standard virtualization technology to consolidate many network equipment types onto standard high volume servers, switches and storage, which could be located in datacenters, network nodes and in end-user premises. It involves the implementation of network functions in software that can run on industry standard server hardware, and that can be moved to various locations in the network as required, without the need for installation of new equipment [24]. Fig. 4 represents an overview of the NFV framework specified by ETSI. The framework consists of the network functions virtualization infrastructure (NFVI) that is composed by hardware resources, the virtualization layer for running the virtual network functions (VNF), the VNFs, and a component named NFV management and orchestration to support orchestration and lifecycle management of physical and/or software resources that support the infrastructure virtualization, and the lifecycle management of VNFs [25]. The following advantages may result cause of NFV deployment: reduced costs for equipment, provisioning and operation; faster introduction of new network features; high scalability; network configuration can be adapted regarding the actual traffic in nearly real-time; lower electrical power consumption.

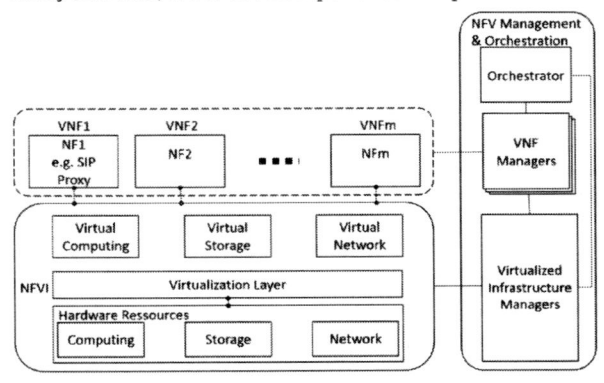

Fig. 4. NFV framework

Mainly two kinds of virtualization technologies are utilized nowadays. Hypervisors-based virtualization and container-based virtualization are common technologies in use now (see Fig. 5). In hypervisor-based virtualization, the hypervisor operates at hardware level, thus supporting standalone virtual machines that are isolated and independent of the host system. So any operating system may be used on top. The disadvantages here are that a full operating system is installed to virtual machine and the emulation of virtual hardware devices incurs more overhead [21]. Two different types of hypervisors are classified – native hypervisors, which operate on top of the host's hardware and hosted hypervisors, which operate on top of the host's operating system. Container-based virtualization can be considered as a lightweight alternative to hypervisor-based virtualization. Containers are running on top of shared operating system kernel of the underlying host machine. An advantage of container-based solutions is that the size of the disk images are smaller compared to hypervisor-based solutions. Container-based virtualization solutions also have some disadvantages, such as that no different operating system can run on top of the host (e.g. Windows on top of

Linux) and containers do not isolate resources, because the kernel is exposed to the containers, which may be an issue of security for multi-tenancy [21].

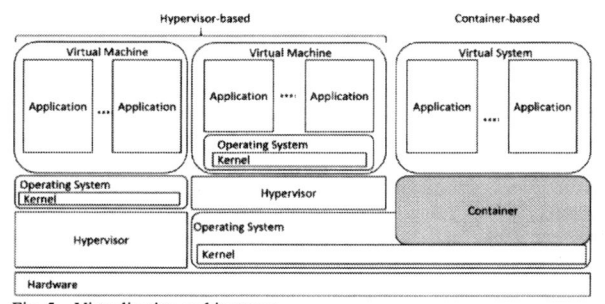

Fig. 5. Virtualization architectures

The specification of NFV primarily focuses on the use of hypervisor-based virtualization, but it also says that further research on container-based virtualization is needed [22] as well as in [23]. With respect to virtualization, container-based solutions offer further advantages such as low latency, low overhead, instant booting and energy efficiency especially in terms of networking [26]. In [22] requirements for energy efficiency are defined to be fulfilled by NFV.

A complement of NFV is mobile-edge computing (MEC), which provides IT and cloud-computing capabilities within the radio access network (RAN) in close proximity to mobile subscribers [27]. In MEC, for instance services and applications can be shifted to the base stations onto a so-called MEC server (see Fig. 6). The MEC server consists of a hosting infrastructure and an application platform. Compared with the NFV framework a real difference between the hosting infrastructure and NFVI is not noticeable. A distinctive difference is the MEC application platform that provides capabilities for the virtualized applications and consists of the application's virtualization manager and application platform services. However as MEC is a complement to NFV it also utilizes virtualization and is focused on benefits such as rapid deployment of new services and placing applications near to consumers to reduce the volume of network traffic to the core network, where normally applications are hosted.

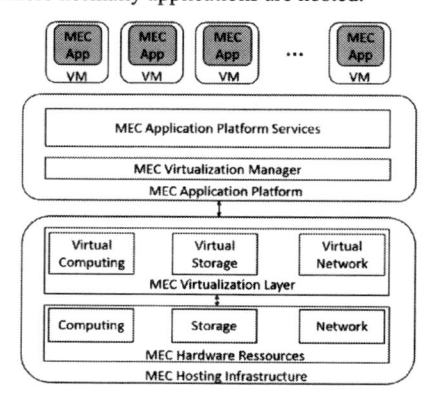

Fig. 6. MEC server architecture

To solve the challenges, sustainability and operability regarding to disaster networks, network virtualization implemented by NFV will help to optimize a wireless mesh network, which will be discussed in the next section.

V. WIRELESS MESH NETWORK FOR OPTIMIZED DISASTER OPERATION

Because several nodes, which span the WMN, are not connected to a fixed power supply, one of the key criterion in this relation is the energy demand of each wireless mesh node. All requested tasks, as for instance sustain of internet access shall accomplished as long as possible even if energy sources such as batteries or generators are used. This leads to an approach, which integrates and utilizes NFV functionalities on basis of a WMN to operate an optimized disaster network. Fig. 7 depicts an overview of a WMN NFV node's architecture. A distinctive difference regarding the already presented NFV framework architecture is that the network part of the underlying hardware resources and operating system implements mesh routing protocols. These routing protocols should be optimized with respect to energy consumption, scalability, reliability, and support of real-time communication, such as voice or video, because these are essential services in disaster scenarios. Through abstraction of network interfaces and mesh routing protocols from the arranged components on top new overlay networks can be constructed, to provide special services in virtually separated networks. Another distinction is the replacement of the hypervisor by a container-based virtualization. This will result in lower latency, lower overhead, smaller disk images, and higher energy efficiency. Further advantages are resulting from NFV utilization, which enables to provide special services and network functions on top of the WMN. A NFV infrastructure contains three elements, virtual network, virtual computing, and virtual storage. The virtual network element is responsible to provide virtual networks for VNFs. These networks can be established between VNFs and to connect them to external networks. Consequently, arbitrary complex networks can be build and combined. Virtual computing supplies the processing unit to each VNF. The virtual storage element represents a virtual disk space for e.g. images of VNFs, which will be utilized by virtual computing. Applying NFV in disaster networks will benefit in terms of flexibility and availability of services and network functions. Furthermore, the proposed infrastructure benefits from the MEC notion by adoption of the idea to place applications and services near to customers to reduce the volume of network traffic, which will lead to reduce power consumption too.

The resulting WMN framework consists of nodes implementing NFV according to Fig. 7 and building a backbone network as represented in Fig. 2. Based on the architecture an optimized disaster network can be established to provide real-time communication services and several other functions such as data communication for water supply or medical help to support disaster response workers effectively. The nodes within the proposed WMN are non- or minimal moving during deployment. They offer an extendable and resilient backbone network to connect other networks such as Internet and provide in addition the possibility to be constructed very fast, because common technologies like Wi-Fi are used [28].

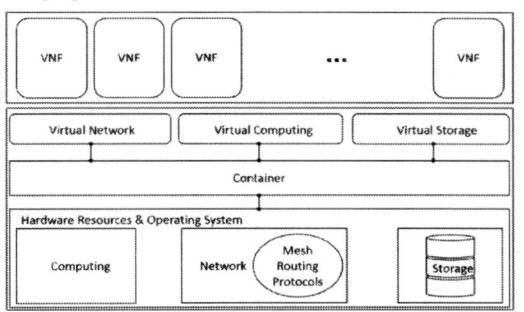

Fig. 7. WMN NFV framework architecture

Utilizing NFV implies the possibility to handle network functions dynamically. VNFs can be switched on and off on demand on any virtual computing instance. The usage of container-based virtualization implicates instant booting of a VNF. Furthermore, VNFs can be relocated to other virtual computing instances near to places where they are needed. For instance, if a session initiation protocol (SIP) proxy server is needed in only one special network segment, e.g. at the edge, it does not make sense to carry the traffic through the whole network. Therefore, it might be helpful to place the SIP proxy server close to the point where it is needed.

The following Fig. 8 shows a set of network functions. Some of these functions are bound to hardware, which makes them immovable. All bound functions are access technologies such as IEEE 802.11 or Ethernet. They comprise different physical layers and provide gateway functionality to the bridge that sits on top of these.

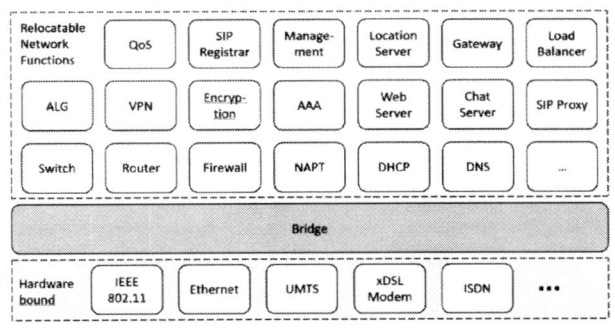

Fig. 8. WMN NFV network functions

The so-called relocatable network functions can be placed on any node within a NFV, because they are virtualized network functions. The fact that VNFs can be relocated will offer a new chance within disaster networks for conservation of energy. Other possibilities to save energy might be to relocate network functions depending on the network load or in dependence of local existing energy resources. Network functions also may be placed on a different node due to computational power or a network function can be distributed onto multiple nodes. The distributed network functions can cooperate through a load balancer for instance. The bridge functionality generally is required in any NFV component, because it serves as basis for all other functions. Through the bridge, any VNF can be directly connected to an access network or different VNFs can be chained to realize a network service.

Another crucial criterion in terms of providing VNFs is the orchestration of them. By orchestration and management for NFV the energy consumption can be monitored and dynamically controlled to be minimized. In [29] the network functions virtualization management and orchestration (NFV-MANO) architectural framework is specified (see Fig. 9). The role of NFV-MANO is to manage the NFVI and orchestrate the allocation of resources needed by the network services and VNFs. NFV-MANO handles the discovery of available services, management of virtualized resources i.e. availability, allocation, release, and virtualized resource fault/performance management. The management and orchestration refreshes and controls the resources within the NFVI that are:

- Compute, including machines (e.g. hosts), and virtual machines, as resources that comprise both CPU and memory.
- Storage, including volumes of storage at either block or file-system level.
- Network, including networks, subnets, ports, addresses, links and forwarding rules, for the purpose of ensuring intra- and inter-VNF connectivity.

The orchestrator particularly is responsible for the network service lifecycle management, which means the registration and instantiation of a network service. In addition, scaling of network services is a responsibility of the orchestrator, i. e. grow or reduce the capacity of network service. Furthermore, network services can be updated and terminated by the orchestrator. As consequence, orchestration is the main factor to achieve reduction of energy consumption by NFV. It is possible to control and manage all virtual elements within NFVI. In disaster networks energy consumption is an important item as already mentioned in section two.

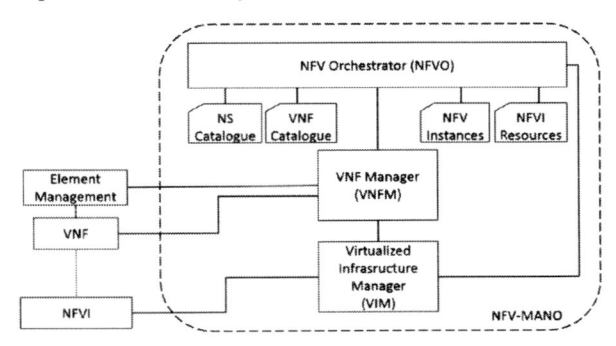

Fig. 9. NFV-MANO framework architecture

Another issue regarding to disaster network's reliability, when using NFV, is the orchestration and management. It would be not beneficial if this component loses connectivity to NFVI. In datacenters, it is possible to implement a centralized

NFV-MANO, however in WMN-based disaster networks utilizing NFV this could be an obstacle. In conclusion, the distribution of orchestration and management over all WMN nodes might be a better solution.

VI. CONCLUSIONS

Due to the characteristic of wireless mesh networks, a disaster network can be setup spontaneously if a previous existing infrastructure and communication system is destroyed after a disaster. Fundamental challenges for disaster networks are presented with special attention to energy consumption. Choosing the right routing algorithm and virtualization of network functions can lower the consumption and increase the performance. As a result, we propose utilizing the advantages of NFV to increase the energy efficiency, so that the devices used in disaster networks will have a long working time, which is a novelty in wireless mesh networks and disaster networks. A further innovation regarding the improvement of the introduced optimized WMN for disaster operation is the distribution of the orchestration and management over all WMN nodes for the NFV.

REFERENCES

[1] International Telecommunication Union (ITU), "Technical Report on telecommunications and disaster mitigation," Technical Report, Version 1.0, June 2013.
[2] N. Marchetti, "Telecommunications in disaster areas," River Publishers Series in Communications, vol. 12, pp. 1-9, 2010.
[3] K. Kanachana, A. Tunpan, M. A. Awal, D. K. Das, T. Wongsaardsakul, and Y. Suchimoto, "DUMBONET: a multimedia communication system for collaborative emergency response operations in disaster-affected areas," Int. Journal of Emergency Management, vol. 4, pp. 670-681, 2007.
[4] D. G. Reina, M. Askalani, S. L. Toral, F. Barrero, E. Asimakopoulou, and N. Bessis, "A survey on multihop ad hoc networks for disaster response scenarios," Int. Journal of Distributed Sensor Networks, vol. 2015, Article ID 647037, 16 pages, 2015.
[5] J.-S. Huang and Y.-N. Lien, "Challenges of emergency communication network for disaster response," in Proc. IEEE International Conference on Communication Systems (ICCS), Singapore, pp.528-532, Nov. 2012.
[6] K. Ali, H. X. Nguyen, Q.-T. Vien, and P. Shah, "Disaster management communication networks: challenges and architecture design," in Proc. IEEE International Conference on Pervasive Computing and Communication Workshop (PerCom Workshop), St. Louis, pp. 537-542, Mar. 2015.
[7] N. Gondaliya and D. Kathiriya, "An application of ad hoc networks in disaster area for search and rescue operation: a survey and challenges," International Journal of Advanced Research in Computer and Communication Engineering, vol. 3, no. 3, pp. 5711-5714, Mar. 2014.
[8] C. B. Nelson, B. D. Steckler, and J. A. Stamberger, "The evolution of hastily formed networks for disaster response," in Proc. IEEE Global Humanitarian Technology Conference (GHTC), Seattle, pp. 467-475, Nov. 2011.
[9] K. Doppler, M. Rinne, C. Wijting, C. B. Ribeiro, and K. Hug, "Device-to-device communication as an underlay to LTE-advanced networks," IEEE Communications Magazine, vol. 47, no. 12, pp. 42-49, Dec. 2009.
[10] N. Pratas, N. Marchetti, N. R. Prasad, A. Rodrigues, and R. Prasad, "Self-organizing cognitive disaster relief networks," River Publishers Series in Communications, vol. 12, pp. 95-125, 2010.
[11] I. F. Akyildiz, X. Wang, "A survey on wireless mesh networks," IEEE Communications Magazine, vol. 43, no. 9, pp. 23-30, Sept. 2005.
[12] M. Abolhasan, T. Wysocki, and E. Dutkiewicz, "A review of routing protocols for mobile ad hoc networks," Elsevier Journal Ad Hoc Networks, vol 2, no. 1, pp. 1-22, Jan. 2004.
[13] D. G. Reina, S. L. Toral, F. Barrero, N. Bessis, and E. Asimakopoulou, "Evaluation of ad hoc networks in disaster scenarios," in Proc. 3rd IEEE International Conference on Intelligent Networking and Collaborative Systems (INCoS), pp. 759-764, Fukuoka, Japan, Dec. 2011.
[14] D. G. Reina, S. L. Toral, F. Barrero, N. Bessis, and E. Asimakopoulou, "Modelling and assessing ad hoc networks in disaster scenarios," Journal of Ambient Intelligence and Humanized Computing, vol.4, no. 5, pp. 571-579, 2013.
[15] C. Raffelsberger and H. Hellwagner, "Evaluation of MANET routing protocols in a realistic emergency response scenario," in Proc. 10th International Workshop on Intelligent Solutions in Embedded Systems, pp. 88-92, July 2012.
[16] L. E. Quispe and L. M. Galan, "Behavior of ad hoc routing protocols, analyzed for emergency and rescue scenarios, on a real urban area," Elsevier Journal Expert Systems with Applications, vol. 41, no.5 pp. 2565-2573, 2014.
[17] A. Sharma and N. Rajagopalan, "A comparative study of B:A:T:M:A:N: and OLSR routing protocols for MANETs," International Journal of Advanced Trends in Computer Science and Engineering, vol 2, no. 5, pp. 13-17, 2013.
[18] V. M. Sarabu and N. Kasiviswanath, "Routing protocols for wireless mesh networks," International Journal of Scientific and Engineering Research, vol. 2, no. 8, pp. 42-46, 2011.
[19] D. Seither, A. König, and M. Hollick, „Routing performance of wireless mesh networks: a practical evaluation of BATMAN advanced," in Proc. 36th IEEE International Workshop on Local Computer Networks (LCN), pp. 897-904, Oct. 2011.
[20] M. Liechti, "Real-world evaluation of ad hoc routing algorithms," Semester Thesis SA-2012-35 ETH Zürich, 2013.
[21] R. Morabito, J. Kjällman, and M. Komu, "Hypervisors vs. lightweight virtualization: a performance comparison," in Proc. IEEE International Conference on Cloud Engineering (IC2E), Tempe, pp. 386-393, Mar. 2015.
[22] ETSI Group Specification, "Network functions virtualization (NFV); infrastructure; hypervisor domain," NFV-INF 004, V1.1.1, Jan. 2015.
[23] S. Natarajan, R. Krishnan, A. Ghanwani, D. Krishnaswamy, P. Willis, and A Chaudhary, „An analysis of container-based platforms for NFV," IETF Draft, Oct. 2015.
[24] ETSI ISG NFV, "Network functions virtualization – an introduction, benefits, enablers, challenges & call for action," SDN and OpenFlow World Congress, Oct 2012.
[25] ETSI ISG NFV, "Network functions virtualization – network operator perspectives on industry progress," SDN and OpenFlow World Congress, Oct. 2013.
[26] R. Morabito, "Power consumption of virtualization technologies: an empirical investigation," to appear in Proc. 8th IEEE/ACM International Conference on Utility and Cloud Computing (UCC), 2015.
[27] ETSI ISG MEC, "Mobile-edge computing – introductory white paper," White Paper, Sept. 2014.
[28] R. Miura et al., "Disaster-resilient wireless mesh network – experimental test-bed and demonstartion," in Proc. 16th International Symposium on Wireless Personal Multimedia Communications (WPMC), pp. 1-4, June 2013.
[29] ETSI Group Specification, "Network functions virtualization (NFV); management and orchestration," NFV-MAN 001, V1.1.1, Dez. 2014.

Evaluating Framework for Monitoring and Analyzing WebRTC Peer-to-Peer Applications

Marco Schindler, Christian von Harscher, Johannes Kinzig, Sergej Alekseev
Computer Science and Engineering
Frankfurt University of Applied Sciences
Frankfurt am Main, Germany
{mschindl|harscher|kinzig}@stud.fra-uas.de, alekseev@fb2.fra-uas.de

Abstract—Web Real Time Communication (WebRTC) technology becomes more and more popular, because it enables Communication between web browsers and mobile applications without the need for plug-ins or other apps. This makes it interesting for a wide range of use cases such as call center or online webshop. Our expectation is, that in the near future a lot of commercial and free applications based on this technology will be developed.

This paper presents an environment for prototyping of p2p WebRTC based applications, monitoring and analysis of their behaviour. The basic idea of this environment is to provide a possibility to visualize connection graphs containing connected peers of a WebRTC session and to collect statistics for monitoring and analysis.

Index Terms—peer-to-peer (P2P), Web Real Time Communication (WebRTC), Connection Graph, Monitoring

I. INTRODUCTION

Web Real-Time Communication (WebRTC) [1] is a new standard and industry effort that extends the web browsing model. It provides the ability of putting real-time communication capabilities such as audio, video and data communications into web browsers without the need of installing additional software or plug-ins. Undoubtedly, one of the most common and frustrating issues of companies, who offer products that make use of real time communication, are missing diagnostic tools for testing and troubleshooting the WebRTC connectivity. The WebRTC services are typically p2p applications and thus the troubleshooting process is even more difficult.

In this paper we present a framework for prototyping of WebRTC based applications, monitoring the WebRTC connectivity by collecting the analysis of various statistics. Furthermore the framework visualizes all gathered information including the connection states, statistic and geographical location of involved peers.

II. RELATED WORKS

Considerable prior work has been done on the subject of WebRTC state analyzing in [2]. We are motivated by the fact that this cited work described how to analyze WebRTC connections by looking at therefor collected events. These events are generated by a state change of a WebRTC peer concerned in the connection process. The essential approach of this cited work is rest upon finite-state machines in accordance with the WebRTC specification. We are using this state analyzing concept to monitor and evaluate WebRTC sessions. Additionally we gather various statistics including the peer topology.

It is important to mention that an API named *getStat()* for getting WebRTC statistics exist. This API can be used within JavaScript code to return several WebRTC statistics such as *round-trip-time, packets-send, packets-lost* etc.

The API is used by several projects (on github, etc.) which claim to be "analyzing libraries" for WebRTC. These libraries mostly lack the infrastructure component to collect and maintain the statistics at a local place for error-handling and analyzing. An example for such a library can be found under https://github.com/muaz-khan/getStats.

There exist one more framework named "callstats.io" which offers the infrastructure to collect and analyze the statistics in one single place but this is a proprietary framework. They offer client libraries for integration in the application. The library then takes care for transmitting the WebRTC statistics to the callstats.io's servers. Customers then can access their gathered statistics through a web interface. (cf. [4])

In contrast to the already existing possibilities offers our solution a complete framework (based on open source tools and libraries) which can easily be installed on a linux server. The framework does not only collect the statistics, it additionally collects the WebRTC events generated by the clients.

III. SYSTEM OVERVIEW AND GENERAL STRUCTURE OF THE PROPOSED FRAMEWORK

Figure 1 shows the overall system architecture of the proposed framework. All software components are running in a linux server environment. *Nginx* is used as a proxy to the backend applications such as application and signaling server. The application server includes a *PHP* and *MySQL* installation to run the *Moodle Platform* (see section III-A) and the *WebRTC Monitor* (see section VI). For the server side implementation of P2P algorithms two signaling services are provided, one for running the algorithms written in *Java* and one for running the algorithms written in *JavaScript* (see section III-C for further details).

A. Application Server

The basis for the evaluating and benchmarking framework is the *Moodle eLearning Platform* [5]. The reason for implementing the benchmarking framework partly as a *Moodle Plugin* is

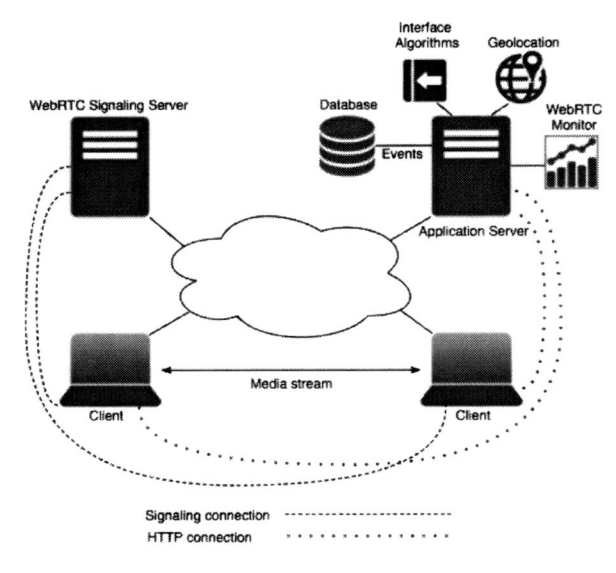

Fig. 1. System Architecture

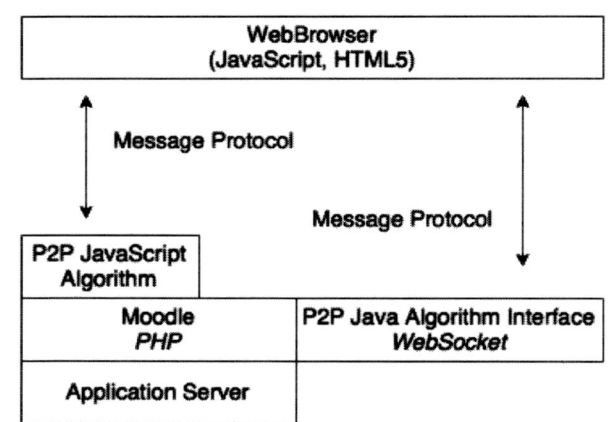

Fig. 2. Description

the easy administration of users and sessions. The evaluation of the different P2P algorithms was done with real users all over the world. Therefore it was necessary to have a simple solution for adding and maintaining users and "classrooms".

The *Moodle Plugin* basically provides the client functionality for the P2P algorithm framework and the WebRTC Monitor application, which is responsible for displaying the collected data and statistics.

Our framework provides several iunterfaces for implementing P2P algorithms in *Java* and *JavaScript*.

B. WebRTC Signaling Server

WebRTC enables peer to peer communication between browsers, but also needs a mechanism to coordinate communication. This process is known as signaling. Signaling methods and protocols is not part of the WebRTC API [1] .

There are several commercial cloud messaging platforms that provides an API for WebRTC signaling such as Pusher [1], Kaazing [2], PubNub [3], and vLine [4]. There are also several open source solutions based on Socket.io [7] such as webRTC.io, easyRTC and Signalmaster.

We decided to implement our own WebSocket based signaling server running in node.js [6] rely on channels. A Channel is a namespace which allows broadcasting messages to make sure the signaling data is exchanged among relevant users.

C. P2P Algorithm Server - RSWebSocket

In our proposed solution, two different algorithm servers are implemented, but both are based on the Web-socket principle.

[1] Pusher - https://pusher.com
[2] Kaazing - https://kaazing.com
[3] PubNub - https://www.pubnub.com
[4] vLine - https://vline.com

They differ in the programming language, the way how they handle the communication and they accept different types of incoming requests. One is implemented in Java and the other one in JavaScript.

IV. SOFTWARE INTERFACES AND PROTOCOL DESCRIPTION

A. Signaling Server for Java based algorithms - RSWebSocket

For evaluating algorithms written in Java the RSWebSocket has an interface called *IP2PJoinAlgorithm* which declares the methods needed for implementing a P2P joining algorithm. The interface can be seen in the following listing:

```
IP2PJoinAlgorithm.join
IP2PJoinAlgorithm.peerLeave
IP2PJoinAlgorithm.getSerachTreeGraph
IP2PJoinAlgorithm.getSearchTreeRoot
IP2PJoinAlgorithm.getP2pTreeGraph
IP2PJoinAlgorithm.getPeer
```

The *join* method takes two arguments, as first argument an object of the type*TopologicalCooridante* and as second argument *peerId* of type *int*.

The *peerId* is the unique identifier for the user which should be inserted in the topological tree structure. The *Topological-Coordinate* is an object which consists of the following data and types:

```
TopologicalCoordinate.continent
TopologicalCoordinate.country
TopologicalCoordinate.city
TopologicalCoordinate.ip1xxx
TopologicalCoordinate.ip12xx
TopologicalCoordinate.ip123x
```

The returned element by the *join* method is an object of the type *JoinPeerResult*, which holds all the information necessary for a peer to be attached to or included in the peer tree structure. The *JoinPeerResult* object holds an ArrayList which contains *Reconnect* objects.

The *Reconnect* object has two integer attributes, *peerId* and *reconnectId*. In case a peer leaves the session or a new peer is inserted between two peers, this reconnect list is transmitted to the clients. The clients then do a reconnect and update the tree structure because peers were added or removed from the recent structure. Additionally *JoinPeerResult* contains an integer object called *parentJoinId*, which holds the peerId where the new peer should connect to.

The third method is named *peerLeave*, it takes the *peerId* as an input argument and returns an object of the type *PeerLeaveResult*. The *peerId* is the peer which is going to be disconnected from the tree structure. This peer's children then need to be reconnected to the remaining peers. The type *PeerLeaveResult* holds an array list with *Reconnect* objects (as described above).

The fourth method is called *getSearchTreeGraph*, it takes no arguments and returns an object of the type *SearchTreeGraph*. The *SearchTreeGraph* object represents the whole search tree and implements several methods such as *getAsDot* which allows to print the search tree in the dot language format.

The fifth method is named *getSearchTreeRoot*, it does not take any arguments and returns an object of the type *TVertex*. The *TVertex* class is used to represent the nodes in the search tree.

The sixth method is called *getP2pTreeGraph* and returns an object of the type *P2PTreeGraph*, it does not take any arguments as input. The *P2PTreeGraph* class is used to represent the P2P tree.

The last method is called *getPeer* and takes the *peerId* as an input. The return type is an object of the *PeerVertex* class, it represents a node in the P2P topology.

B. Message Protocol Description - Implementing custom signaling server

When implementing a custom signaling server to work with the framework, the described messages in this section should be taken into account. Developing a custom signaling server becomes important when trying to evaluate algorithms written in another language than Java or JavaScript.

The signaling mainly takes place by exchanging messages between the client (session initiator, included as demo.js into the Moodle Plugin) and the signaling server. These messages are based on the JSON data format. JSON is widely used and can easily be processed by major programming languages and frameworks.

Generally the application is using two different JSON messages, one for each communication direction:

```
signaling server -> session initiator
signaling server <- session initiator
```

The important data fields for *session initiator → signaling server* can be seen in this listing:

```
type: NewSession: [sessionid, algorithmID]
      join: [peerid]
      onLeave: [peerid]
```

When a new websocket connection is opened by the session initiator the signaling server checks for the message *type*. In case it is *NewSession* a new session is internally added to the sessions map and the *sessionid* and *algorithmID* is taken from the JSON message. The *algorithmID* is only important for the testing architecture where you can chose between several algorithm implementations.

In case the message *type* is *join* the peerid is taken from the JSON message and the algorithm's join method is called. In case the message *type* is *onLeave* the peerid is taken from the JSON message to disconnect this peer from the structure and reconnecting the other peers which have been connect to this peer.

The data fields used for communicating in the opposite direction: *signaling server → session initiator (demo.js)* are described in the following listing:

```
type: join_return:
    [peerid, connectto, reconnectList]
    LeaveResult:  [peerid, reconnectList]
    reconnectList[peerid, reconnectid]
```

When the session initiator requests a *join* the signaling server answers with a *join_return* which contains the *peerid*, *connectto* and *reconnectList*. The *peerid* is the current peer, *connectto* is the peerid which the current client should connect to and the *reconnectList* contains the peers which need to reconnect in case the new peer is attached in between two other already connected peers. The *reconnectList* contains name value pairs of *peerID:reconnectID*.

C. JavaScript client side implementation

The client side implementation for the algorithm evaluating framework is part of the Moodle eLearning plugin (cf. section III-A). It is a JavaScript class for interacting with one of the signaling servers mentioned in section III-C. The class is implemented with the shown methods in the listing below:

```
P2PAlgorithm.prototype.init
P2PAlgorithm.prototype.join
P2PAlgorithm.prototype.onLeave
```

With these methods a point of intersection between the client and the algorithm is defined. Through this construction it is possible to use distributed algorithms running in the browser of each client as well as centralized algorithms running on the server. The communication of these algorithms is done over a WebSocket connection with a specific message format (cf. IV-B).

The *init* method is initializing the algorithm instance. The join method is called by clients entering the WebRTC session. The join method communicates the client's session-ID to the session initiator. The session initiator is then requesting the position for the new joining client from the signaling server. The client is joined after the session initiator receives the position information and extends the tree structure by the client's ID.

If a session is ending the *onLeave* method is called automatically by the corresponding client. This happens even if the browser window is closed by the user. The client is sending the *onLeave* information to the session initiator. The session initiator is then requesting the reconnection list from the server by sending the client-ID. On response the reconnection list is processed by the session initiator and the reconnect is executed.

V. GATHERING EVENTS AND STATISTICS

For the analysis of the WebRTC sessions the WebRTC states are gathered. The current system state of each WebRTC connection is represented through the states of the three following Finite State Machines. According to [2, section III] these finite state automatons are the signaling state machine, gathering state machine and connection state machine. For persisting the systems' state we are using a MySQL database in combination with the WebRTC Analyzer mentioned in [2, abstract].

A. Raw events

The so called raw events are the WebRTC events reflecting the state of the connection. Not only the three states for signaling, gathering and connection finite-state automatons are displayed, but also the peer-id, the room-id of the virtual classroom, the session-id, the user-id and the method which fired the event. The given user-id is utilized for creating a link to the corresponding Moodle user. An database excerpt with sample events are displayed in table I.

B. WebRTC Statistics

The WebRTC traffic is transmitted over the best-effort IP network, which is inherently vulnerable to network congestion. Audio, video and data packets can be lost during transmission and congestion also increases the network latency and the delay of the transported packets. High packet loss and long delays affect the quality of the WebRTC media stream.

A statistics API of the WebRTC standard provides features to return peer connection stats. These statistics can be used to guarantee the best possible quality of WebRTC calls. The JavaScript library used in this environment, enables performance monitoring features for audio and video calls in WebRTC-based endpoints. By using this library, the following statistics of a client can be gathered.

```
audio_video_out_RoundTripTime,
audio_video_out_packets_sent,
audio_video_out_bytes_sent,
audio_video_out_packets_lost,

audio_video_in_target_delay_ms,
audio_video_in_jitter,
audio_video_in_discarded_packets,
audio_video_in_packets_received,
audio_video_in_bytes_received
```

TABLE III
DATABASE EXCERPT WITH GEOLOCATION TRANSMITTED BY THE PEERS

UserID	Longitude	Latitude	City	Country	IP
18	13.381347	52.5496360	Berlin	DE	79.218.211.X
22	13.952636	51.1793429	Dresden	DE	141.30.66.X
25	7.4047851	51.5565821	Dortmund	DE	217.237.151.X
7	6.3500976	51.4813828	Essen	DE	132.252.3.X
13	8.692041	50.1287105	Frankfurt am Main	DE	194.95.82.X

Table II shows the statistics gathered for session 10. This table shows an excerpt generated by the monitor (cf. VI) and displays values necessary to analyze the session's quality.

C. Geolocation

Additionally to the gathered events described section V-A and V-B the geographical position of each peer is determined. When a peer enters a session the browser requests the current geographical location using the HTML5 geolocation service. This geolocation service replies with the geographical coordinates of the current location. The client then uses the Google Maps Geolocation API to translate the retrieved coordinates into city, and country. As soon as the client has received this information, it stores them in the database.

Fig. 3. Screenshot of the WebRTC monitor showing its functions and capabilities

VI. MONITOR

Our gathered WebRTC events can be evaluated with the WebRTC Monitor module inside of Moodle. The module must be enabled for each Moodle course in which the virtual classroom is used as an activity module. The monitor features a selection dialog for each classroom. After selecting a classroom the WebRTC sessions are displayed. These sessions are adjustable in the settings of a classroom. The start and ende time as well as the session-id are displayed in the session overview. In addition to that information buttons for various actions are displayed. These buttons provide links to the raw events, to the map, to the location and bandwidth information and to the browser based WebRTC statistics. A screenshot of the monitor can be seen in figure 3.

VII. CONCLUSION

Since WebRTC does not provide a standardized opportunity to monitor and evaluate sessions, this article describes a framework, introducing a solution for the missing analyzing

TABLE I
DATABASE EXCERPT WITH WEBRTC RAW EVENTS GENERATED BY THE MONITOR

UserID	PeerID	RoomID	Timestamp	sid	Eventhandler	Signaling State	Gathering State	Connection State
18	1443149221164_587393171153963	61	1443149276	10	start	stable	new	new
18	1443149221164_587393171153963	61	1443149276	10	onsignalingstatechange	have-local-offer	new	new
7	1443149221678_318042188814992	61	1443149276	10	start	stable	new	new
7	1443149221678_318042188814992	61	1443149277	10	onsignalingstatechange	have-remote-offer	new	new

TABLE II
DATABASE EXCERPT WITH WEBRTC STATISTICS

course	time_stamp	sid	userid	peer_id	video_out_rtt	video_out_packets_sent	video_out_packets_lost
2	1443149231696	10	7	1443149221678_318042188814992	-1	347	null
2	1443149232029	10	18	1443149221164_587393171153963	8	375	0
2	1443149241689	10	7	1443149221678_318042188814992	-1	875	null
2	1443149242048	10	18	1443149221164_587393171153963	1	953	0

option. This framework includes different possibilities to assess past sessions (see section VI). There are still some slight improvements of the monitor necessary, such as implementing the option to show the peer graph of a particular session (VIII). But all in all it is an operative framework to find errors and problems in WebRTC applications.

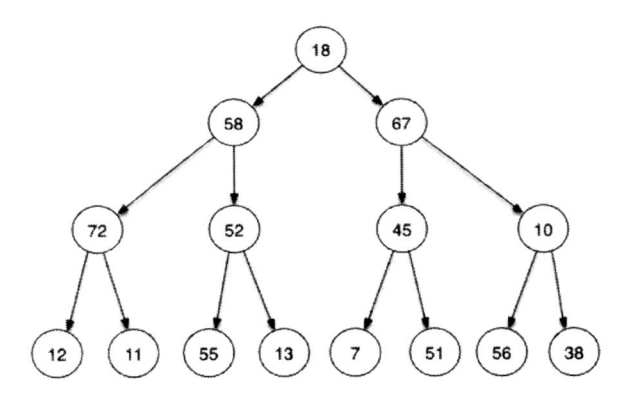

Fig. 4. Sample graph for a WebRTC session; shows the tree structure and peers

VIII. FUTURE WORK

The next steps for the project consist of defining algorithms for automated event examination and graphical displaying. As described in section VI the monitor is able to show the gathered events (cf. V) as a table. Important information such as the tree structure or the state of a peer can be determined by looking at the events but for a fast and easy evaluation a graphical solution would be helpful. At the current state of the project, these graphs were generated manually by examining the database relations. Results can bee seen in figure 4. The graph shows the tree structure of the participating peers and important information about the connection between the peers.

Therefore the next steps include defining an algorithm which is able to draw a graph displaying the participants as nodes and the connection direction as edges. Additionally the statistics can be included in the graph such as showing the *round trip time* for packets from one peer to another, showing the video and audio packets send from one client to another and showing the lost packets between the peers.

REFERENCES

[1] Adam Bergkvist, Daniel C. Burnett, Cullen Jennings, Anant Narayanan, *WebRTC 1.0: Real-time Communication Between Browsers*, W3C Working Draft 10 February 2015 https://www.w3.org/TR/webrtc/
[2] S. Alekseev, C. von Harscher and M. Schindler, *Finite State Machine based Flow Analysis for WebRTC Aplications*, Fourth International Conference on Innovative Computing Technology (IEEE INTECH), University of Bedfordshire, Luton, UK, 2014
[3] S. Alekseev, J. Schfer, *A New Algorithm for Construction of a P2P Multicast Hybrid Overlay Tree Based on Topological Distances*, The Seventh International Conference on Networks and Communications, 2015
[4] Nemu Dialogue Systems Oy, callstats.io, *callstats.io monitors and manages the performance of video calls in an WebRTC application.*, Helsinki, Finland, 01.2016.
[5] Martin Dougiamas and Moodle Community, *Moodle free and open-source software learning management system - Release 3.0*, 16 November 2015 https://docs.moodle.org/dev/Moodle_3.0_release_notes
[6] Node.js Foundation, *Node.js*, Version 5.5, 20. Januar 2016 https://nodejs.org
[7] Guillermo Rauch, *Socket.io*, Version 1.3.6, 15 July, 2015 http://socket.io Socket.IO is a JavaScript library for realtime web applications.

Proceedings of the Eleventh International Network Conference (INC 2016)

A Mobile Solution for Linguistic Communication with Deaf-Blind People Using Arduino and Android

Anderson Luiz Nogueira Vieira, Felipe Félix Novaes, Douglas Machado Silva,
Lucas Santos, Saymon Belozi, Tarik Castro
University Center Estácio Juiz de Fora
Juiz de Fora, Brazil
anderson.vieira@gmail.com, felix3designer@yahoo.com.br, douglas.machado@estacio.br

Abstract— Nowadays technology has been used for numerous purposes and it is still possible to find applications and solutions not explored before that could bring benefits to part of the population that has not received attention from many researches yet. This paper aims to present the main needs of deaf-blind people, their demands and a proposal of a mobile solution to facilitate and expand interpersonal communication with deaf-blind people, including those people who do not have familiarity with the methods of communicating with deaf-blind people by specific sign language.

Keywords— Deaf-blind, Multi-sensory disabilities, Interface, Arduino, Android.

I. Introduction

Multisensory disabled people are people with visual impairment and hearing impairment, associated with other conditions, whether in the field of physical, mental or emotional and learning subjects. [1].

As children, for instance, they demonstrate serious difficulties such as difficulty understanding routines of day-to-day gestures or other forms of communication, of course, also demonstrating difficulty recognizing people who are around them. There is little response to sound, movement, touch and other stimulation.

The complexity in anticipating events or what is happening around them makes each new experience looks like something scary, like simple actions as going from one place to another or even eating or touching food. In addition, their interest in recognizing the environment is decreased due to these physical and psychological barriers which they have to deal with. They actually should be encouraged to create their communication and recognition method to compensate their visual and hearing impairment, and to develop the creation and maintaining of interpersonal relationships.

II. The Deafblindness

Among people with multi-sensory disabilities are the deaf-blind people. According to the Decalogue of the deaf-blind, a declaration adopted at the Fourth "Helen Keller" World Conference, held in 1989 in Stockholm, "deafblindness is a single disability rather than the simple sum of the deafness disability and blindness disability, requiring specialized services." Miles and Riggio [8] classify deaf-blind people as:
- profoundly deaf and blind people
- deaf people with low vision;
- people with low hearing and who are blind;
- people with low vision and poor hearing.

These multi-sensory disabilities can be obtained congenitally or acquired, "congenital when the individual is born with this unique disability; acquired when the individual is born listener, seer, deaf or blind, and because of different biological or external factors, acquires deaf-blindness" [3]. Its causes are associated with many situations but mainly "due to congenital rubella, meningitis and Usher Syndrome" [3]. Regardless of whether congenital or acquired, the study and creation of communication methodology is needed to facilitate the interaction of these people with the society, allowing them to decrease their difficulty in socialization, following the Decalogue of the deaf-blind [12], which states that "Communication is the biggest barrier to personal development and education of the deaf-blind, therefore the teaching of effective communication methods should be prioritized."

Nowadays, deaf-blind people still need the support of a guide and they also need those guides to interpret signals and to communicate with people for them. This dependence can decrease the socialization ability and conversational possibilities with those who can't communicate using specific sign language for deaf-blind people, as well as the dependence of the interpreter that is not always available to people with this disability.

Ampudia [2] says that the great difficulty deaf-blind children have is precisely in developing a learning mode to compensate the visual and hearing handicap and allow the relationship with the world. So, it is essential to explore the potential of remaining senses (touch, taste and smell) for orientation and perception, which justifies furthermore the possibility of using technologies that leverage the remaining senses and offer the individual some communication independence and socialization with others. Therefore, it is necessary to look for tools that can assist them in communicating due to the fact that there is a weakness in the very essential senses that enables the communication process.

177

III. Technology as an Aid to Communication

Nowadays, it is noticeable the growth in technology usage by society, including creating a dependent relationship with these technological resources that facilitates the daily lives of human beings. A topic that has been a research focus in many countries is the Internet of Things, where not only men interact with machines, but also where objects communicate with themselves through the Internet. "The internet of things will revolutionize our daily life, turning tasks that today are complicated in simpler tasks, thanks to the use of micro-controllers that will assist in various areas ranging from industrial automation to the field of medicine, for example. Cities will become increasingly intelligent thanks to this technology, and communication between the government and people will be facilitated, even environmental disasters can be avoided thanks to the use of this new technology. "[10].

Arduino plays an important role in this whole process. It is one of the main instruments nowadays to the study and development of technologies that will be used in the Internet of Things, and which has allowed the improvement of various areas of society, regardless of social and financial class, always focusing on supply or optimize human needs.

Conceived in 2005 by Massimo Banzi, Arduino, which is an "Open Source Hardware", is based on a microcontroller that is easy to use and program, initially created to facilitate the teaching of electronics, but because of its simplicity, it has been used in schools for teaching to children, adults and researchers, inspiring many people around the world to develop ideas that used to be impossible without having a great knowledge in electronics, "aiming to encourage this open innovation, creating an aura around the technology that helps to sell it, cutting radically development costs and allowing projects that are always one step ahead, thanks to the skills and dedication of thousands of specialists all over the world "[11].

IV. The Deaf-Blind Interface Development

Due to the motivation presented by this paper, and to contact with a philanthropic and non-profit civil organization specialized in caring for people with multiple disabilities, we have identified the possibility of developing a device that could help this institution and their patients in teaching and in linguistic communication with deaf and blind people, just using the enhancement of the touch sense, creating possibilities for communication with any individual using Morse code, originally created for use in telegraphs, "where each letter of the alphabet and each number has a sequence of dots and dashes (long and short pulses), with a stroke 3 times longer than a period "[4], in order to use this communication standard using the vibration technology as a means of reception of a signal by the disabled person.

Using an Arduino microcontroller connected to a vibrating micro-engine (as used in smartphones that has vibrating mode), command buttons, and a Bluetooth HC-06 Module, often used with Arduino, we started the development of a prototype, respecting hardware limitations, but creating an interface that could somehow send and receive messages via Bluetooth, so that at the end of the translation to the device, the disabled person could "read" the message using the vibration of Morse code.

We decided to use the Bluetooth communication because in addition to low power consumption and its easy configuration when used with the Arduino board, it also can be directly paired to another interface without additional parameterization, which does not occur with a wireless module 802.11 where routers and their wireless networks need to be set up directly via Arduino programming, which would not allow flexibility in use of the device by the disabled, for example, for entering an authentication password for a specific SSID.

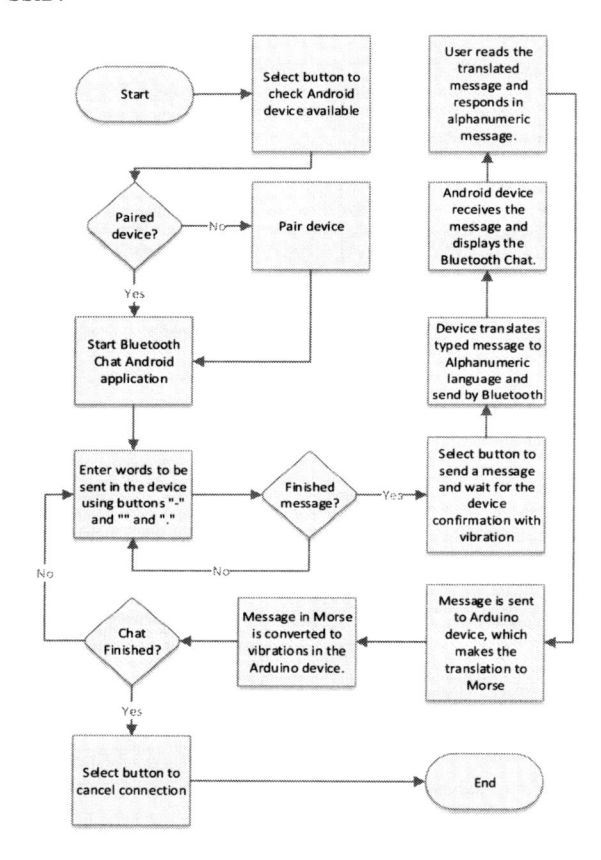

Figure 1. Diagram demonstrating the operation of the interface

In addition to these components, since the goal of the device is to provide mobility, the final prototype will have a rechargeable battery, so that it works without the need to be plugged into any outlet.

Thinking about the usability and practicality of the device as well as its portability, it would have the following buttons:
- Button 1: Connect
- Button 2: "." Morse code for dot

- Button 3: "_" Morse code for dash
- Button 4: "ok" - a confirmation used to complete a letter, a word or a phrase, sending the message, having the following functions:
  - 1 click (end of letter)
  - 2 clicks (end of the word)
  - 3 clicks (end of sentence)
- Button 5: "Cancel or Search Bluetooth devices" having the following functions:
  - 1 click (search)
  - 2 clicks (cancel connection to all devices).

In order to include the whole process of data transmission and reception on the interface created using Arduino, the prototype will be responsible for receiving the text sent through the application, to be presented in the following paragraphs, as well, as the translation of the text received in Morse code, and vice versa, in order to convert all text vibrations, or converting the Morse code into intelligible text to others.

This process can be seen in the Table 1, which shows a small code of Arduino programming [5] [6], specifically the process of typing a message in Morse and his conversion on the device with Arduino.

TABLE I.   ARDUINO SOURCE CODE FOR MORSE TRANSLATION IN THE PROTOTYPE

```
void loop()
{
// Character Array
char letters[36] =
{'A','B','C','D','E','F','G','H','I','J','K','L','M'
,'N','O','P','Q','R','S','T','U','V','W','X','Y','Z'
,'0','1','2','3','4','5','6','7','8','9'};
// Morse Array
char ditdit[36][36]= {{'.','-'},{'-
','.','.','.'},{'-','.','-','.'},{'-
','.','.'},{'.'},{'.','.','-','.'},{'-','-
','.'},{'.','.','.','.'},{'.','.'},{'.','-','-','-
'},{'-','.','-'},{'.','-','.','.'},{'-','-'},{'-
','.'},{'-','-','-'},{'.','-','-','.'},{'-','-
','.','-'},{'.','-','.'},{'.','.','.'},{'-
'},{'.','.','-'},{'.','.','.','-'},{'.','-','-'},{'-
','.','.','-'},{'-','.','-','-'},{'-','-','.','.'
},{'-','-','-','-','-'},{'.','-','-','-','-'},{'-
','.','-','.','-','.'},{'.','.','-','-','-'},{'-
','.','.','-','-'},{'.','.','.','-','-'},{'.','-
','.','.'},{'-','-','.','-','-','.'},{'-
','.','.','.'},{'-','-','-','-'}};
char message[] = "";   // Array that stores the whole message.
char palavra[]= "";   // Array that stores each word.
noTone(Buzz);   // Interrupts vibration

// Reading the Arduino device
 while (!digitalRead(BTEsp)){
// While the BHTEsp is not tight, the array will be mounted morse
  if(digitalRead(BTTrac))
// When BTrac tight, insert the character _ in the message array.
  {
   strcat(message,"-");
   Serial.println(message);
```

```
// displays the contents of the message array
// Does the vibrate over _ the morse for the user to identify the tight Button
   tone(Buzz,1500);
   delay(750);
   noTone(Buzz);
  }

  else if(digitalRead(BTPont)) // When BTPont tight, insert the character _ in the message array.
  {
   strcat(message,".");
   Serial.println(message);

// Does the beep / vibrate short of "." Morse for the user to identify the tight Button
   tone(Buzz,1500);
   delay(250);
   noTone(Buzz);
  }
```

V. PROTOTYPE FOR LINGUISTIC COMMUNICATION WITH SMARTPHONES

Based on the features offered by the prototype and on the possibility of bluetooth's module usage in full-duplex communication (sending and receiving data), the continuity of the project could be the pursuit of developing an application for smartphones.

This application is necessary to allow smartphone users who do not have disabilities neither know methods of communicating with deaf-blind nor the use of Morse code can, via a mobile device, type a message in the application and the same can be sent to the interface created, which will convert the text into Morse code, and then immediately it turns into vibrations to the deaf-blind person.

This application allows a range of communication possibilities with deaf-blind people. It respects the Decalogue of the Deaf-Blind previously mentioned: the possibility of communication of a deaf-blind to any individual who has a mobile phone could break a big barrier existent today and would limit the disabled communication only with a small number of people.

For application development, initially we choose mobile devices using Android as operating system. According to IDC Institute [7], is responsible for 82.8% of smartphones sold today in the world market, which can be seen in Figure 2.

Period	Android	iOS	Windows Phone
2015Q2	82.8%	13.9%	2.6%
2014Q2	84.8%	11.6%	2.5%
2013Q2	79.8%	12.9%	3.4%
2012Q2	69.3%	16.6%	3.1%

Figure 2. Smartphone OS Market Share. IDC, Aug 2015

After choosing the operating system for starting the application development, a research led to the project *BluetoothChat* source code, available on GitHub website [9], a code example available to demonstrate the use of Bluetooth Android API that can be run by two Android devices at the same time, to establish chat over Bluetooth between these devices, among the already available functions, also allows to:
- Set up Bluetooth;
- Search for other Bluetooth devices;
- Pair the local Bluetooth adapter to another device;
- Transfer data among the devices.

Based on this code, some changes were made. Among them, we changed the application source code to allow it to be compatible not only with Android devices, but also with Bluetooth interface HC-06, used in the Arduino, responsible for interpreting and the conversion for Morse code messages.

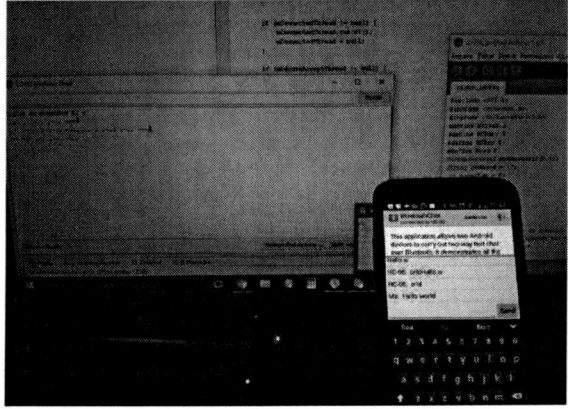

Figure 3. Running tests with BluetoothChat and Arduino

We have performed tests and confirmed the feasibility of the project. The application and prototype will be tested in the partner institution in order to identify potential improvements, as well as to allow future implementations, as planned, in the final version.

VI. FUTURE IMPLEMENTATIONS

Given that in the current phase of the project we decided to focus on the implementation of the application and its interaction with the deaf-blind interface, new implementations were inserted in it at a later stage, but that we can not fail to mention due to the usefulness of these resources.

For the final step in the implementation of the project we will include:
- Changes in the Application interface, improving the usability to the end user of the Android device
- Ultrasonic sensor: for the use of the interface to detect objects and obstacles near the deaf-blind to keep their safety and avoid accidents. The sensor use the same mechanisms of the parking sensor used in today's cars.
- LED and Buzzer: For the use by deaf-blind people that can still see, although through a limited vision, or hear, in a limited way.

CONCLUSION

This paper is the result of the researches made by a scientific initiation group that studies and researches automation possibilities using Arduino at the University Center Estácio Juiz de Fora. During the research and focusing on projects that can help people with difficulties and shortcomings, it is clear that there is a range of possibilities where the *Internet of Things* have not been targeted.

It is necessary that researchers identify ways that benefit these disabled people and that can benefit from small solutions but that make a big difference in theirs lives. This proposal, created using inexpensive resources as Arduino and other devices and the Android app, allows the facilitation of the socialization of these disabled people and will certainly make a difference in their lives.

However, this first prototype is not intended for commercial use. The main goal is to help the institute where we identified the initial demand. Even so this solution can be easily implemented in any other institutions and could be an initiative that can motivate the creation of new solutions for the multisensory disabled people.

REFERENCES

[1] PERREAULT, Stephen. Alguns pensamentos sobre atendimentos a crianças com múltipla deficiência. In: MASINI, Elcie F.S. (Org.) Do sentido... pelos sentidos...para o sentido. Brazil. São Paulo: Vetor Editora, 2002. pp. 113-118

[2] AMPUDIA, Ricardo. Revista Nova Escola. O que é surdo cegueira. 2011. Brazil. Retrieved August 22, 2014 from http://revistaescola.abril.com.br/formacao/surdo-cegueira-deficiencia-multipla-inclusao-636397.shtml

[3] Sousa, Cláudia. Rocha, Patricia. Lourenço, Nehemias. O ensino a crianças surdas e a crianças cegas: A prática pedagógica de Anne Sullivan em Foco. Brazil. 2014

[4] Sampaio, Adovaldo. Letras e Memória: Uma breve história da escrita. Ateliê Editorial. Brazil. 2009.

[5] McRoberts, Michael. Arduino Básico. 456. Editora Novatec, Brazil, 2011

[6] Margolis, Michael. Arduino Cookbook. 662. O'Reilly Media, 2011.

[7] IDC Institute. Smartphone OS Market Share, 2015 Q2 http://www.idc.com/prodserv/smartphone-os-market-share.jsp

[8] Miles, B. & Riggio, M. (Ed.) (1999). Remarkable Conversations: A guide to developing meaningful communication with children and young adults who are deafblind. Perkins School for the Blind.

[9] Bluetooth Chat source-code. Retrieved in 04 Feb 2016 from https://github.com/googlesamples/android-BluetoothChat

[10] KALIL, Fahad e RODRIGUES, Kelvin. Tecnologia e o futuro: internet das coisas, microcontroladores e webservices. Núcleo de Estudo e Pesquisa em Computação Aplicada - NEPCA, IMED, Brazil.

[11] VIDIGAL. Antonio. Arduino e o Open Source. Arduino. Retrieved May 15, 2015 from http://www.antoniovidigal.com/drupal/cd/O_Arduino_e_o_hardware_open_source

[12] FABRI, Rozi. LEME, Carolina. A importância do guia intérprete para o aluno surdocego no processo de inclusão na escola de ensino regular. Brazil. November 2009 from http://www.uel.br/eventos/congresso multidisciplinar/pages/ arquivos/anais/2009/034.pdf

Author Index

Adda M	109	Khambari N	85
Alekseev S	147, 171	Kinzig J	147, 171
Al-Obaidi S	3	Kirkagac Y	153
Alshathri SI	9	Klein D	135
Ambroze MA	3	La Blunda L	159
Atkinson S	79	Lancaster D	85
Aversente F	135	Lehmann A	165
Ball F	13	Li C-M	91
Bansod D	97	Lin B-SP	31
Basu K	13	Liu Z	55
Belozi S	177	Mishra A	97
Bouché J	19	Mühlhäuser M	73
Castro T	177	Novaes FF	177
Chawla J	25	Novinskiy A	103
Chen C	55	Owen G	109
Chundrigar SB	31	Picking R	37
Crowcroft J	73	Regier S	67
Cunningham S	37	Santos L	177
Dai H-N	43	Schäfer J	135
Davies J	37	Schindler M	147, 171
Dawood M	141	Shieh M-Z	31
Dogan G	49	Silva DM	177
Fadhil M	109	Simsek S	153
Fan C	55	Steinheimer M	115
Fengel J	79	Stengel I	67
Fischer-Hellmann KP	121	Sultani S	135
Frank H	63	Sun L	85
Frömmgen A	73	Tchinda AP	165
Fuhrmann W	63, 115, 121, 127, 141	Trick U	115, 127, 165
		Tsokanos A	3
Ghita B	3, 63, 85, 115, 127, 141	Tung L-P	31
		Vieira ALN	177
Giakoumidis E	3	Vo TH	121
Gribel L	67	von Harscher C	147, 171
Grout V	37	Vronski D	135
Haribabu K	97	Wacht P	127
Harriehausen-Mühlbauer B	79	Wagner M	25, 159
Heuschkel J	73	Wang H	43
Heuss T	79	Wu F-M	91
Hock D	19	Xiao H	43
Houlden N	37	Xiu B	55
Humm B	79	Yang Y	55
Kappes M	19	Yavas D	153